Advance praise for *Japan Rising*

"As usual, Ken Pyle has provided the most intellectually acute and policy-relevant assessment of recent adjustments in Japanese foreign and security policy and the domestic institutions that support them. He does so with exceptional judgment and clear prose that reflects a rare combination of emotional empathy and analytic detachment. This valuable and timely book reminds us that the 'rise of China' is not the only—or even necessarily the most important—development American officials must take into account in adapting U.S. policy to a rapidly changing Asia."—Michael Armacost, former U.S. Ambassador to Japan

"Japan's economy has recovered and its security policy has begun to move in new directions. Ken Pyle's *Japan Rising* analyzes these recent shifts within a 150 year perspective. The book makes it clear just how much transformation has taken place and yet how much remains an outgrowth of long standing geo-strategic necessities. The clarity of his argument makes this an easily accessible and rewarding book that will be anxiously read by policy makers and academics alike."
—T. J. Pempel, Professor of Political Science, University of California Berkeley

"In this learned, comprehensive, and up-to-date book one of the world's leading specialists on Japan sends a strong message. Kenneth Pyle argues that international structural changes in world politics and domestic generational changes in Japan are now beginning to affect a major reorientation in Japan's foreign policy. Henceforth Japan's traditional pursuit of economic realism will be enriched with a strong dose of political realism. The return of Japan to great power politics has been predicted many times—wrongly—in the last half century. This book may be more on target. In *Japan Rising* the realist argument has found an advocate with admirable skills and an unrivaled depth of understanding. At this historical juncture all serious students of Japan, East Asia and American foreign policy should heed this book's message."—Peter J. Katzenstein, Walter S. Carpenter Jr., Professor of International Studies, Cornell University

"In the most comprehensive history of Japan's international relations to date, Kenneth Pyle chronicles the changing sense of national purpose underlying Japan's integration into the world order. He tells the remarkable story of the rise and fall of the modern era's first non-Western great power, postwar Japan's equally ambitious economic expansion, and the nation's precipitous loss of purpose in the 1990s. Most provocative, Pyle examines recent developments that may lead to a resurgent Japan in the present century."—Sheldon Garon, Professor of History and East Asian Studies, Princeton University

"Ken Pyle's excellent new book is just in time. Amidst changes in Northeast Asia that are reshaping the policy and political landscape, Japan has been the 'quiet power.' No more. Pyle explains the 'puzzle' of Japan's past, its capacity to surprise, and how historically Japan's rulers have sought security by shrewdly (and rapidly) adjusting to changes in the external international order. And it's happening again—right now."—Robert B. Zoellick, former U.S. Trade representative and Deputy Secretary of State

"The land of the rising sun is poised to rise again as a regional, and even world, power. So holds noted Japan specialist Pyle. . . . An interesting thesis, backed by a strong historical narrative."—*Kirkus Reviews*

"In *Japan Rising*, Kenneth Pyle marries the insights of a long dual career as a major historian of modern Japan and a shrewd analyst of Japan's uneasy role in the contemporary world. *Japan Rising* is a grand, thematic, historical overview of the bedrock policy paradigm that lay behind the nation's stunning roller-coaster rise as a powerful state—and how traditional conservative wisdom is finally undergoing fundamental change in response to the challenges of a new Asia and new global economy."—John W. Dower, professor of history, MIT, and author of *Embracing Defeat: Japan in the Wake of World War II*

"Japan's global role, as a political, military and economic bridge between East and West, has never been more vital. Kenneth Pyle's *Japan Rising* gives us an insightful portrait of the ways in which Japan's history and its present policies will shape the world."—Thomas S. Foley, former United States Ambassador to Japan and former Speaker of the House

"Now, as in the last 150 years, except for a brief period in the 1980s, the world underestimates Japan. Kenneth Pyle is a rare combination—a senior scholar of Japan who is also a foreign policy analyst. He here wrestles with the big issues, how the deeper processes of history and national character are shaping the new Heisei generation and Japan's role in the world."—Ezra F. Vogel, Professor, Harvard University

"Kenneth Pyle's writings were valuable to me during my term as U.S. ambassador in Tokyo. *Japan Rising* again demonstrates Pyle's extraordinary ability to interpret Japan not only for policymakers but also for a wide audience interested in understanding our key ally."—Walter Mondale, former U.S. Vice President

"Our alliance with Japan must be grounded in a deep understanding of Japanese history and culture. That is why I enthusiastically recommend the thoughtful analysis in Ken Pyle's *Japan Rising*."—George Shultz, former Secretary of State

Kenneth B. Pyle

JAPAN RISING

The Resurgence of Japanese Power and Purpose

A Century Foundation Book

PublicAffairs™

NEW YORK

For Anne, my companion on the journey

BOOK DESIGN AND COMPOSITION BY JENNY DOSSIN
Set in Garamond MT

Library of Congress Cataloging-in-Publication Data

Pyle, Kenneth B.
  Japan rising : the resurgence of Japanese power and purpose / Kenneth B. Pyle.
    p. cm.
  "A Century Foundation Book"
  Includes bibliographical references and index.
  ISBN-13: 978-1-58648-417-0 (hardcover : alk. paper)
  ISBN-10: 1-58648-417-6 (hardcover : alk. paper) 1. Japan—Foreign relations—1945-
2. Japan—Politics and government—1945- I. Title.
  DS889.5.P95 2007
  327.52—dc22

                                                                      2006035616

Paperback ISBN: 978-1-58648-567-2
10 9 8 7 6 5 4 3 2 1

Contents

FOREWORD

The end of the Cold War was cause for rejoicing and, as it turns out, for a series of erroneous conclusions about the "new world order." In the West, there was a widespread expectation that the demise of the Soviet Union heralded the beginning of an era of peaceful economic competition and U.S. military predominance. The global triumph of democratic capitalism seemed assured. History was over. Walls between nations and cultures would fall, and security would be largely a problem for local police forces. Pundits wrote glowingly and certainly that past differences among the peoples of the world would fade away as humanity slowly blended into a common international race of consumers and voters. For the foreseeable future, Americans could do what they liked best: go about their business without concerning themselves about the rest of the world.

The nagging cloud on that rosy horizon was the emerging economic power of two former adversaries that had now become staunch U.S. allies: Japan and Germany. Of the two, the true powerhouse clearly was the same Asian island nation that had stunned the world in the twentieth century by its rapid industrialization and outsized ambitions. By 1990, Japan, in fact, seemed well on its way to creating a "Greater East Asia Coprosperity Sphere," without a strong military at all.

Now, a decade and a half later, new dangers are at large in the world, and past concerns about industrial competition seem greatly overblown. So, too, do the expectations of relentless Japanese economic progress. That nation's growth has turned remarkably sluggish despite several significant government programs designed to reenergize it. Today, Japan's continued economic significance is obscured, to some extent, by the phenomenal growth of other Asian economies and, especially, the spectacular emergence of China as a global power. Not surprisingly, basic questions about Japan—present and future—are being asked.

In this context, The Century Foundation seized the opportunity to work with Kenneth B. Pyle, the Henry M. Jackson Professor of History and Asian Studies at the University of Washington, on an in-depth study of Japan, with a special emphasis on Japanese-American relations. Pyle writes from a long life of deep understanding of and sympathy for Japan. His book is thorough, filled with insights about Japanese history and current politics, and he deftly places his subject in the larger context of international relations, past and present.

This volume is the latest in a long history of studies of East Asia sponsored by The Century Foundation. In 1968, we published Gunnar Myrdal's landmark study *Asian Drama: An Inquiry into the Poverty of Nations*. More recently, we have supported a number of works looking specifically at U.S. policy in the region, including Morton Abramowitz and Stephen Bosworth's *Chasing the Sun: Rethinking East Asian Policy;* Selig Harrison's *Korean Endgame: A Strategy for Reunification and U.S. Disengagement;* and Patrick Tyler's *A Great Wall: Six Presidents and China.*

Looking back, Kenneth Pyle reminds us of the miracle of Japan's astonishingly swift industrialization—an achievement that created the impression of modernity for a culture that was in many ways still quasi-feudal. However, as Pyle points out, "To achieve national power the Meiji leaders were willing to swallow cultural pride, even risk their national identity, to borrow massively from an alien civilization."

Even today, the scale and pace of that accomplishment is unmatched. Japan's modernization put in place a foundation that even the ravages of World War II could not erase. Arising from the ashes of total defeat of the past regime's fervent, aggressive, and militarized nationalism, Japan ascended to near the top of the world economy, a tribute to its single-minded public policy, and a reward for its rejection of rearmament. To be sure, in many areas the ruthless necessities of global market capitalism have clashed with the traditional obligations and mores of Japanese culture. But in most respects, the priority given to economic strength has persisted.

In one area, however, Japan remains somewhat outside the Western consensus. As Pyle notes, "Democracy is not an indigenous phenomenon that Japan has ever sought to export. The Japanese have not achieved a democratic revolution on their own; it is not in their life's blood. These were not values the Japanese themselves had struggled for and made their own." Indeed, Japan is still essentially a one-party state. And yet, it generally satisfies the definition of a democracy despite the lack of consistent and effective party competition.

Pyle reviews the many current foreign policy challenges facing Japan. He offers a succinct and insightful review of the major issues, including one of the persistent threats to regional tranquillity, North Korea. Pyle suggests that the debate over nuclear weapons is only the symptom of a deeper condition. Moreover, he argues that Korea may prove the "catalytic event [to] trigger the emergence of a new international order," perhaps precipitating a major U.S. force draw-down from the region.

While Washington geostrategists are fixated on China, Pyle describes how there is a new Japan emerging, a "Heisei" generation that has come of age since the accession of the current emperor. Pyle writes:

> The Heisei generation, which emerged after Japan was widely recognized as having caught up with the West, is more at home in the world than any earlier generation in modern Japan. . . . Typically, having studied and traveled abroad, they are less constrained by traditional practices and mores. Instead, they are attuned to the lifestyle changes brought on by globalization and technological change.
>
> They constitute the first generation whose entire schooling has been under the democratic principles mandated by the Fundamental Law of Education of 1947, which the Occupation drafted.

Of course, those on the Right in Japan had sought, as early as the 1950s, to repeal the "renunciation of war" written into the Japanese constitution by the Americans, but public opinion for half a century was so intensely in favor of the renunciation that they could not touch it. Now, however, encouraged by U.S. policymakers who see Japan as a counterweight to China's rise, a new generation without direct memories of war is more open to considering the use of military power.

Pyle reminds us that, while the Bush-Koizumi axis has bound the two countries closely together, the Japanese political elite has different goals in mind than Washington does. Japan is not making its determined drive for a permanent seat on the UN Security Council in order to be a rubber stamp for Washington.

Americans often have seen Japan as doing considerably less than it could well afford to do in international matters. Now, after fifteen years in the doldrums and deepening debt, Japan's economy appears to be expanding. Pyle's book is a timely reminder not to write Japan off based on that slump and the contraction of its population that is under way. As he aptly puts it, "Japan still seeks its place in the sun. . . . The way in which the constitution is revised, the reshaping of the party system and the political structure, and the reform of Japan's economic institutions will be worked out, to a very considerable degree, by external developments that impact Japan's national interest."

Wise counsel, as is *Japan Rising: The Resurgence of Japanese Power and Purpose* generally. On behalf of The Century Foundation trustees, I thank Kenneth Pyle for this important work.

RICHARD C. LEONE, *President*
The Century Foundation
August 2006

Acknowledgments

This book is the result of many years of study and reflection on the nature and meaning of modern Japanese history. An invitation to deliver the Edwin O. Reischauer Memorial Lecture at the International House of Japan in 1997 initially prodded me to gather my thoughts. A grant from the Century Foundation provided support to work my thoughts into this book. I would especially like to acknowledge former ambassador to Japan Walter Mondale, the late Michel Oksenberg, and Princeton professor emeritus Robert Gilpin for their early encouragement in this project.

A subsequent opportunity to develop my thinking came in a collaborative project on "how the great powers shape the world," organized by Robert Pastor and published as *A Century's Journey* (Basic Books, 1999). Further opportunities came in presentations at the Reischauer Institute at Harvard University and the Mansfield Freeman Memorial Lecture at Wesleyan University.

Sections of Chapters 9, 10, and 11 draw on research and writing that I undertook for the National Bureau of Asian Research (NBR) with former ambassador to Japan Michael Armacost. These studies, published by NBR, analyzed Japanese attitudes toward Korean unification and toward the rise of China. I thank Mike Armacost for permission to use material from our essays.

The chairman of NBR's board of directors George Russell has been a constant source of encouragement for my work. I am also indebted for the long-time friendship and support of my colleague Rich Ellings, the president of NBR.

The book manuscript was read at different stages by valued friends Sheldon Garon, T. J. Pempel, Dick Samuels, and the late Jim Palais. At the Century Foundation, Beverly Goldberg made important suggestions. I am grateful to Peter Osnos, founder and editor-at-large of PublicAffairs, for the special interest he took in this project, and to Lindsay Jones for her careful editing of my manuscript.

I have been fortunate to be part of a vibrant program of Asian studies at the University of Washington. The opportunity to develop my thinking over many years with both students and colleagues, especially Don Hellmann and Kozo Yamamura, has been of great value.

My work has benefited from the generous support of the Henry M. Jackson Foundation. My own horizons were broadened by my five years of friendship and travel in Asia with Senator Jackson before his untimely death.

My greatest obligation is, as it always has been, to my wife Anne for her constant support, inspiration, and love that have sustained my work and being. This book is dedicated to her.

THE JAPAN PUZZLE

O ne of the most demanding challenges for the historian of any country is to explain the underlying processes of history and national character, what the British historian A. J. P. Taylor referred to as "the profound forces," that impel a nation along one course rather than another.[1] Modern Japan's history has been particularly difficult to explain and understand. Japan's international behavior has fluctuated widely and wildly—from isolation to enthusiastic borrowing from foreign cultures, from emperor worship to democracy, from militarism to pacifism. Since the middle of the nineteenth century, when its leaders abruptly ended national isolation and undertook the reorganization of their institutions after the model of the West, Japan has been marked by its pendulum-like swings in national policy. None has been more dramatic than the 180-degree turn from a brutal imperialism to withdrawal from international politics and a sustained drive for commercial prowess after World War II.

Japan's role as a merchant nation brought astonishing results. Staying on the sidelines of the Cold War, it recovered rapidly from wartime devastation to become the world's second-ranked economic power. Through its widely envied choice of avoiding the military spending and involvements that encumbered other nations, Japan was able to make the long-term investments in science, education, and technology that would speed its advancement. Japan's financial markets garnered massive wealth and influence. Its mastery of the skills of organizing a modern industrial society provoked universal admiration as foreign observers grasped for superlatives to describe its achievement. In 1979, a Harvard sociologist ranked Japan simply "number one" in the world. Two years later, a popular French writer regarded it as "a model to all the world."[2]

After 1990, however, the nation again surprised the world. Japan abruptly entered into a puzzling period of paralysis; its economic ascent stalled and its government ceased to function as effectively as it once had. Foreign observers were at a loss to explain Japan's failure to take steps to revive its moribund economy. U.S. policymakers spared no opportunity to advise their slumping ally on the reforms required. The "Japanese economic miracle" was soon eclipsed by the rise of the neighboring colossus. The 1990s became Japan's "lost decade," and China's emergence as an economic giant dimmed the memories of Japan's achievement.

In retrospect, this period of stagnation may well be seen as a transition time. Early in the new century there are many indications that Japan is on the verge of another sea change in its international orientation. The belligerence of North Korea, the growing rivalry with a newly powerful China, and the uncertainties of an age of terrorism all have awakened Japanese security consciousness. A new generation of Japanese leaders is impatient with the low political profile that came with Japan's role as a merchant nation. Japan is moving from a period of single-minded pursuit of economic power to a more orthodox international role in which it will be deeply engaged in political-military affairs. After more than half a century of national pacifism and isolationism, the nation is preparing to become a major player in the strategic struggles of the twenty-first century.

These recurrent wide swings in national policy raise persistent questions about the motivations of the Japanese in their national life. What are the common threads that bind together the divergent strategies of modern Japan? Japan's national purpose and the perceived traits of its national character are subjects of scrutiny among its neighbors and can be sources of distrust. Japan's imperialist depredations are still fresh in the minds of Chinese and Koreans. Memories of their bitter experience as victims of Japanese expansion are stoked by their rising nationalism. Signs that Japan might be abandoning its postwar pacifism are disturbing and cause for outcry.

For Americans, in contrast, the apparent readiness of Japan to adopt a more active security role is a welcome change and the fulfillment of a goal long pursued. The alliance with Japan, now extending more than half a century, has often frustrated U.S. leaders because it seemed to provide Japan with unfair economic advantage: While the United States provided security guarantees for Japan, Japan pursued economic growth, often in competition with U.S. interests. Preoccupied with the war on terrorism and the proliferation of weapons of mass destruction, and at the same time aiming to maintain an effective balance with China, a rising power, the United States now seeks to rework the alliance with Japan to meet new conditions. Drawing Japan into a more active role in its global strategy is a major objective of U.S. policy.

Despite more than a century of alliance experience, American understanding of Japanese character, motivation, and purpose remains shaky. Japanese patterns of behavior have been a source of frequent puzzlement for Americans, whose history has been tightly intertwined with Japan but whose social values and national experience are utterly different. As Henry Kissinger pointed out, Japan's unique civilization presents the United States with an ally possessing "intangibles of culture that America is ill-prepared to understand fully."[3] What are the driving forces that influence how Japan will act in the international system? Are there recurrent patterns in Japan's modern experience that will help to explain how its leaders may respond to the emerging environment of world politics? These questions are relevant not only in looking back at Japan's remarkable history but also in observing contemporary Japan and pondering its future at a critical time of change and uncertainty in Asia and the world. U.S. policymakers have been wrong about—or surprised by—Japan's behavior many times in the past. As Japan returns to great-power politics and the alliance enters a new and problematic phase, a clear understanding of Japanese character and purpose and its new role takes on renewed importance.

HIGH EXPECTATIONS

When the Cold War came to an end, there was widespread expectation that Japan would assume international leadership in a world where economic and technological prowess, more than military strength, would be the decisive measures of power. At the beginning of the 1990s, Japan, in the judgment of a chorus of foreign observers, was the model of a nation with the kind of focused goals that would bring success in the twenty-first century. "The Cold War is over," wrote more than one observer at the time, "and Japan has won." One of the most influential academic theorists of international relations wrote: "Now Japan is ready to receive the mantle [of a new great power] if only it will reach for it."[4] *Newsweek* observed, "In boardrooms and government bureaus around the world, the uneasy question is whether Japan is about to become a superpower, supplanting America as the colossus of the Pacific and perhaps even the world's No. 1 nation."[5]

The Yale historian Paul Kennedy, in a best-selling work published in 1987 chronicling the rise and fall of the great powers over the previous 500 years, boldly suggested that Japan was about to emerge as the new world power. The book jacket showed a jaunty Japanese businessman carrying the Rising Sun, mounting the stage of world history, as a tired Uncle Sam followed an aged John Bull off the stage. Japan, according to Kennedy, possessed the combination of advantages required of the next great power. While Cold War powers had poured their resources into arms competition, Japan had husbanded its resources, making the shrewd, long-term investments in research, education, and development that would prepare it for a new industrial hegemony. "Just how powerful, economically, will Japan be in the early twenty-first century?" Kennedy asked. "Barring large-scale war, or ecological disaster, or a return to a 1930's style world slump and protectionism, the consensus answer seems to be: *much* more powerful."[6]

Americans were angry and worried. The Japanese were buying up trophy real estate, like the Pebble Beach Golf Course and Rockefeller Center. They were running mounting trade surpluses and outcompeting venerable U.S. companies. A majority of Americans, according to a 1989 Newsweek/ Gallup poll, believed that Japan represented a threat comparable to the Soviet Union.[7] "Is Japan Out to Get Us?" the *New York Times* asked. A "great tide" of books analyzed the danger Japan posed.[8] Michael Crichton dramatized the threat in his best-selling novel *Rising Sun,* a thriller (later made into a movie) depicting the intricate web of Japan's evil conspiracy to take over the United States. The *New York Times* reviewer compared the novel to *Uncle Tom's Cabin* for its similar ability to use popular fiction to awaken America's consciousness to the dangers its society faced.

These forecasts of Japan's impending dominance were extrapolated from a startling record of Japanese recovery from defeat and rapid acquisition of economic power and influence. When Japan went to war in 1937, it accounted for less than 4 percent of world manufacturing output. By the 1960s it had recovered to this level, and in the 1980s it became the world's second-largest economy, with more than 15 percent of world product. By 1990, Japan had become the "greatest creditor nation the world has ever known" and the world's leading donor of foreign aid.[9] A study by the World Bank concluded that Japan had evolved a unique form of capitalism that in its efficiency and focus would make it the model system for the future.[10]

The Japanese themselves reveled in these high expectations for their future. A majority of Japanese respondents polled in a highly regarded national survey in 1983 believed that they were superior to westerners.[11] As for the United States, once the unfailing model, the Japanese regarded it as debt-ridden, bereft of its work ethic, and plagued by crime, declining productivity, and social malaise. "Watching the United States suddenly losing its magnificence," wrote an *Asahi* editor in 1980, "is like watching a former lover's beauty wither away. It makes me want to cover my eyes."[12] This exuberant self-assurance was the hallmark of the prime ministership of Nakasone Yasuhiro (1982–1987). The tide of history was now in Japan's favor. "Having 'caught up' [with the Western nations]," the dynamic and colorful Nakasone said, "we must now expect others to try to catch up with us. We must seek out a new path for ourselves and open it for ourselves."[13]

Nakasone had an impressive grand design to ready Japan for global leadership that called for reforming Japan's institutions, restoring national pride in Japan's history, and, above all, adopting an active role in strategic affairs. He aimed to replace the country's politically passive policies with an activist foreign policy that envisioned a Japan engaged in international strategic issues, participating in its own defense, and possessing its own goals and values. In photo sessions at G-7 meetings, Nakasone pushed to the center and stood tall, chatting affably with Margaret Thatcher and Ronald Reagan. He struck up a first-name relationship with the American president. The "Ron-Yasu" era was a heady time, and the rest of the world was duly impressed.

These high expectations for Japan's emergence as the world's new leader were confounded. By the turn of the century, a decade after the Cold War had ended, and in defiance of the nearly universal anticipation of Japan's emergence as an international leader, not only had Japan not assumed the mantle, it had sunk into economic and political doldrums. Japan was a puzzle.[14] A country that for so long had been driven by the clear national purpose of catching up to the world's major powers and overtaking them, and that seemingly had brought this goal within reach, had gone adrift and lost its way. Paul Kennedy, who had forecast that owing to American imperial overstretch the Pax Americana would be replaced by Japanese international leadership, observed in the *Financial Times* that instead of assuming its expected preeminence, Japan had "entered a puzzling era of economic malaise."[15] Mired in prolonged economic stagnation and political gridlock since the early 1990s, Japan suffered a precipitous loss of prestige and influence. What had happened to Japan?

A SYSTEMIC CRISIS

In the 1990s a veritable tide of troubles swept over Japan as the nation experienced the worst political and economic crisis since the end of World War II. The economic boom at the close of the 1980s proved to be a bubble. Alarmed by runaway stock prices and land values, the Bank of Japan raised the discount rate in 1990. Soon after, the Nikkei stock index began to plummet and the price of land, which had been the principal collateral for bank loans, followed suit. Nonperforming loans mounted to over $1 trillion and dozens of financial institutions were bankrupted. As the decade proceeded, the real growth of gross domestic product (GDP) hovered at 1 percent. Unemployment rose to new highs. Government policy vacillated between fiscal restraint and fiscal stimulation.

The economic slump produced mounting frustration as Japanese economic officials tried varying solutions to the nation's problems. Finance officials tried to reignite the economy through massive deficit spending, but with no sustained effect. By 2002, Japan's national debt as a proportion of GDP was approaching the highest level that any major industrialized country had faced in half a century. As the economy sank into the doldrums, Japan suffered a dramatic diminution of its international stature. Moody's Investors Service in 2002 downgraded Japanese government bonds one grade below the African nation of Botswana. For the status-conscious Japanese to be rated below a country that was a recipient of Japanese aid provoked public outrage. "Half of the people of Botswana are AIDS patients," fumed the Japanese trade minister. "It is outrageous the rating is lower than such a country."[16]

Most of the media and scholarly attention was focused on the need to reform Japan's closed economic institutions, but the problem was not simply the prolonged economic slump, the uncertain progress of deregulation, and the unresolved banking crisis. The economic crisis was only part of a much bigger problem. Japan faced a systemic crisis—a system-wide failure exacerbated by a paralysis of leadership in the face of the troubles at hand. The political system was in disarray. In 1993, when the Liberal Democratic Party (LDP) was overthrown after thirty-eight years of uninterrupted rule, a dizzying series of party realignments ensued. Politics drifted in a rudderless state. In the space of ten years, Japan had nine prime ministers. Although determined reformers came to power with soaring public support, they failed in their purpose. The bureaucracy, once revered as an incorruptible elite that guided Japan's rise, became the source of a long string of scandals and major policy blunders, leading to an unprecedented loss of public confidence in it.

As the Japanese economy and political system suffered, the society lost its competitive vitality and was gripped by malaise. An aging society and a rapidly declining fertility rate presented a demographic dilemma of unusual proportions. After 2005, the nation's population was forecast to begin a dramatic decline. A very sizable portion of young people began to drop out of the once well-ordered progression of social life. Known as "parasite singles," they chose to remain unmarried, live with their parents, take only temporary jobs, and just enjoy life. The school system, once internationally acclaimed for its achievements, encountered a rampant breakdown of classroom order and discipline.

Foreign policy, too, was in disarray. In a succession of crises throughout the decade, the Japanese system and its leaders exhibited a peculiar pattern of passivity, indecisiveness, and incapacity to come to grips with the strategic issues facing the nation. In the Persian Gulf War of 1990–1991, in which a UN-sanctioned coalition of nations was assembled to counter Saddam Hussein's aggression against Kuwait, the Japanese government became paralyzed, unable to muster coherent policy. Asked to contribute to the coalition and return stability to the Gulf on which it was dependent for its energy needs, the Japanese floundered. Chagrined, the government could only write checks to support the coalition, and even though these totaled $13 billion, Japan received little thanks and much derision.

Normally a proud, independent, spirited people, the Japanese continued to live under a foreign-imposed constitution, which they interpreted as denying them the ability to engage in collective defense—a right that the UN Charter extended to all nations. The Japanese remained reliant on the United States for its security, unable to agree on what steps to take to provide for many of the elemental needs of national security. Japanese leaders failed to lay to rest the burden of the nation's militarist past, at great cost to Japan's international standing and its own self-respect. Issues of acknowledging responsibility for Japanese atrocities of the World War II era—especially those associated with "comfort women," germ-warfare experiments, and the Nanjing massacre—continued to fester and divide the Japanese people and to spark intense distrust and criticism abroad.

The country that had only recently seemed destined to become the new world leader entered the new century mired in immobilism and gridlock. What had happened to the motivation that drove this restless people? Why had Japan failed to make the reforms in its institutions that were widely recognized, both among Japanese and outside observers, as essential to restoring its historic drive for national power and influence? As the economist Edward Lincoln observed, "The fact that the malaise spawned calls for reform is encouraging. The continuing puzzle to many foreign observers has been the lack of vigor in that [reform] process."[17]

JAPAN'S CAPACITY TO SURPRISE

This was by no means the first time Japan had confounded foreign observers, but a repeat of the many times Japan had baffled the world. Since the thirteenth century, when Marco Polo wrote a hearsay account of a mysterious "Zipangu," as he called Japan, the Western world has found the Japanese and their behavior difficult to interpret. The first Western visitors to Japan who tried to understand its civilization were genuinely perplexed. As part of their proselytizing effort, Jesuit missionaries, who began arriving in Japan in 1549, made a genuine effort to understand Japanese manners and customs. One Jesuit, in exasperation, finally concluded of the Japanese:

> They have rites and ceremonies so different from those of all the other nations that it seems like they deliberately try to be unlike any other people. The things which they do in this respect are beyond imagining and it may be truly said that Japan is a world the reverse of Europe; everything is so different and opposite that they are like us in practically nothing. . . . Now all this would not be surprising if they were like so many barbarians, but what astonishes me is that they behave as very prudent and cultured people in all these matters.[18]

Two centuries later Japan seemed no more comprehensible to European visitors. Rutherford Alcock, the first British minister to Japan (1859–1864), concluded that "Japan is essentially a country of paradoxes and anomalies, where all—even familiar things—put on new faces and are curiously reversed. Except that they do not walk on their head instead of their feet, there are few things in which they do not seem, by some occult law, to have been impelled in a perfectly opposite direction and a reversed order."[19]

A century later, in 1961, President John F. Kennedy sent Edwin Reischauer, America's leading academic expert on Japan, to Tokyo to try to open a strategic dialogue with the Japanese. After serving for five years as U.S. ambassador to Japan, Reischauer returned to academic life. Reflecting on his experience, he wrote of modern Japanese foreign policy: "It is a subject of bewildering complexity and also vagueness. . . . It is hard to come to grips with and almost impossible to pin down in fixed words. . . . It is like the exploration of the surface of the moon or some distant planet." Rather than try to characterize it as a whole, he said, it was better, as in studying the moon's surface, to make "a selection of pictures from diverse angles and different degrees of closeness" in order to get "a better concept of the lay of the land."[20]

Observers at the turn of the twenty-first century wondered why Japan seemed so incapable of change and reform. It had not always been so. Quite the contrary. Japan astonished observers by its historic examples of rapid change. The achievements of the Meiji period (1868–1912) are still remarkable to historians. The massive cultural borrowing that the Japanese undertook in that era is without parallel in world history. And it is not just historians of Japan who make this claim; those who study other national histories find the Meiji transformation stunning. The late French historian at Princeton, R. R. Palmer, once wrote that the "Westernization of Japan" during the Meiji period "still stands as the most remarkable transformation ever undergone by any people in so short a time."[21] The British historian John Keegan described the Meiji reforms as "one of the most radical changes of national policy recorded in history."[22] The political scientist Michael Mandelbaum defined Japan's achievement in sweeping terms:

The Meiji Restoration . . . transformed a traditional society . . . in the span of a few decades. This is the most remarkable accomplishment by any nation in modern history. Because it represented the first occasion on which a non-Western country mastered the techniques of modernity and so served as an example for many non-Western societies of the periphery, it is also arguably the most influential modern national accomplishment. Certainly it ranks with the emergence of the United States as the world's most powerful country, and behind only the French and industrial revolutions themselves, as the most important events in history.[23]

U.S. policymakers have frequently misperceived and misjudged Japan's behavior over the past century and a half, and the results have often been costly. One particularly notable example was the misjudgment of Stanley Hornbeck, the State Department's principal architect of policy toward Japan for more than a decade prior to the Pacific War. In November 1941, contemptuous of the Japanese capacity to challenge U.S. strength, Hornbeck dismissed the fears of a young Foreign Service officer that Japan might initiate war out of desperation over the oil embargo imposed by the United States. "Tell me," Hornbeck said, "of one case in history when a nation went to war out of desperation."[24] Then, ten days before Pearl Harbor, after drafting with Secretary of State Cordell Hull a hard-line memo laying down conditions for relaxation of the sanctions, Hornbeck wagered that Japan would relent and that war was not imminent. The note Hull sent the Japanese on November 26, 1941, said that Japan would have to withdraw from Southeast Asia and China before the United States would resume the oil shipments. Confident that his tough approach would cause Japan to back down, Hornbeck wrote in a memorandum the following day:

> In the opinion of the undersigned, the Japanese Government does not desire or intend or expect to have forthwith armed conflict with the United States. . . . Were it a matter of placing bets, the undersigned would give odds of five to one that the United States and Japan will not be at "war" on or before December 15 . . . ; would wager three to one that the United States and Japan will not be at "war" on or before the 15th of January . . . ; would wager even money that the United States and Japan will not be at "war" on or before March 1 (a date more than 90 days from now, and after the period during which it has been estimated by our strategists that it would be to our advantage for us to have "time" for further preparation and disposals).[25]

Even as Hornbeck wrote this optimistic memorandum, the Kido Butai, the Pearl Harbor Striking Force, had already weighed anchor and was plowing across the north Pacific. Hornbeck later rued what he called his "wishful thinking and gratuitous predicting."[26] In fairness to Hornbeck, who has been derided by historians for this ill-founded wager, it should be said that he understood as well as any other U.S. policymaker the irreconcilable conflict between Japanese and U.S. interests. For more than a decade he had urged a policy of economic pressure on Japan. Had the

United States heeded his recommendations much earlier, Japanese power would have been significantly weakened.[27]

Although the Americans had broken the Japanese code and therefore were already alerted to the likelihood of expanded Japanese hostilities, and although Ambassador Joseph Grew had earlier in 1941 reported rumors of a planned Japanese attack on Pearl Harbor, the United States was somehow brought up short by the bold Japanese attack. U.S. policymakers misperceived the Japanese reaction to the embargo. As President Franklin D. Roosevelt conceived it, the United States would "slip the noose around Japan's neck and give it a jerk now and then."[28] Assistant Secretary of State Dean Acheson felt certain that this policy would not lead to war because "no rational Japanese could believe that an attack on us could result in anything but disaster for his country."[29]

On December 8, the day after the Japanese attack on Pearl Harbor, New York Congressman Hamilton Fish, who had been an ardent isolationist, expressed a reaction common among members of Congress supporting the declaration of war: "The Japanese have gone stark, raving mad, and have, by their unprovoked attack committed military, naval, and national suicide." Winston Churchill likewise observed that Tokyo's decision to attack a country of vastly greater military potential "was difficult to reconcile with . . . prudence, or even sanity."[30]

Pearl Harbor is the most dramatic and memorable example of unexpected Japanese behavior, but there had been many earlier examples and there would be many more both during and after the war. Americans have been repeatedly caught off guard by the major changes of Japanese course. As a consequence, Americans began to regard Japan as inherently unstable. Educated Americans familiar with Japan, the sociologist Nathan Glazer once observed, "have the sense that Japan might very rapidly become something very different—and much more uncomfortable to live with."[31] Ruth Benedict's *The Chrysanthemum and the Sword,* published in 1946, attempted to account for Japan's surprising postsurrender "embrace of defeat" and openness to sweeping change and reform by defining radical paradoxes of Japanese national character. The Japanese, she wrote, were "unprecedentedly polite," but also "insolent and over bearing"; "incomparably rigid in their behavior," but also able to "adapt themselves to extreme innovations." They show a "passion [for] Western learning," she said, but also "fervid conservatism."[32]

As Japan's economic power grew in the 1970s, foreign observers anticipated that Japan might once again undergo abrupt change. A proud and nationalistic people, the Japanese might rearm, they theorized, and even exercise the nuclear option. Zbigniew Brzezinski, President Jimmy Carter's national security adviser, believed the instability of Japanese behavior defined the national character:

> What is striking about these shifts is the suddenness with which they come. . . . As a result of this predilection for abrupt change after considerable gestation, Japanese society can be said to be characterized by a kind of metastability, that is to say, a stability that appears to be extremely solid until all of a sudden a highly destabilizing chain reaction is set in motion by an unexpected input. . . . Once instability is set in motion, insecurity tends to intensify the instability.[33]

George Ball, undersecretary of state in the Kennedy and Johnson administrations, described the Japanese as repeatedly unpredictable and irrational. In the midst of the Nixon administration's rough treatment of the Japanese in 1971, when it administered the twin shocks of a surprise opening to China and trade sanctions designed to force revaluation of the yen, Ball cautioned indelicately: "You never know when the Japanese are going to go ape." He described the Japanese as a people motivated by "pride, nationalism, and often downright irrationality." Ball perceived a pattern in Japanese history of sudden, careening changes of national course: "Japanese history has never been charted by the same kind of wavering curve that has marked the progress of other countries; instead it resembles more a succession of straight lines, broken periodically by sharp angles as the whole nation, moving full speed, has suddenly wheeled like a well-drilled army corps to follow a new course. There is nothing in all human experience to match it."

The historic, lightning-like changes of Japanese national policy that baffled Ball included the way it had suddenly reversed its closed-country policy of rejecting foreign contacts in the mid-nineteenth century and embarked on a course of unrestrained westernization. He was also reacting to the way in which in the twentieth century, after a period of rabid militarist expansion, Japan had suddenly become a pacifist nation, unwilling even to provide a minimal defense for its own security. Ball was convinced that the Japanese were at heart a dangerously unpredictable people.[34]

Yet Ball, like so many others who anticipated that Japan might revert to assertive nationalist policies during the post–World War II period, was mistaken. He expected that Japan's pacifist stance might at any time give way to an activist policy that would redeem Japanese nationalist pride. But throughout the last half of the twentieth century, Japan avoided involvement in international political strategic affairs and shunned controversial issues in foreign relations. During this time, Japan single-mindedly pursued its own commercial interests. Its behavior often seemed more appropriate to an international trading firm than to a nation-state. Foreign observers ordinarily interpreted Japan's passivity as a result of wartime trauma, unconditional surrender, popular pacifism, the nuclear allergy, and the restraints of an imposed peace constitution. To an extent, this understanding is accurate. These factors clearly established the parameters within which postwar Japanese political leadership had to operate.

However, Japan's fundamental orientation toward economic growth and political passivity was also the product of a carefully constructed and brilliantly implemented foreign policy. It took U.S. policymakers a long time to recognize this. Belatedly, they realized that Japan's purpose in the postwar world was the result of an opportunistic adaptation to the conditions in which the Japanese leadership found their nation and a shrewd pursuit of a sharply defined national interest within the constraints that the postwar international order placed upon them.

THE EDUCATION OF HENRY KISSINGER

The U.S.-Japan alliance has been a peculiar relationship, repeatedly marked by American misperception of Japanese purpose and motivation. Despite more than half a century duration, the alliance has rarely produced close personal relations between its leaders. The Reagan-Nakasone friendship and the recent friendship of George W. Bush and Koizumi Junichirō may have been exceptions, although those relationships no doubt have been exaggerated by media hype and probably have not been as close as has been portrayed. In terms of cultural connection and affinity, Japan is alone in the world. Among the world's great civilizations, it is sui generis. As Samuel P. Huntington put it: "Japan is a civilization that is a state."[35] It cannot count on another country for automatic backing in the way that Britain and America rely on each other. Genuine communication between the leaders of Japan and other countries remains difficult. The Japanese have historically been poor communicators, and few U.S. leaders have had the interest, much less the background, to understand the intricacies of

Japanese culture. Japanese leaders abroad tend to be stiff and formal.[36] Ill at ease and resigned about ever making themselves understood, they often appear dull and lifeless to boisterous and informal Americans. The nuances and subtleties of Japanese expression are usually lost in this cultural mismatch. Although their modern histories have been deeply intertwined, no two societies are more different in their fundamental mores than the United States and Japan. Little wonder, then, that the alliance often has lacked genuine understanding. During the Nixon administration, the strains latent in this peculiar relationship were striking.

Henry Kissinger, who served as chief foreign policy architect in the Nixon and Ford administrations, was, like many U.S. policymakers, slow to appreciate the Japanese strategy and purpose. "When I first came to office," Kissinger later confessed, "there was no major country I understood less than Japan. . . . I did not grasp Japan's unique character."[37] In his memoirs, Kissinger recalled: "Neither I nor my colleagues possessed a very subtle grasp of Japanese culture or psychology."[38] Nor did he have the time or the inclination to try to understand them. Japan seemed of limited importance in the great-power calculus. During his tenure as national security adviser and as secretary of state, he gave short shrift to Japan.[39] Privately, Kissinger derided the Japanese as "little Sony salesmen," or "small and petty bookkeepers" whose diplomatic documents were nothing more than trading ledgers. Their leaders were so inarticulate that he deemed them unworthy of his attention.[40] Because they seemed to him not a part of the international power calculus, he was said to have disdained them as "prosaic, obtuse, unworthy of his sustained attention." His contempt was scarcely concealed. He detested invitations to the Japanese embassy in Washington because, he said, they always served him Wiener schnitzel.[41]

With his realist fascination with the politics of the traditional power balance, Kissinger had no patience for the intricacies of Japan's "opaque" decisionmaking. Kissinger's indifference was reflected in the Nixon administration's brusque treatment of Japan, its principal Asian ally, when it undertook the surprise opening to China in 1971 without advance notice to the Japanese prime minister. Subsequently, in his many visits to Beijing, Kissinger had little time for Tokyo, stopping there only briefly. The alliance that had been forced on Japan as the price of its independence was now taken for granted. Japan's lack of military and political power gave Kissinger confidence that it could be slighted.[42]

Even Mao Zedong, in a remarkable exchange shortly after Kissinger opened relations with Beijing, lectured Kissinger on his slighting attitude toward the Japanese. "When you pass through Japan, you should perhaps talk a bit more with them. You only talked with them for one day [on your last visit] and that is not good for their face."[43] Unlike Kissinger, Mao was not disposed to underrate the Japanese. Having spent many years as a guerrilla fighter against the Japanese invaders, Mao had learned an unforgettable lesson. Japan was not to be taken lightly. He wanted the Americans to pay close attention to Japanese intentions. Kissinger recalled that on his subsequent visit to Beijing, Mao "applauded my decision to spend a few days in Tokyo on my way home. Japan [Mao continued] must not feel neglected by the United States; Japan was inherently insecure and sensitive."[44]

Kissinger's failure to understand Japanese motivating principles is particularly ironic because he was the unswerving proponent of founding foreign policy on the principles of realism, and yet he failed to notice that these very principles were deeply embedded in postwar Japanese foreign policy. The reason for his obliviousness was that Japanese postwar foreign policy was characterized by economic realism, and Kissinger had little interest in economics as a source of power. National Security Council staff members under Kissinger observed that he had a "profound lack of knowledge and interest in economics" and that discussing economic issues with him was akin to discussing military strategy with the pope. He perceived Japanese diplomats as "not conceptual" in their thinking, lacking long-term vision, and making decisions only by consensus.[45] "The Japanese do not yet think in strategic terms," he told Deng Xiaoping in 1974. "They think in commercial terms."[46] The implication was that pursuing economic advantage was not a means of strategic pursuit of power. Kissinger was no less insightful than most other U.S. leaders in his failure to see that Japanese economic policy was profoundly rooted in strategic thought.

After Kissinger's term as secretary of state ended and Japan's economic power and influence grew so dramatically, he came to see how deeply he had underrated Japanese power and purpose. When he wrote his memoirs many years later, Kissinger professed to have gained an understanding and appreciation of Japanese political leaders and their unique, culturally rooted patterns of decisionmaking:

The Japanese system has not been easy for Americans to comprehend. It took me a long time to grasp how decisions are made. . . . One of the features of the Japanese system is its opaqueness to outsiders. . . . A foreigner underestimates the Japanese at his peril. It is true that they are not as conceptually adept as, say, the Chinese, as articulate as most Europeans, or as boisterously open and forthcoming as Americans. [Japanese leaders] have not been selected for any of these qualities. They gather intelligence about foreigners; they do not seek to persuade them with words. They chart future actions for their society; they do not need to articulate its purposes in rhetoric.[47]

Belatedly, Kissinger came to see that Japan had as clear a foreign policy strategy as any other power. Indeed, he recorded, "in my view Japanese decisions have been the most farsighted and intelligent of any major nation of the postwar era even while the Japanese have acted with the understated, anonymous style characteristic of their culture."[48]

Kissinger's new understanding of Japan was an important realization. Contrary to what American policymakers have often thought, Japan is no more "unpredictable" and "irrational" than any other country. To understand Japan's international behavior we must grasp the profound forces of history, geography, and culture that have shaped the country's approach to the outside world. Far from being erratic, Japan demonstrates recurrent patterns that give a consistency to its foreign policy and make it intelligible.

WHITHER JAPAN?

In the post–Cold War period, when Japan's leadership abruptly lost its sense of purpose and sank into a protracted malaise, U.S. policymakers were stunned. The Armitage Report, a bipartisan study authored by leading U.S. officials and informed academics in 2000 that aimed to energize the U.S.-Japan alliance and to press Japan to reform its slumping economy, observed that "the Japanese tend to be averse to radical change except in circumstances where no other options exist." The authors expressed frustration with Japan's "risk-averse political leadership" and with "a national character resistant to abrupt shifts in established practices."[49] U.S. policymakers in the post–Cold War period quickly grew impatient with Japan's resistance to change in the face of massive policy failures. This was ironic in light of the fact that in earlier decades U.S. officials had been puzzled by Japan's instability and proclivity for abrupt and sudden change.

Nevertheless, after a decade of indecisiveness, at the beginning of the new century, Japan began to change in quiet, almost imperceptible ways. The country took small steps toward what could be a major reorientation of the nation in ways that may once again surprise outsiders. Adjusting and reshaping its institutions to new conditions in the international economy, Japan turned the corner in its economic recovery. Policy innovations restored healthy growth. In the face of more insecure regional politics and the specter of terrorism, the government steadily abandoned many of the prohibitions on a proactive military that were in place throughout the Cold War. Japanese Self-Defense Forces were deployed abroad, even to combat areas in the Middle East. The ability to project power abroad was broached.

The changes received popular support. A distinct majority of Japanese favored revision of the pacifist constitution. The greater assertiveness was most evident in a new generation of Japanese political leaders with a view less constrained than that of their elders by memories of defeat and occupation. In the midst of flux and upheaval in the political system, they worked to loosen the hold of past practice and to reform institutions to meet the new conditions of globalization and insecurity.

No one can be sure how these changes will play out. That will depend upon the course of events in the coming years. What does seem clear is that after more than half a century of withdrawal from international politics, Japan is revising its domestic institutions and preparing to become a major player in the strategic struggles of the twenty-first century.

CHAPTER ONE

NEW INTERNATIONAL ORDERS

An island nation with its own distinctive civilization, modern Japan is frequently characterized as introverted and parochial. Nothing stirs greater exasperation among foreign observers, even those who have devoted their lives to explaining Japanese culture, than Japanese ethnocentrism. The literary critic Edward Seidensticker in his last column for the *Yomiuri* newspaper in 1962 concluded that "they are not like other people. They are infinitely more clannish, insular, parochial, and one owes it to one's self-respect to preserve a feeling of outrage at the insularity." The late Edwin Reischauer, the leading interpreter of Japan in his day, wrote in 1978 that the Japanese people "must overcome their sense of separateness and, to put it bluntly, show a greater readiness to join the human race." These were the observations of scholars who deeply admired Japanese civilization. In the era of globalization in the twenty-first century, Japan still remains notable for its insularity, as evident, for example, in its reluctance to accept foreign workers, political refugees, or even foreign investment.

However, though it is true that Japanese society often seems closed, it is also true that Japan has experienced periods of astonishing receptivity to foreign culture, foreign ideas, and foreign advisers. This paradox lies at the heart of all the puzzling aspects of this country's behavior. Despite its ethnocentrism, Japan at certain times has been extraordinarily open to the outside world. Over the past century and a half, Japan has almost always taken its cues from the international system, set its priorities, even formed its self-identity, in relation to the international order. At such periods of openness, in the well-known observation of G. B. Sansom, "the power and prestige of a foreign culture seem as if they would overwhelm and transform Japan, but always there is a hard non-absorbent core of individual character, which resists and in its turn works upon the invading influence."[1] Periods of remarkable receptivity to the outside world contrast greatly with other times of equally remarkable resistance to foreign influence.

The key to understanding modern Japan's abrupt changes and wide swings of international behavior lies in two major factors: the nature of the external order, and the distinctive strategy and style of Japan's ruling elite for dealing with that order. The interactivity of these two factors has heavily determined the course that Japan has taken since the beginning of its modern history in the middle of the nineteenth century. The outside-in influence of the international system on any nation is strong, but because of the extraordinary responsiveness of Japan's leaders to its external setting, that influence was especially strong. The conservative elite developed a strategy that had deep roots in Japan's culture and history. Japan's leaders are sensitive to the configuration of power in the international system and its implications for Japan's interests. Major changes in the balance of power engage their intense concern. When fundamental changes have taken place in the international environment, they have often proved skillful at adapting their policies to these changes and using them opportunistically to further the nation's interests and ambitions. Whenever the system has changed, Japan has also changed: Japan's leaders adjusted their foreign policy and refashioned their domestic institutions to fit the new circumstance. Therefore, an understanding of Japan's international behavior must begin with the influence of the international environment.

The Outside-In Influence

Japan has sometimes been described as a reactive country. In this view, it simply responds to events in its external environment—such as the arrival of the U.S. Commodore Matthew Perry, who demanded Japan end its seclusion, or the onset of the Great Depression, or the outbreak of world war in Europe, and so on. Japanese government policy in the 1980s was often seen as reactive to outside pressure (*gaiatsu*), as when the United States used the leverage of its market access or security guarantee to bring about a change in Japanese policy.[2]

There is, however, a more fundamental and persistent external pressure for change. In the modern world, the outside-in influence of the international system is inexorable. Because of its unforgiving, competitive nature, it has the power to shape the behavior of an individual state. The competition of states seeking wealth and power requires each to look to its own security and integrity. The international system is "a self-help system . . . in which those who do not help themselves, or who do so less effectively than others, will fail to prosper, will lay themselves open to dangers, will suffer."[3] Those states that do not heed the cues of the international system, that ignore the distribution of power in the world and do not take the necessary steps to adopt the institutions and techniques of the strong states, will suffer harm and may lose their independence as a result. The fundamental parameters of a nation's foreign policy are established by its relative power within the international system. Hence Thucydides's well-known dictum, "The strong do what they can and the weak suffer what they must."

The way in which the strong states organize and structure order in the world inevitably impacts the other, weaker states. Structure influences behavior. It socializes states, "rewarding some types of behavior and punishing others," as the political theorist Robert Gilpin put it. Gilpin added, "Through socialization of the actors and through competition among them, structure channels the behavior of actors in a system."[4] The core domestic institutions of the most successful nations are emulated by other nations.

The influence of the international system is found not only in a nation's struggle for security but also in the drive to enhance the productive capacity upon which national power depends. Along with the international state system, the international economy exerts great force in shaping domestic institutions. The interaction between economics and strategy became especially close in the nineteenth century with the rise of industrial civilization in Europe. Industrial civilization conferred great power on a few states and established a steep gradient of power and hierarchy of prestige that underwrote the rise of Western imperialism. States keenly recognized the need to be both rich and strong, to enhance their wealth and power, and to use their productive economic resources as efficiently as possible.

The Industrial Revolution in England altered the international environment of all other countries. A gap of wealth and power opened between the early industrializers, on the one side, and all other countries, on the other, which transformed the external setting of these other countries, challenging them to bridge the gap and overcome their backwardness. The world was divided between advanced and "follower" societies. The disparity stimulated a competitive struggle for survival by the follower states that impelled them to emulate the institutions of the great powers. They scrutinized the developments that had increased the political and economic strengths of competing states and that could be emulated to better their position in a setting of international struggles. In the economically backward states, perceptive leaders grasped the advantage in borrowing from the very states by which they felt threatened.

Moreover, to catch up, to come up from behind and close the gap, they looked for shortcuts by which they could develop more rapidly than the advanced states had.[5] Follower states introduced the most modern, capital-intensive technology in order to close the gap as rapidly as possible.[6] Leaders of economically backward societies sought the benefits of an industrial society, but they wanted to achieve them by a speedier and less costly transition than that which had occurred in the pioneering industrial societies. In the ensuing international struggles, there were even some advantages for follower states. The advanced countries not only became models of the economic and political techniques up for adoption, they also provided examples of mistakes made, warning of problems that the first industrializers had encountered and that the follower societies could seek to avoid or mitigate.[7] The Industrial Revolution and the consequent realization that economic power mattered as much as military strength further bolstered the outside-in influence on the modern state.

The international system provides incentives and constraints for all modern nations, but the course of modern Japan has been influenced and shaped to an unusually large degree by the international system and by the changes through which that system has passed since the middle of the nineteenth century. Few countries in modern history have been as subject—and as sensitive, responsive, and adaptive—as Japan to the forces of the international environment. The international system has had a powerful effect on Japan's foreign policy, and it has exercised an extraordinary role in shaping Japan's domestic institutions. Repeatedly, Japan has sweepingly revised its domestic order to meet the needs of new configurations of the international order.

JAPANESE ELITES AND THE INTERNATIONAL ORDER

From the beginning of its modern history, Japan's external setting exercised a decisive influence on the course of the nation. Nevertheless, there was never anything inevitable or determinist about the result. Japan's international behavior emerged from the choices its leaders made.[8] And no matter how constraining the international system might have been, Japan did have choices to make in dealing with its position.

The structure of the international system, however powerful in its pulls and constraints, does not alone determine a state's behavior. The perceptions and abilities of decisionmakers drive foreign policy choices. States occupying similar positions in the international system often react differently to its challenges. Even where the influence of the external environment is the strongest, a considerable margin of choice remains.

In different countries, statesmen react differently to the same environment. Even during the foreign occupation of their country after World War II, the most constraining impact that the international system could conceivably exert, the Japanese made critical choices. Since there was always more than one way to respond to the external environment, elite politics often revolved around competing responses. Japanese leaders had to assess the workings of the external order. They had to determine how best to adapt. Making choices was often contentious and the source of heated debate in Japanese political life.

States vary in their skills, attitudes, and perceptions toward international affairs. Some states are more responsive and sensitive to the workings of the international system and what will serve their national interest than are others. Some states ignore external threats; others may hide from them by taking refuge in their inherited institutions and by reaffirming and strengthening tradition. The choices that states make depend on domestic politics, especially their leadership, their perceptions, and the strength of their institutions. To succeed in the international system, states must respect the sources of power and must perceive impending shifts in power in the world.

The realism with which leaders perceive and act upon the constraints and opportunities of the international environment is a critical determinant of state behavior. As the political writer Fareed Zakaria put it, "Statesmen, not states, are the primary actors in international affairs, and their perception of shifts in power, rather than objective measures, are critical."[9] The international system shaped modern Japan not only because of its inherently powerful outside-in influence, but also because modern Japanese leadership was sensitive to the system. Japan made it a matter of strategy to act in accord with the movements of the international system, designing policies and institutions to take advantage of its conditions.

Conservative elites have ruled Japan for its entire modern history. These elites possessed extraordinary latitude to manage the nation's course in the world. Although the makeup of this elite leadership has changed from one era to another, reflecting the needs of the times, and it has recruited new talent into its midst, it has managed to preserve its dominance over society and has remained consistent in its fundamental approach to the international system. The resilience of this conservative elite was never clearer than in the days after World War II, when it clung to power even though it was utterly discredited by the catastrophic defeat, and America, the occupying power, sought to displace it.

Americans are not accustomed to a political system that allows so much latitude to an elite in managing foreign policy, setting strategic priorities, committing national resources, and determining the workings of the political system. By dividing powers between the branches of government, the American system is, in Edwin Corwin's famous phrase, "an invitation to struggle."[10] The founders sought to avoid the abuse of power by dispersing it and creating checks and balances. Although this safeguards domestic democracy, it complicates the conduct of U.S. foreign policy. Tocqueville's well-known judgment followed that "especially in their conduct of foreign relations, democracies appear to me decidedly inferior to other governments."[11]

In contrast, the Japanese values of hierarchy, status, and the sanctity of the authority held by central governing institutions ensured steady support for a strong state. The impact of opinion outside of government was muted. Articulate opinion contributed to the structuring of debates among the elite, and the mass mood set the parameters for debate. But it was the elites who set Japanese policy. Their traditions of realism, with its respect for power, its opportunism, and its pursuit of status and autonomy, persisted through the century and a half of Japan's modern history.

For reasons found deep in their inherited strategic culture, Japan's conservative elites gave priority to the challenges from the outside, keenly aware that Japan's precarious position in the international system required it. Modern Japanese leaders have regarded the structure of the international system as an established condition to which they must respond as deftly as possible in order to pursue the nation's interests. Their realist pursuit of national power, and their opportunistic adaptation to the configuration of power in the world, meant that concern with preserving the ideals of Japan's cultural heritage generally took second place. Henry Kissinger aptly remarked that "it seemed as if Japan had a finely calibrated radar that enabled it to gauge the global balance of power and to adapt its institutions to its necessities, confident that no adaptation could disturb the essence of Japanese society."[12]

This strategic style of modern Japan's leadership is a legacy of premodern influences and the formative experience of the Meiji Restoration of 1868, Japan's modern revolution that brought it into the international system. Japan's long isolation and feudal experience implanted in its modern conservative leaders a bold realist approach to its international environment. Carried out from above by a party within the old Tokugawa samurai class, the Restoration bequeathed a pragmatic conservative tradition that has held sway over policymaking ever since. Emerging from the lower ranks of the samurai class, the Meiji leaders were galvanized by the encroaching dangers posed by the Western powers at the time of Commodore Perry's arrival. They strongly felt the need to protect the security of the homeland in the face of the threat to the nation's existence, and they gave priority to foreign policy above all else. Foreign policy *was* domestic policy. The Meiji leaders responded to the weight of outside influences with a full mobilization of internal organization.

Japan's conservative revolutionaries in 1868 restored the emperor to the center of government as a symbol of a new national unity. Obsessed by the massive threat that Western imperialism posed to Japan's sovereignty, they moved resolutely to replace the old feudal political organization of the state with new institutions modeled after the institutions of the Western imperialist powers. Intensely aware of their nation's economic backwardness and strategic vulnerability, Japanese leaders determined to accept the external order as a given and to seek to advance their interests in a pragmatic and opportunistic fashion. Where other countries facing the challenges of imperialism resisted and reaffirmed their traditions, Japan chose to adapt. This realist approach was striking for the primacy it gave to foreign policy and to the acquisition of national power and for the readiness to abandon inherited ways even to the extent of risking Japanese identity.

The modern Japanese state therefore, to a great extent, had its origins in meeting the challenges of the external order. It was charted out of an opportunistic response to the external order and did not grow spontaneously and naturally out of domestic circumstance. And if that order changed, Japan would adapt its policies and internal organization to the changed order. For the full length of Japan's modern history, the Meiji paradigm held sway: The demands of foreign policy set Japan's course.

The reaction of Japanese leaders to the danger posed by Western encroachment had much in common with the reaction of nineteenth-century realists in the continental European tradition who were engaged in an intense struggle for survival. The geopolitical vulnerability of Prussia to the dangers posed by the rivalries and warfare of the European state system led advisers to the Prussian monarchy to counsel "the primacy of foreign policy" (*der Primat der Aussenpolitik*). Faced with the threat of being conquered, occupied, and made subservient, they asserted that all aspects of state policy must address the external challenges.

The historian Leopold von Ranke wrote in his famous 1833 essay on *die grossen Mächte* ("the great powers") that the struggles among great European powers had become so intense that the domestic character of a state must be shaped above all to meet the constant challenges that these rivalries and wars posed. He stressed the determining force that foreign policy exercised in the life of states. The phrase *der Primat der Aussenpolitik* came out of Ranke's view. Later, counseling the Prussian state, Ranke urged that it organize itself internally so as to succeed externally. Competing to survive in the international system, states must rely on themselves. "The world has been parceled out," he said: "To be somebody you have to rise by your own efforts. You must achieve genuine independence. Your rights will not be voluntarily ceded to you. You must fight for them." Domestic policy had to be subordinated to the exigencies of foreign affairs; the dangers of war and defeat required that foreign policy take precedence. "The position of a state in the world," he wrote, "depends upon the degree of independence it has attained. It is obliged, therefore, to organize all its internal resources for the purpose of self-preservation. This is the supreme law of the state."[13]

In the same vein, the famous social historian Otto Hintze, who counseled the German government early in the twentieth century, held that the state was less a reflection of the internal evolution of society than a creature of the external environment:

> The state is by no means solely determined by society. For the state is not merely a government internally but a sovereign power externally. Throughout history power has been the main goal of the activities of the state; hence its structure depends at least as much on the conditions of its external power position as on the social-structural conditions of its internal governing activity. Since the state must adjust itself not only internally, but also externally to the conditions of its existence, the external setting must surely influence the internal social development.[14]

Hintze drew the grand conclusion that "throughout the ages pressure from without has been a determining influence on internal structure." By this he meant that it was external threats more than internal social structure or class conflict that shaped the state: "If we want to find out about the relations between military organization and the organization of the state we must direct our attention particularly to two phenomena, which conditioned the real organization of the state. These are, first, the structure of social classes, and second, the external ordering of the states—their position relative to each other, and their overall position in the world. It is one-sided, exaggerated, and therefore false to consider class conflict the only driving force in history. Conflict between nations has been far more important; and throughout the ages pressure from without has been a determining influence on internal structure."[15]

In counseling the German government, Hintze, like Ranke, argued that it was necessary for the state to organize itself internally so as to succeed externally. Like Ranke, he stressed that a strong military posture, political organization, and foreign policy are essential to the external security of the state, but he also maintained that the government should direct all activities, including education and especially economic activities, that could strengthen Germany against foreign powers.[16] The exposed position of Germany in Central Europe required it to adapt all of its domestic institutions to the exigencies of constant military conflict.

Such realist thinking was also characteristic of the Meiji leaders in Japan. They came to the same conclusions by their own cultural path, but there can be no doubt that they shared common assumptions with their Prussian counterparts who also came out of a military and feudal background. It was no accident that Tokyo Imperial University, where the great majority of Japan's modern mandarins were trained, invited one of Ranke's disciples to come to Japan in 1887 and establish a history department. During his sixteen-year tenure, Ludwig Riess educated a generation of students in Ranke's views.[17]

The trauma of Japan's entry into the international system—that is, the forced opening of the country by Western gunboats—provoked Japan's modern revolution and set a pattern whereby it would cast its internal structure to meet the demands of the outside order. Because the Restoration evoked the deeply embedded values of the Japanese in their struggle for the radical change that was required to preserve their national existence, it cast a long shadow over their subsequent history. The Meiji Restoration established a pattern of characteristic Japanese interaction with the international system.

Although the internal developments of Tokugawa society paved the way for change, domestic developments are an insufficient explanation for the form that the new Meiji state took. Long-term economic and social change had undermined the vitality of Bakufu rule. The rise of a market economy, the spread of education, social unrest, and new currents of thought all prepared the way for revolutionary change. The shogunate had become a weak and uncertain polity. The remarkable responsiveness of Japan to the Western challenge is thus to be understood in part as resulting from the gradual buildup of social and economic problems during the preceding century. Had Tokugawa rule not been characterized at this time by institutional incapacity, widespread social unrest, and anxious groping by political leaders for new reform measures, the Japanese response would have been more measured. However, without the foreign intrusion, the demonstration of new sources of power, the new examples of institutional capacity, and the competitive challenge, Japan's leaders would have formulated a very different set of policies and constructed a very different set of institutions. The new Meiji state was by no means simply a reflection of Japanese society.

The nature of a nation's modern revolution illuminates a great deal about the national character, the strategic principles, and the logic of a people. Just as 1776 tells Americans so much about themselves—the ideals and purposes that they have held central—so the Meiji Restoration reveals much about the nature and purpose of modern Japan. The Restoration was a nationalist revolution driven by the competitive demands of the international system and the determination to adapt the nation's policies and institutions to succeed in that system. Japan's entire domestic infrastructure was remodeled to respond to the challenges of the imperialist order.

The formative experience of Japan's entry into the modern world established a pattern of extraordinary sensitivity to the workings of the international system, a readiness to accommodate to its changing demands, and an unusual degree of opportunism in the nation's approach to its external environment. Repeatedly, through the course of the 150 years of its modern history, each time the structure of the international system underwent fundamental change, Japan adapted its foreign policies to that changed order and restructured its internal organization to take advantage of it.

THE NEW ORDERS IN EAST ASIA

An international order is dynamic. Nations rise and decline owing to their uneven rate of growth and to the technological and organizational breakthroughs that bring advantage to one state or another. Some states grow more rapidly than others. The strong states must constantly see to their sources of power lest they become wedded to the status quo and lose their vitality. Weaker states are motivated to improve their position in the system by emulating the sources of strength of the dominant powers. Eventually a newly risen power may find its interests unsatisfied by the existing order. It may seek to revise that order and even come to believe that its interests lie in contesting and overthrowing the order and its rules and institutions. If it succeeds in challenging the old order, typically through warfare that results in a new distribution of power among states, a fundamental change in the organization and governance of the international system occurs.

Few countries have revised their domestic orders so sweepingly to meet the needs of new configurations of international order as Japan. Since entering the modern world, Japan has experienced five fundamental changes in the international order:

1. the collapse of the Sinocentric system and the establishment of the Western imperialist order in the mid-nineteenth century;
2. the end of the imperialist system after World War I and the beginning of a new American-inspired system based on several treaties negotiated at the Washington Conference in 1921–1922;
3. the disintegration of this U.S.-led system and the anarchy of the 1930s, which enticed Japan into attempting to create its own East Asian order;
4. the crushing defeat of Japan's new order and the establishment of a new U.S.-dominated liberal order after 1945 and the beginning of the Cold War;
5. the end of this Cold War bipolar system with the collapse of the Soviet Union in 1989.

Each of the first four transitions in the international system resulted in fundamental and profound changes in Japan's foreign policy as well as in its domestic institutions. The fifth transition in the external order, which came with the end of the Cold War, set in motion great changes in the international system that have yet to produce a settled new international order in East Asia and the world. But Japan is already responding to the flux by moving steadily away from the policies that guided it during the Cold War and initiating a major restructuring of its domestic institutions, including revision of its constitution.

Each of the successive new international orders in East Asia that Japan confronted had its own distinct characteristics, its own configuration of power, and its own legitimating norms and values. Each was in a sense a regional extension of the prevailing international system. In each case, the dominant powers constructed a framework of rules and practices to secure their interests. The rules of the system covered the conduct of diplomacy and political relations as well as economic and trade relations, and the values and interests of the dominant states were woven into an ideology that served to legitimate the authority they exercised. Reflecting the balance of power, a clear hierarchy of prestige prevailed, and the weaker states in the system were compelled to play by the rules of the game established by the dominant powers.

On particular issues, domestic circumstance in Japanese foreign policy decisionmaking might prevail, but in the long run and in the bigger picture of calculating strategy and shaping the society's institutions, it was the paradigm of international order and its fundamental changes that influenced the deeper processes of modern Japan. The primacy of foreign policy did not mean that the appropriate course was immediately agreed upon by the elite leadership. Fundamental change in the international system often occasioned debate about the best strategy to adopt. But once consensus was achieved, Japan adapted in a fundamental and pervasive way to all aspects of the external order. It is particularly at the moments of change in the structure of international orders that Japanese adaptation is so telling. In these periods of transition lies the explanation for the wide swings in Japan's international behavior that have baffled foreign observers.

Prior to the arrival of the Western imperialists, Japan had not been a part of an international system. In its island isolation, it was able to stand apart from the Sinocentric system that had held sway over much of Asia for centuries. With the arrival of Western power in the middle of the nineteenth century, the Sinocentric system collapsed. The first new order in modern East Asia, the imperialist system was the longest lasting of the succeeding orders. Owing to the huge preponderance of power that the Industrial Revolution gave to the Western powers and to the cooperative framework that they worked out among themselves, the system lasted nearly eighty years, from the Treaty of Nanjing of 1842, which ended the Opium War, to the end of World War I.

The system of tributary relations by which imperial China had maintained its central place in regional relations could not cope with the raw military might that industrial civilization bestowed. Nor could the already declining Tokugawa regime in Japan, which was now finally delegitimized by its acquiescence in the demands of the imperialist system. Imperialism integrated East Asia into the world economy, subjected the regional states to Western dominance, and created the first truly international system. Japan entered the international system as a weak actor, a victim of the system, but never a passive actor. Despite its traditional isolation and aloofness from the Sinocentric system, Japan responded quickly and dramatically to the imperialist system, accepted its rules and norms, reformed all its domestic institutions, and so began an intense drive to reorganize every aspect of its core domestic institutions in order to meet the competitive demands of the international system into which Japan had been suddenly thrust.

It would be difficult to find a more profound example in world history of the *Primat der Aussenpolitik* than Meiji Japan. While other Asian states resisted the new international order that Western imperialism imposed, Japan alone responded through all-out emulation of the institutions of the great powers. Western law, banking systems, military organizations, scientific knowledge—all aspects of the imperial powers' civilization became models for the rapid transformation of Japan. Playing by the rules of the game, within the space of a generation Japan became itself an active participant in the system. Ultimately, by the time of the Russo-Japanese War of 1904–1905, Japan had achieved major power status with its own expanding empire.

World War I undermined the imperialist system in East Asia and led to the creation of the next new regional order. The United States emerged from the war as the new world power and asserted a new set of organizing principles that would revolutionize the system. Woodrow Wilson's principles were intended to do away with the norms of imperialism, to end reliance on balance-of-power politics and secret treaties, and to replace them with ideals of international liberalism. Compared to the imperialist order, this new order, known as the Washington Treaty System, was weak and short-lived, lasting scarcely a decade. Nevertheless, Japan's initial response was similar to its earlier one. Japan chose to accommodate to the demands of the new order. It accepted the prevailing rules of the Washington System even though its principles were designed to contain Japanese power and had no basis in Japanese experience. Japan's conservative elite not only revised its foreign policies, it sanctioned a newly proclaimed democratic politics at home that would accord with the new international norms.

The Washington System, however, soon lost its credibility and authority. The Anglo-American powers failed to underwrite the new system. They themselves abandoned the principles upon which the system was based by retreating into isolationism and adopting protectionist measures. The Washington System crumbled under the impact of world economic depression. The resulting vacuum of power and anarchic regional environment opened the way for the next order.

Inspired by the emergence of regional blocs elsewhere in the world, Japan's leaders declared their determination to create "a new East Asian Order." Within the space of a decade, from 1932 to 1942, Japanese military power brought much of East and Southeast Asia under its hegemony and proclaimed ideals of pan-Asian solidarity and the end of Western colonial influence. Once again Japan reorganized its domestic institutions to support its foreign policy. Fascism appeared to represent the wave of the future, and Japan drew inspiration for reworking its domestic institutions from Germany. This abortive order asserted Japanese values of familial hierarchy, whereby each nation would find its own place in a Japanese-led system, but under wartime conditions the order relied on military control to maintain itself. Japan's bid for regional hegemony ended in catastrophic defeat and the most extreme form of outside-in influence: a foreign occupation and the remaking of all of Japan's domestic institutions in the image of the occupier.

The United States emerged from World War II with unprecedented power to remake the international order. The Americans set out again to create a system based on international liberalism, but one more resilient than the Washington system. They hoped that the new system would embrace the other victorious powers, including the Soviet Union. But the almost immediate collapse of agreements reached between Franklin D. Roosevelt and Joseph Stalin at Yalta in 1945 led to the beginning of the Cold War. The result was a bipolar system in the world and in Asia.

The Yalta Conference envisioned a regional order—the Yalta system—that would enshrine U.S.-Soviet cooperation in East Asia. The Chinese revolution and the Korean War doomed this vision. The United States responded by negotiating a series of alliances in Asia and confronted a Soviet–led East Asian group of states in a regional version of the Cold War system. U.S. leaders held together this network of bilateral alliances in Asia with security guarantees, massive aid, and access to the U.S. market. During this period, Japan formulated a unique response to the system, known as the Yoshida Doctrine. This strategy capitalized on a Cold War structure that allowed Japan to depend on U.S. security guarantees and concentrate exclusively on the rapid economic growth that would restore Japan's standing in great-power competition. Japan's domestic institutions were reworked to maximize its ability to exploit the free-trade regime sponsored by the Americans. This Yoshida strategy, named after the veteran diplomat who was the postwar prime minister and a great admirer of the Meiji paradigm of pragmatic adaptation to the international order, worked brilliantly until 1989, when the Cold War system came to an abrupt end with the implosion of the Soviet Union.

The post–Cold War order is still in the making. It is not yet clear what the new order in East Asia in the twenty-first century will look like and how Japan will fit with it. U.S. power was unchallenged after the Cold War, and the Americans proclaimed the victory of the principles of international liberalism, asserting their universal validity for a new order. In East Asia, remnants of the Cold War persisted in the divided Korea, the Taiwan issue, the absence of a Russo-Japanese peace treaty, and the continuation of America's bilateral alliances throughout the region. But this "interregnum" will eventually give way to a very different structure of regional order. The rise of China and the rapid economic growth and political awakening of former colonies signals a proactive Asia. Japan, which has always gained its sense of purpose and the character of its domestic political-economic institutions through relating to its external environment, is moving cautiously in the uncertainty of this regional interregnum. Adjusting incrementally to the emerging trends, it began to move away from the Yoshida strategy in the 1990s and to rethink the organization of its domestic structure. But without a clear vision of what shape the new international order would take, Japan's leaders have been cautious in implementing their characteristic strategy.

These successive changes in the structure and nature of order in East Asia are what have given direction to the course of modern Japan's history. It is indeed ironic that a nation that had enjoyed a unique isolation and security for nearly all its history prior to the modern period should have been more responsive to its international environment than other countries whose cultures seemed more open and amenable to change. Yet it is the interplay of these two distinct historic forces—a relentless and dominant external influence and an opportunistic strategy of adapting skillfully to the outside influence—that explains so much about modern Japan's behavior.

CHAPTER TWO

JAPAN'S NATIONAL STYLE

F oreign policy," it has been said, "is the face a nation wears to the world. The minimal motive is the same for all states—the protection of national integrity and interest. But the manner in which a state practices foreign policy is greatly affected by national peculiarities."[1] The behavior of nations, like that of individuals, is shaped by elements of heredity and environment, which through history respond to problems and experiences and in time build up relatively stable patterns of response. These patterns, although persistent, are by no means immutable; rather, they evolve as a people absorb new experiences and encounter changes in their environment. They may change gradually over time, but they are not erased. There is innovation in the patterns as new challenges are encountered, but there is great conservativeness too. These recurrent patterns of behavior constitute a distinctive set of national attitudes, habits, and principles that are brought to bear as a people approaches its problems. They show themselves in the nation's foreign policy and in the interaction the nation has with its external environment.

As the eminent French authority on international politics Raymond Aron observed, states acquire different "styles of being and behaving" that persist through time.[2] A nation's style springs in part from intrinsic factors of geography and the nation's natural endowments. "A position on the map imposes upon the diplomacy or upon the strategy of a state," Aron said, "certain orientations which are likely to be lasting, if not permanent."[3] Within that geographical setting, the centuries of experience are transformed over time into second nature, producing cultural traits that

Montesquieu called "the spirit of a nation." This *esprit* crucially influences a nation's international behavior and, as Aron allowed, gives a "relative consistency in the 'style' of foreign policy," but it must not be used as a sufficient explanation of any particular policy. As Aron wisely observed,

> The "spirit of a nation" which Montesquieu speaks of is a notion as equivocal as that of national character, but perhaps preferable because it emphasizes the share of culture and the historical heritage. . . . The French nation was not born as it is now, it has become what it is as a result of the events which it has lived through, of the customs which have been slowly established and of the mode of government. A result more than an origin, the spirit of a nation renders a destiny intelligible as a particular act, but it must not constrain investigation; it helps understanding, but it must be explained.[4]

The wellsprings of modern Japan's international behavior lie in the long years of isolation during Japan's premodern history. Japan's insular setting and geographic isolation ordained a distinctive culture, a keen sense of uniqueness and independence. Its civilization was built on the constricted islands largely in isolation from the outside world. Through most of its history prior to the nineteenth century, Japan did not participate in an international society that acted on it with great intensity. Japan is separated from the Eurasian continent by more than 100 miles, five times the distance that separates England across the Straits of Dover from the Continent. This distance across the Korean Straits is surpassed by the 450 miles of open seas that lie between Japan and China. Thus a distinctive strategic culture, shaped by Japan's domestic political and social currents and its values, emerged from the long years of isolation.

SINOCENTRISM VERSUS JAPANESE INDEPENDENCE

In the premodern period, Japan occasionally participated in the Sinocentric system, and at times it had regular interactions with Korea and other states, but for the most part it held aloof from the external world. Geography allowed Japan to enjoy a largely self-sufficient isolation. In the thirteenth century, Khubilai Khan mounted the largest overseas expedition in world history prior to modern times, but the Kamakura feudal government (*bakufu*) rejected the messengers from the Mongols and their demand that the Japanese submit to a tributary relationship. The bakufu even ordered the execution of the messengers. The first Mongol invasion attempt, in 1274, was broken up by a great sea storm that was later celebrated as the *kamikaze* or "wind of the gods" shielding the divine homeland. The subsequent Mongol invasion, in 1281, composed of a massive force of 140,000 men, likewise was ultimately done in not by samurai forces defending the shores of Kyushu but again by a great storm. The Mongols are said to have lost 100,000 men.

Sometimes premodern Japan's isolation and natural security are exaggerated. Historians of premodern Japan, according to Ronald Toby, are prone to overlook the way in which "changes in the strategic balance in continental East Asia have often affected Japan in significant ways."[5] Although geography afforded Japan free security through much of its premodern period, there were periodic security threats. Toby and several leading Japanese historians now argue that not only was premodern Japan affected by the strategic balance on the continent, but its sense of insecurity led it to import political institutions from the continent. Undoubtedly, in light of this new interpretation, the most surprising and significant way in which the strategic balance on the continent affected Japan was in the seventh century, when, as some historians now think, the rise of an expansive China spurred Japan to adopt Chinese institutions and create the first unified Japanese state.[6]

Until recently, historians described the influence of Chinese culture in the early centuries of Japanese history as arising simply through Japanese awe and admiration of China's high cultural achievements. Describing the missions that Japan sent to China in the seventh and eighth centuries to bring back knowledge of its religion, art, architecture, and philosophy, Edwin O. Reischauer wrote that it was "the glory of China before their eyes" that led the Japanese to try "to create in Japan a small replica of China."[7] Similarly, Arnold Toynbee and even the eminent historian of Japan, Sir George Sansom, approached Japan's cultural borrowing in this period of classic institutional development as evidence of a Japan "overwhelmed by the example of China and thus driven to imitation and emulation."[8]

Undoubtedly, there was an awe that stimulated Japan's borrowing and institution-building modeled on China, but more recent research suggests that Japan's motivation in importing knowledge and institutions to establish a Chinese-style bureaucratic state during the seventh century was fundamentally driven by the Japanese perception of a *strategic* threat from the continent. During the 660s, an internally disunited Japan feared the specter of an expansive T'ang China empire that in alliance with Japan's old enemy, the Korean kingdom of Silla, destroyed the other two Korean kingdoms of Paekche and Koguryo. Subsequently, beyond the specter of Chinese power on the Korean peninsula, Japanese leaders felt threatened—one can see parallels to the contemporary developments on the peninsula—by the possibility of a unified and hostile Korea. "In 672 . . . an even more threatening situation emerged in Korea," wrote one Japanese historian. "Silla, Japan's old enemy, was breaking its ties with T'ang and moving to seize control of the entire Korean peninsula." Painfully aware that Japan's internal disunity made it vulnerable, Emperor Tenmu sought to unify and strengthen the state through adoption of Chinese central institutional models.[9]

If it is true that the period of great cultural borrowing from China in the early history of Japan was brought on by Japanese concerns over the threat in Japan's external environment, then it would constitute a compelling precedent for the later Japanese reaction to the West. "In both cases," wrote a prominent historian, "the Japanese felt threatened by foreign powers and responded by adopting an array of reforms needed to strengthen their state."[10] Although he emphasized the ambitions of domestic actors and their drives for power as the force behind the borrowing from China, the historian John Whitney Hall could not help wondering "whether Japan of the seventh century felt a sense of foreign crisis comparable to that which agitated the Japanese of the nineteenth century."[11] It seemed the external environment and domestic political struggles were inextricably linked. Cultural borrowing was motivated and legitimated by its strategic value and by the power it brought to the Japanese state and its leaders. In the short run, Japan then, as later, was willing to risk its cultural identity if it would strengthen national power.

In any case, threats from the continent did not succeed. Neither in the case of the T'ang foray into Korea and the specter of a unified Korea in the seventh century, nor in the memorable invasion attempts of Khubilai Khan in the thirteenth century, was the security of the Japanese state violated. By the time of these great Mongol invasions, the imperial bureaucratic state had declined and Japan had become a society ruled by samurai schooled in the tasks of warfare and strategy. On this occasion, there was less need for institutional innovation because the society was pervaded by institutions of warfare and defense. As one authority wrote, "The Mongol invasions were a meeting between a people with strong tendencies toward conquest and a society governed by warriors."[12]

Japan therefore entered the modern period with an extraordinary sense of self-reliance, a fierce determination to maintain its independence, and an almost religious belief in its distinctive identity. It was virtually unique among East Asian countries in the degree of its fixed resistance to inclusion in the Chinese world order.[13] The Japanese pragmatically drew from the continent the technology and institutions needed to develop the power of their government, but they were resolute in their refusal to defer to Chinese political claims. With rare exception, Japanese leaders refused to accept a subordinate position in the Chinese world order centered on the theory of the universal preeminence of the Chinese emperor. In contrast to the Westphalian concept that developed in Europe, whereby a number of independent nations were in theory considered equal, each with its own independent legitimacy and sovereignty, the Sinocentric concept dictated that the countries of East Asia were subsumed within the Chinese sphere of civilized society. Rulers of the various countries within this sphere were expected to present themselves to the Chinese emperor for investiture as "kings." With rare exception, Japanese leaders refused to accept this subordinate position.

To have accepted such a position would not only have acknowledged China's superior civilization but would have signified acquiescence to China's claims to represent civilization itself. The Japanese saw their sovereignty, independence, and, most important, their way of life at stake. In the Sinocentric order, the Chinese emperor had to be acknowledged not only as the preeminent temporal power but also as a power of cosmic significance who mediated between heaven and earth. To have accepted tributary status would have required the Japanese emperor to be invested with his authority, to receive a seal symbolizing the authority granted, to date all memorials according to the Chinese calendar, and to make regular visits to the Chinese imperial court to reaffirm this subordination. On numerous occasions, however, Japanese leaders ostentatiously dispatched messages from the Japanese emperor to the Chinese emperor on the basis of equality. At the beginning of the seventh century, to take one example, Empress Suiko dispatched an official mission to the Sui court with a memorial that began, "The offspring of heaven in the land where the sun rises offers a letter to the offspring of heaven in the land where the sun sets."

In only one relatively brief period during the premodern millennium did Japan acknowledge subordination to the Chinese emperor. In the fifteenth century, Japan's feudal leader, the shogun Ashikaga Yoshimitsu, accepted investiture by the Ming emperor, referring to himself as "Your subject, Minamoto King of Japan." By entering into a subordinate relationship, Yoshimitsu thereby gained Chinese sanction for official trade, which proved immensely profitable. It should be noted that it was not the Japanese imperial court that accepted investiture. Yoshimitsu, who is generally thought to have been motivated by a desire for economic gain, was, in fact, criticized by the court nobility for accepting this subservient status.

Although most historians have emphasized the profit motive for this aberration from Japan's customary aloofness, one prominent historian has offered an explanation that credits Japanese strategic concerns in the international system of the time. The Japanese historian Sasaki Ginya sees Yoshimitsu's motivation as stemming partly from concern over Ming intentions and "the insecurity caused by fear of a Chinese invasion."[14] In fact, after Yoshimitsu's death, when his son became shogun and discontinued diplomatic relations with the Ming, the Emperor Ch'eng-tsu contemplated sending troops to attack Japan. The next shogun restored relations with China, and the official trade continued for more than a century before ending in 1547. A half-century later, as Japanese central feudal power coalesced, the great general and unifier Toyotomi Hideyoshi launched an abortive invasion of the continent designed to extend his overlordship to the Sinocentric world. This was an instance of not only resisting the Chinese world order but actually contesting it.

Throughout the Tokugawa era (1600–1868), the Japanese tried to establish their own international system on a limited scale. Japan claimed a central position in the East Asian sphere and sought legitimacy by asserting that the Ryukyus, Korea, Siam, and other states were sending tribute to Japan. As Toby wrote, the Tokugawa shored up their own legitimacy at home by declaring that "Japan dealt only with ritual peers and inferiors, and was not subordinate to any other power. . . . Japan relied on no external agency, such as China, for its definition of itself or for its location in the cosmos, except insofar as these agencies either recognized the bakufu as a peer, as Korea seemed to do, or as a suzerain, as Ryukyu did."

The spectacle of China's fall to barbarian Manchu rule confirmed Japan's pride in its ability to resist conquest. A leading Confucian scholar, Yamaga Sokō, asserted that China had thereby forfeited its claim to centrality. In contrast, Japan had not only defied barbarian control, it had never changed dynasties. China was merely another foreign country. Yamasaki Ansai, another prominent Confucian scholar, observed that every country must regard itself as "central" and other countries as "barbarian." And in a famous anecdote that prefigures the pragmatic Japanese nationalism of the modern period, Yamasaki declared that if Japan were attacked by a Chinese army commanded by the sages that Japan revered, Confucius and Mencius, it would be the duty of a loyal Japanese Confucian to resist and to capture the sages and put them in the service of Japan.[15]

THE LEGACY OF FEUDALISM

Although these intermittent experiences with the external environment that upheld Japanese resistance to foreign authority became a part of the national political tradition and contributed to Japan's strategic culture, for most of premodern history Japan was a closed system. The dynamics of change were largely lived out within the islands. Given the prevailing isolation, the most important legacy for modern strategic culture grew out of the long feudal experience that helped prepare Japan for the modern international system. Along with Europe, Japan is often regarded as one of "only two fully proven cases of feudalism" and even as "the classic case of feudalism."[16] The origins of Japanese feudalism are traced to the twelfth century, and its forms continued to characterize the political system until the Meiji Restoration in the nineteenth century.

The mechanisms of feudalism were excellent preparation for the international system.[17] During Japan's prolonged experience of anarchic conditions and weak central authority, feudal states competed with one another for both political and economic power. In its dynamics, Japan's own internal political system was in many ways a miniature of the modern international state system. One historian described Japanese feudalism at its high point in the sixteenth century as a "society where each lord was the potential enemy of every other lord and every vassal a potential lord, power and its symbols, even more than money and its symbols in modern society, were the sources of almost all security and prestige. In the struggle between fiefs only the fittest survived, and those domains that did not actively attempt to increase their strength were eliminated by a military process of natural selection."[18] The six centuries during which feudalism persisted in Japan left this legacy of an overriding concern with the maximization of military power as a condition of survival.

In 1950, the political scientist John Herz introduced the concept of "the security dilemma" to describe the dynamics of nation-state competition in a condition of anarchy. The dilemma is created when states, seeking to ensure their security by taking measures to enhance their power, arouse the suspicion, distrust, and insecurity of their neighboring states, whose leaders, in turn, feel compelled to take corresponding measures, thereby stimulating an ongoing competition for power and security. Herz wrote that owing to the anarchic condition of international politics, states, "striving to attain security from . . . attack, . . . are driven to acquire more and more power in order to escape the impact of the power of others. This, in turn, renders the other more insecure and compels them to prepare for the worst. Since none can ever feel entirely secure in such a world of competing units, power competition ensues, and the vicious circle of security and power accumulation is on."[19] Herz concluded that this competition constituted a struggle for survival that was the inherent and inexorable condition of international relations. The logic of the security dilemma perfectly described the political experience of the Japanese feudal elite. This was especially so in the Warring States Period (1467–1568), when there was a complete breakdown of central authority, but even afterward, to the very eve of the modern period, this competitive dynamic persisted among the feudal domains.

During the final phase of Japanese feudalism, from 1600 to 1868, a peace was imposed on the system by a coalition of feudal lords. They froze the feudal structure in a complex equilibrium under the Tokugawa central administration, but the competition among the semiautonomous domains or feudal states persisted. Although the substance of feudalism was often less apparent than the form in this final phase, the military traditions were preserved and actually persisted strongly in the outlying domains that finally overthrew the Tokugawa. The competition was increasingly of an economic sort. Among the more powerful of the roughly 250 domains in the Tokugawa feudal system, for example, the concept of *kokueki* (state interest) became common. The major domains were continually concerned about maintaining and increasing their material capabilities in relation to other domains. They competed for wealth, power, and prestige. The Confucian scholar Kaiho Seiryō observed in 1813 how competition among domains had come to focus on trade in a zero-sum affair akin to warfare:

> This is an age when one must not let his guard down toward other domains and must carefully cultivate his own country. One must be on guard not from his neighbor's violent attack, but rather from loss of trade. . . . If a domain does not innovate to increase its land's produce relative to its neighbors, the neighbor will grow rich and the domain will grow poor.

And if the neighbor becomes prosperous and the domain is impoverished, gold and silver will flow to the prosperous land.[20]

Here we can find rudiments of modern Japan's subsequent economic strategy in such practices as the retention of experts in new product development, import substitution, promotion through subsidies of crops and products for export (to other domains), mastery of the most advanced technologies, and so on. Mercantilist thought in the Tokugawa era, according to a study by historian Luke Roberts, "developed out of the internal dynamics of the miniature 'international' economic order within the Japanese islands." When Perry arrived and the imperialists imposed the demands of trade and the restrictions of sovereignty of an international system on Japan, "many domains had much experience in 'internationally' organized commercial development, [and] their leaders and their merchants were better situated than the shogunate to appreciate and enact this new pattern of foreign relations. The strongly mercantilist concepts that were part of *kokueki* thought possessed numerous similarities to the economic nationalisms of the nineteenth century West."[21]

The persistent fragmentation of political authority in the feudal structure accustomed the Japanese to dealing with competing political units and with the hard knowledge that survival depended on mastery of the sources of power. It is striking how often, even today, Japanese strategists will make analogies to the Japanese feudal period to explain events in the international system. It would be hard to think of better historical training for the modern international system and its competitive dynamics than Japan's prolonged feudal experience. As Joseph Strayer wrote in his essay on Japanese feudalism in the Tokugawa period, "Feudalism was what distinguished Japan from its neighbors; feudalism best expressed the values which were peculiar to Japan."[22] The prolonged Japanese experience of feudalism defined many of the assumptions and beliefs and much of the reasoning behind the modern elite's decision to adapt to the modern international system.

REALIST PATTERNS IN THE JAPANESE RESPONSE

A distinctive logic and set of strategic principles drawn from the premodern era, especially the political values instilled by feudalism, informed Japanese conduct in the international system. The Japanese response, in its essentials, was based in the logic of Realpolitik, whereby "the state's interest provides the spring of action, the necessities of policy arise from the unregulated competition of states, calculation based on these necessities can discover the policies that will best serve a state's interest, success is the ultimate test of policy, and success is defined as preserving and strengthening the state."[23]

There are six closely interrelated and overlapping patterns of response to the international system that define Japan's realist approach. Though not immutable, they constitute persistent traits, propensities that last over time. They are not in themselves unique except as they are combined and embedded in Japanese elite culture. They are products of history and therefore not immune to the subsequent course of historical events, the influence of new social forces, and the hard trials of the international system. However, owing to the momentum of the past, they change only slowly. The persistence of these core characteristics also owes much to the continuity and staying power of the modern Japanese political elite and its roots in the premodern ruling class. These characteristics are what made Japan so responsive to structural change in the international system. They underlie the approach taken by the conservatives who have dominated modern Japanese foreign policymaking.

Attentiveness to Power

Thomas Hobbes wrote in *Leviathan* that the first "general inclination of mankind" is "a perpetual and restless desire of power after power, that ceaseth only in death."[24] All temporal orders lust for power; the pursuit of power is universal and ubiquitous in international politics, but for the past 150 years Japan's pursuit has been peculiarly determined and persistent. Japan is striking for its fundamental realism, that is, its respect for the power distribution and for the sources of power in the international system, for its readiness to adapt its policies and institutions in order to accommodate itself to the conditions of the external world.[25]

How was it that Japan alone among Asian countries reacted so swiftly to the challenge of Western power, sacrificing so much of its own institutional heritage and restructuring its political and economic policies in order to prepare the ground for the far-reaching reforms required to build an industrial society in the course of a single generation? To put the question another way, Why did Japan's leaders, during the Meiji era and later, give primacy to foreign policy?

A compelling answer to these central questions is found in the fundamental values held by the new Meiji leaders. Japan's modern revolution, the Meiji Restoration, was carried out "from above" by members of the traditional samurai ruling elite. Owing to their feudal background, the Meiji leaders instinctively gave priority to the value of power and its symbols. The overriding concern in feudal society with the maximization of military power as a condition of survival meant that power and its symbols were the source of security and prestige.[26] As a consequence, there was little restraint on the exercise of power. This was in sharp contrast with the situation in China and Korea, where the value system imposed limits on power.[27] In Japan, Buddhism flourished, but it did not resist the warrior ethos. Nor did Confucianism; indeed, Confucianism served to buttress loyalty to superiors and subordinated knowledge to practicality, educated scholars to warriors. It therefore developed in Japan as only a shadow of what it meant to the continental states. There is no trace in Japan of the Confucian emphasis on the ethical restraint on absolute power.

Fukuzawa Yukichi, the leading advocate of reform in the early Meiji period, wrote in his widely read essay published in 1875, *An Outline of Civilization,* that the overriding concern with power was the defining characteristic of Japanese society:

> Comparison of Japanese civilization with Western civilization reveals that the greatest difference between the two is this imbalance of power. Imbalance of power pervades the entire network of Japanese society. . . . This imbalance of power is one element in the Japanese spirit. . . . We shall find this imbalance pervading the whole of life in Japan, public or private. It is as though thousands of scales were hung in Japan, and all of them were always out of balance, none ever in equilibrium. . . . Wherever there are social relationships there you will find this imbalance.[28]

The long experience of the feudal system, with its competition among political units for survival and position, bred a preoccupation with power. The Meiji Restoration brought to power young samurai from the domains of Chōshū and Satsuma, and they were the group in Japanese society with the keenest sense of the need to maximize power and the means by which it was achieved. They were not satisfied simply to consolidate their power against internal opposition. "The Meiji leaders . . . represented in an extreme form this concern of the traditional society with power," wrote Albert Craig. "In their eyes the existence on Japan's doorstep of the superior

Western powers was intolerable. . . . Their main task was to create a state sufficiently powerful to cope with the foreign powers of which they were so conscious. . . . That the values or goals of the [feudal] period continued to function with so little change explains the strength of Japan's obsession to equal the West."[29] This primary commitment to the achievement of power imparted to Japanese foreign policy a fundamental realism that became one of its defining characteristics throughout the modern period.

Besides having strong realist values to guide their response to the international environment, Japan's leaders presided over state structures that gave them the ability to pursue these values. Through much of its modern period, Japan has had a strong state with the resources at its command to carry out a realist foreign policy. This was particularly true in the Meiji period, when the new leaders overcame domestic opposition and created the most highly centralized government in Japanese history. In addition, the Meiji government was ruled by a small, coherent group of oligarchs with a strong consensus on their nationalist goals and the means to achieve them. Throughout modern Japanese history, Japan has had a conservative ruling elite to carry on the strategic principles of the Meiji leaders. This conservative elite has never been dispossessed—not even by the U.S. Occupation.

Japan's modern conservative elite has consistently manifested an impulse to maximize Japan's share of world power. Distrustful of the intentions of other powers, these leaders sought to improve the nation's position. The nature of Japan's entry into the international system provided an indelible historical lesson that confirmed their distrust. At the mercy of the great powers, Japan was compelled to accept a series of unequal commercial treaties that infringed its sovereignty for the first time in the country's history.

Through the past 150 years, this conservative elite was rarely satisfied with the distribution of world power. The seemingly insatiable appetite for power sometimes seemed impervious to reason, but it was at the same time highly sensitive to the logic of force. It is certainly significant that Japan has been inclined to side with the powerful. As a matter of self-interest, Japan has repeatedly allied itself with the dominant ascendant power: with Great Britain from 1902 to 1922, with Germany from 1936 to 1945, and with the United States since 1952.

Pragmatism and the Weakness of
Transcendent and Universal Ideals

Japan's role in the international system has not been driven by great transcendent ideals or universal principles. Instead, Japan's international behavior has been marked by its pragmatic, often opportunistic pursuit of power. Neither during the Meiji Restoration nor subsequently has Japan been motivated by utopian visions of the future or by transcendent and universal ideals (for example, the victory of a classless society or the spread of democracy). The historian Akira Iriye argued that generally Japanese foreign policy has been pragmatic (*genjitsuteki*) and opportunistic (*jit-sumuteki*). He characterized it as "a foreign policy without ideological principles" (*mu-shisō no gaikō*):

> The Japanese government's foreign policy for a long stretch of time has been pragmatic and does not unfold according to fixed ideas and principles. The government's foreign relations are not controlled by ideology or an ethical view, rather it is exclusively through the pursuit of the fundamental concept of national interest. Outside of government, however, there has been from early on a segment of public opinion that holds that Japan should have a policy based on ideals and moral values.[30]

Political leaders (as opposed to opinion leaders) have been extraordinarily opportunistic, moved not by dogma or abstract principles, but rather, by what will enhance the power of the Japanese state. Their only ideology has been in fact devotion to the power of the state (*kokkashugi*). Nationalism and the national identity have been undeniable determinants of their policies.

Modern Japanese leaders have consistently displayed opportunism in pursuing national power. Each international order that they faced presented them with dangers and exposed them to vulnerabilities. The sense of insecurity was persistent, and as a rising power, Japan always looked for opportunities to expand its power. Attentiveness to the relations among the great powers could pay huge dividends. World War I and the preoccupation of the powers in Europe gave Japan an extraordinary opportunity to expand its power in East Asia. Similarly, when war broke out in Europe in 1939, British, French, and Dutch colonies in East Asia were left exposed to Japanese exploitation. A more elaborate opportunism during the Cold War allowed Japan to take advantage of the U.S.-Soviet confrontation to formulate a foreign policy that relied on U.S. security guarantees while pursuing economic power.

This opportunistic approach is reflective of currents that run deep in Japanese civilization. There is broad agreement among students of Japanese religion and political philosophy that in the Japanese value system there is a relative weakness of transcendental and universalistic orientations.[31] As Nakamura Hajime pointed out, in the world of Japanese religion, the native creed that came to be called Shinto (lit., "the way of the gods") is remarkable for its emphasis upon the "fluid and arresting character of observed events [which] regards the phenomenal world itself as Absolute and rejects the recognition of anything existing over and above the phenomenal world."[32] Accordingly, as Robert Bellah concluded, in Japanese society loyalty was typically to a social nexus of human relationships and not to a set of abstract ideas: "There was not, in the Japanese tradition, a strong philosophical or religious orthodoxy such as existed in China, the Islamic world, or the West."[33] Buddhism, the dominant religion in feudal Japan, never attained an ascendant position or had an institutional center equivalent to Rome from which it could propound norms for the political world.[34]

Moreover, the political world of feudal Japan did not witness implacable conflicts over great ideological principles in the change of regimes. Once the imperial hegemony was established in early times, there were no competing power hierarchies. Since the political and geographical boundaries of Japan coincided with Japanese civilization, there was no separate space from which an ideological challenge could be mounted. Political change came from within the existing oligarchic group, and there was little occasion for ideological confrontation and struggle over principles of legitimacy. There was always a pattern of continuity and compromise in feudal rule. "Five times powerful military families arose to political hegemony," wrote John W. Hall, "Yet in each instance these families achieved their victory as a result of a military conquest which carried through from within the oligarchic structure."[35]

Modern Japan inherited a value system based on the mundane order and on the nexus of human relationships. This is in stark contrast to the many civilizations that conceived the mundane order, and especially the political order, as an inferior or incomplete version of a transcendental order. In such cultures, politics might therefore witness movements to reconstruct the mundane order according to a transcendental vision. The most familiar example is the Western tradition, where the Christian transcendental vision exercised a strong influence in creating universal values. "In all these [other] civilizations, in other words, there developed an urge to implement in the mundane institutional arenas the precepts of the higher metaphysical order," according to S. N. Eisenstadt.[36] Thus, the great revolutions of modern history have typically aimed at the "destruction of the symbols of the old, hierarchical order and the assertion of a strong egalitarian ethos oriented to the future and rooted in universalistic premises."[37] The Meiji Restoration, however, involved no missionary urge to remake humankind according to transcendent ideals. Instead, the Meiji leaders legitimated their revolution by emphasizing the sanctity of an ostensibly "older primordial-sacral hierarchical order." When the founders of the modern Japanese state sought to create an ideology to unify and mobilize the nation for the competitive demands of the inter-state competition, they recognized that, having no religious orthodoxy to draw on, they would have to construct one around the person of the emperor. All the little loyalties that were traditional in Japanese society would lead up to one great loyalty. The oligarchs produced the ultimate example of Japanese orientation to the mundane order: "the fusion of deity and ruler, the divine king, the emperor as a living deity."[38]

Modern Japan's conservative leaders were exemplars of the maxim that conservatism is the negation of ideology. They did not cling to any particular conservative theory. They did not vest their "confidence in any general political or economic principle equally applicable to—and equally abstracted from—all societies."[39] They did not begin with a grand design for refashioning the social order from top to bottom. Theirs was a conservatism of the concrete and particular. They invariably favored the pragmatic to the doctrinal approach. Although foreign policies might from time to time be given ideological justifications, they were more pretext than motivation.

No doubt the greatest contrast with the Japanese approach may be found in the sources of American conduct. The prominent contemporary Japanese social scientist Murakami Yasusuke, an adviser to Prime Minister Nakasone, observed that "more than any other country in the world, the United States is a country in which transcendental thought is strong and a country that believes in a single justice, and does not doubt progress in the modern sense."[40] It was precisely the American style of transcendental thought that repeatedly puzzled the Japanese as they interacted on a world stage. Over the past century and a half, the Japanese conservative elite has had to cope with the unfamiliar reality of international liberalism and the assertion of universal values as the legitimating principles of the international order.

When initially confronted by these principles at the time of the Versailles Peace Conference in 1919, the Japanese reacted with confusion and skepticism; many concluded that these principles must be no more than a sugarcoating for Anglo-American self-interest. In the Hull-Nomura negotiations that preceded the Pacific War, Japanese leaders confronted the same principles as justification for rejecting a Japanese–led East Asian order. The universal ideals of international liberalism were again the basis for legitimating the post–World War II American system, to which Japan had to adapt as best it could. The Constitution of 1947 that was imposed on Japan contained these same principles. Murakami observed ruefully in 1992 that for their entire modern history the Japanese people have been compelled to live in a world where the transcendental, abstract values of Western civilization, rather than the familiar norms of their own value system, ruled.[41]

Bellah, summarizing the dominant orientation of the Japanese value system, wrote that "ethics consist mainly in acting as one should in one's group—there is no universal ethic."[42] The prominent anthropologist Nakane Chie, recognized for her work on the structure of Japanese society and for her theory of an unchanging Japanese character, gave a startlingly brutal characterization of Japanese motivation:

> The Japanese way of thinking depends on the situation rather than principle—while with the Chinese it is the other way around. . . . We Japanese have no principles. Some people think we hide our intentions, but we have no intentions to hide. Except for a few leftists or rightists, we have no dogma and don't ourselves know where we are going. This is a risky situation, for if someone is able to mobilize this population in a certain direction, we have no checking mechanism. . . . If we establish any goal we will proceed to attain it without considering any other factors. It is better for us to remain as we are. For if we are set in motion toward any direction, we have just too much energy to check its direction.[43]

Outside of government, to be sure, there was genuine adherence to ideological principle. During the Meiji period and the challenge of Western imperialism, for example, pan-Asianism held an appeal for some Japanese intellectuals, but political leaders were characteristically motivated by pragmatic nationalism rather than fixed principles. Later, liberalism and Marxism found many adherents outside of official circles. In the post–World War II period, the nonideological nature of Japanese policymaking was made explicit—even consciously stressed as a matter of strategy. Miyazawa Kiichi, Japan's most durable postwar leader, defended Japan's pragmatic and nonideological course, arguing that for Japan as a merchant nation, "the only value judgments we can make are determining what is in Japan's interest. Since there are no real value judgments possible we cannot say anything. . . . We watch the world situation and follow the trends."[44] This demeaning view of Japanese selfhood at the heart of Japan's Cold War foreign policy revealed a fundamental dilemma caused by the characteristic opportunism of Japan's political leaders.

One of contemporary Japan's leading strategic thinkers, Ambassador Okazaki Hisahiko, responding to an American journalist who asked him if there were any fixed principles in Japan's foreign policy, once said: "The histories of our two countries are different. Your country was built on principles. Japan was built on an archipelago."[45] Okazaki did not elaborate on this Delphic assertion, but it is easy enough to surmise what he meant. An island nation further from the continent than England, with a homogeneous population and few natural resources, Japan was shaped by its geography as well as the unique history that was the legacy of this geography, and its modern outlook on world affairs reflects that. Japan was a natural nation-state, not one forged by drawing lines on a map or constructed from common beliefs. Ambassador Okazaki doubtless also had in mind Japan's "strategic geography."[46] The long distances to its primary suppliers of energy, raw materials, and food made Japan, after it industrialized, constantly dependent on the security of its sea lanes. Japan could not afford to take a stand on principle: Its island economy and geopolitical position made it too vulnerable; and its peculiar dependence on trade left it with a feeling of insecurity that engendered a persistently opportunistic foreign policy. Resource poor and a late arriver in the modern world, Japan was uniquely vulnerable to shifts in the international system.

Adaptation and Accommodation

Given this characteristic sensitivity to the balance of power, the pragmatism, and the weakness of universalistic ideals as a motivation for Japan's international behavior, it is not surprising to find a pattern of adaptation, even accommodation, to changes in the structure of the international order. Japan's leaders learned to be adaptable and pragmatic, to adjust to conditions in order to offset their vulnerability and insecurity. Peter Katzenstein has shown how in Europe, "the domestic political arrangements of small states are determined by their vulnerable position in international markets; conversely, the domestic structures of large states determine their strategy in world markets."[47] Or, to put it more simply, "Whereas great powers adapt their foreign strategies to their domestic circumstances, small powers adapt their domestic circumstances to the strategy that their foreign environment dictates."[48]

Japan's leaders have always had to have the competitive demands of their external environment uppermost in their minds when planning for the future. With impressive flexibility, Japanese leaders have taken their cues from the framework that surrounds them. The late Professor Kōsaka Masataka, a leading authority on Japanese foreign policy, emphasized the passive, situational, and reactive patterns in the Japanese approach to international norms. Its source, he believed, lay in Japan's particular experience as an island nation:

> In [Japanese] eyes, norms are something that are either given from above or called forth by the situation. They are not created by men through multilateral action. . . . This passive view toward norms can be understood as a reflection of the Japanese view of society. Japan is a natural nation-state; the idea that a state is created by a common will and contract has not existed in Japan. Japan has existed and will exist, regardless of the will and action of its people. Hence, norms are considered to be created by nature, not men. Given the tradition of authoritarian rule in Japan, moreover, to the extent that a norm is created by men, it is by superiors and not by the common efforts of all citizens. . . . The logical conclusion from such a view of the world is that the task for the Japanese is to adapt wisely to the international situation to secure its national interests, and not try to change or create the mysterious framework.[49]

The distinguished political scientist Kyōgoku Jun'ichi has written, in the same vein, that in Japan's experience, "the world has been a 'given' surrounding Japan, which makes a real impact on Japan, but which cannot be modified by the efforts of the Japanese. The world is nothing but the 'framework' or the setting which can change only mysteriously."[50]

This adaptive approach that Japan's political class took toward its external environment is apparent in the readiness to revise Japan's domestic institutions to serve its foreign policy needs. To take just one example, the institutions of Japanese fascism, in contrast to those in Europe, where they came about through upheavals that overthrew the political system, were introduced from above by the existing elites. A leading political scientist of the 1930s, Rōyama Masamichi, said it had always been characteristic of Japan's political institutions that they changed and adapted to meet the circumstances of the time.[51]

To what antecedents does Japan owe this propensity to accommodate itself to its external environment? The logic of this approach is intimately related to the characteristics of realism and pragmatism, but its roots may also be traced to another aspect of Japan's premodern culture. From the middle of the nineteenth century on, Japanese statesmen repeatedly perceived Japan as vulnerable to historic forces too powerful to tame and control, and they tried to operate in accord with these forces and use them to Japan's advantage. In part this sense of vulnerability sprang from an immediate recognition that Japan was a late-developing nation in an international system organized and dominated by the Western powers. Modern Japan's accommodative approach to its external environment was enhanced by its position as a late industrializer forced to follow the trends set by the advanced economies, but it was already deeply embedded in Japan's premodern historical experience.

In their realism Japanese leaders always sought to read the direction of the flow of events, what they called "the trend of the times," and to act in accordance with it—seeking not to change it but rather to move with it in ways that would work to their own nation's advantage. In this sense Japanese leaders resembled sixteenth-century Italians, especially Niccolo Machiavelli, who exhibited great respect for external forces of nature that impacted politics. Machiavelli called the workings of these forces "Fate" or "Fortune." "I would compare her [Fortune]," Machiavelli wrote in *The Prince*, "to an impetuous river that, when turbulent, inundates the plains, casts down trees and buildings, removes earth from this and places it on the other; everyone flees before it, and everything yields to its fury without being able to oppose it." Machiavelli held that while these great, impersonal forces seemed beyond a ruler's capacity to manage, he must nonetheless seek to master them by foresight: "And yet though it [Fortune like an impetuous river] is of such a kind, still when it is quiet, men can make provision against it by dykes and banks, so that when it rises it will either go into a canal or its rush will not be so wild and dangerous. So it is with Fortune, which shows her power where she knows that no dykes or barriers have been made to hold her."[52]

Japan's political leaders similarly displayed a deep respect for the great impersonal forces of history and saw themselves maneuvering within the constraints of these great forces. They referred to the powerful forces controlling their environment as *sekai no taisei* (trends of the world), *jisei* (trends of the time), *shizen no ikioi* (natural forces), or *hitsuzen no ikioi* (inexorable forces), all terms denoting the dynamic force in human affairs impelling events that is beyond the ability of leaders to control. The Japanese judged their leaders by their capacity to gauge the trend of the times and to react to the opportunities that presented themselves. Japanese leaders tried to operate in accord with these trends and use them to their own advantage. The ability to adapt, which is essential to a pragmatic, opportunistic, and realist pursuit of power, drew strength from this tendency of the Japanese to regard conformity to the trend of the times as a supreme virtue.

Many distinguished scholars writing on Japanese national character have observed this tendency. Yanagita Kunio, the eminent scholar of Japanese folkways, stressed the Japanese deference to the great impersonal forces referred to as *taisei*. He pointed out that while the term *taisei* had long been common in Oriental languages, it assumed special significance for the Japanese. Without the influence of a frontier to help shape the national character by offering a haven for original and unusual views, the Japanese have always had an unusually strong tendency to assimilate. Yanagita discerned in the Japanese political tradition a climate of respect for the ability to change easily and adapt to the dominating trends, to read the feelings of others, to sense the atmosphere of a given situation, and to protect oneself by allying with the powerful. He observed a tendency in Japanese history to regard adaptation to the trend of the time as a great virtue: "The emergence of a new trend would produce the urge to comply before it was too late, without thorough evaluation. In scholarship and politics, as well, the tendency to join in and assimilate was strong. . . . People increasingly sought positions at the vanguard of the trend."[53]

Maruyama Masao, the leading political scientist of the post–World War II period in Japan, cited this tendency to conform to the environment as a key aspect of Japanese political psychology. Foreigners, he observed, were often baffled by two contradictory tendencies in Japanese politics: the difficulty of making change, and the rapidity with which change took place. Maruyama's explanation was that a reluctance to break with the present was set off by a readiness to accommodate to the realities of the time. This readiness, he wrote, was the hallmark of the pragmatic and nondoctrinaire nature of Japanese conservatism, which stood in contrast to the stubborn and principled conservatism of Europe. In Japanese politics, he added, it was difficult to take the lead in reform, but once reform was under way, change tended to spread rapidly.[54]

The Meiji leaders frequently characterized their adaptive and emulative policies as impelled by great impersonal forces. The term *jisei* was a key concept in the widely read *Nihon gaishi* (Unofficial History of Japan), written in 1837 and read by all the Meiji leaders. In this book, often said to be the most popular history of Japan in the nineteenth century, the author Rai San'yō used the concept to denote a trend in human affairs, generated by past events, which if ignored could frustrate the aspirations of even the most able and virtuous of men. The perceptive statesman understood the nature of these forces, foresaw the outcome of change, adapted to it, and so paradoxically was even able to direct and control change. San'yō's writings were favored by the Meiji leaders, especially Itō Hirobumi. Itō's readiness to emulate Western forms of government was undergirded by San'yō's understanding of the role of *jisei*. Itō, the drafter of the Meiji Constitution, was a self-proclaimed admirer of San'yō, and he justified Japan's adoption of constitutionalism as adjusting to the inevitable trend in human affairs. In his *Opinion on Constitutional Government,* written in 1880, Itō explained why Japan must change its domestic structure and adopt constitutional and representative institutions:

> Today conditions in Japan are closely related to the world situation. They are not merely affairs of a nation or a province. The European concepts of revolution, which were carried out first in France about 100 years ago, have gradually spread to the various nations. By combining and complementing each other, they have become a general trend (*taisei*). Sooner or later, every nation will undergo changes as a result. . . . The trend of the times has brought [this] about, and human efforts cannot control it.[55]

The disposition to acknowledge the inevitable force of the currents of international affairs was again apparent when the international system was transformed after World War I. Having striven so fiercely to accommodate to the rules and mores of the imperialist system, the Japanese were stunned by the abrupt changes that took place in the international system under the leadership of U.S. President Woodrow Wilson. Indeed, the revolution in the structure, mores, and governance of the international system in East Asia undertaken by the Americans at the end of World War I was as remarkable as any that one might encounter in world history. The imperialist system was replaced by a new U.S.-inspired order, the Washington

Treaty System, with its opposition to balance-of-power principles and its commitment to universal ideals of self-determination and the Open Door. With their characteristic realism, the Japanese leaders accepted the new order in East Asia, even though one of its principal objectives was the containment of Japan. Prime Minister Hara Kei declared that Japan must act in accord with the trend of the times and accept the Wilsonian redefinition of the international order and its new norms. This acceptance of the norms of the new system was, in the first place, a reflection of Japan's relative power position, but as Hara's repeated references to world trends showed, it was reinforced by instinctive attitudes deeply embedded in Japan's historical experience.

Only once, in the 1930s, did Japan appear to abandon this reactive and accommodative approach, but even then many Japanese leaders thought they were acting in accord with the trend of the times. As they saw the liberal international order crumbling, their external world anarchic and devoid of rules or enforcers, their security concerns and strategic objectives reasserted themselves. Other powers were forming closed regional spheres, the international system was collapsing, and fascism seemed to be the wave of the future. They did not want to miss the bus.

During the fateful policy conferences of 1941, when they were deciding whether to gamble the nation's future by going to war with a country eight or ten times more powerful, Japan's leaders repeatedly spoke of being impelled by great impersonal forces. In his valuable study of the Japanese decision for war, Nobutaka Ike observed this theme running through decisionmaking: "It is easier to make decisions in the face of uncertainty if one is a fatalist. If a decision maker believes, for example, that human affairs are ultimately controlled by super human forces, then he is not really a free agent, and so is ultimately not responsible for his actions. Fatalism of this kind was common among Japanese high officials."[56]

When the campaign to create a Japanese order came to a disastrous close in 1945, the emperor's surrender edict to his people began, "After pondering deeply the trends of the world (*sekai no taisei*) . . . we have decided to effect a settlement of the present situation by resorting to an extraordinary measure." It went on to intone that surrender was necessary because "the war situation has developed not necessarily to our advantage, while the trends of the world [*sekai no taisei*] have all turned against our interest. . . . It is according to the dictate of time and fate that we have resolved to pave the way for a grand peace." Japan's leaders attributed defeat not to disastrous and mistaken policies, but to historical forces that could not be surmounted. Such being the case, the emperor's subjects were enjoined in the final words of the edict to "work with resolution to not fall behind the progress of the world."[57]

Autonomy and Regional Hegemony

Before the arrival of the West, Japan had been wholly self-sufficient, and restoration of its own autonomous sphere became a persistent but elusive goal for the modern state. With an almost religious sense of its own distinctive identity, Japan had resisted inclusion in the Sinocentric world. Thrust into the international system after an entire history of virtual isolation, Japanese leaders from the start saw the outside world whole. That is, coming to the international system de novo, they saw it not so much as Thomas Hobbes did, as a state of nature, nor as statesmen among the great powers saw it, as competing nation-states, nor as students of international politics see it, as anarchic. Rather, they saw the outside world as a single great unitary threat to national survival. They faced the international order in its entirety as a force of encroaching danger and harm that they must countervail via all-encompassing planning. From the outset of the modern period, the Meiji leaders stressed that self-reliance was essential because Japan was surrounded by predatory imperial powers. One Restoration leader, writing to his fellow oligarchs in 1869, said, "All countries beyond the sea are our enemies."[58] This did not preclude forming alliances; on the contrary, these alliances were marriages of convenience to pave the way to autonomy.

The infringement of Japan's sovereignty for the first time in its history stimulated determination among the Japanese to restore their domestic autonomy and escape dependency on the foreigners. Japan's leaders were determined to end the unequal treaties by all possible means, including acquiring Western scientific and technological knowledge, but at the same time they were intent on preventing the foreigners from gaining a foothold. The imperative of self-reliance was widely held. The founding statement of the Maruzen Company in the early Meiji period foreshadowed Japan's persistent recognition that trade represented another form of struggle in which Japan must assert its independence:

> The foreigners did not come to our country out of friendship; their reason for being here is to trade. . . . Their main object is to seek profits through trade. When we sit idly by and allow them to monopolize our for-

eign trade, we are betraying our duty as Japanese. If we once allow them to take over our foreign trade, if we are aided by them, if we rely on them, if we borrow money from them, if we are employed in their companies, if we invite them into our companies, if we respect and admire them, if we run around at their orders, if we fall into that kind of condition, there could not possibly be a greater disaster to our country. A country in that situation is not a country.[59]

From that day on, the Japanese have gone to extraordinary lengths to preempt the establishment of any kind of foreign foothold in the Japanese domestic economy.

In the face of an East Asian system dominated by the Western powers, an ambitious Japan was bound to be a revisionist actor. Both in domestic affairs and in their region, the Japanese leadership has sought to establish their nation's autonomy. Premodern writers had advocated Japanese domination of Asia, but in early Meiji it became a refrain of national purpose. Fukuzawa, among many others, advocated that Japan become "the leader of Asia" (*Tōyō no meishu*).[60] The Japanese empire grew like topsy because its leaders were never satisfied with their share of regional power. In 1890, Japan's most astute strategic thinker, the founder of the Japanese army, Yamagata Aritomo, explained that Japan must not be satisfied with the line of sovereignty but must always seek to advance the line of advantage.[61]

Japan's leaders consistently sought to shift the balance of power in their favor, believing it was imperative to gain more power to enhance the nation's security. Following the Russo-Japanese War, when Japan had joined the ranks of the great powers, there were prominent Japanese outside of government who called on their leaders to turn back from any further expansion. But the conservative leaders were no more content with the status quo than they had been a half-century before. They were ever watchful for opportunities to gain power at the expense of their rivals. Japan was beset by a combination of insecurity and ambition that drove it to undertake policies to secure regional hegemony that were so aggressive that they galvanized Anglo-American determination to contain Japanese expansion. Weighing the risks of the pursuit of hegemony, Japanese leaders took their biggest gambles when their rivals were bogged down with other matters during the two world wars. In both cases, however, the gambles backfired.

Modern Japan's all-consuming drive for wealth and power was intended to restore Japan's autonomy. It was therefore ironic that industrialization and military power actually increased Japan's reliance on the external world.

The Japanese built a great navy, but after World War I, battleships were powered by oil, a commodity that Japan lacked and had to import in huge quantities. Japan discovered too that it was almost wholly devoid of the raw materials required for modern industry and had to import them. At the beginning of the twenty-first century, it had to import a range of strategic resources, including 99 percent of its oil, 96 percent of its liquefied natural gas, 100 percent of its iron ore, and 96 percent of its copper.[62] Japan became the world's largest importer of raw materials and had to export finished goods to pay for them. The security of its sea lanes was a matter of life or death. From the outset of the modern period, Japan's conservative leaders always confronted a precarious international position. Japan now had to overcome this vulnerability and restore self-mastery.

As a late developer that was heavily dependent on trade to exist, Japan lacked the buffer from the pressures of international competition that many great powers enjoyed. As Michael Barnhart wrote in describing Japan's drive for autonomy and autarky in the 1930s, "The United States was what Japan sought to be. Interwar America was self-sufficient in every major respect, from food and energy to coal and iron. . . . American views about the essentials of national security, therefore, were strikingly different from those of the Japanese."[63] The United States, which had immense reserves of strategic materials and a vast internal market, could face the security environment without the vulnerability that the Japanese always confronted. The Great Depression—the collapse of the international trading system, with the rush to create economic blocs and beggar-thy-neighbor policies—presented a huge challenge to Japan's precarious international position, threatening not only loss of foreign markets and massive unemployment but even social revolution. For Japan's conservative leadership, these were unthinkable alternatives.

The Pacific War was fought in part to establish Japan's economic autonomy. When that failed, Japanese postwar leaders formulated a political-economic strategy designed to assure it access to the raw materials, markets, and technology required to restore the nation's independence. Japan's concept of comprehensive security, developed in the aftermath of the oil shocks of the 1970s, placed great emphasis on economic security. Seeking to limit Japan's external vulnerability, it stressed diversifying sources of energy supply and "maintaining a high level of domestic technical competence."[64] Many other policies, such as limiting foreign direct investment in Japan, were similarly designed to shield the economy from foreign dependence. Still, no matter how persistent the pursuit or how brilliant the strategy, reaching the goal ultimately proved elusive. Toward the end of the twentieth century, in the words of one economist, "[Japan's] dependence on foreigners for the necessities of life is greater than that of any other major industrial country."[65]

Japan's pursuit of regional hegemony and the autonomy that would accompany it were evident again in the 1980s in a new economic form. The economic power that Japan had amassed could be used in the form of foreign aid, loans, investment, technology transfer, and preferential market access to dominate East Asia. Japanese bureaucrats conceived a well-coordinated plan to implement a comprehensive integration of the economies of Asia, with the Japanese bureaucracy serving as the "Asian brain" that would mastermind the region's economy and structure a regional division of labor under Japanese leadership. "Flying geese" became a favorite metaphor for a pattern of development designed to achieve regional hegemony. The phrase, actually coined in the 1930s as part of Japan's prewar pan-Asian ideology, prescribed a lead economy with others ranked behind in the order of their economic strength and technical sophistication. For a time, it appeared that Japan's quest for dominance would succeed. The collapse of the bubble economy and the disarray in Japanese politics in the 1990s, however, put the ambition for regional leadership in abeyance.

Emulation and Innovation

No state in history better exemplifies the logic of emulating the successful practices of the great powers than does modern Japan. It could be said that the international system impels states to do this, and that all states must eventually bend to this logic. But why was Japan so swift to pick up on it? Japan is widely noted for its tradition of cultural borrowing. Many observers have described the extraordinary degree of openness to borrowing as essential to the nature of Japanese culture. The early twentieth-century philosopher Nishida Kitarō is said to have defined Japanese culture as a "formless form" (katachi ga nai katachi). Similarly, Maruyama Masao described Japanese tradition as an "empty bag," a container whose contents were largely of foreign origin; and he famously observed that "there is no history of Japanese thought as such but only a history of the reception of foreign systems."[66] The Meiji leaders often cited the first great period of borrowing from China—it has been called "perhaps the most systematic effort in world history before modern times of a less developed society to learn from a more developed one"[67]—as powerful precedent for their own emulation. Still, what motivated this borrowing?

Japan's premodern experience of an intensely competitive feudal system prepared them for the logic of emulation. In the late Tokugawa period, the various domains competed with one another to adopt the most successful practices of economically and militarily powerful domains. Accordingly, the Meiji leaders wasted no time in turning to the West and selecting from an array of national models the institutions best suited to bring Japanese power into the new era. The historian James Crowley observed of the Meiji responsiveness that "to a degree unparalleled in western Europe, with the possible exception of Imperial Germany, [Japanese] domestic politics were structured by foreign affairs."[68] The Meiji leaders went to extraordinary lengths to emulate the successful institutions of the Western world and to accommodate to the international system. In the same way that the Japanese crafted their reform of domestic institutions to fit the needs of the international system, they also designed their imperialist policies to match the practices of the Western imperialist system. As Peter Duus wrote, "Japanese imperialism, like so many other aspects of Meiji development, was an act of mimesis. The Meiji leaders, who avidly monitored world politics, crafted their expansionist policies along Western lines, deployed the same gunboat tactics to establish domination in Korea, and appealed to the same legal justification to legitimate it."[69]

The Japanese brought a distinctive style of learning to their participation in the international system. The anthropologist Thomas Rohlen, in his study of Japanese learning processes, stressed a pattern in the premodern period whereby students developed skills in their highly developed arts, crafts, and manufactures through a protracted apprenticeship and imitation of the master. In fact, the verb "to learn" (*narau*) carries in addition the meaning "to imitate." Only after long years of copying had brought mastery of the technique did Japanese teachers encourage real creativity and originality. Cultural borrowing was not disparaged as slavish. On the contrary, it was seen as a natural and essential aspect of national advancement. The Japanese did not have the same barriers of cultural and religious self-absorption that in other countries impeded learning from other civilizations. Effective borrowing and adaptation rested on their tradition of learning, which gave them the disposition to "scan the external environment objectively" and the capacity to "grasp the essence of other social and technological orders." Of the qualities that made the Japanese attentive to the outside world, Rohlen wrote:

We might also distinguish between societies preoccupied with expressing their own "reality" to the rest of the world and those oriented toward perceiving carefully what lies outside. *In Japan's case, the accommodative inclination has been dominant.* . . . While some nations perfect the art of communicating their own virtues and worldview for political or religious reasons, Japan has emphasized listening and detailed observation. . . . This "objectivity" starts, I think, with *a basic cultural disposition to an adaptive posture and with a fundamental epistemology that emphasizes exterior rather than interior truth.* The "other" orientation and context-specific qualities of the language and of Japanese social relations are relevant here, just as is the generally nonproselytizing nature of the Japanese approach to religion. That is to say, the fundamental character of the Japanese cultural pattern is strongly oriented to learning from others.[70]

Rohlen's analysis of this culturally embedded Japanese approach to learning offers yet another valuable insight into the sources of Japan's unique responsiveness to change in its external environment. As each new international order has emerged, Japan has shown remarkable receptivity to the practices and institutions of the dominant power. Although emulation was never so intense as when Japan first entered the international system, and hence had the most to learn and adopt, still each new international order has been marked by a keen Japanese attention to the "best practices" of the dominant power or powers. The democratic practices of the United States were studied and became widely influential in the politics of the post–World War I era. But in the 1930s, with the apparent shift in world trends, Japan found the institutions of fascist Germany more appealing and took them as the inspiration for wide-ranging institutional and policy innovation.

Emulation did not mean convergence. In the Japanese tradition of learning, as Rohlen added, "a successful apprentice is one who finds the best teacher, learns diligently all there is to know, and ultimately surpasses the master's skill. . . . The place of originality is properly found at the end of the apprenticeship when mastery is attained."[71]

The Japanese thus adopted institutions and made them fit into their society. Moreover, as part of the process, the Japanese looked for ways to improve the efficiency of those institutions. The Japanese leaders were not only attuned to the need to emulate the institutions and practices of the great powers, they were also remarkably perceptive in trying to find shortcuts out of their backwardness in order to develop more rapidly than the advanced countries had; they were equally perceptive in trying to avoid the errors and learn from the mistakes of the powers. In this strategy they had "the advantage of followership."[72] Japanese leaders seemed instinctively aware of what Leon Trotsky called "the privilege of historic backwardness" in his *History of the Russian Revolution:* "Although compelled to follow after the advanced countries, a backward country does not take things in the same order. The privilege of historic backwardness—and such a privilege exists—permits, or rather compels, the adoption of whatever is ready in advance of any specified date, skipping a whole series of intermediate stages."[73] Japanese leaders, then, could try to prevent the social disruption and dislocation, the struggle between labor and capital, that attended the earlier industrializations. The economist Thorstein Veblen, writing in 1915 of "Japan's opportunity," observed that by importing modern technology and preserving feudal values intact Japan would avoid much of the social cost of industrialization. Personal ties and vertical relations of loyalty and obedience would permit a much smoother industrialization than could have occurred had economic individualism taken hold.[74]

But years before Veblen published his famous essay, the Japanese already understood that they could go beyond emulation to innovate a more efficient course. A prominent official, Kaneko Kentarō, wrote in 1896 that the Japanese should learn from the "sad and pitiful" history of British industrialization. "It is the advantage of the backward country," he said, "that it can reflect on the history of the advanced countries and avoid their mistakes."[75] The economist Kawakami Hajime put it this way in 1905: "The history of the failure of the advanced countries is the best textbook for the follower countries."[76]

It was Japan's vulnerable international position that gave urgency to averting the class antagonisms to which industrial civilization in the West had given rise. Japanese leaders developed a powerful nationalist orthodoxy to underwrite the forced march to industry and empire, wealth and power. "The groups in control of the state," Thomas C. Smith concluded, "had no choice but to sustain orthodoxy as best they could. . . . If that effort should collapse, so must Japan's precarious international position, bringing loss of foreign markets, unemployment, perhaps social revolution."[77]

As time went on, Japanese leaders moved from emulation to innovation, that is, they "found clever ways to gain power at the expense of their rivals."[78] They regarded the international system as something to be studied and made use of it to improve Japan's position. In this way they adopted German institutions to promote an effective industrial policy in the 1930s. In the postwar period, Japanese leaders fashioned these institutions into a distinctly Japanese set of institutions to promote high economic growth in ways that took advantage of the international free-trade order sponsored by the Americans.

Rank and Honor

A final recurrent characteristic of the Japanese response to the international system is a persistent obsession with status and prestige—or, to put it in terms the Japanese would more readily recognize, rank and honor. Thomas Hobbes, in *Leviathan*, recognized that human nature breeds a competitive striving for honor and dignity because honor confers power. Honor and power, in his view, are intimately related. "Reputation for power," Hobbes wrote, "is power."[79] Honor, as such, may be attributed to an individual, but it can also be attributed to groups and to nations.

In the workings of the international system, the status and prestige attached to the great powers play a critical role in the governance of the system. Many scholars have observed the function of a hierarchy of prestige in governing and establishing order in the system. Hans Morgenthau, for example, devoted a chapter in his classic work *Politics Among Nations* to prestige as a primary goal of nations in the struggle for power. Power and prestige are closely linked, and yet they are distinct. Prestige is the reputation for power. It is the equivalent of authority in domestic politics. As E. H. Carr concluded, prestige is "enormously important" because "if your strength is recognized, you can generally achieve your aims without having to use it."[80] The prestige that a country deserves is subjective and difficult to measure other than by a successful display of power. The international system is said to be stable when the hierarchy of prestige is widely accepted and acknowledged.

Once again, Japan's feudal experience prepared the way for its understanding of the workings of the international system. The conservative elites immediately recognized the importance of status and prestige, but their concern had a distinctive flavor and peculiar intensity. Japan brought to its participation in international society a highly developed and elaborate culture of honor. "Although the notion is apparently universal," wrote Eiko Ikegami, "some societies have more elaborate and more highly developed sets of honor-related cultural idioms as dynamic symbolic social complexes. Japan is one such society."[81] Codes of honor had long since declined or disappeared in Europe, but in Japan in the middle of the nineteenth century, honor was still a vital ethos.

Feudal Japan was an "honor-ridden society."[82] The ethos of the professional military class that dominated Japanese politics and society through the long centuries of feudal life effectively wove the culture of honor into the structure of power. The samurai ethos that took shape in the medieval period provided the warrior with his identity. With their emergence as a ruling elite, samurai defined themselves as the class, unlike the nobles and the commoners, that would risk their lives to defend their honor. Codes of honor were the unique cultural style of a class whose dominance originated in the ability to use violence. These codes exalted fighting and were based on physical strength, martial skills, valor, power, and self-discipline. Individual warriors were attentive, even obsessed, with preserving their reputation, self-esteem, and personal dignity. Honor was fragile. Because honor entailed their very identity as a class, the samurai were hypersensitive and vulnerable to slights and gossip. They were protective of their own pride, which was preserved by an elaborate set of honor-related symbols of their reputation for power. In its most extreme form, this concern for reputation was ritualistically embodied in *seppuku,* or disembowelment in self-willed death. "Rather than incurring the shame of being taken as captives by the enemy," Ikegami wrote, "the samurai could testify to their autonomy through their complete control of the body in the final moments of life."[83]

When the endemic warfare of the medieval period gave way after 1600 to the sedentary life of the Tokugawa period, the new shogunate set out to tame samurai violence, its quarrels and vendettas, and in a time of unfolding peace, to transform the samurai into bureaucrats and administrators and to regulate them by their organization into strict hierarchical structure. The result was a highly stratified order of status based on honor ranking, which was determined by each vassal samurai's military title and relationship with his lord. In the new conditions, these rankings became hereditary, and honor became less a matter of performance and more of status. All forms of behavior were meticulously governed by codes of conduct: manners, etiquette, conventions of speech, seating order, dress code, styles of residential housing, gift giving, styles and scale of wedding ceremonies, and many other visible differentiations of status. "Consequently," Ikegami wrote, "politeness and good manners in the Tokugawa samurai community acquired political importance; the samurai's stylized forms of courtesy were by no means simply indicators of breeding and refinement, but direct and explicit idioms of power."[84] The locus of honor and loyalty came to be focused less on the individual and more on his lord and his domain and thus became more state focused.

The honorific ethos of the heroic samurai of an earlier period never lost its grip on the identity and imagination of the Tokugawa warrior, but it was sublimated and kept alive through the traditions, practices, and institutions of his life. The Tokugawa system, in fact, maintained a tension between the older ideal of the warrior, whose full-blooded devotion to honor was won through heroic feat of arms, and the new ideal of the disciplined bureaucrat acting within a cooperative vassalage where honor was attached to status in a highly stratified hierarchy. Either way, society remained deeply suffused with the honorific culture.

At the time of the Restoration, this honorific culture was revitalized, but now with a focus on the nation itself, prompting samurai activists to confront the challenge of Western imperialism. The national crisis created a dynamic new fusion of honor and nationalism.[85] Meiji Japan's leaders came from the lower reaches of the samurai class, and their biographies show their training in the honorific values and norms essential to that class's identity. Japan's subsequent competition in the anarchic struggles of the international system was marked by a distinctive "honorific nationalism." This culturally embedded notion of state-centered honor meant that the concern with prestige and a reputation for power that characterized all nations in the system was accordingly more sensitive, fragile, and vulnerable for the Japanese.

Throughout its modern history, Japan has measured its standing against other major powers. Its goal was always to be recognized as a first-rank country (*ittō-koku*). Moreover, how the great powers perceived Japan was always critical. The Japanese needed confirmation that the evaluations of others included the recognition of their superior qualities. They discovered that the reputation for power alone was not sufficient to provide the recognition they sought. The mistreatment of Japanese immigrants in Western countries even after Japan was accorded great-power status came as a huge blow to Japan's national standing. So also, the perception of Japan as successful in emulating the institutions of the more advanced countries reflected poorly on Japan's own cultural heritage and weakened international respect for Japan.

One of the most puzzling aspects of modern Japan's international history was its readiness to go to war with a country that was eight to ten times more powerful than itself. To a considerable degree, Japanese leaders took this action because in the end they saw their standing in the international hierarchy at stake. Roberta Wohlstetter, in her classic work on Pearl Harbor, concluded that "war with the United States was not chosen.

The decision for war was rather forced by the desire to avoid the more terrible alternative of losing status or abandoning the national objectives."[86] Faced with U.S. insistence on withdrawal from China as a price for ending the U.S. embargo, Prime Minister Tōjō declared that compliance would render Japan a third-rate power. To make so fateful a choice, in the face of Japan's own realist traditions, bespoke the extent to which prestige and status in and of themselves were goals for which the leadership was willing to gamble the future of the nation. The foreign minister in 1941, Tōgō Shigenori, explained in his autobiography:

> But he who argues that Japan would nevertheless have been in better case by bowing to the American dictate, and thus escaping the ravages of war, while plausible, is wholly sophistical, for he fails to allow weight to either the honor or the prestige of the nation. Entirely aside from the question whether Japan had or had not been engaged in aggression, had or had not invaded foreign rights and interests, it has to be remembered that she was struggling to maintain her status as a Great Power.[87]

Any power will dread an injury to its prestige, but for Japan, whose standing in the world was an essential aspect of its national identity and purpose, the importance of prestige was critical.

CONCLUSION

These six intertwined aspects of the Japanese approach to its external environment are rooted in Japan's past, especially its long feudal experience, but they emerged and took shape according to Japan's encounters with new forces and struggles. The international system, with its constant, competitive struggle, served to reproduce them—and also to transform them as the international order itself evolved and presented new challenges. As the Japanese became more self-conscious of them, they were quietly honed, refined, and articulated into principles of national strategy. Instinctive style became calculated strategy. At the beginning of the twenty-first century, these core characteristics are still evolving and changing. Yet the accumulated experience of history constitutes a powerful momentum, and although these characteristics are still changing, the impetus of the past persists. These national qualities provide the key to understanding Japan's remarkable receptivity to change in the structure of the international system.

CHAPTER THREE

THE WORLD JAPAN ENTERED

I n the middle of the nineteenth century, the forces of the international system broke in upon the natural isolation and free security that Japan had always enjoyed. Thrust from island remoteness onto the stage of world history, Japan was now subject to vast new forces. Heretofore, except for the occasional influence of events on the continent, Japan had been able to stand free of external forces; it could choose if and when it would receive foreign influences. Its wars were almost always civil wars. Premodern Japanese history was, as John Whitney Hall, one of its preeminent interpreters, said, "almost completely an indigenous affair, and the roles and motivations of its main actors were created and sustained by the conditions of the Japanese environment." Hall added, "To this extent Japan offers the ingredients of a closed system in which the norms of political life have been relatively fixed and in which influences intruding from outside have been few and easily identified."¹ Japanese life was lived within the islands.

Although the driving forces of Japan's premodern history were overwhelmingly internal, this did not preclude important contacts with the external world. Japan did have such contacts, but it controlled them. A leading cultural historian, Haga Toru, wrote of the Tokugawa seclusion policy, "The shogunate could bring in the things it needed and keep out what it didn't. It could take in all the information it needed and keep out what it didn't. It could take in all the information it found useful without letting out any information it didn't want to. In this way it ensured the nation's security. . . . For all the talk of seclusion, Japan was probably receiving more information from other countries than any other non-Western country of the time."[2] But those self-sufficient days, when Japan's leaders could determine the nature of its foreign relations, came to an abrupt end. Beginning in the mid-nineteenth century, external pressures became a constant influence on Japanese decisionmaking. Drawn abruptly into the maelstrom of international politics, its sovereignty infringed for the first time, Japan lost control of its relations to the outside. The island nation's era of free security disappeared, and it became subject to forces that were beyond its reach. Japan had been able to remain aloof from the Sinocentric system, but not the new order imposed by Western imperialism. The gap in military and industrial power was too great to resist.

Only with the arrival of the modern world did there exist a single international system.[3] The Industrial Revolution brought waves of technological advances in transportation and communication that made possible the first truly global international system. Steam propulsion, railways, and telegraphs all contributed to this end. The new technology also brought with it a revolution in firepower and mobility. Faster-firing guns and armored warships marked the new era of modernized military and naval technology. Most important, the Industrial Revolution brought spectacular increases in productivity and the prospect of an international economy. Inherent in the imperialist international system was the interrelationship of economics and security, of wealth and power. The advent of industrial civilization made the sustained economic growth that came from modern science and technology essential to the power of the state. "Economic wealth and military power," Robert Gilpin wrote, "became increasingly synonymous." As the relative importance of productive technology in the generation of wealth and power grew, "the position of state in the world market (the so-called international division of labor) became a principal determinant, if not the determinant, of its status in the international system."[4]

In 1853, Commodore Perry arrived on Japan's shores with his flotilla of American ships to demand trade, setting off a tumultuous and chaotic period. As debate in Japan focused on how best to respond to the foreign crisis, armed conflict among factions revealed the full scale of the Tokugawa Bakufu's weakness. The arrival of this new international system played a major role in delegitimizing Japan's ancien regime, leading to its overthrow by two powerful domains, Chōshū and Satsuma. In many respects, Japan was ripe for radical change. There was discontent in all social classes owing to the dislocations caused by long-term social and economic change. But it took an external threat to shape the forces that led to the overthrow of the Tokugawa and the establishment of the new Meiji government. The fifteen-year period from 1853 to the Meiji Restoration of 1868, when Japan established a new government and set about the pursuit of national power, is one of the most turbulent in the recorded history of the country. When this period was over, however, Japan had in place a vigorous young ruling clique with a fierce determination to meet the challenges of the new international environment in which Japan found itself.

Although it has not generally been interpreted this way, the Restoration proved to be a revolutionary event designed to accommodate to the norms, rules, and institutions of a new international order. The new leaders themselves had no clearly formed plan for a reformed institutional structure; rather, determined to do whatever was necessary to restore Japanese sovereignty and build national strength, they took their cues from the institutions of the great powers.

With the coming of the imperialist international system, Japan was forced to face all at once time three major interrelated developments that were essential to the modern pattern of international relations: the triumph of the nation-state, the new role of industrialization in underwriting national power, and the emergence of a world market economy. The highly centralized nation-state was the wave of the future. Japan would have to cast aside the Tokugawa feudal structure with its fragmented and inefficient divisions. A strong nation-state would dominate in the modern system because it could generate the revenue required for the technological revolution and for modern warfare. Its fiscal and war-making capabilities made the nation-state essential. Moreover, it could mobilize loyalties, foster nationalism, establish social cohesion, and form an effective political organization to deal with the new set of military and economic conditions.

The Meiji leaders instinctively grasped the interaction of economics and security. Thus it was not only the international state system and the distribution of power among states that had powerful effects upon the character of Japan's domestic regime, but the international economy as well. From the time in the mid-nineteenth century when Japan's leaders realized the extent of Western industrial as well as military power, the determination to overcome Japan's economic backwardness dominated their policy-making. For more than a century thereafter Japan saw itself as a follower society seeking to catch up and overtake the advanced nations of the West. To protect its own security, and to compete in the anarchic realm of international relations, Japan had to adopt the most efficient and effective weapons, strategies, and technologies. Japan was socialized into the international system by emulating the practices of the more successful states in the system.

Accepting rather than resisting the challenges of the system, Japan was drawn ineluctably into its workings. It was incorporated into the world economy. To survive and compete in the new economic environment, Japan had to import all manner of new technology and finished manufactured goods. More important, it had to emulate the institutions of the most successful nations, which it did with astonishing skill, diligence, and attention to detail. Thus the exigencies of the new international system determined in fundamental ways the makeup of Japan's domestic Meiji regime.[5]

PAX BRITANNICA

The states of the North Atlantic and particularly Britain dominated this first truly international system. The Pax Britannica—the era of Britain's hegemony beginning in 1815 after the Napoleonic wars—established the general structure of international relations that enveloped Japan in the middle of the nineteenth century. British power, which was at that time at its height, determined the character of the system, the way it was governed, and its rules and mores.

The Industrial Revolution, which began in England in the eighteenth century, changed the material life of humankind more than anything since the beginning of the Neolithic Age or even since the discovery of fire. Substituting inanimate for animate sources of power, the use of machines brought forth stupendous and self-sustaining increases in productivity. Over the span of a few generations, life in the first industrial nation was transformed in sweeping fashion. The technological changes were of so great a magnitude that they gave Western peoples a military and economic advantage large enough to transform their relationship to other peoples of the world. Asia, which by virtue of its larger population had previously accounted for a far larger portion of world manufacturing output than Europe, was now abruptly relegated to a position of backwardness. Owing to new economic forces and improvements in transport and communication, Asia was drawn increasingly into an integrated global economy centered on Great Britain. To the detriment of Asia and other regions, industrial developments translated into greatly enhanced military power, and Europeans, who in 1800 had controlled 35 percent of the world's land surface, increased this figure to 67 percent in 1878 and 84 percent by 1914.[6]

As "the first industrial nation," Britain was a different kind of power than the world had known. It became the trading center of the world. With only 2 percent of the world's population, Britain conducted one-fifth of the world's commerce, possessed one-third of the world's merchant marine, and was responsible for two-fifths of the world's trade in manufactured goods.

After the Industrial Revolution and the extension of an international market economy around the globe in the nineteenth century, market power became a principal means by which the imperial powers sought to organize the international system. Britain, along with other European powers, already had colonial empires, but acquisition of colonies was now less attractive than it once was. The use of force to maintain territorial control and administer colonies at a distance of many thousands of miles was not efficient if the economic benefits could be achieved in a more economical way. The British were interested in commercial gain and did not want to take on the burdens of government unless it became necessary to do so in order to engage in commerce. Intent on gaining economic advantage without incurring the responsibilities of political control, the principle of British strategy was to "trade with informal control if possible; trade with rule when necessary."[7]

Thus, whereas in India Britain had taken a ruling position, in East Asia its primary purpose was not territorial control. Subjugating and establishing colonial political controls over China, Japan, and Korea would have been an onerous task. Instead, the British brought to bear sufficient force to exercise "informal imperialism," imposing treaties that assured "free trade." They could exploit their comparative industrial advantage and technological superiority by insisting on rights of free trade, a unified international monetary system, and a set of international rules protecting private property.[8] British naval supremacy provided the force necessary to implement and enforce the requirements of informal empire.

Free trade was the ideology of the strong, a dogma preached by a nation in the firm confidence that no other economy could compete with it. To other nations unable to compete, the British ideology of free trade smacked of hypocrisy, to say the least. The British, after all, decades earlier had protected their own domestic industries from foreign competition until they were strong enough to outperform the competitors. The German economist Friedrich List, who later exercised great influence in Japan, in a memorable indictment of this free-trade ideology, wrote:

It is a very common clever device that when anyone has attained the summit of greatness, he kicks away the ladder by which he has climbed up, in
order to deprive others of the means of climbing up after him. In this lies
the secret of the cosmopolitan doctrine of Adam Smith . . . and of all his
successors in the British Government administrations. Any nation which
by means of protective duties and restrictions on navigation has raised her
manufacturing power and her navigation to such a degree of development
that no other nation can sustain free competition with her, can do nothing
wiser than to throw away these ladders of her greatness, to preach to other
nations the benefits of free trade, and to declare in penitent tones that she
has hitherto wandered in the paths of error, and has now for the first time
succeeded in discovering the truth.[9]

British free-trade principles were, in short, nothing other than the self-
serving ideology of the economically strong. By imposing treaties of
"amity and commerce," the British set a pattern that the other powers followed. These unequal treaties assured them of trading enclaves by which
the backward economies of China, Japan, and Korea were opened to the
machine-made goods of the industrially advanced nations.

With Britain promoting free trade, the interdependence of the world
economy expanded, producing a fourfold increase in world trade from
1870 to 1913. During the same period, Britain and other European industrial powers exported great quantities of capital in order to develop new
markets for machines, railroads, and other capital goods and to develop
sources of raw materials for primary product-exporting nations. The
world was experiencing the first great wave of globalization, which was
marked by a rapidly growing economic integration. Markets became inter-
connected owing to improved communication. By the mid-nineteenth
century, an integrated global economy had drawn East Asia into a trading
and financial network centered in the North Atlantic. Steamships were increasing the West's trade with the Far East. The opening of the Suez Canal
on November 17, 1869, brought Asia closer by hastening the transition
from the sailing ship to the steamship. London also managed the international monetary system, which was an important element of the interdependent world economy.

To legitimate imperialism and provide a form of control or governance
essential to any international system, the imperial powers needed "a set of
rights or rules that govern or at least influence the interaction among
states."[10] The dominant states, relying on their military, economic, and even

cultural power and prestige, shaped the system's processes and interactions—both political and economic—to further their own interests. They shaped a distinct body of rights and rules that reflected the values and interests of Western civilization. Then they called this body of rules "international law" and considered it a code of conduct providing the basis for cooperation among modern states. Recognizing that in order to restrict violence, they had to respect the sovereignty of individual states in European international society, they banished the notion of a "just war" among themselves. But this notion did not apply to the non-European world.

The political theorist Hedley Bull wrote that "as the sense grew of the specifically European character of the society of states, so also did the sense of its cultural differentiation from what lay outside: the sense that European powers in their dealings with one another were bound by a code of conduct that did not apply to them in their dealings with other and lesser societies."[11] Theorists of international society by the middle of the nineteenth century had formulated a "standard of civilization" that had to be met if non-European states were to be admitted to this society. A "civilized state" guaranteed the rights of private property, freedom of trade, travel, and religion through an effective system of law, courts, and political organization.

THE FIRST NEW ORDER IN EAST ASIA

This was the world Japan entered. It was an order characterized by an "informal imperialism" embodied in the unequal treaty system. The institutions of this first new order in East Asia, a subsystem of the Pax Britannica, were devised initially by the British to satisfy the demands of commercial opinion in the House of Commons. British merchants wanted unfettered access to trade in East Asia, especially China, for which they had the greatest hopes and expectations. As Lord Clarendon, who served as foreign secretary, said in 1870, "British interests in China are strictly commercial, or at all events only so far political as they may be for protection of commerce."[12]

The essential technique of control was the imposition of treaties, actually "unequal contracts" permitting the imperialists to gain economic penetration without having to bear the cost or the responsibility of governing the population. The East Asian states, in any case, had complex and historical institutions capable on the whole of maintaining social stability. There was therefore little disposition to annex territory outside of the treaty port, thus leaving political and administrative affairs to the existing government. Needless to say, before establishing their "informal" control, the British initially had to demonstrate their ability to enforce their will on the Asian peoples. Rutherford Alcock, the British minister in Japan, wrote: "All diplomacy in these regions which does not rest on a solid substratum of force, or an element of strength, to be laid bare when all gentler processes fail, rests on false premises, and must of necessity fail in its object."[13]

Although imperialism was "informal" in its exercise, the unequal treaty system did infringe sovereignty. Indeed, Japanese historians refer to Japan's status at that time as "semi-colonial"(*han-shokuminchi*). Ports were opened to trade, territories for foreign settlements were leased therein, tariffs were placed under international control and fixed at minimal levels, and foreigners had extraterritorial privilege. The system took on a multilateral, cooperative, collaborative character as a result of the most-favored-nation (MFN) clause inserted in the treaties. Rights and privileges granted to one power were to be extended to the others.

The British fought two naval wars with China to achieve these ends: the Opium War of 1840–1842 and the Arrow War of 1856–1858. The treaties ending these wars established the fundamental institutions and legal structures of the imperialist system that lasted into the twentieth century. The provisions of the Treaty of Nanjing (1842) followed the advice that the China coast merchants gave to the British Foreign Office. Hong Kong was ceded to Britain, as the British negotiator said, to provide "an emporium for our trade and a place from which Her Majesty's subjects in China may be alike protected and controlled." Five other ports were opened where the British could trade "without molestation or restraint." Under a separate commercial agreement concluded the following year, customs duties were fixed at low rates, averaging 5 percent ad valorem.[14]

Chinese sovereignty was most obviously infringed upon through the principle of extraterritoriality, which provided that British subjects would be subject to their own country's law as administered through consular courts established in the treaty ports. The legal structures of this commercial imperialism were extended and systematized through the MFN clause, which provided that the British would be granted any privileges that other foreign powers might subsequently extract from the Chinese. Great Britain forced China to sign another treaty in 1858 at the conclusion of the Arrow War that greatly expanded the number of treaty ports to the north and in the interior. By the twentieth century, eighty ports had been opened in

China. Once their treaty rights were secured, the Western nations, led by Britain, sought to shore up the Ch'ing government in order to maintain a stable environment for trade and investment.

Because the British were preoccupied with compelling further concessions from China, it fell to the Americans to press Japan to submit to this new order. Perry resolved in 1853, as the official narrative of his expedition recorded, "to adopt a course entirely contrary to that of all others who had hitherto visited Japan on a similar errand—to demand as a right, and not as a favor, those acts of courtesy which are due from one civilized nation to another." Still, the Americans imposed British-inspired institutions of informal empire on the Japanese. It was, moreover, the ever-present threat of British naval power that gave credibility to U.S. demands. And it was the British ideology of free trade that Perry drew on to legitimate his intrusion. As he later recorded, "Japan has been opened to the nations of the west. . . . It belongs to these nations to show Japan that her interests will be promoted by communication with them; and, as prejudice gradually vanishes, we may hope to see the future negotiation of commercial treaties, more and more liberal, for the benefit, not of ourselves only, but of all the maritime powers of Europe, for the advancement of Japan, and for the upward progress of our common humanity."[15]

Perry negotiated a treaty in 1854 that provided ports of refuge and supply for American ships but did little to promote trade. Townsend Harris, America's first diplomatic representative stationed in Japan, arrived in 1856 with orders to negotiate a commercial agreement of the kind Britain had imposed in China. He had firsthand experience of the British method. Harris came to Japan by way of Siam, where the British had just concluded a Treaty of Friendship and Commerce between Her Majesty and the King of Siam providing for all aspects of informal empire. Using the British model, Harris negotiated a treaty between the United States and Siam. In Japan, he proceeded to implant the institutions of informal empire that the British had previously imposed in China. Meanwhile, the British were preoccupied in China with events surrounding the Arrow War, and it was the example of force used against China at the time that gave Harris the leverage he needed. (The British and French ultimately used impressive force to compel Chinese acceptance of treaties in 1858. These treaties permitted their ministers to reside in Beijing on terms of diplomatic equality, thus ending Chinese traditions of superiority. The British used 41 warships and 10,500 troops; the French used 60 ships and 6,300 troops.) Harris played on the specter of such force to compel the Japanese to negotiate with him, telling them that "if Japan should make a treaty with the ambassador of the United States, who has come unattended by military force, her honor will not be impaired. There will be a great difference between a treaty made with a single individual, unattended, and one made with a person who should bring fifty men-of-war to these shores."[16]

The treaty that Harris succeeded in negotiating with the Tokugawa Bakufu "transplanted the treaty port system from China to Japan."[17] Five ports were opened to trade: Hakodate, Nagasaki, Hyōgo (Kobe), Kanagawa (Yokohama), and Niigata. Consuls would reside there, and extraterritoriality was agreed to, as were fixed import and export tariffs. Osaka and Edo were opened to foreigners. The British and other Western powers in short order extracted similar treaties, and Japan was thereby incorporated into the imperialist order in East Asia. Under the treaties imposed by the powers, "Japan switched from virtual autarky to free trade in 1858."[18] Japanese tariffs were placed under international control and at such a low level that the domestic economy was thrown open for the import of Western manufactured goods.

THE JAPANESE RESPONSE

The challenge of the international system to Japan's sovereignty sparked the overthrow of the old Tokugawa government and set Japan on a new course. Unlike most other modern revolutions, the Meiji Restoration was a profoundly conservative event; it was a nationalist revolution that set out Japan's determination to acquire the power to be the equal of the Western world, or even to overtake the Western world. Led by young, low-ranking members of the traditional samurai elite, it was motivated by the values of Japan's long feudal period—values of power, status, realism, and respect for hierarchy. The new Meiji leaders responded to the challenge of the international system not with resistance, but with a marked realism, pragmatism, and opportunism. As a result, the Japanese alone among Asian peoples accommodated quickly to the norms, principles, and mores of the imperialist system. Recognizing and respecting the superior power of the Western nations, Japan's new leaders were determined to play by the rules of the game, adapt them to their own purposes, and rise within the existing system.

The influence of Japan's long feudal experience would have been weakened if the samurai elite had been displaced by a new ruling class intent on acquiring political voice and influence. Had Japan's modern revolution been carried out by a rising middle class that had decided to overthrow the old elite in the name of new values, demanding political rights, its modern history would have taken a different direction. But this was not the case. The Meiji Restoration was carried out by a party within the old ruling class, and it was precipitated by Japan's forced entry into the international system. Weakened by long-term economic and social change, Tokugawa rule was finally delegitimized by its inability to cope with the challenge posed by Western imperialism. The young samurai who took power in 1868 instinctively grasped the reality of the competitive struggle that must be waged for the nation's survival. In the face of this challenge, they were remorseless in their readiness to sacrifice Japan's own time-honored institutions to the demands of foreign policy.

In spite of the initial turmoil that transpired in Japan, what was remarkable was how short-lived the resistance was to the demands of the international system. During the fifteen-year interval between Perry's arrival in 1853 and the overthrow of the old regime in 1868, at varying times and under varying circumstances, Japan's future leaders came to the realization that the external threat could not be resisted. The demonstration of Western military superiority was an essential part of this realization, but so was the long-accumulated knowledge of Western science and technology.

No doubt an essential element in Japan's responsiveness was the timing of the international challenge. Japan was ripe and ready for change. Momentum for change had been gathering for many decades. Profound social and economic change and pervasive discontent among all classes had already, before the arrival of Western power, undermined the foundations of Tokugawa rule. Its institutions no longer seemed adequate to cope with the new social and economic conditions. The foreign crisis brought into sharp focus the impotence of the old system, delegitimized it, and prompted revolutionary action to create a new order. Two of the most powerful feudal domains, Chōshū and Satsuma, took the lead in toppling the regime and provided the new young political leadership from the lower ranks of the old samurai elite. At first, they appeared resolutely conservative in choosing to restore the emperor, the traditional source of political legitimacy, to the center of government. Yet at the same time they proved keenly perceptive of Western military strength and its basis in scientific and technological achievement. Their attention to the sources of power in the new environment sanctioned wholesale reforms and the importation of Western civilization.

The new leaders of the government that came to power in 1868 were determined to give primacy to foreign policy. They became obsessed with the goal of overtaking the West and doing whatever was necessary, even risking Japan's very cultural identity, to achieve that goal. In the first important official document of this new Meiji era, the Imperial Charter Oath of 1868, which the Meiji leaders had the boy emperor Mutsuhito issue in 1868, they declared: "Knowledge shall be sought for all over the world, and thereby the foundations of imperial rule shall be strengthened. . . . All absurd customs of olden times shall be abandoned and all actions shall be based on international usage." Where other Asian countries remained committed to their traditional knowledge and institutions, Japan undertook to accept and adhere to the rules and practices of the international system.

As we have seen, the long feudal experience of Japan produced realist values and assumptions that were paramount in the inherited strategic thinking of the new leaders.[19] It is significant that among the new Meiji leaders, many were young military commanders. Raised in martial discipline, trained in swordsmanship, they were men of action. In the outer domains of Chōshū and Satsuma, from which generations of Japan's modern leadership sprang, the samurai code kept alive a strong sense of pride in physical strength and martial skills and a conscious respect for master-follower relationships of vassalage. Boys from samurai families in Satsuma, for example, were taught to comport themselves "with dignity," and they "learned to be prickly about their honor," wrote Albert M. Craig in an analysis of the Meiji leaders' character. "[They] quizzed each other on how they would behave in complex hypothetical situations involving their duty or honor, and gathered together to read and discuss through the night the *Military Record of Sekigahara*, the tale of the forty-seven rōnin, or other heroic literature."[20] Their future concern with Japan's national honor and dignity was a value implanted from their early days of schooling.

As a whole, the samurai class throughout the country had often become demoralized and effete, transformed into bureaucrats who were often underemployed. However, the young, generally low-ranking samurai who led the overthrow of the old regime fought their way to power as commanders of military units, making use of commoners and new weapons bought from the West. Thus, as Craig said, in an understatement, "a largely civilian interpretation of the Restoration is probably mistaken."[21]

It was this realist pursuit of power that led the Meiji leaders to destroy institutions that stood in the way of establishing Japanese power. For them, when push came to shove, the importance of power and the preservation of the nation took precedence over the preservation of Japan's own cultural practices. This willingness to sacrifice old and comfortable ways was at the root of the Meiji leaders' pragmatism and strategic thinking. Finally, it was their attentiveness to power that drove them to catch up with the West.

The new Meiji elite, rising out of the lower reaches of the old, grasped the significance of the new possibilities and brought the vision and the energy that Japan required to reorder their society so that it could thrive in the international system. They quickly recognized that the practices of the old Sinocentric order were outmoded. The imperialist powers had made clear from their first appearance that they would not accept the prevailing ethos of the old East Asian order, which stressed suzerain-vassal relations and elaborate rituals of exchange. The powers insisted on adherence to a system of international law that purported to treat all members of the society of nations as equal.

With their military background and the primacy they gave to the pursuit of power, the Meiji leaders were extraordinarily endowed to understand the nature of the challenge that lay before them. They readily adopted the vocabulary of Social Darwinism and spoke of *jakuniku-kyōshoku* (the strong devour the weak) to describe the mores of international politics. They understood that the state that failed to be socialized into the prevailing norms of this new order might be deprived of its very existence.

ADAPTING TO INTERNATIONAL PRACTICE

What is notable about the Japanese reaction is not simply the ready realization of the superiority of Western technology and the irresistibility of Western power, but the fact that Japanese leaders also quickly discerned advantage in accommodation to the governing principles of the external order that was enveloping them. On the eve of the Restoration, the most powerful feudal lords, whose domains had initially led resistance to foreign intrusion, submitted a joint memorial to the imperial court urging acceptance and accommodation to the international order that the foreign powers were imposing. Writing at the end of February 1868, they counseled that Japan must avoid "the bad example of the Chinese, who fancying themselves alone to be great and worthy of respect, and despising the foreigners as little better than beasts, have come to suffer defeat at their hands." Recognizing that resistance to the powers would be fruitless, they advised pursuing "relations of amity" with the foreigners and summoning their representatives to imperial audiences "in the manner prescribed by the rules current among all nations."

Ten days later, the emperor responded in phrases marked by similar determination to accommodate to the realities of the system: "The stipulations of the treaties . . . may be reformed if found to be hurtful, but the public laws observed by all nations forbid wanton disturbances of those arrangements as a whole. . . . The imperial government feels itself therefore compelled to entertain amicable relations under the treaties concluded by the Bakufu."[22] In the space of fifteen rapid years, the Japanese leaders had moved from determined resistance to the Western powers to acceptance and accommodation to the rules and mores of their system.

The unequal treaties imposed upon Japan by the powers assumed the superiority of Western civilization. Henry Wheaton's classic *Elements of International Law* in its first edition of 1836 had said that international law was "limited to the civilized and Christian people in Europe or to those of European origin."[23] Extended to the non-Western world, international law would deal with the practical problems of protecting Western interests. It would also determine which countries merited legal recognition. When the Meiji leaders tried to revise the unequal treaties, they were told that Japan must reform its institutions to meet the standards of civilization.

The Meiji leaders accepted these new rules and sought to use them to their own advantage in East Asia. It is noteworthy how quickly the Meiji leaders picked up on the principles of the system, which had been used against Japan, and applied them in their relations to their neighbors in East Asia. As Alexis Dudden wrote in describing Japan's role in Asia at that time, "Japanese officials determined to establish their newly reorganized nation in the terms of international law, thus relocating Japan's place in the world and redefining power in Asia."[24]

Wheaton's *Elements of International Law* was translated into Japanese in the mid-1860s, and the Meiji leaders, although well aware that it was an instrument of Western power and influence, nonetheless accepted international law as the prevailing norm by which relations among states would be conducted. In his diary, Kido Kōin, the prominent new leader from Chōshū, in 1868 identified international law as the instrument of the powerful: "There is an urgent need for Japan to become strong enough militarily to take a stand against the Western powers. As long as our country is lacking in military power, the law of nations is not to be trusted. When dealing with those who are weak, the strong nations often invoke public law but really calculate their own gain. Thus it seems to me that the law of nations is merely a tool for the conquest of the weak."[25]

The Meiji leaders grasped the significance of the "vocabulary of power" and the way in which the terms of international law played a central role in creating international order by legitimizing the use of force and the establishment of the instruments of imperialist governance.[26] Only a few short years after it signed the last of the unequal treaties in 1866, Japan itself sought to apply these principles and conclude a similar unequal treaty with China. The Japanese sent an envoy to China to negotiate a treaty based on the new concepts, which would thereby force the Chinese to acknowledge the new practices. The newly established Japanese Foreign Ministry drafted in 1871 a typical unequal treaty that sought to gain from China by virtue of the MFN clause all the concessions made to the Western powers.

The Chinese, however, rejected the Japanese draft. Li Hongzhang, China's principal diplomat, dismissed the Japanese proposal: "We cannot do anything about Western nations, but we should not allow any such treatment from Japan. The Japanese are poor, greedy, and untrustworthy. Because the proximity of the two countries facilitates intercourse, and because both peoples are of the same stock and use the same script, it would be very much more disadvantageous for us to grant the Japanese permission to go into China's interior than it was to give such rights to the Westerners."[27] Much to the exasperation of the Japanese, they were only able to achieve a Treaty of Amity and accompanying trade regulations in 1871. Although the Japanese did not win acceptance of MFN status from China, they nonetheless weakened the old order because the treaty established Japan's titular equality with China. It was the first treaty signed between two East Asian countries on the basis of Western international law.

The Japanese leaders persisted in their determination to apply the rules and mores of the imperialist system to Korea in the face of Korean defiance. It was evidence that the Japanese were already prepared, as Fukuzawa Yukichi later counseled, to dissociate from Asia and treat other Asian countries in the same way that the West treated them. The Japanese embarked on this treaty negotiation in part to compel the Koreans to accept a new relationship with Japan. The Koreans had rejected Japanese attempts to open relations based on Western concepts of international law, insisting on the retention of the old Sinocentric system. In this context, Korea, as a tributary state of China, would not recognize Japan's emperor as being equal in status to the Chinese emperor.

After extended controversy, in 1876 a Japanese force arrived and demanded treaty relations based on the "law of nations." The Treaty of
Kanghwa of 1876 that the Japanese forced on the Koreans in effect fore-
told the end of the Sinocentric order in East Asia by declaring that Korea,
China's most faithful vassal, was now "an independent nation."[28] Moreover, modeled in its provisions on the treaties that Japan itself had been
forced to sign, it accorded Japan the privileges of open ports, extraterritoriality, and (by supplementary treaty) tariff controls. This was the first successful opening of Korea to foreign intercourse. It also marked an
important milestone in Japan's accommodation to the new international
order. In 1879, the incorporation into the Meiji state of the Ryukyu Islands, which had once had tributary relations with both Japan and China,
was another nail in the coffin of the old Sinocentric order.

The Japanese went to extraordinary lengths to use international law to
assert their power in their relations with their Asian neighbors. In 1885
when Itō Hirobumi met with Li Hongzhang in Tientsin to resolve disputes
over the stationing of Japanese and Qing troops in Seoul, and a decade
later when the same two met at Shimonoseki to negotiate the peace treaty
ending the Sino-Japanese War, Itō ostentatiously chose to negotiate in
English, the European language he knew best, in order to make the maximum impression with concepts of international law. If he had conveyed
these concepts in Chinese characters, it would have allowed the Qing representative to quarrel with their meaning from the viewpoint of traditional
Sinocentric referents. By invoking the "law of nations" and negotiating in
English, Itō effectively delegitimated the old diplomatic lexicon and defined power in a new way.[29] After centuries of Chinese domination of East
Asia in which states legitimated themselves with reference to Chinese concepts, Japanese officials, by mastering the terms of international law,
"wrested power away from the continent and became the definers of the
new terms of exchange," in Dudden's words.[30]

EMULATION AND INNOVATION

During the reign of the Meiji emperor (1868–1912), Japan's revolutionary leaders laid the foundations for the national drive for military and
industrial power by creating domestic institutions that would prepare
Japan to deal with the forces of the international system. Although the
Meiji leaders initially thought that building military power was what was

required, they soon perceived that the challenge they confronted was much larger and more inclusive than that. With extraordinary insight born of long feudal experience, they soon grasped the immensity of the task. They would have to build military power and strengthen the state. They would have to import modern industry. But they soon realized that even all this would not suffice. Above all, they grasped the multifaceted sources of power in the new system:

> The power of the nation-state by no means consists only in its armed forces, but also its economic and technological resources; in the dexterity, foresight and resolution with which its foreign policy is conducted; in the efficiency of its social and political organization. It consists most of all in the nation itself, the people; their skills, energy, ambition, discipline, initiative, their beliefs, myths and illusions. And it consists, further, in the way all these factors are related to one another. Moreover, national power has to be considered not only in itself, in its absolute extent; . . . it has to be considered relative to the power of other states.[31]

The Meiji leaders learned that the challenge of the international system could not be met simply by acquiring its military and industrial technology. To succeed externally they would have to reorganize all aspects of domestic society. It meant harnessing the energies of the people and giving them a vision of the national goals in terms that would command their belief and loyalty. It meant committing the nation to the competitive struggle with other nations similarly motivated and increasing Japan's power in relation to them. It meant, ultimately, not only the pursuit of industry but also of empire. Foreign Minster Inoue Kaoru summed up Meiji policy in 1887: "What we must do is to transform our empire and our people, make the empire like the countries of Europe, and our people like the peoples of Europe. To put it differently, we have to establish a new, European-style empire on the edge of Asia."[32]

If Japan was to be a full participant in the new East Asian order, it would have to bring to an end the unequal treaties imposed upon it at the end of the Tokugawa period. Revision of the unequal treaties forced on Japan by the Western powers required adapting quickly to the rules of the system. For twenty-five years after the Restoration, from 1868 until 1894, when the goal was achieved, the primary goal of Japanese foreign policy was revision of the unequal treaties so as to stand on equal footing with Western countries and escape the semi-colonial status to which extraterritoriality and tariff control had relegated Japan. Since the great powers would only agree to the elimination of the treaties when Japan had reformed its domestic legal institutions, foreign policy became a matter of transforming Japan's domestic institutions.

The most remarkable diplomatic mission in Japanese history, the Iwakura Mission to the United States and Europe from 1871 to 1873, ostensibly to make preliminary soundings for revision of the unequal treaties, was more fundamentally about discovering "the great principles which are to be our guide in the future."[33] This mission, which has few, if any, parallels in world history, took more than half of the Meiji leadership abroad for almost two years. Its final report was a massive 2,000-page, five-volume chronicle of the mission's observations. Comprising more than 100 members, many of whom had never before been abroad, the mission was headed by Prince Iwakura Tomomi, the most prestigious member of the new ruling group; included the key leaders Ōkubo Toshimichi, Kido Kōin, and Itō Hirobumi; and permitted a thorough examination of the world's most advanced nations. The group's members wanted to discover the sources of Western power and wealth so that a plan for strengthening the Japanese state could be worked out. They began with visits to nine cities in the United States, followed by sojourns in England and Scotland, France, Belgium, the Netherlands, Germany, Russia, Denmark, Sweden, Italy, Austria, and Switzerland.

What they learned ultimately convinced the Meiji leaders that they must not only centralize the nation-state and adopt new technology from the West, but must in addition remake Japan's domestic institutional structure to meet the competitive demands of the international system. The question was, How far was it necessary to go in reorganizing Japanese institutions? The Meiji leaders were not ideologues. They approached the task with a characteristic pragmatism. As one of the key leaders, Ōkuma Shigenobu, told a promising associate in the days after the Restoration, "Our duty [now] is to advance further and build a new Japan. . . . It is not only you who does not know where to start. No one does."[34] The guiding motivation was to overtake the power of the Western nations.

Although pragmatism and realism ultimately carried the day, Japanese leaders had intense debates over the appropriate strategic response to the imperialist system. In the contentious years after Perry's arrival there were bitter struggles over the choices facing the nation. Advocates of armed resistance and protecting the cultural heritage confronted reformers who favored opening the country to Western influences. Those who subsequently became leaders of the new government moved steadily from resistance to reform as they gained firsthand experience of Western power. Similarly, after the Restoration the new leaders who went on the Iwakura Mission had to face down opposition from the formidable Satsuma warrior ("the last of the samurai") Saigō Takamori and others who had supported centralization of the government and restoration of the imperial institution but had opposed a full-scale adoption of Western practices. Later, in the political crisis of 1881, the choice between a liberal, English-style form of Western government and a more authoritarian, Prussian-style one occasioned more debate and contention among the elite. The demands of foreign policy, in the final reckoning, once again settled the decision to make Germany the preferred model of government.

The Iwakura Mission strongly confirmed the Meiji leaders' views of the predatory nature of international politics. Above all, they came back convinced of the need for national self-reliance. The European tradition of political realism strongly resonated with their own experience. Both Ōkubo and Itō subsequently recalled the advice that German Chancellor Otto von Bismarck had given them. He spoke the language of Realpolitik—the notion that relations among nations are determined by raw power and that the mighty will prevail—which they readily understood. The Iron Chancellor, who had solved the problem of German unification through a foreign policy based on calculations of power and the national interest, cautioned the Meiji leaders to prepare Japan for the intense competition among nation-states. The official narrative of the Iwakura Mission records that Bismarck counseled them that "although people say that so-called international law safeguards the rights of all countries, the fact is that when large countries pursue their advantage they talk about international law when it suits them, and they use force when it does not."[35] Bismarck concluded that everything he had learned convinced him that a nation-state could preserve its independence only through policies of strength and the cultivation of patriotism among the people.

Bismarck's words reinforced what the Meiji leaders had already decided: that Japan must rely on itself. They must look to their own interests. This was a world of struggle not just for survival but for superiority over other states. Two years before the departure of the mission, Iwakura had written, in a memorandum on foreign affairs,

Although we have no choice in having intercourse with the countries beyond the seas, in the final analysis those countries are our enemies. Why are they our enemies? Day by day those countries develop their arts and their technology with a view to growing in wealth and power. Every country tries to become another country's superior. Country A directs its efforts at country B, country B at country C—they are all the same. That is why I say, all countries beyond the seas are our enemies.[36]

The members of the mission concluded that it was imperative for Japan to become self-sufficient in its economy and in its military strength and that a sharply focused, but long-range view of Japan's national interest must be the foundation of comprehensive plans for Japan's development.

All members of the mission were impressed by the industrial muscle of the West and its essential part in national power. They also recognized that the people must be mobilized to provide an educated, disciplined, loyal foundation for the hard tasks of industrial and military power. As Kido Kōin, the young samurai leader from Chōshū, recorded in his diary,

> Unless we establish an unshakable national foundation, we will not be able to elevate our country's prestige in a thousand years. The creation of such public morals and the establishment of such a national foundation depends entirely on people. And the supply of such people in endless numbers over a long period of time clearly depends on education, and on education alone. Our people are no different from the Americans or Europeans of today: it is all a matter of education or lack of education.[37]

The mission's final report is striking for its pervasive optimism. One might suppose that the visitors would have been overwhelmed by Western civilization and the task of trying to match its achievements. Instead, one finds a bold self-confidence that what the West had accomplished was of recent origin and that Japan, through careful planning and hard work, could catch up. The report said:

> Most of the countries in Europe shine with the light of civilization and abound in wealth and power. Their trade is prosperous, their technology is superior, and they greatly enjoy the pleasures and comforts of life. When one observes such conditions, one is apt to think that these countries have always been like this, but this is not the case—the wealth and prosperity one sees now in Europe dates to an appreciable degree from the period after 1800. It has taken scarcely forty years to produce such conditions. . . . How different the Europe of today is from the Europe of

forty years ago can be imagined easily. There were no trains running on the land; there were no steamships operating on the water. There was no transmission of news by telegraph. . . . Those who read this should reflect upon the lesson to be drawn for Japan.[38]

The Meiji leaders thus set out to organize the nation internally so as to achieve its external goal of catching up with the West. Ōkuma Shigenobu, one of the prominent Meiji leaders, later wrote that "to attain an equal footing with the other powers . . . has been the impulse underlying all the national changes that have taken place."[39]

The Meiji leaders shrewdly created the most highly centralized state in the nation's history and adopted a broad program of reforms to enhance its power. Universal conscription, a universal system of compulsory education, and an efficient new land tax all came in rapid order. The government hastened the adoption of the new technology and institutions by hiring more than 3,000 foreign advisers over the course of the Meiji period. The Meiji leaders concluded from discussions with Western diplomatic representatives that revision of the treaties depended not only on the development of national power but on legal and administrative reforms that would make Japan a "civilized" country capable of proper treatment of foreign nationals.

They went to great lengths to accommodate to the rules and mores of the international system. They pressed for adoption of westernized legal codes in order to impress on the powers the civilized progress of Japan and so to hasten treaty revision. They adopted European legal codes and drafted a constitution modeled after Prussia's. The government moved quickly to plan such reforms. Committees appointed to compile penal and civil codes took French law as a model and engaged the French jurist Gustave Emile Boissonade to advise them in compiling laws. A German legal expert, Hermann Roesler, was entrusted with drafting a commercial code. The desire to impress the West was likewise a constant stimulus to the establishment of constitutional government. The Meiji leaders were pragmatic in adopting the long-range view that however humiliating accommodation might be, along this road lay national power. In a way, they fully understood the Western demand that Japan reform its laws and institutions. "After all," confessed Foreign Minister Inoue Kaoru, "would we expect Japanese subjects to subject themselves to Korean law and courts?"[40]

The task of building a modern nation-state engaged the Meiji leaders for the entire period of their hold on government, from 1868 through the turn of the century. The decentralized, diffuse, divided Tokugawa state was replaced by the most highly centralized government Japan has known—then or since. Everything the Meiji leaders did in their domestic agenda was directed at building a strong state that could mobilize their nation's human and material resources behind the foreign policy they had set for Japan.

Ultimately, the policy of the Meiji leaders bore fruit; in mid-1894 the Western powers recognized the effectiveness of their reforms and agreed to sign treaties providing for the end of their extraterritorial privileges in Japan. By now the program of reforms that had begun after the Restoration was in place, and the Meiji leaders perceived the power of the state sufficiently centralized, sovereignty restored, and society stabilized. It has been said that "nations try to expand their political interests abroad when central decision-makers perceive a relative increase in state power."[41] Such a moment was at hand. Little more than two weeks after revision of the unequal treaties was achieved, Japan declared war on China and embarked upon its first great foreign adventure in three centuries. The Sino-Japanese War of 1894–1895 worked fundamental changes in the imperialist system, bringing Japan fully into the system as a new imperial power. Furthermore, by demonstrating the weakness of Chinese government, it generated increased rivalry among the powers and began to erode the cooperative nature of the regional order.

The New Imperialism

At the end of the nineteenth century, the rise of several new powers and the resulting relative decline of Great Britain brought about a change within the imperialist system in East Asia, though not a change of the system itself.[42] The Meiji reforms culminated and the treaty revision movement succeeded at a time when the intensity of the competition among the imperialist powers was increasing and the practices of cooperative imperialism breaking down. This new phase, sometimes referred to as the "new imperialism," saw the rise of new states in the governance of the system and the relative decline of a formerly dominant power. The imperialist system remained intact, but the dominant role of Great Britain began to fade as new powers engaged in intense competition for position in the regional system. Substantial changes in the way the imperialist system functioned took place. By the middle of the 1880s, the United States had a greater share of the world's manufacturing production than Great Britain, and by 1906–1910, Germany, too, had surpassed England.[43]

Rather than investing in its own industrial infrastructure, Britain increasingly put its capital into overseas investments that paid a greater short-term return. Furthermore, Britain lost its technological lead as innovations of the "second industrial revolution" in electricity, chemicals, and steel began to form the industrial basis of economic development in the United States and Germany. Accustomed to the success of the past, Britain found it hard to change and to throw off the inertia that had set in. Britain was, as Veblen observed, paying the price for having taken the lead earlier.[44] More youthful industrializers, the United States and Germany, pressed ahead to develop new technologies. They were able to learn from the British experience, import the more advanced technology, use it more efficiently, and—without the rigidities of labor and vested interests that had plagued the British—move ahead. At the close of the century, England had become, in the famous words of its first lord of the admiralty, Joseph Chamberlain, "the weary titan [struggling] under the too vast orb of its fate."

While in command of the seas, Britain had restrained colonial competition in order to maintain free access to the world markets and sources of raw materials. But after 1880, with the emergence of French and German naval power, the British Navy was no longer able to rule unchallenged. The first lord of the admiralty warned, "The United Kingdom by itself will not be strong enough to hold its proper place alongside of the U.S., or Russia, and probably not Germany. We shall be thrust aside by sheer weight."[45]

European rivalries were shifting to the colonial field, and East Asia became the site of these rivalries. Russia's decision to build the Trans-Siberian Railway, undertaken in 1891, was a notable indication of the rivalries opening up in the region. The intensification of great-power rivalry meant a decline of the cooperative features of the earlier informal imperialism of free trade. In its place, in the 1890s, came the new imperialism with its competition for more exclusive concessions in the form of spheres of influence, leaseholds, and protectorates. These arrangements gave the powers sole access to raw materials, markets, and naval stations from which they could exclude others. The British, with the support of the Americans, sought to preclude this carving up of the region into exclusive enclaves through the doctrine of maintaining the "Open Door." Eventually, on the eve of World War I, stability was restored to the imperialist system in East Asia, but not before two decades of intense rivalry had created a more complex system. It was during this time that Japan, having completed its domestic transformation begun after the Restoration, entered the race for concessions and became a full participant in the system.

The Sino-Japanese War of 1894–1895 was the event, more than any other, that revealed the full extent of China's weakness and set off an intense competition among the imperial powers for control of the resources and markets of East Asia. Yet the race for exclusive concessions, as Duus pointed out,

> was quickly halted by the reluctance of the treaty powers to upset the advantages of shared or collective imperialism. The rules of collective informal empire were reformulated in the doctrine of the Open Door. The treaty powers realized that maintaining a balance-of-power equilibrium in China was less costly than risking conflict through competition, and they reaffirmed the basic rules of the game under the same free-trade ideology that had justified the establishment of the treaty system in the first place.[46]

No longer able to contain the ambitions of its rivals, Great Britain engaged in what Gilpin called "a massive effort of 'preclusive' imperialism."[47] It sought to shore up its diplomatic and strategic position in East Asia through closer ties with the United States and the conclusion of the Anglo-Japanese Alliance of 1902.

THE MOTIVATION OF JAPANESE IMPERIALISM

Japanese imperialism in the Meiji period was notable for the degree to which it was prompted by the international system.[48] Japan was socialized into the system by the hard struggles its leaders undertook to restore its sovereignty. Japan entered the system as a victim, an object of imperialism, almost a subject nation. After a brief period on the eve of the Restoration in which they attempted to resist Western incursions, Japanese leaders chose to adapt to the international order. They picked up quickly on the cues and incentives that the system offered. This was not inevitable. Japan could have resisted, as other Asian nations did, but the strategic culture that the Meiji elite possessed gave them a keen sensitivity to the imperatives of the competitive struggle to survive. They believed that if Japan did not heed the cues of the international system and emulate the sources of strength of the strong states—their institutions and techniques—it would continue to suffer harm at their hands.

Before the Meiji period, Japan had not been an expansionist country. Hideyoshi's brief and abortive invasion of Korea in the sixteenth century was an exception to a premodern history that lacked experience in the overseas conquest of alien peoples. Meiji imperialism was, in the first instance, defensive and preemptive. Japan's relative power and its position as a late developer in the international system determined its strategic needs. The power vacuum in East Asia, and the encroachment of the imperial powers, made it imperative that Japan look to its strategic interests.

The prevailing political instability of East Asia outside of Japan created both problems and opportunities. Japan's more rapid development, together with the institutional backwardness of other countries in East Asia, created a situation in which Japan could almost expect to dominate its neighbors. In Korea and China at the end of the nineteenth century, old impotent governments were being undermined by revolutionary movements. The impending collapse of these weak governments caused a pervasive insecurity in Japan because they might be replaced by Western control, with consequent jeopardy to Japan's security. In addition to the geopolitical danger of allowing neighboring states to fall under the sway of other powers, maintaining access to the raw materials and markets of East Asia was also critical. Japan had to look for favorable circumstances in which it could thwart the designs that the powers would likely have on these weak neighbors.

Japanese imperialism was prompted more by strategic military considerations than by economic incentives. The latter were significant but in no way comparable to the commercial motives of the other powers. The historian Mark Peattie wrote:

No colonial empire of modern times was as clearly shaped by strategic considerations. . . . Many of the overseas possessions of Western Europe had been acquired in response to the activities of traders, adventurers, missionaries, or soldiers acting far beyond the limits of European interest or authority. In contrast, Japan's colonial territories . . . were, in each instance, obtained as the result of a deliberate decision by responsible authorities in the central government to use force in securing territory that could contribute to Japan's immediate strategic interests.[49]

Outside-in influences in the genesis of Japanese imperialism are unmistakable. This is not to say that domestic forces supporting expansionism were absent. Internal forces unleashed by industrial society played a role in impelling imperialism. The search for markets and investment opportunities, the growing involvement of the masses in politics, and the influence of a nationalist press prodded expansionism. Still, these were secondary influences. The Meiji leaders' pursuit of strategic advantage was primary as they sought to displace Chinese influence in Korea and then preempt Russian influence there and in southern Manchuria. In the 1880s, it became a cardinal principle of Japanese foreign policy that the security of the Japanese islands depended on preventing Korea from falling under the control of a third country. As the Prussian adviser to the Meiji army put it, the Korean Peninsula was "a dagger thrust at the heart of Japan."[50] The General Staff concluded that the "independence" of Korea could only be secured via control of the neighboring Port Arthur and the Liaotung Peninsula. With those strategic objectives in mind, the government steadily built up the nation's military power.

The "new imperialism," marked by intensified competition among the Western powers for spheres of influence and territorial concessions, heightened Japan's strategic anxiety. Japan embarked on expansionism following a kind of inexorable realist logic that was hinted at by Japan's leading military strategist, Yamagata Aritomo, who, addressing the Diet as prime minister at its opening session in 1890, explained: "The independence and security of the nation depend first upon the protection of the line of sovereignty and then the line of advantage. . . . If we wish to maintain the nation's independence among the powers of the world at the present time, it is not enough to guard only the line of sovereignty; we must also defend the line of advantage . . . and within the limits of the nation's resources gradually strive for that position."[51]

In other words, Japan's security depended not only on protecting the actual territorial limits of the nation, but also on establishing Japan's dominant influence in the areas beyond. In 1890, Yamagata had Korea in mind as the neighboring area that fell within the "line of advantage." Subsequently, when Japanese control of Korea was achieved, the line of advantage extended into southern Manchuria, where, to ensure the security of Korea, Japan also needed to establish its dominant influence. Such strategic thinking was not unique to Japanese leadership, but it was unusually influential in Japan, partly because the Japanese empire, unlike the far-flung European and American empires, was in close proximity to the home islands.

In the same way that Japanese leaders crafted domestic institutions to fit the needs of the international system, they also designed their imperialist policies in emulation of the practices of the Western imperialist system.

Peter Duus, in his study of Japanese penetration of Korea in the period 1895–1910, wrote:

Japanese imperialism, like so many other aspects of Meiji development, was an act of mimesis. The Meiji leaders, who avidly monitored world politics, crafted their expansionist policies along Western lines, deployed the same gunboat tactics to establish domination in Korea, and appealed to the same legal justification to legitimize it. In the same way, residency-general officials poured out annual reports filled with complaisant statistics on new roads laid, hospitals built, trees planted, crops harvested, railway lines extended, and trade promoted that were not so very different from reports produced by their counterparts in Western colonial regimes. And Japanese settlers, like Western colonials, carefully cordoned themselves off in segregated neighborhoods named after places back home and even established in Seoul a Nihon Club much like the clubs that dotted the British empire.[52]

By 1894, intrigue and chaotic politics in Korea were creating tense relations between China and Japan, each of which sought to assert influence over the course of Korean politics. The Japanese foreign minister, seizing the opportunity provided by the problems in Korea as a *casus belli*, moved to resolve the situation, writing in a personal memoir that he "sensed that the wisest course to follow now was to precipitate a clash between ourselves and the Chinese."[53] The superior planning and readiness of the Japanese military brought quick victory. By the time the Treaty of Shimonoseki was signed in 1895, Japan had become a full participant in the framework of the imperialist system.

In addition to ceding Taiwan and recognizing Korean independence, which amounted to a strategic edge for Japan on the peninsula, in this treaty the Chinese gave the Japanese a lease on the Liaotung Peninsula in southern Manchuria, a location the Japanese leaders had recognized a decade earlier as being of key strategic importance. The treaty also gave Japan a large indemnity and an impressive array of commercial concessions, which through the most-favored-nation clause were also accorded the other powers. Japan was playing by the rules of the imperialist game. Understanding the "vocabulary of power," and knowing that "international terms empower the strong," Japanese politicians and translators were meticulous about legitimating the seizure of Korea in terms of international law.[54] As Foreign Minister Mutsu Munemitsu instructed the Japanese minister in Seoul: "We must be extremely cautious not to take any action which may substantially overstep the rules of international law either diplomatically or militarily."[55] Each step of the way, Japan cast its position in Korea using the legal concepts sanctioned by international law.

Japan was immediately caught up in intense competitive rivalries among the imperial powers. Shortly after the conclusion of the treaty, the nation went through one of the most devastating and memorable experiences of its modern history as European powers sought to contain its sudden expansion of power. In an incident known as the Triple Intervention, Russia, France, and Germany, on April 23, 1895, demanded that Japan retrocede the Liaotung Peninsula to China. Too weak and isolated to oppose the joint demand of the three powers, Japan capitulated. Shortly afterward, Russia seized the peninsula for itself. As a result of this humiliating event, Japan set about preparing for conflict with Russia, whose interests lay in thwarting Japanese ambitions on the continent. One of Japan's leading diplomats, Hayashi Tadasu, described with bitter determination in the weeks after the Triple Intervention what Japan's strategy must be:

> We must continue to study and make use of Western methods; for among civilized nations applied science constitutes the most important part of their military preparations. If new warships are considered necessary we must, at any cost, build them; if the organization of our army is inadequate we must start rectifying it from now; if need be our entire military system must be changed. We must build shipyards for the repair of our vessels. We must build steelworks to provide us with guns and munitions. Our railway networks must be enlarged to enable us to carry out a speedy mobilization of our troops. Our merchant fleet must be expanded to enable us to transport our armies overseas. . . . At present Japan must keep calm and sit tight, so as to lull suspicions nurtured against her; during this time the foundations of her national power must be consolidated; and we must watch and wait for the opportunity in the Orient that will surely come one day. When this day arrives Japan will decide her own fate; and she will be able not only to put into their place the powers who seek to meddle in her affairs; she will even be able, should this be necessary, to meddle in their affairs.[56]

The Triple Intervention, in addition to being a lesson of power politics, demonstrated the need for alliances. Japan had been vulnerable because it was isolated. Japanese diplomats set out to rectify this situation, producing the Anglo-Japanese Alliance in 1902. The agreement promised British assistance if Japan became embroiled in conflict with more than one power. It was a triumph of diplomacy, setting a pattern in Japanese foreign policy for most of the twentieth century of seeking to ally with the ascendant world power. With this alliance, the first military pact arranged on equal terms between a Western and non-Western nation, Japan overcame its previous diplomatic isolation. The alliance was a great symbol of Japan's newfound respect among the imperial powers, and it strengthened Japan's hand in its rivalry with Russia.

In the decade following the Sino-Japanese War and the Triple Intervention, the Japanese government made comprehensive plans for military buildup, intelligence penetration, and diplomatic cover for what was regarded as almost inevitable conflict. The Russo-Japanese War, which began with a surprise Japanese submarine attack on the Russian fleet at Port Arthur on February 8, 1904, established Japan's sphere in southern Manchuria, brought Japan great-power status, and won it worldwide acclaim. Throughout Asia, leaders of subjected peoples drew inspiration from the Japanese example. Jawaharlal Nehru described the Japanese victory as "a great pick-me-up for Asia"[57] that kindled his nationalism, and Sun Yat-sen, recalling the profound impression the event made on Chinese revolutionaries, said, "We regarded that Russian defeat by Japan as the defeat of the West by the East."[58] Japanese leaders, with their realist concerns, were never strongly attracted to the ideals of pan-Asianism. Their preoccupation was with strengthening their strategic advantage. They had little sympathy or even understanding of nationalist movements elsewhere in Asia. In fact, the Japanese brutally suppressed a nascent Korean nationalism to ensure control of the Korean peninsula, which was annexed in 1910.

Among U.S. leaders, Theodore Roosevelt was exceptionally attentive to the implications of Japan's rise. He had presided over America's own rise as a world power, but he was conscious of U.S. weakness in Asia. The United States could have its way in the Western Hemisphere, but great-power rivalry in East Asia was more complex. "I was thoroughly pleased with the Japanese victory," Roosevelt recalled, speaking of the Japanese challenge to Russia's imperial ambitions, "for Japan is playing our game." But once Russian power was rolled back in Northeast Asia, Roosevelt, with his keen sense of the balance of power, became concerned. He was, to be sure, prepared to accept the reality of Japanese domination of Korea. He dismissed the hopes of the Koreans, who had suffered the first step in the loss of their country, saying: "Korea is absolutely Japan's. To be sure, by treaty it was solemnly covenanted that Korea should remain independent. But Korea was itself helpless to enforce the treaty, and it was out of the question to suppose that any other nation . . . would attempt to do for the Koreans what they were utterly unable to do for themselves."[59] Once a proponent of acquiring the Philippines, the U.S. president now recognized that their distance from the United States made them "our heel of Achilles."[60]

Roosevelt mixed conciliation with firmness in dealing with Japan's evident new power. On the one hand, he sanctioned agreements with Japan that mutually recognized U.S. interests in the Philippines and Japanese interests in Northeast Asia. At home, when the San Francisco School Board angered Japan with its order to establish a separate school for "Oriental" children, Roosevelt summoned school officials to the White House to resolve the issue. On the other hand, he also dispatched the U.S. fleet on a world tour to demonstrate American power and resolve to the Japanese. It was at this time that both the U.S. and Japanese navies began to regard each other as primary hypothetical enemies.

It is possible to regard Japanese imperialism prior to the Russo-Japanese War as defensive and preemptive. The power vacuum in Northeast Asia created by decaying regimes in China and Korea drew the great powers into an intense competition for strategic advantage from which Japan could stand aside only at its own peril. To preempt the powers, particularly Russia, from domination of the Korean Peninsula, and to acquire bases and markets that would ensure Japanese security, there was no other choice but to compete in the imperialist fray. Japan established its position in the regional system through necessity.

There was a time after the victory over Russia in 1905 when Japan might have been satisfied with its new position in the system, having dispatched the threats to its security and recognizing that to extend its imperial ambition might impel other powers to balance against it. Some of Japan's most noteworthy writers advocated acceptance of the status quo. A prominent journalist, Ishibashi Tanzan, argued for a "little Japan" that would eschew further territorial expansion and instead concentrate on becoming a trading state.[61] The Christian writer Tokutomi Roka, in a memorable address to the First Higher School in 1906, oppressed by a foreboding of disaster should Japan continue to compete with the great powers, called on his country to turn away from reliance on military power: "Awake Japan, our beloved fatherland! Open your eyes and see your true self! Japan repent!"[62]

Yet, although the earlier motivations of Japan's leaders were primarily defensive and preemptive, the drive for more advantage and influence was not easily satiated. The strategic requirements of Japan's empire now included both insular possessions and continental territory. The navy sought to expand to an "eight-eight fleet"—that is, eight dreadnought battleships and eight armored cruisers—and the army insisted on revising its objectives to take account of Japan's expanding role in the region. Lieutenant General Tanaka Giichi of the Army General Staff wrote in 1906, "We must disengage ourselves from the restrictions of an island nation to become a state with continental interests."[63] The Imperial Defense Strategy of 1907, in its definition of Japan's grand strategy, avoided choosing between the two imposing sets of interests and recognized the importance of both services. The army was accorded force levels necessary to pursue a forward position on the Asian continent, and the navy was allowed to begin a building program designed to fulfill a big-navy ideology.

Even after Japan achieved power sufficient to offset Russian encroachment on the peninsula, Japanese leaders were still moved by a combination of ambition and insecurity. Committed to state power, they were not content with the status quo. More frequently now, Japanese leaders spoke of attaining regional hegemony. "It is not always easy to say," observed the Cambridge historian Herbert Butterfield, "when a given State moves from an originally defensive policy, and then from a reasonable demand for securities, to actual aggrandizement. . . . The State which at a given moment becomes strong enough to assert what it regards as its rights may go a long way in aggrandizement without feeling itself to be an aggressor at all."[64]

At the end of the Russo-Japanese War, Japan had established a strong position in Northeast Asia. If Japan were motivated simply by defensive intentions, one might expect to find a certain relaxation of security concerns after 1905. The historian Hata Ikuhiko spoke to this very point: "In retrospect, it can be said that the Russo-Japanese War brought Japan to an important crossroads in the path of its national destiny. The basic issue was whether Japan should be satisfied with a limited success as a solid middle-sized nation or should drive toward becoming a great military power dominating the Asian continent. . . . Greater Japanism implied continued expansionism, whereas little Japanism implied satisfaction with the postbellum status quo." Adherents of the former, especially the army, wanted to push on toward hegemony on the continent, whereas advocates of the latter wanted to give priority to the navy and concentrate on development as a trading nation and on building a modern welfare-oriented society at home. It was indeed a turning point. In the end, those supporting a greater Japanism carried the day, driven "by the popular nationalism induced by two victorious wars in 1895 and 1905, by the displacement of older leaders by a younger generation, and by the army's increasing vociferousness and influence."[65]

What is striking about this period is that, despite having fulfilled, even surpassed, the goals they had earlier set for the nation, the Meiji leaders were beset by a keen sense of insecurity. Karl Deutsch's observation applies well to this moment: "[There is] a kind of Parkinson's law of national security: a nation's feeling of insecurity expands directly with its power. The larger and more powerful a nation is, the more its leaders, elites, and often its population increase their level of aspirations in international affairs. The more, that is to say, do they see themselves as destined or obliged to put the world's affairs in order."[66]

This observation captures the Japanese mood after the Russo-Japanese War. Along with the newfound pride was an enhanced sense of vulnerability and the fragility of Japan's position. Despite having fulfilled the Meiji vision by escaping the unequal treaties, acquiring strategic overseas possessions, and joining the ranks of the great powers, Japan's leaders pressed on to further strengthen Japan's imperial position. The primary initial motivation, which had been defensive and preemptive, was steadily turning to ambition and aggrandizement. Although threats to its security were now diminished, there could be no relaxation in the drive to improve Japan's position. Japanese imperialism was thus driven by a continuing preoccupation with strategic advantage and a peculiar combination of nationalist ambition and insecurity.[67]

CHAPTER FOUR

STATURE AMONG NATIONS

I n the conclusion to his book on America's unplanned rise to world power at the beginning of the twentieth century, the historian Ernest May wrote, "Some nations achieve greatness; the United States had greatness thrust upon it."[1] May described the way in which Americans, without seeking it, had international leadership thrust upon them because of their material wealth. Japan's national experience was quite the opposite. Stature among nations was a goal to be achieved. It was not bestowed. From the time of the Meiji Restoration, Japan strove and struggled for status as a great power. Other countries in Asia were aware of their own backwardness, but nowhere else was this awareness so intense and so paramount that it drove a people with such single-minded determination. It became a national obsession in Japan to be the equal of the world's great powers. The Japanese acquired international influence because they tirelessly and relentlessly pursued it. National power was to be achieved by the unremitting hard work, unity, and sacrifice of the Japanese people. Japan's rise as a great power in the twentieth century was the outcome of an all-absorbing struggle, the result of long-term goals set by the Meiji leaders to enhance the power of the Japanese nation and to overcome Japan's status as a latecomer in the industrial world. The Japanese were a driven people.

Unlike the United States, whose material wealth and industrial might awaited only a strong state to mobilize it for international influence, Japan's rise was less the result of its industrial power relative to other countries than it was the result of a strong state apparatus that mobilized the will and purpose of the nation. In relation to the other great powers in the pre–World War II period, Japan never had startling increases in its industrial economy. Its share of world manufacturing output between 1860 and 1938 grew only from 2.6 percent to 3.8 percent.[2] Japan's rise did not come about through its size or wealth. It happened because its leaders galvanized the determination of the nation. The Japanese displayed a willingness to sacrifice all other goals to achieve national power. No government could ask for greater devotion from its people. Japan's rise was a feat of national will and determination.

Japan's success in its forced march to industry and empire depended critically on restricting consumption in the interests of maximum economic investment for growth. Indeed, the economic historian Sydney Crawcour observed that "consumption over the whole [modern] period to 1945 appears so low and so weakly correlated with national income as to be difficult to reconcile with the usual experience in a free economy."[3]

How was Japan able to achieve such purposeful cohesion in pursuing its foreign policy? What motivated Japanese citizens to work with such devotion to build a national empire? Placing the Japanese economic achievement in comparative context, the economic historian David Landes wrote that there is "one aspect . . . that has not caught the attention of celebratory historians: the pain and labor that made it possible." The Japanese farmer or laborer was "willing to put up with hours of grinding, monotonous labor" that his counterparts in other industrializing societies would never have tolerated.[4]

The state was able to link work and patriotism. In a society where regular religious instruction was absent, it was the responsibility of the schools to inculcate the morality of sacrifice and hard work. As one textbook put it: "The easiest way to practice one's patriotism [is to] discipline oneself in daily life, help keep good order in one's family, and fully discharge one's responsibility on the job."[5]

The international system exerts powerful forces on nation-states, impelling them toward certain courses of action, channeling their behavior, and socializing them into its ways. But despite the strong pull of systemic pressures on nations, there is nothing fixed, determined, or inevitable in the courses that they choose. Nations react differently to the challenges that the hard realities of struggle in the world pose. In a state system, as Kenneth Waltz put it, "some do better than others—whether through intelligence, skill, hard work, or dumb luck."[6] Or, one might add, through stronger motivation.

What was it that drove the Japanese with such relentless determination?

The usual answer is "nationalism." But nationalism is very nearly a universal phenomenon in the international state system. Without it, a state cannot exist. To say that Japan was motivated by nationalism leaves unexplained the distinctive complex of ideas, norms, and values that constituted this people's extraordinary motivation. It says nothing about how Japan conceived its national purpose and mission, its formulation of national interest, after it entered the anarchic international system. "Anarchy," in the memorable phrase of Alexander Wendt, "is what states make of it."[7] Although universal ideals and abstract principles were relatively weak in Japan, shared ideas of national identity and the Japanese social construction of the world they had entered were powerful determinants of their international behavior.

POWER INITIALLY TRUMPS CULTURE

To Restoration leaders, national power trumped culture. Initially, Japan was driven by the need to acquire the power that would restore Japanese sovereignty and preserve its security. The Meiji leaders were prepared to do whatever was necessary to build national power—even if it entailed discarding the cultural institutions and practices of the past. Their obsession with gaining power to attain security and wealth in international society outweighed preserving Japan's traditional mores. Strategic interests outweighed cultural pride. They cared less than other Asian leaders did about preserving the customary institutions and practices of their inherited way of life if sacrificing them was necessary to acquire national power. The primacy of foreign policy and the pursuit of power and status legitimated the sweeping destruction of old institutions and the adoption of new ones from another civilization. Taking a long view of the future, they reassessed all their cultural values and institutions.

The overriding commitment to material power and strategic interest led Japanese leaders to jettison their traditional institutions and practices and thereby even to risk their own cultural identity. This willingness to swallow cultural pride plunged Japanese national life into a period of all-out emulation of Western civilization. Western clothing was made compulsory for government officials in 1872. The following year, in his second official photograph, the emperor is seen wearing European court attire. At the same time, the Western calendar was adopted. Education, banking, the postal system, accounting methods, and nearly everything else fell under the sway of Western models. Western music, art, and architecture came in vogue. Knowing that revision of the unequal treaties required legal and administrative reforms that would satisfy the foreign powers, the government moved quickly to adopt laws—and in 1889 a constitution—all of which emulated Western models.

Today Japan is often criticized for its inhospitableness to immigrants and foreign workers, but in the Meiji period the Japanese sought out foreign advisers and accorded them special treatment—for a time. They were to be the teachers of civilization to which the Japanese would apprentice themselves. The government hastened the adoption of the new technology and new institutions by hiring more than 3,000 foreign advisers over the course of the Meiji period. They included engineers, technicians, military consultants, teachers, and financial and legal advisers. In all, they contributed the equivalent of 10,000 years of service. Most of this work was during the first fifteen years after the Restoration. Then, once the Japanese had fully exploited the westerners' expertise and learned the new ways, they replaced the foreigners with Japanese. At times, the salaries of foreigners accounted for a third of the Ministry of Industry's budget and a third of the budget allocated to the new Tokyo Imperial University. Itō Hirobumi, at the 1873 opening of what became the university's engineering department, urged Japanese students to absorb everything the foreigners could teach them:

> It is imperative that we seize this opportunity to train and educate ourselves fully. On this solemn occasion, I urge all ambitious youths to enroll in this school, to study assiduously, to perfect their talents, and to serve in their various posts with dedication. If this is done, then as a matter of course, we will be able to do without the foreigners. We ourselves will fill the realm with railroads and other technological wonders that will form the basis for further developments to continue for a myriad generations. The glory of our Imperial Land will shine forth to radiate upon foreign shores, while at home, high and low will share in the benefits of a great civilization.[8]

At the same time, in what Marius B. Jansen called "the first great student migration of modern times," more than 11,000 passports were issued for overseas study between 1868 and 1902. More than one-half of the government-sponsored students went to the United States, but increasingly they were sent to Germany once it became the preferred model in organizing Japan's governmental, legal, and military organizations.[9]

The readiness to emulate the institutions of the strong grew out of the traditional Japanese attitude toward learning, which entailed a long apprenticeship in which one meticulously followed the practices of the master. Japan, in effect, apprenticed itself to the West—except that its citizens were motivated largely by an instrumental use of their borrowings. And, of course, the Meiji "westernizers" were anti-Western in their purpose. For them, westernization was a means to an anti-Western end. By adopting the techniques and institutions of Western society they hoped to eliminate all manifestations of Western power, especially the unequal treaties, from their country. The institutions that were adopted were means at the service of the nation, but often not considered to have intrinsic value in and of themselves.

As the first non-Western nation to industrialize, Japan had no road map, no guide to understanding what was essential to adopt from the West in order to succeed. What was the key to Western power? Was it only science? Was it political and social institutions as well? Was it the values that lay behind them? Was it the religious beliefs? There were no ready answers. Many of the leading Meiji thinkers concluded that the answer lay in the full adoption of civilization. If universal laws of nature governed human behavior, Japan must develop in accord with these laws and thus progress in the same way that Western nations had. Progress, in other words, was unilinear; it was determined by universal forces of historical development rather than by the particular trends of national history.

During the period of "civilization and enlightenment" that held sway in the 1870s and 1880s, as an essential part of this self-strengthening effort, the full sweep of European Enlightenment and nineteenth-century liberal thought was introduced into Japan in a very short space of time. This all-out opening left a permanent mark on modern Japan, for Western liberal civilization challenged Japan's traditional beliefs, social organization, and system of government with such ceaseless persistence as to throw every area of life into a state of turmoil.

From the outset of its entry into the modern world, Japan's historical cultural values and institutions were treated as backward, feudal, and irrelevant. The Meiji Enlightenment's leading exponent of laissez-faire economics, Taguchi Ukichi, wrote in his *Short History of Civilization in Japan* (1877)[10] that civilized development meant not only that people would use similar machines, but also that they would think and behave in similar ways, eat the same kinds of food, wear the same kinds of clothing, live in houses of similar architecture, and enjoy the same kinds of art. In his widely read essay "An Outline of Civilization" (1875), Fukuzawa wrote that the fundamental flaw of Japanese culture was its most basic institution—the Japanese *family* system. The Meiji Enlightenment writers blamed the family for destroying the spirit of individual initiative and independence upon which, they believed, modern scientific civilization depended.

So extreme was the cultural submission of Japan at the outset of Japan's modern period that Fukuzawa wrote in 1875: "If we compare the knowledge of the Japanese and Westerners, in letters, in techniques, in commerce, or in industry, from the largest to the smallest matter . . . there is not one thing in which we excel. . . . In Japan's present condition there is nothing in which we may take pride vis-a-vis the West. All that Japan has to be proud of . . . is its scenery."[11] In the opening chapter of Natsume Sōseki's novel *Sanshirō* (1908), the student Sanshirō encounters a man aboard the train to Tokyo, who says to him of Mt. Fuji, as they pass in sight of it, "There it is. It is the finest thing Japan has to offer, the only thing we've got to boast about. The trouble is, of course, it's just a natural object. It's been sitting there for all time. We certainly didn't make it."[12] The one thing that could bring Japanese pride in their country, its scenery, was not something they themselves had created.[13]

Many of the foreign advisers who came to Japan found much to admire in its traditional culture. But in the early Meiji days, the Japanese had no time for Japanophiles and took no pleasure in the patronizing compliments of foreign visitors. Many Western visitors, then and since, have fallen in love with aspects of Japan's arts and have viewed it as a nation of unique artistic and aesthetic bent. But such an identity, the Japanese believed, would not serve to raise Japan's stature among nations. Prestige in the international system was accorded to states with military and economic strength. The British poet Sir Edwin Arnold on a visit to Japan in 1891 was rebuked by the Japanese when he lavished praise on their traditional aesthetics. He told an audience of Japanese journalists, politicians, and officials that Japan

appears to me as close an approach to Lotus-land as I shall ever find. By many a pool of water lilies in temple grounds and in fairy-like gardens, amid the beautiful rural scenery of Kama-kura or Nikko; under long avenues of majestic cryptomeria; in weird and dreamy Shinto shrines; on the white matting of the teahouses; in the bright bazaars; by your sleeping lakes, and under your stately mountains, I have felt farther removed than ever before from the flurry and vulgarity of our European life. . . . Yet what I find here more marvelous to me than Fuji-san, lovelier than the embroidered and gilded silks, precious beyond all the daintily carved ivories, more delicate than the Cloisonne enamels, is . . . that almost divine sweetness of disposition which, I frankly believe, places Japan in these respects higher than any other nation. . . . Retain, I beseech you, gentlemen, this national characteristic, which you did not import, and can never, alas, export.[14]

Arnold's praise was not accepted with quite the "sweetness of disposition" that he had remarked upon; for, as another Englishman present, a longtime resident in Japan, Basil Hall Chamberlain, observed, "The educated Japanese have done with their past. They want to be somebody else and something else than what they have been and still partly are." Chamberlain recorded that the day after Arnold's address, one newspaper acknowledged

the truth of Sir Edwin's description but [pointed] out that it conveyed, not praise, but condemnation of the heaviest sort. Art forsooth, scenery, sweetness of disposition! cries this editor. Why did not Sir Edwin praise us for huge industrial enterprises, for commercial talent, for wealth, political sagacity, powerful armaments? Of course it is because he could not honestly do so. He has gauged us at our true value, and tells us in effect that we are pretty weaklings.[15]

Sir Edwin could not have given a more unwelcome compliment.

Preserving Japan's cultural essence was not a priority for the Meiji leaders. In their eyes, it was not Japan's traditional self, but rather, national power that would raise Japan's stature. Success in foreign policy was essential to national pride. Not only were Japan's historical and cultural values and institutions dismissed as backward and irrelevant, everything Asian was rejected as even more objectionable. Accommodation to the Western-dominated international system led the Japanese to turn their backs resolutely on any kind of identification with the rest of Asia. In the best-known essay on Japan's view of its Asian neighbors at this time, Fukuzawa urged in 1885 that Japan "escape from Asia":

Today China and Korea are no help at all to our country. On the contrary, because our three countries are adjacent we are sometimes regarded as the same in the eyes of civilized Western peoples. Appraisals of China and Korea are applied to our country, . . . and indirectly this greatly impedes our foreign policy. It is really a great misfortune for our country. It follows that in making our present plans we have not time to await the development of neighboring countries and join them in reviving Asia. Rather, we should escape from them and join the company of Western civilized nations. Although China and Korea are our neighbors, this fact should make no difference in our relations with them. We should deal with them as westerners do. If we keep bad company, we cannot avoid a bad name. In my heart I favor breaking off with the bad company of East Asia.[16]

Far from making common cause with its Asian neighbors, Japan aimed to become a "first rank country," which inspired expansionism. In the mind of Fukuzawa, this supposed liberal reformer, building national power, imposing Japan's will on its neighbors, and gaining international status were paramount. In a highly revealing moment in 1882, he confided his feelings:

Whenever I go abroad and stay in Europe or in the United States, I frequently have unpleasant experiences because the peoples of these nations tend to treat me less than cordially. Recently I took a voyage across the Indian Ocean. During that trip, I saw the English officers land on many places in China and elsewhere that they controlled. They were extremely arrogant and their attitude to the natives was so brazen that it was not possible to believe the English were dealing with the same human beings. In seeing all of this, my reaction was a mixture of pity for the natives and of envy for the English. Even now I cannot forget the promise I made secretly in my heart. We are Japanese and we shall some day raise the national power of Japan so that not only shall we control the natives of China and India as the English do today, but we shall possess the power to rebuke the English and to rule Asia ourselves.[17]

Fukuzawa was convinced that Japan must first become so strong that no nation could impose its will on it. Then, in time, Japan would be so powerful that it could impose its will on others. It could do what it was determined to resist itself.

NATIONAL PURPOSE: HONOR, STATUS, AND PRESTIGE

Power was clearly a primary value for the Meiji leaders, but it was not an end in and of itself. Their aims were more complex than that. Pursuit of national power had a purpose beyond the achievement of security. They sought power to defend a vulnerable nation and to extend its influence. As political theorist Raymond Aron wrote in describing the mixture of motives that constitute a state's goals:

Might we, finally, define power as the capacity to impose one's will on others? In that case, power is not a final goal, either for the individual or for collectivities. Policy is always ambitious, it aspires to power because political action involves, in essence, a relationship among human beings, an element of power. Yet grand policy wants such power not for itself, but to carry out a mission. Similarly, a collectivity does not desire power for itself, but to achieve some goal.[18]

For Japan's new leaders, their aim was more than restoring the national sovereignty that the unequal treaties had infringed, more than securing Japan's territory from the dangers of imperial encroachment, more even than acquiring empire. The purpose of acquiring power ultimately was to bring Japan dignity and recognition as a first-class nation. This preoccupation was reflected in Japan's keen attention to its rank and status from the time it entered international society. Fukuzawa observed in 1875 that Japanese

sights are now being reset on the goal of elevating Japanese civilization to parity with the West, or even of surpassing it. Since Western civilization is even now in a process of transition and progress day by day, month by month, we Japanese must keep pace with it without abating our efforts. The arrival of the Americans in the 1850s has, as it were, kindled a fire in our people's hearts. Now that it is ablaze, it can never be extinguished.[19]

The ambition to gain equality with Western powers and to surpass them, which in retrospect we call "the catch-up drive," became an obsession of Japan's leaders at the very outset of the nation's entrance into the international system. Even before the Restoration, once the gap between the power of the West and Japan was perceived, Bakufu officials spoke of one day overtaking the West.[20] This determination was announced on every kind of occasion at which it was appropriate to speak of national goals.

The obsession of the Meiji leaders became over time a national consensus, a goal repeatedly held up as one toward which all Japanese must aspire. For example, in rhetoric common to the time, Takahashi Korekiyo, who later became finance minister and prime minister, exhorted his students in

an 1889 farewell address at Tokyo Agricultural College: "Gentlemen, it is
your duty to advance the status of Japan, bring her to a position of equality with the civilized powers and then carry on to build a foundation from
which we shall surpass them all."[21] This oft-repeated vision was supported
by optimism and by a fierce determination to exert whatever effort was required to achieve the goal. Mori Arinori, who became minister of education in 1885, argued that education was the key to Japan's ascent in the
hierarchy of nations. "Our country," he often said, "must move from its
third-class position to second-class to first; and ultimately to the leading
position among all countries of the world. The best way to do this is by
laying the foundation of elementary education."[22] We have already noted
the optimism that pervaded the Iwakura Mission's report—the belief that
what the Western powers had achieved in their industrial and scientific advances could be equaled by Japan through hard work and diligence. Those
qualities, honored in domestic society, were seen as critical in international
competition. In 1874, one of Japan's leading reformers wrote, "How will
we catch up with and overtake the Western powers if we allow Sunday to
be a holiday for our people?"[23]

   Japan's worldview, the way in which it conceived of or constructed the
world of nation-states that it entered, was a projection of the ideas it held
of its own internal society. Its hypersensitivity to its rank in the world owed
much to its distinctive honor culture nurtured over centuries of feudal life,
as already mentioned. That is, it brought to the international system what
Ruth Benedict called a "confidence in hierarchy." But the ideas that it held
about order in its domestic society were undergoing important changes.
Respect for hierarchy remained the dominant view of how order was
maintained, but the determinant of hierarchy was becoming less predetermined by heredity and more a function of competition in which hard
work, diligence, and ability—in a word, merit—were the new determinants. As Japan entered the international system, its sense of hierarchy was
strong, and its sense that positions in the hierarchy were achieved by merit
was keenly felt. As a result, the awareness of hierarchy as an ordering principle was bound to be unusually strong in the Japanese consciousness. It
was this widely shared frame of reference in their social thinking that the
Japanese brought to their participation in the international system.

   During the peaceful and stable rule of the Tokugawa, the violent aspects of the culture were tamed and transformed into a highly stratified order that gave priority to virtuous service in the administrative hierarchy of
the lord's domain. The source of honor was no longer performance on the

battlefield, but rather status and position in an elaborate power structure. Still, despite the sedentary conditions, constant attention was given to maintaining, through appropriate forms of conduct, the personal dignity, self-esteem, and reputation appropriate to one's rank and to the relative standing of the lord's domain among the more than 250 domains in the Tokugawa order.

The meticulously defined hierarchy was reflected in "rituals and ceremonies [that] are expressions of the most essential values of Japan," wrote the literary historian Masao Miyoshi. He added, "In the great chain of being that—theoretically—connects the Emperor to the humblest laborers via the Shogun, lords, and myriad ranks of samurai, artisans, and merchants, all must perform ceremony so that order may be maintained and reaffirmed throughout."[24] The identity of each individual was determined by his responsibility to some particular individual higher than himself in the hierarchy. Rank in the social hierarchy was reflected not only in the distribution of goods and services, in the stipend warriors were paid, and in social relations, but in myriad other ways as well—in invidious distinctions among occupations, in the many levels of honorifics in the language, in the elaborate details of etiquette, and in the stream of regulations and expected social practice concerning clothing, domicile, and personal deportment.

Consciousness of rank and observance of status distinctions were maintained in every institution throughout society. Fukuzawa described over a hundred different levels of distinction in the samurai class in Nakatsu, the small domain in Kyushu in which he grew up and which had only 1,500 samurai.[25] Minute gradations of hierarchy existed within the samurai class in every domain in the Tokugawa period. In Chōshū, for example, "more than 5,000 samurai (including foot soldiers) were divided into 70 honor rankings. . . . Although these [honor rankings] derived primarily from military functions, the titles became merely honorific rankings in daimyo domains everywhere, describing precisely each samurai's position in the hierarchy of the daimyo's vassal organization."[26] So pervasive was the respect for status and the power it implied that in itself it provided the basis for political authority in the Tokugawa state—what John W. Hall termed "rule by status."[27] Dan Fenno Henderson, the eminent authority on Tokugawa law, observed that "nothing was of more constitutional import to the Tokugawa law than the rigid, heritable hierarchy of statuses established to classify the entire Tokugawa populace. The barriers were maintained between these statuses by Edo decrees and the Confucian thought patterns."[28]

The Meiji leaders came from a feudal ruling class in which constant attention to preserving the respect appropriate to rank was bred from the earliest days of childhood. At the time of the Restoration, the honorific culture was revitalized and focused on the nation. The reaction of Tokugawa Nariaki, the lord of Mito, was typical of the daimyo: "The Americans who arrived recently, though fully aware of the bakufu's prohibition . . . were arrogant and discourteous, their actions an outrage. Indeed, this was the greatest disgrace we have suffered since the dawn of our history."[29] Samurai activists were prompted to confront the challenge of Western imperialism as a stain on Japan's national honor. Sakuma Shōzan, one of the most influential of the activists, recalled that when "the American barbarians arrived . . . their deportment and manner of expression were exceedingly arrogant, and the resulting insult to our national dignity was not small."[30]

The indignity awakened the passionate and self-assertive side of the samurai ethos latent throughout the Tokugawa years. The national crisis created a dynamic new fusion of honor and nationalism; entry into competition in the anarchic struggles of the international system was marked by a distinctive "honorific nationalism." This culturally embedded notion of state-centered honor meant that the concern with prestige and reputation that characterized all nations in the system was accordingly more intense and sensitive, and also more fragile and vulnerable, for the Japanese. Concern for national dignity and respect for Japan's standing in the world had peculiar intensity. The strength of Japan's inherited rank consciousness prompted an instinctive need for recognition of its status in the hierarchy of nations, and the values of hierarchy provided a behavioral norm that focused and intensified the realist drive for national power. Establishment of Japan's honor, of its reputation for power in relation to other nations, became a goal sanctioned by inherited values and norms.

The new demands of foreign policy, requiring knowledge and abilities of a new kind, radically revised the criteria for status in domestic society and encouraged competition for status. During the long years of the Tokugawa regime, the hierarchy had become frozen. Official appointments in government had come to be determined largely by hereditary succession. It was the rigidity of the old status system, rather than the hierarchy itself, that motivated the opposition of ambitious young samurai to the Tokugawa order. In his famous tract entitled *The Encouragement of Learning* (1872), Fukuzawa declared that a person's place in society should be determined by mastery of the new practical learning taught in the schools.

Thus, merit based on possession of useful, scientific learning should become a criterion for determining social rank. The Meiji Restoration was not intended to overthrow Japan's hierarchical social system itself but rather to strengthen and legitimate it by promoting greater mobility within the hierarchy. The reforms that abolished the old class restrictions, made education universal, and opened government service to all men of talent were not true democratic reforms but rather the means to legitimate social hierarchy by making its determination dependent on merit and ability.

Once status in the social hierarchy was unfrozen by the new conditions, a fierce competitive ethic took hold in Japan's domestic society. It may well be that the greater fluidity and mobility that abruptly emerged in Japanese society at this time contributed to the heightened awareness of relative ranking.[31] And although mental acuity now trumped heredity, it was not thought that success in the world could be determined by that alone; rather, success came from "diligence, sacrifice, mastery of detailed information, endurance over many years, willingness to postpone gratification, and competitive spirit."[32] The Japanese brought all of these same virtues, all of this stamina and determination, to their marathon struggle as a people to see Japan rise in the world. The new competitive ethic was absorbed into Japan's behavior in the international system. Just as, through energy, initiative, and hard work, one could now rise in Meiji society, so Japan could by perseverance rise in international society. And as social mobility increased, the new talent required to increase Japan's national power emerged.

HIERARCHY OF PRESTIGE

The prominent social values and norms that the Japanese people shared inevitably shaped the way in which they constructed the international system, its workings, and their place in it. Belief in hierarchy as the basis of order, whether in the family, in Japanese society, or in the international system, was embedded in the Japanese worldview. In particular, their honorific culture implanted the importance of acquiring a reputation for power because with it came respect, honor, and authority—or what those in the West also call "prestige."

Prestige in the context of international relations is the reputation for military and economic power. The hierarchy of prestige provides order and authority and is an important element of the governance and legitimacy of the dominant states. Prestige and power are intertwined. As

Robert Gilpin wrote, "Whereas power refers to the economic, military, and related capabilities of a state, prestige refers primarily to the perceptions of other states with respect to a state's capacities and its ability and willingness to exercise its power."[33]

Because of its concern for national honor and power, Meiji Japan frequently took measure of its standing against other nations. For example, *Kokumin no tomo,* a leading magazine read by educated young Japanese, observed in 1891 that Japan was catching up with Western countries: National wealth had increased five or six times in the two decades since the Restoration, population was increasing more rapidly than in most European countries, and most Japanese were getting an education comparable to that received by Europeans. In short, "if one impartially compares our country with European countries, we are above Spain and abreast of Italy."[34]

But taking measure of their own successes was not enough; the Japanese needed confirmation that westerners perceived Japan's superior qualities. In the international system, how others saw them was critical to their self-image. One theorist expressed this phenomenon in current social science terms: "The basic idea is that identities and their corresponding interests are learned and then reinforced in response to how actors are treated by significant Others. This is known as the principle of 'reflected appraisals' or 'mirroring' because it hypothesizes that actors come to see themselves as a reflection of how they think Others see or 'appraise' them, in the 'mirror' of Others' representations of themselves."[35]

Kokumin no tomo complained in 1893 that westerners praised Japan only for its ability to imitate their ways. This was condescending: "They regard us as only a step above Fiji or Hawaii." The magazine balked at the fact that Japan was so often compared to Siam and Annam and seen in a positive light because of the contrast, rather than viewed for its own positive qualities as seen from the long view of history: "They observe only the developments of the thirty years since the opening of the country. They do not know of our 2,500-year history. They do not know that for 2,500 years our society, people, culture, and resources have developed splendid national qualities. . . . They do not know that we have the talent to assimilate the virtues of Western civilization and to put them to our own use."[36] Earlier in the same year, the magazine had complained that despite the nation's progress in adopting civilized institutions and developing its national strength, Japan had not received the respect that it deserved from the rest of the world: "The most progressive, developed, civilized, intelligent, and powerful nation in the Orient still cannot escape the scorn of white people." The magazine observed that in terms of respect there was a hierarchy among nations. In the first rank were strong, civilized (*bunmei ryoku*) countries like the United States. In the second were countries like Russia, which, though lacking in civilization, nevertheless commanded respect because of its barbarian strength (*yaban ryoku*) and lust for conquest. Finally, at the bottom, were countries like Egypt and Korea, which lacked both civilization and barbarian strength. Unfortunately, Japan was still regarded in the third rank.[37]

It can be difficult to perceive changes in the balance of power in the international system. They might be based on the changing size of militaries or on industrial progress. The most important measure of changed power relations, however, is warfare and its outcomes. As Gilpin wrote, "Power and prestige are ultimately imponderable and incalculable; they cannot be known absolutely by any a priori process of calculation. They are only known when they are tested, especially on the field of battle."[38] For Japan, the demonstration of military prowess in the Sino-Japanese War of 1894–1895 and in the Russo-Japanese of 1904–1905, and the spoils of victory that it received, served to mark Japan as a new great power that must be accommodated in regional and world calculations. Such impressive demonstrations of newly acquired national power brought Japan a rapid increase in prestige and standing in the international hierarchy.

Wars demonstrate in concrete and undeniable ways the relative power of combatants. They show how the distribution of power has changed. They establish the prestige of the victors, which is the currency of power in the international system. Prestige is, as Gilpin put it, "the functional equivalent of the role of authority in domestic politics." That is, as E. H. Carr observed, prestige is "enormously important" because "if your strength is recognized, you can generally achieve your aims without having to use it."

A country gains prestige from the possession of economic and military power. These are matters partly of fact and partly of opinion. . . . It is not possible to measure either the wealth of a country or the degree of its mobility, and even if the military force that could be maintained were precisely known, there are imponderables to take account of, the military qualities of the men, the proficiencies of the leaders, the efficiency of the administration, and, last, but not least, pure luck. The result is there is a wide margin of error. . . . In the last resort prestige means reputation for strength in war, and doubts on the subject can only be set at rest by war itself.[39]

The hierarchy of prestige as determined by war in turn determines which states will govern the international system.

When war between China and Japan broke out in August 1894, the general opinion among Western powers was that China's size and immense resources, together with its navy and the powerful fortifications it had constructed under foreign supervision, would prevail. Almost at once events belied this expectation. The Japanese Army pressed immediately to a series of victories, and the navy won a decisive engagement off the Yalu. Shortly after, Port Arthur fell, and losses to the Japanese were light. The war lasted only eight months. The uninterrupted success of the Japanese Army and the surrender of Weihaiwei convinced China of the futility of further resistance.

Victory brought an outpouring of national pride. Fukuzawa expressed a common sentiment when he pointed out that the triumph in the war had demonstrated Japan's new power and vindicated the Meiji reforms. "One can scarcely enumerate," he wrote in 1895,

all of our civilized undertakings since the Restoration—the abolition of feudalism, the lowering of class barriers, revision of our laws, reform of the military, promotion of education, railroads, electricity, postal service, printing, and on and on. Yet among all these enterprises, the one thing none of us scholars who were influenced by the West ever expected thirty or forty years ago was the establishment of Japan's imperial prestige in a great war. . . . When I think of our marvelous fortune I feel as though in a dream and can only weep tears of joy.[40]

The Sino-Japanese War was significant for Japan because victory brought the kind of honor—that is, a recognition of status and power—that was the essence of Japanese national purpose. As the journalist Tokutomi Sohō wrote, westerners had been scornful of Japan because the Japanese had seemed incapable of doing anything but imitating the institutions and practices of the West: "They regard the Japanese as a race close to monkeys, or as monkeys who are almost human." After the Japanese victory in war, the new recognition that the West accorded Japan confirmed to the Japanese that the hierarchy of prestige in the world rested, above all, on the exercise of military power. It showed them that prestige was acquired through the reputation for strength. Tokutomi wrote that "now we are no longer ashamed to stand before the world as Japanese. . . . Before, we did not know ourselves, and the world did not yet know us.

But now that we have tested our strength, we know ourselves and we are known by the world. Moreover, we *know* we are known by the world!"[41]

The victory over Russia a decade later in the Russo-Japanese War of 1904–1905, which set Japan on a path to colonize Korea and to establish its sphere of influence in Manchuria, brought even more national pride and self-assurance. As Gilpin observed, "The most prestigious members of the international system are those states that have most recently used military force or economic power successfully and have thereby imposed their will on others."[42] No event contributed so much to Japan's rising international prestige and influence as the Russo-Japanese War.

Defeat of a Western power by an Asian nation captivated the world's attention and brought the Japanese endless pride in their newly found identity as a world power. In that war, no event was so significant in establishing Japan's new prestige as the naval battle in the Sea of Japan in what the naval historian Julian Corbett described as "the most decisive and complete naval victory in history."[43] Thirty-eight ships of the Russian Baltic Fleet steaming through the Korean Strait near the island of Tsushima on May 27–28, 1905, were routed by the Combined Japanese Imperial Fleet commanded by Admiral Tōgō Heihachirō. Only four of the Russian ships emerged intact at the other end of the strait. The Japanese Navy, with stunning speed and precision, had sunk, captured, or scuttled the other thirty-four; moreover, 4,830 Russian sailors had been killed and nearly 6,000, including two admirals, had been captured. The Japanese lost three torpedo boats and 110 men.

More than any other event, the battle of Tsushima marked international recognition of the emergence of a new power in East Asia. On the other side of the world, in the White House, Theodore Roosevelt was filled with admiration at the Japanese victory. Impressed by Japan's new power, he wrote to Henry Cabot Lodge in 1905: "As for Japan, she has risen with simply marvelous rapidity, and she is as formidable from the industrial as from the military standpoint. She is a great civilized nation. . . . In a dozen years I think she will be the leading industrial nation of the Pacific."[44] And writing to a Japanese friend, he said:

This is the greatest phenomenon the world has ever seen. Even the Battle of Trafalgar could not match this. I could not believe it myself, when the first report reached me. As the second and third report came, however, I grew so excited that I myself became almost like a Japanese, and I could not attend to official duties. I spent the whole day talking with visitors about the Battle of the Japan Sea, for I believed that this naval battle decided the fate of the Japanese Empire.[45]

Roosevelt was subsequently persuaded by the Japanese and Russians to mediate a peace treaty between the two belligerents. The rise of Japan's international reputation was due not only to its demonstration of power but also to its implementation of Western norms and institutions. The first edition of Henry Wheaton's *Elements of International Law*, published in 1836, said that international law was "limited to the civilized and Christian people in Europe or to those of European origin." But Japanese perseverance in adhering to the rules of the game established by the West bore fruit in the agreements reached with the powers in 1894 providing for the termination of the unequal treaties. With its sovereignty now fully recognized, Japan had gained—at least formally—equal status. It was a first for a non-Western nation. Legally, Japan had made it into the West's world. The fourth edition of *Elements of International Law*, published in 1904, described the great significance of the "acquisition by Japan of full international status" in a new section of the book entitled "The International Status of Non-Christian Nations."[46]

In countless ways, Japan courted international recognition of its newly demonstrated power. The Japanese government went to extraordinary lengths to try to establish its international status through exhibitions at the World's Fairs. Carol Ann Christ, describing these events, said, "They were grand arenas in which nations established or bolstered their status by demonstrating a strong, centralized government, industrial and economic might, military potency, and a capacity for cultural leadership—all the requisite characteristics of a colonial power of the era."[47] Already in 1876, in Philadelphia, Japan expended great effort to impress the Western nations. And at the Columbian Exhibition in Chicago in 1893, the Japanese went to such efforts that they said their displays should entitle them to, as one Japanese author wrote in the *North American Review*, "full fellowship in the family of nations, no longer deserving to labor under the incubus which circumstances forced upon her," referring to extraterritoriality.[48] Japan's display also served to demonstrate Japan's status at the St. Louis Exhibition of 1904, especially in comparison to a weak and poorly arranged Chinese exhibit.

The annexation of Korea in 1910 was further evidence of Japan's rising stature among nations. Nitobe Inazō, principal of the elite First Higher School, spoke to his students of this "unforgettable event" and of their place in the world: "Such an occurrence takes place only once in a lifetime. Overnight, our country became bigger than Germany, France, and Spain. Many people will comment and make speeches, [but no matter how you look at it] all of a sudden we grew by ten million people. . . . Our nation has become more of a Great Power than many European countries, and you have become much more important. Japan of a month ago and Japan of today are completely different."[49]

Realism and the Cultural Dilemma

To recover Japan's national independence and establish its place in the world, the Meiji leaders risked Japan's cultural identity. Over time, however, there was a price to be paid for such unalloyed realism. Power and strategic interest were not sufficient to provide the self-assurance and dignity that a positive national identity requires. Although in the light of their own traditional attitude toward learning this wholesale adoption of foreign practices was not regarded as slavish or demeaning, in an age of imperialism and intense international competition this cultural borrowing easily came to be seen as servile. For a follower nation it was necessary to emulate the institutions of other countries, but the emulation itself implied fundamental shortcomings in one's own civilization. Power acquired by imitation of another civilization was not so satisfying as power achieved by the creative efforts of one's own cultural talents. This dilemma did not go unnoticed. There was contention over the issue within the original Meiji elite. Some of the leaders of the Restoration, most notably Saigō Takamori, vehemently opposed the far-reaching cultural revolution. But their resistance was overridden. Outside of government, too, many writers advocated a more evolutionary approach that would preserve Japan's unique cultural identity, but their views were also ignored.

There was a profound irony in the strategy of imitation. Although it was a great success in realist terms, at the same time it undermined the sense of cultural identity upon which Japanese self-confidence and self-esteem depended. The implied acceptance of the superiority of Western civilization created a persistent uncertainty about Japan's own self-image. While other Asian nations resisted the Western intrusion and defended their values and institutions, Japan's leaders in the Meiji period prodded the nation to remake itself in the mold of the West. Koreans, for example, scornful of such seemingly unprincipled behavior, posted a wall notice in 1873 at the outpost where Japanese traders were customarily received: "[The Japanese] do not feel shameful in adopting institutions from the foreigners and changing their appearances as well as their customs. We should not consider them as 'Japanese' any more."[50]

Accommodation to the norms of the international system became a deeply divisive issue that went to the very heart of modern Japanese life, and the nation has been struggling with it ever since. Ready accommodation to the demands of the international system, though designed to advance Japanese power and raise its status and prestige among nations, inevitably set up a conflict with Japanese cultural traditions, which were sacrificed at the altar of realism. Whatever the success in regaining their sovereignty through emulation of Western institutions, the Japanese remained emotionally attached to their own ways.

Even for Fukuzawa, this greatest of the advocates of Western civilization, it was impossible to be wholehearted in such a sweeping sellout of Japanese culture. However much he espoused the total transformation of Japan, he remained emotionally tied to the old ways of his own lifestyle. He was proud of his samurai heritage. Albert Craig, in an analysis of Fukuzawa, wrote that he:

liked to live in Japanese style, wearing Japanese dress and eating Japanese food. He pounded his own *mochi* [sweet rice cakes]. He was extremely fond of *sake* and only with great reluctance gave it up for reasons of health in his later years. He liked walking and horseback riding. He was proud of his quick draw with a sword and would demonstrate his prowess by flipping a coin into the air, drawing, and cleaving the coin before it struck the ground. A tireless partisan of women's rights, he was quite traditional in the education of his own daughters and conservative in most respects in his own home.[51]

Fukuzawa, in fact, once confessed regarding his own reform writings: "A wine merchant is not always a drinker, a cake dealer does not always go in search of sweets. You should not make hasty judgment of the dealer's taste by what he sells in his shop."[52] Like Fukuzawa, modern Japan has strained to reconcile the demands of the international system with living according to the comfortable old ways.

Still, given the primacy of foreign policy, there was no way to go but ahead. Trading in their own cultural heritage and replacing it with the accoutrements of modern military and industrial power, the Japanese sought to reclaim whatever national pride was lost by successfully demonstrating its new instruments of power. The exercise of military power therefore took on special meaning. It compensated for the cultural insecurity they felt from borrowing so extensively from the West. The journalist Kinoshita Naoue observed after the Russo-Japanese War that the Japanese had been "seduced" by military victory and the acclaim it brought Japan from abroad; those who fell victim to this temptation, he said, had earlier been humiliated at the thought that "since the opening of the country the Japanese people have done nothing but import and copy foreign things."[53] The philosopher Miyake Setsurei cautioned his countrymen that "although a modern nation must depend first of all on military strength, the true measure of its worth is determined mostly by cultural elements."[54] Power brought prestige, and prestige pride. But this pride was not sufficient to lay to rest the insecurities that the Japanese were experiencing in an international society dominated by the values of Western civilization.

The most sensitive Japanese were keenly aware of the cost of the single-minded pursuit of power. The art critic and philosopher Okakura Tenshin despaired that modern Japanese citizens took pride in the exercise of military prowess and the respect that it won abroad. In the *Book of Tea*, published the year after the Russo-Japanese War, he wrote that the West had called Japan "barbarous while she indulged in the gentle arts of peace," and now called her "civilized since she began to commit wholesale slaughter on Manchurian battlefields." He went on to observe that "much comment has been given lately to the code of the Samurai,—the Art of Death which makes our soldiers exult in self-sacrifice; but scarcely any attention has been drawn to Teaism, which represents so much of our Art of Life." Okakura was referring to the Muromachi period (1333–1568), particularly in the culture of Kyoto, especially the aesthetic world of tea and the Zen elements of the culture, which he argued had humanized the Japanese military tradition. He believed, as the historian Fred Notehelfer observed, that by "setting out to emulate the West in the Meiji period Japan was following Europe and America down the very path of raw unbridled military power that Japanese culture had so valiantly overcome" in the Muromachi age.[55] The honor, prestige, and status that Japan sought in an international system dominated by the West could not be acquired by military and economic power alone. The thoroughgoing realism of the Japanese elites was always problematic.

CONSTRUCTING A JAPANESE IDENTITY

The Meiji leaders quickly perceived the Hobbesian nature of the competitive struggle that must be waged in the international system, but they interpreted this struggle in light of the cultural values that had characterized their feudal society. From the outset, they perceived it as a struggle not just for survival and security but for superiority over other states and for the self-esteem that would result from that superiority. National power and the honor and status that would come with it were what initially motivated Japan's new leaders—and they were prepared to focus every institution of national life on the achievement of this purpose. Once they had introduced the apparatus of the modern state, including a constitution, a parliamentary system, political parties, a national bureaucracy, a standing army, and public education, they realized that to achieve their goals they must find ways to mobilize their people with an ideology that would inspire them. After spending decades attempting to build national strength through adoption of Western institutions, they turned to the task of motivating the Japanese people and mobilizing them in support of the nation's foreign policy goals.

The goals of the nation had to be articulated in terms that the Japanese people could understand, with ideals that would rally them to the self-sacrifice and commitment required. For a country as economically backward as Japan was in the mid-nineteenth century to achieve its goal of becoming a great power as rapidly as Japan did required the government to bring the people to a new pitch of effort. It entailed forging a nationalist ideology that would motivate the people, create a national consensus, and provide them with a sense of cultural identity. A prominent journalist in the Meiji period, Kuga Katsunan, put it this way:

If a nation wishes to stand among the great powers and preserve its national independence, it must strive always to foster nationalism. . . . Consider for a moment: If we were to sweep away thoughts of one's own country, its rights, glory, and welfare—which are the products of nationalism—what grounds would be left for love of country? If a nation lacks patriotism how can it hope to exist? Patriotism has its origins in the distinction between "we" and "they" that grows out of nationalism, and nationalism is the basic element in preserving and developing a unique culture. If the culture of one country is so influenced by another that it completely loses its own unique character, that country will surely lose its independent footing.[56]

The demands of international competition led the nation's leaders to construct a political myth from a complex mix of ideas, attitudes, and emotions that was the legacy of their particular history. They had to integrate the masses into a new political system that would capture their loyalties and win their hearts. Lacking the great transcendental principles that other civilizations drew on to underpin their political ideas, they turned to Japan's "primordial-sacral hierarchical order" for inspiration. The Meiji statesman Itō Hirobumi, drafting a constitution for the nation, asked:

> What is the cornerstone of our country? This is the problem we have to solve. . . . In Japan [unlike in Europe] religion does not play such an important role and cannot become the foundation of constitutional government. Though Buddhism once flourished and was the bond between all classes, high and low, today its influence has declined. Though Shintoism is based on the traditions of our ancestors, as a religion it is not powerful enough to become the center of the country. Thus in our country the one institution which can become the cornerstone of our constitution is the Imperial House.[57]

Observing the ways in which Western nations achieved social cohesion and support for their foreign undertakings, Japan's leaders proved adept at "the technology of nationalism."[58] They "invented tradition" to focus popular sentiment on the imperial institution and instill nationalism. That is, they manipulated and reworked ideas, institutions, and cultural symbols from the past to forge a nationalist ideology. To build support for the modern state they were creating, the Meiji leaders resorted to the traditional language of loyalty and obligation and called on the values of social solidarity and respect for authority, drawing on a mythical past to kindle a competitive nationalist spirit.

They steadily elaborated the concept of the family state (*kazoku kokka*), proclaiming Japan as a nation-state unique among nations for its bonds of kinship and its imperial dynasty descended from the sun goddess. Such a state, embracing the sacred qualities of a divine-human continuity, was worthy to be the sole source of value. For the masses, most of whom were just emerging from rural village life, the religious imperatives for sacrifice and repayment of blessings received were powerful indeed. The conflation of national community and state left no room for a civil society, voluntary associations, or competing sources of value. All work was justified for its contribution to the well-being of the nation, and self-fulfillment was not recognized except in the arts, skills, and mysticism. Ethics texts, which now became a common part of school study, stressed acting as one should in the group, especially the nation. There was no universal ethic.

In 1890, just after the promulgation of the Meiji constitution and with the opening of the new legislature, the government issued a document of vital importance, the so-called Imperial Rescript on Education, which set forth the cardinal principles of this ideology. Beginning with the basic Confucian relationships, it exhorted the people to: "Be filial to your parents, affectionate to your brothers and sisters; as husbands and wives be harmonious; as friends, true; bear yourselves in modesty and moderation; . . . always respect the constitution and observe the laws; should emergency arise, offer yourselves courageously to the state; and thus guard and maintain the prosperity of Our Imperial Throne coeval with heaven and earth." The Rescript, which became part of daily school exercises, marked the beginning of the purposeful inculcation of orthodoxy. Education became a primary tool of indoctrination. The Meiji oligarch Yamagata Aritomo, the key foreign policy strategist, envisioned that "in due course, the nation will become one great civil and military university."[59] In readying the nation for war with Russia, Yamagata emphasized education as the most important preparation.[60]

Soon, the newly established professional bureaucracy took on the challenge of mobilizing the populace. It went far beyond education to include many kinds of grassroots organizations, including youth groups, veterans associations, and women's groups, as well as Shinto shrines. All were harnessed to the work of inculcating the national mission and the supporting ideology and of imbuing the foreign policy goals of the state with an aura of sanctity and legitimacy that would inhibit political opposition and dissent. At the same time as it undertook thought guidance on a widening scale through education and local organizations, the bureaucracy also undertook social policies designed to dampen unrest, preempt radical ideologies, and integrate the lower classes into the political community. Village headmen, Shinto priests, elementary-school principals, prominent landlords, and other local actors were imbued with the ideology and charged with responsibility for achieving Japan's imperial destiny. They became interpreters of the national mission to the masses. Because reverence for the emperor, the values of the family, and suspicion of foreigners struck a responsive chord and resonated with long-held values of the social system, people outside of the government became some of the most fervent purveyors of the ideology.

In the newly emerging industrial sector, bureaucrats and managers also invented tradition as part of their determination to maintain the order and motivation required by their foreign policy goals. Managers invoked "Japan's beautiful customs" of obedience, loyalty, and harmony to conciliate labor and strengthen the social cohesion required for imperial goals. As one leading bureaucrat charged with maintaining a peaceful industrial labor force intoned:

> In the future, our capitalists . . . will be steeped in the generous spirit of kindness and benevolence, guided by thoughts of fairness and strength. The factory will become one big family: the factory chief as the eldest brother and the foreman as the next oldest. The factory owner himself will act as parent. Strikes will become unthinkable, and we can look forward to the increased productivity of capital—the basis for advances in the nation's wealth and power.[61]

Bismarckian social policy was influential in helping the Japanese bureaucrats understand that industrialism would inevitably undermine social solidarity and impede an energetic *Weltpolitik* unless labor peace was maintained. Max Weber, for example, at this very time was expounding the ideas of the newly unified and rising German state. In his inaugural lecture at Freiburg in 1895, he declared, "It is not the purpose of our work in social policy to make the world happy, but to unite socially a nation split apart by modern economic development, for the hard struggles of the future." He added, "Not peace and human happiness we have to pass on to our descendants, but the maintenance and up-breeding of our national kind."[62] Japan's leading disciple of German social thought, Kanai Noburu, who had studied in Germany in classes where one of his fellow students was in fact Weber, not surprisingly was of the same mind, explaining that social policy "is not just a noble human ethic, *it is an effective method to achieve success in foreign policy.*"[63] It was the work of the bureaucracy, he said, to see that Japan did not become "a nation split apart by economic development." If that effort should collapse, and the wrenching changes required for industrialization result in spreading social malaise, as it had in other countries, Japan's always precarious international position would be imperiled.

War and the prospect of hostilities were a constant prod to the people's efforts and self-sacrifice. In the half-century beginning with the Sino-Japanese War of 1894–1895, Japan was at war for half of the time, and in the remainder of the time, it was in readiness.[64] Nonetheless, even when the country was neither at war nor getting ready for war, Japan's "social managers," as Sheldon Garon called them, repeatedly invoked the image of war and the country's vulnerability. Nothing confirms the principle of the *Primat der Aussenpolitik* better than war and the threat of war. The awareness that Japan lived in a hostile international environment, and that the nation could only depend upon self-help, daily promoted ideological indoctrination. As the scholar and ideologue Inoue Tetsujirō importuned in 1891, promoting a thoroughgoing nationalist education, "We must consider the whole world our enemy . . . [for] foreign enemies are watching for any lapse on our part, and then we can only rely upon our forty million fellow countrymen. Thus any true Japanese must have a sense of public duty, by which he values his life lightly as dust, advances spiritedly, and is ready to sacrifice himself for the sake of the nation."[65]

The pursuit of empire and of status as a great power shaped all aspects of Japan's national development, illustrating Charles Tilly's dictum that "war made the state; and the state made war."[66] The wars with China and Russia had transformed Japan. A successful imperialist policy required a unified nation at home, with every part of society subordinated to the whole and with the state taking precedence over individual citizens and social groups. Taxes, conscription, mobilization of the population, and the acceptance of the leaders' values of national power all transformed Japan by the time the Meiji emperor died in 1912. The emerging industrial society was shaped in nearly every way by political and military ambitions formulated for the nation by the Meiji leaders. Landlord-tenant relations, moral instruction in the schools, allocation of economic resources, employer-employee relations—everything was to be subordinated to national greatness, to Japan's status as a first-rate power.

Following both the Russo-Japanese War and World War I, the Japanese public was warned again and again of Japan's "coming peacetime economic war" with the Western powers and of the need to work hard, make sacrifices, and rally behind the state. Initially, it was a matter of the state intervening in society, but as society became awakened to the challenges that the nation faced in achieving its goals, ideologues in the media and the true believers in the communities took up this role.

Typical of the tone set by the nation's leaders to rally support for Japan's foreign policy goals was a speech that a civil servant gave as he traveled around Yamaguchi prefecture in 1906. As a result of its victory in the Russo-Japanese War, he said, Japan had joined the ranks of the world's first-class nations (*ittō-koku*) and now had to expand its military and diplomatic establishments abroad as befitted this new status. The country needed to invest great sums in industrial growth and education so that its people might develop the resources required to support the Japanese empire. Furthermore, the people had an obligation to contribute to the achievement of Japan's destiny by paying higher taxes. The shooting war was over, but Japan would now be engaged in economic warfare, which would be no less demanding than military combat. He spoke of the coming "peaceful warfare" in which every country would be Japan's enemy. If Japan was to increase its strength, it must inevitably come in conflict with other countries over trade. National unity was imperative. Young men, old men, children, women—all would be in the battles and must obey orders as in any war.[67]

This civil servant's speech incorporates critical elements of the national motivation. Japan must unite because its goal of imperial power requires constant vigilance. Japan is vulnerable and the people must work and sacrifice. The goal is recognition of Japan's international standing: Its honor, dignity, pride, and self-esteem are at stake.

The formulation of a nationalist orthodoxy galvanized the people for the hard struggles of the international competition by interpreting the national goals in terms of values that were already deeply rooted and part of their everyday lives. The myth of a divine emperor at the head of a family state, ruling over a nation knit together by his benevolence and the loyalty of his filial subjects, provided a national consensus, motivating the Japanese people to pursue an international standing in the world that would bring honor and esteem to the nation. Because it expressed ideals central to their history, the imperial myth, as the historian Thomas C. Smith wrote, "called up prodigies of effort and self-sacrifice."[68] And the role that groups within society took in responding to it and even strengthening it testify to the public's receptivity to the myth.[69]

But while this orthodoxy assured them of their own identity, the Japanese found recognition in a Western-dominated world to be an elusive goal. The myth was always tenuous in an international order dominated by the Western world, the very civilization Japan hoped to impress in its pursuit of standing. It was an artificial creation, invented after the fact, and unpersuasive in the light of Japan's massive borrowing, which tacitly acknowledged the superiority of Western civilization. Because it was constantly challenged by the new conditions of industrial life, new and harsher class antagonism, and the spread of rationalist thought, the orthodoxy had to be constantly reinforced. The political myth was fragile.

THE PSYCHIC WOUND

Modern Japan sustained a "psychic wound" at the time of its birth. The discovery of Japan's impotence in the face of Western civilization, and the determination to borrow from this civilization everything necessary to overcome this impotence, left the Japanese with a persistent self-doubt that could not be overcome by the artificial creation of a cultural identity. The nationalist orthodoxy that the Meiji leaders instigated could never conceal the fact of Japanese dependence on outside borrowing. Natsume Sōseki wrote without doubt the most memorable and compelling account of the traumatic effect of the international environment on Japan's psyche.

Sōseki, who was once called the equal of Freud "in the sharpness and depth of his psychological observation,"[70] penetrated the mysteries of the Japanese psyche better than any of his contemporaries. In a brooding and despairing speech delivered at Wakayama in 1911, Sōseki gave an extraordinary statement of the outside-in impact on Japan's spiritual life.[71] Remarking on the transition to an industrial economy and Japan's borrowings from Western civilization, he observed that Japan was losing its cultural autonomy. Its sense of self-mastery, its capacity to control its own behavior, and its ability to determine its own institutions were all being lost. Unlike the West, where industrial society had emerged naturally from within societies, Japan's national life was being driven by external forces, he said. In order to survive, Japan had been forced to adopt an alien civilization. Before the coming of the West, "we were a country that had until then developed according to our own internal motivation. But then we suddenly lost our ability to be self-centered [independent] and were confronted by a situation in which we could not survive unless we began taking orders from the external force that was pushing us around at will." In contrast, Western civilization, with its superior science and technology, developed spontaneously out of its own history and inherited values:

> Simply stated, Western civilization (that is, civilization in general) is internally motivated, whereas Japan's civilization is externally motivated. Something that is "internally motivated" develops naturally from within, as a

flower opens, the bursting of the bud followed by the turning outward of the petals. Something is "externally motivated" when it is forced to assume a certain form as a result of pressure applied from the outside. Western civilization flows along as naturally as clouds or a river, which is not at all what we see in the case of Japan since the Restoration and the opening of relations with the West.

The competitive ethic in the international order drove Japanese behavior, socialized it to alien ways, and compelled emulation of the successful institutions of another civilization. Japan had been impelled by forces from the outside in ways that were humiliating, and the result was a superficial civilization that constantly acknowledged Japan's loss of cultural independence and hence of self-worth:

> Just look at the way we socialize with Westerners—always according to *their* rules, never ours. Why, then, do we not just stop socializing with them? Sadly enough, we have no choice in the matter. And when two unequal parties socialize, they do so according to the customs of the stronger. One Japanese may make fun of another for not knowing the proper way to hold a knife or fork, but such smug behavior only proves that the Westerners are stronger than we are. If we were the stronger, it would be a simple matter for us to take the lead and make them imitate us. Instead, we must imitate them. And because age-old customs cannot be changed overnight, all we can do is mechanically memorize Western manners—manners which, on us, look ridiculous.
>
> All of this talk about silverware and manners may seem very trivial and have nothing to do with civilization, but that is exactly my point: everything we do—every trivial little act—is not internally, but externally motivated. This tells us that civilization of modern-day Japan is superficial: it just skims the surface.

Japan, he said, was running a race with Western history; only by reaching the Western nations' advanced stage of development could the nation regain its cultural autonomy and control of its own destiny. But in the meantime, in trying to catch up with the West and "to condense into ten years all the developments that it took the West a hundred years to accomplish," the Japanese would surely suffer "an incurable nervous breakdown; we would fall by the wayside gasping for breath."

But even supposing Japan were by a heroic effort able to catch up by absorbing all the West's knowledge, the result would nevertheless be unsatisfactory, for Japan could be truly independent and self-respecting only if it were creating an internally generated civilization (*naihatsuteki kaika*), one that was the product of its own history and values. As it was, Japan was following a path that had already been broken by those who were in the lead. Building a modern civilization generated by a foreign history and values (*gaihatsuteki kaika*) could never be satisfactory. Such a wretched course, he concluded, was destructive of self-esteem and integrity, for it implied that Japan's own history lacked intrinsic significance.

To compensate for the demeaning dependence on Western civilization, Sōseki observed, the Japanese now boasted of their military achievements. They no longer resorted to "such foolishness as saying to foreigners, 'My country has Mt. Fuji.' But since the [Russo-Japanese] war one hears boasting everywhere that we have become a first-class country." Sensitive to what he regarded as Japan's continuing cultural subservience, Sōseki felt it "frivolous" to claim equality with the West on the basis of military victories.

Sōseki's novels convey a poignant understanding of the toll that the cultural revolution took on Japanese life. In the novel *Sore Kara* (And Then), written 1909, he explored the psychology of the "external enlightenment" and its harmful effects. The hero, Daisuke, a young well-to-do intellectual, speaks bluntly of the society in which he lives:

> The point is, Japan can't get along without borrowing from the West.
> . . . But it poses as a first-class power. And it's straining to join the ranks of the first-class powers. That's why, in every direction, it puts up a façade of a first-class power and cheats on what's behind. . . . And see, the consequences are reflected in each of us as individuals. A people so oppressed by the West have no mental leisure, they can't do anything worthwhile. They get an education that's stripped to the bare bones, and they're driven with their noses to the grindstone until they're dizzy—that's why they all end up with nervous breakdowns. . . . Unfortunately, exhaustion of the spirit and deterioration of the body come hand-in-hand. And that's not all. The decline of morality has set in too. Look where you will in this country, you won't find one square inch of brightness. It's all pitch black.[72]

Sōseki was clearly speaking of the psychological trauma that Japan's entry into international society created. Throughout their modern history the Japanese have been compulsive in their preoccupation with their national character, with the question of what makes them Japanese. Who are the

Japanese? the critic Katō Shūichi once asked. They are a people, he answered, who are always asking who they are.[73] They have been eager for praise of their institutions from Western visitors, but at the same time sensitive to condescension and fearful of being patronized. The goals of their foreign policy have been suffused with this pursuit of recognition in a world made by the West.

Nor would it do to resurrect the old values, as the nationalist orthodoxy sought to do. Although those values attempted to give the Japanese a unique national identity, they could never be satisfying in a modern industrial world that prized science and rationalism. In Sōseki's novel, Daisuke reflected on his father's insistence on living by the old values:

> His father had received the moral upbringing usual for samurai before the Restoration. This upbringing taught a code of conduct utterly removed from the realities of day-to-day living, yet his father believed in it implicitly—and this despite the fact that he was forever being driven by the fierce demands of business life. Over the long years he had changed with these demands, and he now bore little resemblance to what he once was, though he was quite unaware of this. Indeed, he was always boasting that it was his strict warrior education that accounted for his success! But Daisuke thought differently. How could one fulfill the hourly demands of modern life and live by a feudal ethic! Even to try, one must wage war against oneself.[74]

In choosing to promote cultural borrowing while at the same time invoking traditional values, the Japanese leaders subjected their people to searing uncertainty about what world they lived in. Was it the industrial world of the advanced Western countries, with its unfamiliar and uncomfortable standards and values? Or was it the more familiar and comfortable world of inherited Asian practices and values that Japanese history and civilization honored and esteemed? This uncertainty festered at the center of Japanese national life throughout the modern period.

The opportunism of Japanese national policy—reacting to the prevailing conditions around it, taking its cues from the external environment, discerning the trends and adjusting to them, organizing its domestic institutions so as to give primacy to the achievement of its foreign policy goals, and accommodating the historical forces in such a way as to serve the interest of enhancing Japanese power—brought astonishing success in the rise of Japan's stature among nations. But a conflict between the realist pursuit of power and the innate attachment to their own civilization is evident in the lives of many Japanese. The novelist Tanizaki Jun'ichirō, recalling his youth, wrote, "I had come to detest Japan, even though I was obviously Japanese." At the time of the great earthquake that destroyed Tokyo in 1923, he dreamed of a new, wholly Western capital city: "The citizens of Japan will come to adopt a purely European-American style of life, and the young people, men and women alike, will all wear Western clothes. This is the inevitable trend of the times."[75] But Tanizaki was increasingly troubled by the need to yield to the claims of another civilization. In 1934, he wrote plaintively:

> How unlucky we have been, what losses we have suffered, in comparison with the Westerner. The Westerner has been able to move forward in ordered steps, while we have met superior civilization and had to surrender to it, and we have had to leave a road we have followed for thousands of years. . . . I am aware of and most grateful for the benefits of the age. No matter what complaints we may have, Japan has chosen to follow the West, and there is nothing for her to do but move bravely ahead and leave us old ones behind. But we must be resigned to the fact that as long as our skin is the color it is the loss we have suffered cannot be remedied. I have written all this because I have thought there might still be somewhere, possibly in literature or the arts, where something could be saved.[76]

The Sinologist Takeuchi Yoshimi, writing after World War II, reflected on the painful implications of Japan's accommodative path to modernity. For the Europeans, modernization had followed a natural, spontaneous course, he said, growing easily out of their traditions and culture. Modernity entailed the assertion of European civilization's selfhood abroad—the spread of its values and institutions. Except for Japan, the nations of Asia, and particularly China, had resisted this assertion of European influence as a threat to their self-identification. Takeuchi held that by not resisting but instead emulating Western values and institutions and fully accommodating to the international system, Japan had sacrificed its very being. "In other words," he concluded, "Japan is nothing" (*tsumari Nihon wa nani mono de mo nai*).[77]

THE INTERNATIONAL SYSTEM AND JAPANESE IDENTITY

Identities are constructed from two kinds of ideas: those held by the Self and those held by the Other. A national identity is formed and shaped first of all by domestic influences. The new orthodoxy encompassing the family state and the imperial myth was constructed of values and institutions familiar to all Japanese from their premodern past. But although the national identity that the conservative leadership constructed was powerful in its ability to appeal to the Japanese sense of themselves, they needed the reinforcement that could only come from knowing that others saw them in the same way (that is, through the principle of "mirroring," discussed earlier in the chapter). National identities are thus also shaped by participation in the international system. The exercise of national power in warfare attracted the attention of the West, but the identity that the international system ascribed to the Japanese was too often not what they had hoped for. Japanese success in accommodating to the norms of the international system implied that modern Japanese history lacked authenticity because it was imitative, a kind of dwarfed or artificial version of the true linear course that Western civilization had followed. The scornful view that westerners took of an imitative enterprise, their real or imagined slights of this first non-Western power in their midst, and their shabby treatment of Japanese immigrants to their shores magnified the self-doubt and provoked resentment.

In a world dominated by Social Darwinist notions, race was a sensitive issue for the Japanese from the time they entered the imperialist order. It was a world in which Darwinian notions of natural selection and "survival of the fittest" were applied to race and the advancement of civilization. In the 1850s, the French diplomat Joseph Arthur de Gobineau wrote the classic statement of Nordic supremacy. His *Essai sur l'inegalite des races humaines* divided the world into a permanent hierarchy of white, yellow, and black races. In the 1880s, the Scottish natural lawyer James Lorimer set forth the basis of the "law of nations" by relying on the "science of races," dividing humanity into three categories—civilized humanity, barbarous humanity, and savage humanity—and thus justifying unequal relations among peoples. Hedley Bull summarized this view: "Civilized humanity comprised the nations of Europe and the Americas, which were entitled to full recognition as members of international society. Barbarous humanity comprised the independent states of Asia—Turkey, Persia, Siam, China and Japan—

which were entitled to partial recognition. And savage humanity was the rest of mankind, which stood beyond the pale of the society of states."[78] Assumptions of racial inequality were already embedded in the international power structure, and the idea of Social Darwinism quickly spread. Herbert Spencer, the leading exponent of Social Darwinism, wrote in confidence to an influential Japanese leader, Kaneko Kentarō, in 1892:

> The Japanese policy should, I think, be that of *keeping Americans and Europeans as much as possible at arm's length*. In presence of the more powerful races your position is one of chronic danger, and you should take every precaution to give as little foothold as possible to foreigners. It seems to me that the only forms of intercourse which you may with advantage permit are those which are indispensable for the exchange of commodities. . . . There should be not only a prohibition of foreign persons to hold property in land, but also a refusal to give them leases, and a permission only to reside as annual tenants. . . . Regarding the intermarriage of foreigners and Japanese. . . it should be positively forbidden. . . . There is abundant proof, alike furnished by the intermarriage of human races and by the interbreeding of animals, that when the varieties mingled diverge beyond a certain slight degree *the result is inevitably a bad one* in the long run.[79]

In discarding their own civilization in such sweeping fashion, the Japanese undermined their self-respect. This lack of confidence extended to their own abilities and even their physical attributes as a people. Inoue Tetsujirō, a professor of philosophy at Japan's leading university, argued in a well-known essay in 1889 that Japan was not yet fit for competition with the westerners. "Japanese," he wrote, "are greatly inferior to westerners in intelligence, financial power, physique, and all else." The superiority of the westerner, he believed, was evident not only from his greater stature but also from his more highly developed cranium. The shape of the westerner's head was indicative of a superior intellect. "We stand before westerners," he concluded, "exposing our weak and inferior civilization; it is rare that we can hold our heads high and peer down on other races as they do."[80] The implication was that Inoue sought for his country a similarly superior position. It was no accident that he became one of the most rabid exponents of Japanese nationalism.

Accommodation to the international norms to acquire power and status in the hierarchy of prestige was frustrating, too, because despite Japan's achievements it often felt slighted and denied the recognition it deserved for its strenuous efforts. At the turn of the century, Japanese immigration to the United States, Australia, and Canada gave rise to mounting opposition that reflected the fear of a "Yellow Peril" overwhelming local communities. Japan's self-image at the end of the Russo-Japanese War as one of the world's five great powers was undermined by the treatment of Japanese as second-class citizens in Anglo-Saxon countries. The San Francisco School Board's decision in 1905 to establish a separate school for children of Asian descent is well known for provoking Japanese anger. Theodore Roosevelt intervened to resolve the resulting crisis, but the problems continued.

Japanese resentment of the West's racial prejudice was filtered through the strong feelings of hierarchy and status that were deeply ingrained in Japanese culture. The Japanese people did not express anger over the slights in terms of universal principles of racial justice and equality; rather, they responded by becoming more committed to the principles of the Meiji Restoration, with a greater determination to make Japan the equal of the Western powers. As was apparent from Inoue Tetsujirō's views, these feelings of resentment first began to surface as soon as westerners began to mingle with Japanese at home. They became much stronger when the mingling took place abroad. The discrimination against Japanese immigrants in the United States, Australia, and Canada beginning at the turn of the century became an open sore on the Japanese psyche. Despite Japan's rising power and prestige, its people were still not accorded the respect of "high-ranking people." Worse, they were being treated like other Asians. By the time of World War I, the Foreign Ministry regarded the treatment of Japanese immigrants as one of its most pressing concerns.

Japan's hypersensitivity to the treatment of its migrant workers to the United States, Australia, and Canada is best understood within the fusion of honor and nationalism that had taken place after the Restoration. The highly developed and elaborate culture of honor that was a legacy of the feudal experience prompted keen attention to self-esteem, and dignity had become a domain-centered code by the late Tokugawa period. As Eiko Ikegami wrote, "One's honor is the image of oneself in the social mirror, and that image affects one's self-esteem and one's behavior."[81] With entry into the international state system, the culture of honor merged with the rising nationalism. It is precisely in this context that Japanese sensitivity to the treatment of Japanese immigrants arose. At that time a Japanese diplomat explained why the discrimination was so hurtful: "The point which caused a painful feeling in Japan was not that the operation of the prohibition would be such as to exclude a certain number of Japanese from immigration to Australia but that Japan should be spoken of in formal documents, such as Colonial Acts, as if the Japanese were on the same level of morality and civilization as Chinese and other less advanced populations of Asia."[82]

Japan, as Fukuzawa had put it, wanted to "escape from Asia" and be seen as wholly different from the "bad company" of other countries of the region. The California Alien Land Law of 1913 was directed specifically at Japanese immigrants, limiting leases of agricultural lands to maximum terms of three years and barring further land purchases by Japanese aliens. The symbolic implication was that Japan lacked the status equivalent with the powers and that it had not escaped identification with Asia. The foreign minister, Katō Kōmei, was frank in this regard, observing in 1915:

What we regard very unpleasant about the California question . . . is the discrimination made against our people in distinction from some other nations. We would not mind disabilities if they were equally applicable to all nations. We are not vain enough to consider ourselves at the very forefront of enlightenment; we know that we still have much to learn from the West. But we thought ourselves ahead of any other Asiatic people and as good as some of the European nations.[83]

The Japanese had sacrificed so much of themselves in order to achieve power and standing—they had disregarded much of their own history and culture in order to aspire to Western standards. To have their achievement made light of by the rest of the world, to be denied an honored place in the international system, came as a great blow to them. Kōsaka Masataka, one of the most astute Japanese commentators on his country's international relations, often remarked that ever since Commodore Perry appeared in Edo Bay with his fleet in 1853 and Japan was compelled to join the international system on the West's terms, the Japanese had harbored "an intense anger toward the West" at having to play by its rules in a system of its making that devalued their own civilization.[84] In the war crimes trials after World War II, one of the most prominent military strategists, General Ishiwara Kanji, exploded before a courtroom audience when the American prosecutor asked him to justify Japanese aggression:

Haven't you ever heard of Perry? Don't you know anything about your country's history? . . . Tokugawa Japan believed in isolation; it didn't want to have anything to do with other countries, and had its doors locked tightly. Then along came Perry from your country in his black ships to open those doors; he aimed his big guns at Japan and warned that "If you don't deal with us, look out for these; open your doors, and negotiate with other countries too." And then when Japan did open its doors and tried dealing with other countries, it learned that all those countries were a fearfully aggressive lot. And so for its own defense it took your own country as its teacher and set about learning how to be aggressive. You might say we became your disciples. Why don't you subpoena Perry from the other world and try *him* as a war criminal?[85]

To achieve national power the Meiji leaders were willing to swallow cultural pride, even risk their national identity, to borrow massively from an alien civilization. No other people were prepared to sacrifice so much of their own heritage. The power thus acquired often failed to garner the expected praise and prestige or to bring the recognition that Japan sought.

As the Japanese discovered how vulnerable their identity and self-esteem were, they began to desire the self-mastery that would come from autonomy. If they could be masters of their own order, they could not only be independent politically and economically, they could also make their own cultural values paramount. They discovered that in an international system dominated by the West, their quest for status and honor was not easily satisfied.

The Faustian bargain that Japan had struck with the West—this pursuit of the West's science and technology to bring national power—left the Japanese deeply torn and ambivalent, occasioning explosions of rage at their predicament. Take, for example, the father of the sculptor Isamu Noguchi, Yone (Yonejirō). As Ian Buruma wrote, Yone began his career coming to the United States as a young modernist poet who knew William Butler Yeats and Ezra Pound. He published in English and struck up a relationship with his American assistant, Leonie Gilmour, a Bryn Mawr graduate. But he became disillusioned with modernism and returned to Japan before the child they conceived, Isamu, was born.[86] He returned to his own native literary traditions and married a Japanese woman. Buruma wrote, "Something had gone badly wrong with many Japanese artists of Yone's generation. . . . Their initial enthusiasm for European modernism, fueled by a furious rejection of the Japanese past, had led them into a cultural cul-de-sac, from which an equally violent rejection of the West seemed to offer a way out."

In a 1921 essay published in Tokyo and entitled "Japan and America,"

Yone put his finger on the problem: "The Western civilization, generally speaking, intoxicated our Japanese mind like strong drink; and as a matter of course we often found ourselves, when we awoke from our intoxication, sadder and even inclined to despise ourselves."[87] Yone and so many other Japanese people never succeeded in finding a balance or a solid middle ground between Western modernism and aggressive nativism. They harbored an intense anger at having had their national ways of life so challenged and disrupted. This anger rose as the two countries drifted toward war. In the days after Pearl Harbor, it was Yone who wrote one of the most violent and bloodthirsty reactions, a poem entitled "Slaughter Them! The Americans and the English Are Our Enemies!"[88]

The importance of a self-reassuring national identity is critical. As Alexander Wendt wrote:

> Collective self-esteem refers to a group's need to feel good about itself, for respect or status. Self-esteem is a basic human need of individuals and one of the things that individuals seek in group membership. As expressions of this desire groups acquire the need as well. Like other national interests it can be expressed in different ways. A key factor is whether collective self-images are positive or negative, which will depend in part on relationships to significant Others, since it is by taking the perspective of the Other that the Self sees itself. Negative self-images tend to emerge from perceived disregard or humiliation by other states, and as such may occur frequently in highly competitive international environments. ... Since groups cannot long tolerate such images if they are to meet the self-esteem needs of their members, they will compensate by self-assertion and/or devaluation and aggression toward the Other.[89]

The primacy that Japan's leaders accorded foreign policy over culture had profound and lasting implications for Japan's self-assurance and self-respect. And because of the immense importance of status and dignity in the still vibrant honorific code of the Japanese, this psychic wound ran especially deep. In other words, as often happens in life, two values collided. The pursuit of power to establish reputation and rank ultimately clashed with honor and dignity because it robbed the nation of a sense of self-sufficiency, autonomy, and cultural integrity. The result was a tension in Japanese life that was steadily at work in Japan's international behavior. Tokutomi Sohō, the most prominent nationalist journalist, who was purged by the U.S. Occupation, maintained in the Tokyo war crimes trials that Japan began the Pacific War for three reasons—namely, self-existence, self-defense, and self-respect. The war, he said, was a protest, "an explosion of dissatisfaction and malcontent with [the] unfair treatment the World Powers accorded to Japan as an independent state."[90]

Realism and power politics did not provide all the necessary qualifications for a first-rank country. The Japanese discovered that a great power was not defined simply by prevailing in war or acquiring material wealth. A nation's standing, in its own as well as in others' eyes, was also determined by its unique cultural achievements. Recognition as a first-class nation would not come just by accruing material power. It must also be achieved through respect for Japan's civilization. To win recognition that would be truly satisfying, Japan would not only have to catch up and draw abreast of the advanced nations in its technological capability, reaching new levels of wealth and influence, it would have to discover how to live in an order of its own creation, governed by its own norms, thereby restoring its cultural autonomy. Driven in their national life by a complex psychology of ambition, pride, self-doubt, and anger, the Japanese came to believe that their goals could only be fulfilled when they were strong enough to create their own international order. On December 8, 1941, the prominent writer Itō Sei recorded his impression of the momentous events in his diary. In a few words, he expressed the complex psychology of emotions that had driven the Japanese people to risk all that they had achieved in order to attain their ultimate goal: "It is our destiny (*shukumei*) that the only way we will feel ourselves a first-rank people in the world (*sekai ichiryūjin*) is by going to war with the first-class white nations."[91]

CHAPTER FIVE

THE CHALLENGE OF
INTERNATIONAL LIBERALISM

War is a principal mechanism of change in the international system.[1] It is "one of history's great catalysts in rearranging the international distribution of power," wrote John Ikenberry. He continued, "States rise and decline over long stretches of time, but war can speed the process, pushing some great powers dramatically upward and others dramatically downward. Wars do not just produce winners and losers on the battlefield; they also break apart international order and alter the power capacities of states."[2] War, for example, again and again remade the European state system. "At an international level wars and war settlements," Charles Tilly observed, "have been the great shapers of the European state system as a whole. The Peace of Westphalia (1648), the Congress of Vienna (1815), the Treaty of Versailles (1919), and the provisional settlements ending World War II produced incomparably greater realignments of the identities, relations, and relative strengths of European states than any long periods of incremental change between them."[3]

The conflict that broke out in August 1914 was so destructive that it was to be "the war to end all wars." It was not known as "World War I" until much later, when the hopes of ending war were gone. It was simply the "Great War." It inflicted hitherto unimaginable suffering and destruction on the heart of Western civilization. It transformed all the relationships among the leading sovereign states. It claimed the lives of 10 million soldiers, wounded 20 million others, destroyed $300 billion of the West's material treasure, and undermined aging dynasties and empires, leaving widespread political uncertainty. In warfare that had become "total" for its effect on civilian life, the final casualty figures may have reached 60 million people.[4] Domestic polities were transformed, and power relations among nations were reordered.

Raymond Aron, describing the profound changes that World War I brought about in the structure and distribution of power in the international system, termed it a "war of hegemony."[5] Elaborating on Aron's observation, Gilpin wrote that such hegemonic wars have been the source of all fundamental changes in the international order:

> Every international system that the world has known has been a consequence of the territorial, economic, and diplomatic realignments that have followed such hegemonic struggles. The most important consequence of a hegemonic war is that it changes the system in accordance with the new international distribution of power; it brings about a reordering of the basic components of the system. Victory and defeat reestablish an unambiguous hierarchy of prestige congruent with the new distribution of power in the system. The war determines who will govern the international system and whose interests will be primarily served by the new international order.[6]

World War I brought about a stunning change in the international order. The United States emerged from the war as the world's most powerful nation. Its economy was nearly triple the size of Britain's. With its burgeoning industrial output, financial capital, agricultural production, and sufficiency of raw materials, its economic capacity was unrivaled. This preeminence, together with the decisive part it played in ending the European conflict, allowed it to dominate the peace settlement and introduce an American agenda for transforming international affairs.

World War I was a European conflict, but its repercussions reverberated in East Asia. In changing the nature of the international system, it brought fundamental changes to the way it worked in East Asia. There it revealed the greatly enhanced influence of two rising new powers, the United States and Japan. For Japan, the preoccupation of the European powers offered an unprecedented opportunity to expand its economic and territorial influence. Japan not only seized the opportunity to expand its empire, it also took advantage of the conflict to enter markets once dominated by Europe. Japan's exports quadrupled during the four-year conflict. At the same time, Japanese pursuit of regional hegemony undermined the equilibrium and stability that had been reached in the imperialist system and provoked a backlash from the United States. It began a generation of rivalry and antagonism between the two emergent powers.

In the peace settlement at Versailles in 1919, the United States asserted a new conception of international order. Woodrow Wilson's principles of international liberalism attempted a profound change in the framework of power politics. Two years later, in the Washington Conference of 1921–1922, the principles were applied to East Asia. Rather than an international system governed by a balance of power, the Americans favored the application of legal principles. For the Japanese, the changes in the international system that the United States proposed were not only radically different from the international norms and practices that Japan had assimilated over the previous half-century, they had no basis in Japanese experience. In many respects, the principles of regional order asserted at this time formed the basis of U.S. East Asian policy for the remainder of the century. For Japan, with its innate realist understanding of international politics, it was the beginning of a persistent challenge, lasting through the twentieth century, to cope with a liberal internationalist conception of international order.

WORLD WAR I AND EAST ASIA

On the eve of World War I, a relatively stable order prevailed among the imperial powers in East Asia. Although precarious, the imperialist order was sustained by a balance of power. Agreements and alliances were reached among the powers to harmonize their interests. The cooperative character of the imperialist system and the ways in which it served the interests of the powers, despite the rivalries and competition among them, made it the most durable of the East Asian regional orders of the past 150 years. Japan had worked its way into the power structure of the imperialist international system by adapting its mores, building national power, and resorting to military force to expand its territorial sway. It benefited as well from skillful diplomacy. The Anglo-Japanese Alliance of 1902 established a pattern of cooperation with Britain and contributed to the development of an understanding with the United States. In a series of agreements, the latter acknowledged Japan's position in Northeast Asia, in 1905 acquiescing to the Japanese protectorate of Korea. At the same time, Russia and

Japan had by war delimited their spheres of interest, with the former now relegated to protecting its remaining hold on northern Manchuria. The system was in rough equilibrium by this time, with the interests of each power more or less acknowledged by all others: the United States in the Philippines, France in Indochina, Britain in the Yangtze Valley and in South China, Germany in the Shandong Peninsula, and Russia and Japan in Northeast Asia.

World War I upset this balance. Japanese opportunism was to a considerable extent responsible for disrupting the equilibrium. The preoccupation of the Western powers with the conflict in Europe offered an ambitious Japan irresistible opportunities to expand its power. Japanese leaders regarded the Great War as a "gift from the gods" and "a one in a million opportunity." The outbreak of war in Europe in the summer of 1914 allowed Japan, under the guise of fulfilling its obligations to the Anglo-Japanese Alliance, to seize German holdings in Shandong and German-held islands in the South Pacific: the Carolines, Marianas, Marshalls, Palau, and Yap.

Next, Tokyo moved swiftly to resolve the problem of Sino-Japanese relations. On the eve of the war, China had established a weak new republican government over which the imperial powers, especially the United States and Japan, sought to exert a formative influence. U.S. public opinion saw the new government as tuitionary in its potential to absorb American democratic principles; the Japanese saw it as responsive to political domination. In January 1915, the Japanese government delivered a bold set of Twenty-One Demands, which if accepted would have established Japanese domination over the new republican government. They sought Chinese recognition of the transference of German rights in Shandong to Japan; an extension of Japanese rights and holdings in Manchuria; a limitation on China's cession of its coastal areas to other powers; and the employment of Japanese nationals as political, financial, and military advisers in China.

Japan's foreign minister, Katō Kōmei, an Anglophile and admirer of British imperialism, and Foreign Ministry bureaucrats believed Japan could justify its actions within the prevailing framework of the imperialist system.[7] The dominant opinion within the Foreign Ministry was that Japan should not stray far from the imperialist framework, since it was recognized that once the war was over the powers would turn their attention back to East Asia. Though determined that expansion on the continent was "a definite and immutable" policy, Japanese Foreign Minister Komura Jutarō wrote in a memorandum that Japan would "act together with the

Western nations in matters that concern all the powers . . . and, at the same time, have them gradually recognize our special position in Manchuria."[8] Presented, however, as a package at a time when the Europeans were preoccupied and when American domestic opinion was deeply sympathetic with the republican revolution in China, the Twenty-One Demands elicited a sharp reaction in England, and even more so in the United States, where President Woodrow Wilson reached the conclusion that the American people must be "champions of the sovereign rights of China." Japanese policy epitomized the rule-of-power politics that Wilson opposed and helped steel his determination to end the imperialist order and contain Japanese power.

Under pressure from the British and the Americans, the demands were moderated, but the damage done to Japan's image in the United States was amplified by subsequent Japanese policies during the war. Although Foreign Ministry diplomats and their sympathizers in the progressive political parties held to the existing framework of diplomacy, there was another substantial body of elite opinion, particularly within the military, that was less restrained. A second generation of leaders was emerging in Japan without the tempering experience that the Meiji oligarchs had of scrupulous and cautious attention to the position of the Western powers. The new generation of political leaders, less able and less cohesive, presided over a political system that had grown more complex. They practiced Realpolitik with less of the finesse, skill, and restraint that had marked the Meiji leaders. Many in the successor generation, emboldened by past successes, were unreservedly opportunistic in their use of military power. The new leadership of the army—exemplified by Tanaka Giichi, one of the zealous young protégés of the elder statesman Yamagata—had known only the success of repeated applications of national power. This new leadership was determined to continue pressing for expansion of Japan's continental position and to establish a Japanese regional hegemony, and it was intent on seizing the opportunity to resolve the security dilemma that a weak China had long posed.[9]

As the original Meiji leadership passed from the scene, there was evident a growing split within the elite over Japan's future course. Yamagata's protégés believed the war afforded an opportunity to loosen the constraints of cooperative imperialism, including the Anglo-Japanese Alliance, and establish Japan's preeminence in Northeast Asia. They were emboldened not only by the successes achieved in warfare, but also by the growing influence of the military in the political system. Yamagata's followers were in the bureaucracy, in the parties, and in the colonial administration. Their nationalist zeal and ambitions deeply influenced policy circles.

Prime Minister Terauchi Masatake (1916–1918), an army general and another Yamagata protégé in the new generation of leaders, saw the war as an opportunity to restrain the "haughtiness" of the Europeans and make clear that "eventually, all of Asia should be under the control of our Emperor."[10] Terauchi regarded the war in Europe as a "race war," adding, "From our perspective as Asians, it is a war between Christians and, if we borrow their words, heathen peoples. Although we will not insist on excluding Europeans and Americans, it is proper to inform the Westerners that, up to a point, Asia should be under the control of Asians." By establishing Japanese hegemony in China, Japan would be prepared for a racially based conflict with the Western powers.[11]

The Great War provided an additional opportunity to expand Japan's continental position. This time it was in the Russian Far East, where the goals of the Russo-Japanese War had been left unfulfilled. Following the Bolshevik Revolution and the Brest-Litovsk accord by which Russia withdrew from World War I, Wilson reluctantly asked Japan to join an international contingent to land at Vladivostok, protect Allied munitions, and aid the 50,000 Czech troops in the Russian Far East who were making their way westward to join the Allied front in Europe. Wilson suggested a Japanese force of 7,000, but Terauchi soon dispatched nearly 80,000 army troops. As the historian Hata Ikuhiko observed, "By the time World War One ended in November 1918, Japanese military forces were able to operate in a zone that extended from Lake Baikal in the north, into the hinterland of Sinkiang Province to the west, and as far south as the former German-held island territories in Micronesia. . . . It was an area almost equivalent in extent to the regions occupied by the Japanese forces in 1942 in the Pacific War."[12] Whether Japan could retain all of these new holdings would depend on the reaction of the other powers once the conflict in Europe was over.

Relentlessly exploiting the opportunities presented by the European conflict, the successors to the Meiji leaders overplayed their hand. Japan's unilateral pursuit of strategic advantage, a departure from its earlier caution and circumspection in observing the practices of cooperative imperialism, exacted a heavy cost for its future course. First, it threatened the equilibrium of the East Asian imperialist system that had been established among the powers and thereby weakened the system that protected and legitimated Japan's imperial prerogatives. Second, it provoked Chinese nationalism, which took on an anti-Japanese tone, thus prefiguring the problems that beset Sino-Japanese relations for the remainder of the century and beyond. Third, it marked a growing U.S.-Japan estrangement. Already the outcome of the Russo-Japanese War had decisively changed the strategic relations of Japan and the United States. As the new rising power in Northeast Asia, Japan, with its growing naval strength and its designs on Manchuria, became a challenge to U.S. interests.

It is of course possible to date the origins of U.S.-Japan estrangement a decade earlier in the racial tensions raised by Japanese immigration, but the clash of national interests was more sharply drawn by the Japanese wartime expansion. It aroused the deep distrust and suspicion of U.S. and British leaders. When they turned their attention to the postwar settlement in East Asia, they mounted a substantial effort to contain further expansion of Japanese power. The seeds of U.S.-Japan conflict were firmly planted. Finally, Japanese wartime expansion also resulted in the emergence of the United States' role as protector of the new Chinese Republic. It was the beginning of a strategic triangle of relations among Japan, the United States, and China. This triangle went through many phases during the twentieth century, but in this early stage the United States leaned strongly toward support of China. The weak and divided leadership of republican China, in turn, sought U.S. support as a limit on Japanese encroachment.

WILSON'S INTERNATIONAL LIBERALISM

The revolutionary conception of international order that came after World War I was the distinctive product of progressive politics in the United States and the ideals of President Woodrow Wilson. Wilson set out not to restore, reorder, or reform the old international system but to transcend it in accordance with revolutionary ideals growing out of U.S. history. Disdaining the old concepts of balance of power and cooperative imperialism, he advanced ideals of self-determination and collective security as the basis for international order. Wilson's "new diplomacy" was already apparent in his first State of the Union address in 1913, when he declared that international order must be founded on universal law and not the balance of power, on morality and not national interest.

The revolution in the structure, mores, and governance of the international system in East Asia that was undertaken by the Americans at the end of World War I was as remarkable as any that one might encounter in world history. The new order that the Americans proposed reflected a new international distribution of power, a reordering of the components of the system, and a change in the rules of the game. Wilson's "new diplomacy" proclaimed the self-determination and sovereign rights of every people, and he made plain his opposition to international power rivalries at China's expense. He told his European counterparts at the Paris Peace Conference that there was "nothing on which the public opinion of the United States of America was firmer than on this question that China should not be oppressed by Japan."[13] Japanese expansionist ambitions would have to be contained. The balance of power among the imperialists in East Asia would have to be replaced by a new order in which all would refrain from military and political expansion. Although Wilson was no longer president at the time of the Washington Conference of 1921–1922, it was there that his conception was applied to East Asia in the aftermath of the war. Agreements were reached that provided new norms and rules for governing the relations of the Pacific powers. The Japanese initially chose to accommodate to this revolutionary new order; however, the agreements provoked a latent suspicion among many Japanese leaders who regarded them as designed to contain Japan's security goals.

The Wilsonian approach to the world was characterized by moral absolutism and self-righteousness. "America," Wilson believed, "is the only idealistic nation in the world."[14] Later he described what came to be known as Wilsonianism: "This age is an age . . . which rejects the standards of national selfishness that once governed the counsels of nations and demands that they shall give way to a new order of things in which the only question will be: 'Is it right?' 'Is it just?' 'Is it in the interest of mankind?'"[15] Throughout the nineteenth century, the United States had held aloof from the world, believing that its values grew out of its own unique national experience and therefore were exceptional and could not be replicated elsewhere. But in the twentieth century that changed. In his second inaugural address Wilson declared: "We are provincials no longer."[16] He now called on Americans to crusade for democratic institutions abroad, to be "citizens of the world," and insisted that American ideals were "not the principles of a province or of a single continent . . . [but] the principles of a liberated mankind."[17] The ideals that America had cherished for its own political experiment were now to be employed abroad. Principles of individual freedom, accountable government, and the rule of law were of universal value.

Before the end of the war Wilson had already announced the principles upon which peace was to be established. The old diplomacy and the pattern of international relations that relied on a balance of power were blamed for causing the war. Wilson's Fourteen Points sought an end to secret treaties, removal of barriers to international trade, withdrawal of foreign armies from occupied territories, a readjustment of colonial claims, freedom of the seas, reduction of armaments, recognition of the principle of self-determination of nationalities, and an international political organization to prevent war.

Wilson held that his liberal principles must be applied among as well as within sovereign states. His view represented the application of liberal principles to international relations in a triad of reforms that included democracy, disarmament, and free trade. The first principle was fundamental: the establishment of popular governments as an essential condition of world peace. Empires must be replaced by democratic governments, which would adhere to the principle of national self-determination. Peace and order could be maintained by the establishment of democratic politics in domestic and international institutions. The second principle, arms control, was new in Wilson's day. In his view, the accumulation of weaponry was itself a cause of war. He proposed the reduction of all armaments to the lowest level consistent with national safety. Along with democracy and disarmament, a third principle was the removal of restraints on international trade. Where free trade was practiced, he believed, peace would prevail; nations joined in trade would share a common interest in preserving prosperity from the destruction of war.

Finally, if this triad were to endure, the key to a new international order was an institution that would reinforce these three principles and ensure peaceful settlement of disputes. Buoyed by enthusiastic public support when he toured Europe at the end of the war, Wilson believed that the wider world was being drawn to American democratic principles and that this liberal tide would make possible an association of democracies to keep the peace. The centerpiece of his agenda to establish a new international order was the institution of collective security. Peace could be maintained not by constructing a new balance of power but by a "community of power, not organized rivalries but an organized peace."[18] Peace based on principles of democracy, disarmament, and free trade would be preserved by this new overarching concept of collective security. Anarchy in the international system would be overcome by an association of nations committed to these principles that would provide mechanisms for dispute resolution and mutual security obligations.

Under the auspices of the League of Nations, procedures would be established to bring about a reduction in the level of arms so as to preclude wars of conquest. The League would have a parliament or general assembly in which all member states would be represented, a council dominated by the great powers, and an international court of justice. Gathering at Paris in 1919, the peace conference worked out the details of the League, including Article 10 of the covenant, which embodied the new principle of collective security. The article stated: "The members of the League undertake to respect and preserve as against external aggression the territorial integrity and existing independence of all Members of the League. In case of any such aggression the Council shall advise upon the means by which this obligation shall be fulfilled."[19] To keep the peace, Wilson would rely not on an international military force but rather on the deterrent effect of moral commitments; the natural desire of democratic states for peace; arms reduction; public opinion; and diplomatic and economic sanctions.

International liberalism was still embryonic in Wilson's day, but it resonated deeply with the American worldview taking shape in the early twentieth century. Bound up in this worldview at once were liberalism, nationalism, and internationalism. As N. Gordon Levin wrote, "For Wilson, as for many of his successors in the ranks of American decision-makers, the national interest became merged with liberal ideology in such a way that he could act simultaneously as the champion of American nationalism and as the spokesman of internationalism and anti-imperialism."[20] "Born equal" and never burdened by an inheritance of feudalism, as Alexis de Tocqueville had stressed, Americans were destined, in this worldview, to lead the world to an international system of peaceful commercial and political order. In contrast to Germany and Japan, where military and traditional values still held sway, history had prepared America to transform Hobbesian anarchy into a rational, orderly, and peaceful international society.

Such idealism could give birth to great military power to achieve its goals, on the one hand, but on the other hand it was bound to bring disillusionment, as it soon did with the U.S. lapse into isolationism between the two world wars. Nevertheless, international liberalism has always retained its hold on the American sense of mission in the world. Wilson has been roundly criticized for his idealism and naïveté, but he was probably more realistic than many of his critics allow. He recognized, for example, that his ideas and the principles of self-determination and collective security would take hold only slowly.[21] Despite the immediate failures, subsequent disillusionment, and repeated challenges, international liberalism became, as Kissinger wrote, "the dominant intellectual school of American foreign policy"[22] and a new, persistent influence on the international system. And a rising Japan was expected to adhere to this system for the remainder of the century.

Liberalism's adherents disputed the claims of realism. Commercial liberalism, they argued, would create patterns of economic interdependence that would reduce the incentives for conflict. Subsequent theorists elaborated Wilsonian principles to argue from historical studies that "constitutionally secure liberal states have yet to engage in war with one another."[23] In addition to the "theory of the democratic peace," liberals expounded the possibility of progress in international relations, modifying the anarchy of the international system through the rule of law. As the realist Kissinger concluded tartly at the end of the century:

> Woodrow Wilson was the embodiment of the tradition of American exceptionalism, and originated what would become the dominant intellectual school of American foreign policy. . . . Wilson grasped the mainsprings of American motivation, perhaps the principal one being that America simply did not see itself as a nation like any other. It lacked both the theoretical and the practical basis for the European-style diplomacy of constant adjustment of the nuances of power from a posture of moral neutrality for the sole purpose of preserving an ever-shifting balance. . . . Wilson . . . tapped his people's emotions with arguments that were as morally elevated as they were largely incomprehensible to foreign leaders.[24]

THE CHALLENGE TO
JAPANESE CONSERVATIVE ORTHODOXY

Throughout its modern history Japan has had to contend with the hegemony of Western liberal values and institutions. For Japan's dominant conservative elite this was an unhappy reality. The Japanese had no legacy of transcendental and universal values through which to understand international liberalism. The very idea that a nation must be governed by abstract principles that are equally applicable to all societies was scarcely credible. Nevertheless, these values and institutions were backed by greater power than Japan could muster. They were also backed by a claim of universal validity. They applied to all people—including the Japanese. The belief that all societies were subject to the same laws of development was a product of the European Enlightenment. The values of U.S. civilization, the child of the Enlightenment, were deeply at odds with Japanese conservative orthodoxy. They raised divisive and disruptive issues at the very heart of modern Japanese life with which the nation has struggled for the past century and a half. No other country has seen its national life so ceaselessly buffeted, so thrown into incessant turmoil, by the challenge of American liberal values as has Japan. Many peoples have had to submit to the judgment of these values, but none has suffered the harshness and severity of this judgment so much as the Japanese. Japan is a nation that has never on its own achieved a democratic revolution, and the values of international liberalism were utterly at odds with Japanese experience.

Japanese liberals, Christians, socialists, Marxists, and pacifists have been attracted to the Enlightenment. Many Japanese have been internally divided over Enlightenment values, and frequently, Japanese youth drawn to its ideals later abandon them in favor of nationalism. But Japanese nationalists have opposed its claims, and the belief that universal values should guide Japan has confronted a powerful conservative orthodoxy. The values of the Enlightenment have not occupied the mainstream of Japanese political life.

When the Western powers imposed the unequal treaties to open the country in the mid-nineteenth century, requiring the adoption of Western law, constitutional practices, and diplomatic procedures, the Japanese could accept these requirements because they recognized the realist principles that controlled the imperialist system. But the American approach to regional order in the twentieth century, with its assertion of liberal norms and institutions, was anathema to the conservative values that came out of the Meiji Restoration and to the ambitions of a rising power. To the Japanese leaders, the assertion of self-determination, territorial integrity, and the Open Door as principles of universal validity flew in the face of reality when applied to a weak and chaotic Asia.

With their realist traditions of respect for power, the Japanese elite regarded Wilsonian idealism with a combination of skepticism and cynicism. Such liberal norms were wholly at odds with the values of social solidarity embedded in Japanese culture and in the emperor system that constituted the modern Japanese state. As they contended with these values, a generation of Japanese conservative thinkers grew more skeptical. The eminent Japanese philosopher Watsuji Tetsurō, analyzing U.S. civilization at the time of the Pacific War, found its traits of individualism, utilitarianism, and legalistic moralism to be the very opposite—a kind of negative identity—of the values that Japanese culture honored. "The essence of Watsuji's dislike," Robert Bellah wrote, is the *Gesellschaft* (*rieki shakai*) nature of Anglo-American society. It lacks organic unity. It exalts abstract mechanical ideals of which science is the type. It claims that the individual should be independent of social groups. It establishes society in terms of abstract legal rights rather than warm particularistic relationships. It relates to nature through mechanical manipulation rather than intuitive sympathy. In a word, it divides and separates where Japanese culture seeks to unite and fuse.[25]

The universalism of American norms implied an intolerance of cultural diversity and a belief that progress was unilinear, that the success of developing societies could be measured by their convergence with U.S. institutions of law, government, and society.

Again and again through the twentieth century Japan was confronted with American insistence on the univeralism of its values. It was the essence of the last diplomatic notes exchanged between the two governments before Pearl Harbor. It was the essence of the American reforms imposed during the postwar Occupation. It was the essence of American criticism during the trade frictions of the 1970s and 1980s. And it is the essence of Americans' impatient advice to contemporary Japan to reform its economic and political institutions in the post–Cold War period.

Wilson's determination to establish a new regional order founded on norms and institutions so fundamentally at odds with Japanese values was profoundly disturbing. Japan was entering a bewildering new world environment. In some ways, it was more jarring and disorienting an experience than the entrance into the imperialist system had been at the beginning of the modern period. American views of international relations had profound implications for Asia. Japanese leaders had no ideals or categories of thought to prepare them to support such views. The mores of the imperialist system had been readily grasped by the former samurai leaders of the Meiji government, but their successors were on thoroughly unfamiliar terrain when confronted by Wilson's assertion that national interest and security should be entrusted to a new international institution. With their deeply embedded realist principles, the Japanese were hard-pressed to accept, much less to understand, the idealism that underlay the new rules. Having striven to accommodate their policies and institutions to the imperialist system, they were deeply perturbed by the abrupt changes in the system that Wilson advocated.

ADAPTING TO THE TIMES

To the Japanese leaders, the impending change in the international order seemed designed to maintain the international status quo and therefore bound to complicate the achievement of Japanese ambitions. Nonetheless, Japan was determined not to be left isolated and out of step with the changing framework of international politics. The Meiji paradigm of adapting to the external environment as it went through fundamental changes came into play. This change in their international environment was bound to affect not only Japan's international position, but Japan's domestic institutional structure as well. After all, the Meiji political structure had been the product of an adaptation to international norms. Those institutions were not the spontaneous creation of Meiji society. Rather, they had drawn their inspiration from Western practices and models. Therefore, it should come as no surprise that the Japanese would be sensitive to new trends in the prevailing values and norms of the advanced societies.

In the popular media serving an emergent professional middle class, the new norms in international society were widely discussed. Taisho, the name given to the reign of the emperor who succeeded Meiji from 1912 to 1926, became known for its susceptibility to democratic influences in politics and society. Two-party politics, responsible party cabinets, the extension of civic rights to larger numbers of citizens, liberal reform movements, and democratic political philosophies emerged in this era. The sensitivity to the changing norms in international society was most strongly expressed outside of government by liberal intellectuals who wished to see the reform of the political system. Their strongest argument for political reforms was that they were an inevitable force that could not be resisted. They typically argued for liberal political reform less from belief in the intrinsic worth of democratic principles than from the view that these principles constituted the new world trend, the emerging norms of international society. Adherence to these norms would confer legitimacy on Japanese institutions.

The foremost advocate of "Taisho democracy" in the expanding media, Yoshino Sakuzō, a professor of law at Tokyo Imperial University, wrote in the influential magazine *Chūō Kōron* that the world had entered upon a new stage of world history, and it would not do for Japan to go against the trends (*sekai no taisei*).[26] Tetsuo Najita summarized Yoshino's view: "Everywhere, without reference to particular history or racial makeup, all societies had begun to coalesce into a broad and unified movement toward political democracy. . . . This was an irresistible spirit which the ruling class in Japan could not prevent. . . . The 'new politician' of Taisho, therefore, must be one who perceived the inevitable trend and acted accordingly in the processes of government."[27] Yoshino argued for promotion of women's rights as well, because equality for women had become a "natural world trend."[28] The argument was not based on the intrinsic value of popular rights, but on the pragmatic view that the flow of history was moving in this direction and it was expedient to move with the tide. Throughout its history, Yoshino argued, Japan had always been able to adapt to the practices of the most advanced nations in the world.

In 1914, Maruyama Kanji, a leading exponent of domestic liberal reforms, wrote: "The trend of the times demands a new politics, and they demand new men. . . . To resist is like trying to make water run up hill. By new politics, I mean a politics that does not exclude Japan from the rest of the world; by new men, I mean those who will move with the currents in the world. The road the Taisho era must travel cannot veer from the trend toward democracy."[29]

The effect of the external environment on domestic politics in the Taisho period was most markedly evident in the new practice of appointing the head of one of the political parties in the Diet as prime minister. This was not constitutionally required but reflected the acknowledgment by the elder statesmen, who advised the emperor in the selection of the prime minister, of prevailing international practice. In 1918, Hara Kei, the brilliant leader of the Seiyūkai, the strongest party in the Diet, was chosen as the first party prime minister. After his appointment, Hara acknowledged the "new world trends" represented by Wilsonianism and said it was inevitable that Japan should move in accord with them.

Hara had always expressed this fundamental faith in adaptability and pragmatism as a key to political success. As a youthful journalist, he had written in 1881: "Nothing is more conducive of difficulties than not knowing the trend of the times [*jisei*]; nothing is more essential for governance than gauging the *jisei*. . . . To be in a position of power and not know which way the tide is running is very dangerous." After entering the cabinet in 1904, he repeated the wisdom of his younger days: "The greatest need of administration is to be in accord with the forces of nature [*shizen no sūsei*] and to take appropriate measures."[30] Hara had visited the United States in 1908 and had come away convinced of its latent influence in world affairs. As Akira Iriye wrote, "He vowed that an understanding with the United States would be a basic prerogative for Japanese policy. This was because America represented the inevitable trend in human affairs; to him it seemed obvious that the vitality of American people, nurtured by democratic institutions, indicated the wave of the future."[31]

As prime minister, convinced that Japan must now align itself with the historic forces at work in international society, Hara was disposed to overcome the isolation from the victorious powers that Japan's wartime unilateralism had provoked. For him, Japan's interests were served by working with the United States. He was accordingly persuaded that support of the proposed League of Nations was necessary to demonstrate Japan's willingness to cooperate with the Allies. Hara characteristically adopted a wait-and-see pragmatism and advocated adapting to the new conditions as they came to be understood. In a time of stunning transformation in international politics, this characteristic pattern of behavior, the willingness to accept the external environment as a given to which Japan must adapt, seemed appropriate and was expressed by many Japanese leaders, especially in the Foreign Ministry.

A growing sense of the impending revolution in the international system led to the establishment by imperial rescript of the Advisory Council on Foreign Relations (Rinji Gaikō Chōsa Iinkai) on June 5, 1917. This extraordinary resort to a suprapartisan deliberative body was testimony to the emphasis the leadership placed on the prospect of drastic global changes. The council lasted through four cabinets—until the end of the Washington Conference in 1922, which completed the revolution of the regional system.

Ill-prepared to discuss a broad range of issues having to do primarily with Europe, the large Japanese delegation to the peace conference in 1919 at Versailles maintained a low profile. The official leader of the delegation, the elder statesman Saionji Kinmochi, was so reclusive as to encourage rumors that he might not be present. The media referred to Japan as a "silent partner." Instructed to preserve Japan's wartime gains, especially the Shandong concessions, the delegation was left to "follow the general trends of the conference" (*kaigi no taisei o jun'o suru*) on other issues. With regard to the most momentous topic at the conference, the League of Nations, the instructions from the foreign minister were still more cautious: "Postpone as long as you can any definite agreement on a draft; simply receive the draft proposals, but make establishment of the organization a matter for each country to study. Further, put off discussion of a definite draft until some future time, after the matter has been carefully considered."[32]

Makino Shinken perhaps best reflected the council's understanding that Japan must face up to a new order. De facto head of the delegation, Makino commanded respect because of his ties to the founding of the modern state. He was the second son of the early Meiji leader Ōkubo Toshimichi, and he was strongly inclined toward the cautious and accommodative approach that the Meiji oligarchs had adopted toward the international structure. The new order might be bewildering; nevertheless, he believed, Japan had no choice but to align or face isolation. Only through accommodating the new trends, Makino thought, could Japan successfully pursue its interests. He said, "Today it is a worldwide trend to honor pacifism and reject oppression. Everywhere in the world the so-called Americanism is advanced, and conditions have definitely altered from the days of the old diplomacy." Before leaving for Versailles, he told his colleagues on the council that Japan must adapt to the new principles of "fair play, justice, and humanitarianism."[33]

In concrete terms, these principles meant that Japan had to fundamentally revise its policies on China. Cooperation with the United States meant accepting the principle of economic interdependence and abandoning the principles of particularistic pursuit of political advantage. Makino stunned his colleagues by saying this might mean abolition of extraterritoriality in China, withdrawal of foreign troops, and even the return of Boxer indemnity monies. Most members of the council were incredulous. "Are you saying," the future prime minister, Inukai Tsuyoshi, asked, "that apart from economic relations Japan should desist from [territorial] expansionism?"[34] The army general Terauchi Masatake, who had just left the prime ministership, was unmistakably hostile. He countered that Japan had a unique relationship with China and therefore must follow its own principles, which meant an obligation to "guide" that struggling state.[35] Others also doubted that following the American lead would serve Japanese interests. Wilson's proposed League of Nations might be used to impede Japan's legitimate expansion. Makino's response to these objections did not assert his own commitment to Wilsonian principles but rather his belief that they constituted an irresistible force in world affairs.

Among the Japanese leaders, there were few, if any, genuine Wilsonians. Instead, Japan's "internationalists" followed in the diplomatic tradition established by the Meiji leaders, who consistently had held that Japan's interests were best pursued by circumspect policies and Realpolitik that adapted to the prevailing international mores. Particularly among Japan's professional diplomats in the Foreign Ministry, graduates of the Tokyo Imperial

University and widely traveled, there was a disposition to pursue Japan's interests through collaboration with the powers. It was better to work within the system, to use it wherever possible to achieve Japan's purposes, than to resist it. The shrewd young diplomat Yoshida Shigeru, who as post–World War II prime minister was to become Japan's most brilliant politician of the modern era, later described himself as a member of the "clique that makes use of Britain and the United States" (*EiBei ryō ha*).[36] This adaptive approach reveals how conscious Japan's professional diplomats were of Japan's isolation at the end of the war.

Not only was the West suspicious and resentful of Japan's wartime expansionism, Japan was isolated in another direction as well. The new revolutionary government of the Soviet Union repudiated the international agreements negotiated under the old tsarist regime after the Russo-Japanese War. In addition, anti-imperialist nationalist student movements inspired by Wilsonian rhetoric were gathering strength in Korea and China and burst forth in the March first uprising in Seoul and the May fourth uprising in China.

In light of all these uncertainties, the Foreign Ministry was bent on overcoming Japan's isolation. The ministry instructed the Japanese delegation to Versailles to act "in accordance with general world trends" on such issues as secret diplomacy, freedom of the seas, and disarmament. In the Foreign Ministry, the perspective was considerably broader than among Yamagata's protégés in the army. On the eve of the Versailles conference, Komura Kin'ichi, European section chief of the ministry's Political Affairs Bureau and son of the famous foreign minister Komura Jutarō, drew up a memorandum describing the profound changes occurring in the international order. While the Japanese were riveted to Shandong, Siberia, and the Pacific Islands, where Japan had expanded through unilateral military expansion, unstoppable world trends that favored democratic and liberal developments had emerged and undermined the legitimacy of Japan's pursuits. To accommodate these trends, Japan would have to reform its China diplomacy by withdrawing its troops and abandoning its pursuit of spheres of influence.[37]

JAPAN AT VERSAILLES: THE RACIAL EQUALITY CLAUSE

Versailles placed Japanese leaders in a particularly difficult situation. Representing the only non-Western nation among the five great powers, the Japanese delegation was uneasy with the proposed new order. They were ill at ease in a setting of Western leaders who sometimes treated them as strange intruders. French Prime Minister Georges Clemenceau was heard to remark to his foreign minister during one long meeting, "To think that there are blonde women in the world; and we stay closed up here with these Japanese, who are so ugly." Finding themselves at the summit of power in the Western world, the Japanese delegates, according to Wilson's foreign policy adviser, Colonel E. H. House, were "silent, unemotional, watchful."[38]

Although Japan wanted to avoid isolation and was therefore strongly disposed to adjust to the changing tides, its delegation did go to Versailles with several objectives. Japan wanted to retain possession of the German concession in Shandong as well as the German islands north of the equator that they had seized at the outbreak of the war in 1914. Japan also had one original proposal that it cherished for the new international order. This was what came to be called the "racial equality clause" as a way of reassuring Japanese of their status in the world. In the Japanese government's Advisory Council on Foreign Relations, opinion on the League concept was divided and skeptical, but consensus did emerge that the delegation should "so far as the circumstances allow make efforts to secure suitable guarantees against the disadvantages to Japan which would arise . . . out of racial prejudice."[39]

Japan's self-image as one of the world's five great powers was constantly undermined by the treatment of Japanese immigrants as second-class citizens in Anglo-Saxon countries. With such continuing treatment of their nationals, the Japanese understandably felt insecure about a new international organization established under U.S. leadership. Would the Japanese be accorded equal treatment with the other powers? Although Japan was a founding member of the League of Nations, occupying one of the five permanent seats on its council, it was the only one not to have submitted a draft proposal for its organization. Japan sought the permanent council seat for the status it accorded, but there was little expectation that the League would serve Japan's interests. The Japanese remained insecure, keenly sensitive to the fact that despite Japan's standing as one of the great powers, they were in a Western-made international system.

The Japanese delegation proposed a racial equality clause for inclusion in the League of Nations Covenant that would state that members of the League would accord to "all alien nationals of states, members of the League, equal and just treatment in every respect making no distinction, either in law or in fact, on account of their race or nationality." Was this proposal an exception to Japan's characteristic pattern of accepting the norms and rules of the international system and adapting to them? Was Japan in this high-profile moment at Versailles proposing a revolutionary new norm of universal applicability, which, though rejected, later was included in the United Nations Charter? It has often been interpreted this way.

The Japanese intention, however, was not, as it is usually interpreted, to assert a universal principle or even a norm to govern the new order, except insofar as it applied to the relations among the recognized powers. Rather, it was an aspiration to assure Japan of its own great-power status in the new world organization. In addition, the proposal was in part designed to placate domestic opposition to Japanese support of the League. The most careful student of this proposal, the historian Naoko Shimazu, wrote, "The principle of racial equality, as we conceive of it today in the universalist sense, was not even the issue at stake."[40] Instead, the Japanese sought a declaration that Japan, as the one nonwhite great power, would be treated without discrimination. Shimazu argued,

> They were themselves also guilty of a racially discriminatory attitude towards Chinese and Koreans. It was thus a considerable misconception on the part of those at the Paris Peace Conference that the Japanese proposal came to be known as the racial equality proposal, since its universalist label did not at all reflect its original intention. The most important point . . . is that the original demand formulated by the Japanese government referred specifically to Japanese nationals.[41]

Shimazu bluntly concluded that "the Japanese sought to gain the status of honorary whites and nothing more."[42]

Wilson and Colonel House were initially sympathetic to the proposal. House especially was consistently disposed to understand Japan's aspirations as a rising power. Writing to Wilson before Versailles, he observed the importance of accommodating Japanese interests if Japan was to be successfully drawn into accepting the new order: "We cannot meet Japan in her desire as to land and immigration, and unless we make some concessions in regard to her sphere of influence in the East, trouble is sure sooner or later to come. Japan is barred from all the undeveloped places of the earth, and if her influence in the East is not recognized as in some degree superior to that of the Western powers, there will be a reckoning."[43]

Wilson initially offered to help in drafting the racial equality proposal for inclusion as an amendment to his religious freedom article in the covenant.

Sensitivity to the immigration issue, most overtly in Australia, but also in Canada and the United States, caused immediate difficulties for the proposal. Australian Prime Minister Billy Hughes, who was up for reelection and defending a "white Australia" policy, expressed strong opposition to it, arguing that it could justify unrestricted Japanese immigration. Because the British delegation gave the Dominions control over issues relating to immigration, the British opposed the article.

Wilson's priority was the establishment of the League, and he believed that Britain and the United States must be in stride to make the League and the new international order a success. "We, Anglo-Saxons," he observed:

> have our peculiar contribution to make towards the good of humanity in accordance with our special talents. The League of Nations will, I confidently hope, be dominated by us Anglo-Saxons; it will be for the unquestionable benefit of the world. The discharge of our duties in the maintenance of peace and as a just mediatory in international disputes will redound to our lasting prestige. But it is of paramount importance that we Anglo-Saxons succeed in keeping in step with one another.[44]

Believing that strong British support for the League was essential and fearing that British isolation on the immigration issue would weaken its support of the League, Wilson in the end declined to support the Japanese proposal.

Makino, the chief architect of the proposal, sought a compromise that would shift its wording from ensuring "equality of races" to "endorsement of the principle of the equality of nations and just treatment of their nationals." Reluctant to permit controversy that would jeopardize the smooth establishment of the League, the Anglo-American powers withheld their support. In the voting of the committee set up to draft the covenant, Wilson, who was chairing the committee, insisted on unanimity, and when Britain, the United States, Portugal, Poland, and Romania abstained, the proposal died.

Again assigning priority to the success of the League, Wilson, fearing that Japan might not join the League due to rejection of the proposed clause, gave in to the Japanese insistence on keeping Shandong, even though it was a glaring contradiction of his declared principles of anti-imperialism for the new order. Likewise, Japan was permitted to keep the former German-held islands north of the equator, under the guise of the creation of "League mandates."

The rejection of the Japanese proposal is frequently cited as a source of Japanese disaffection from the international order created by Wilson and the Americans. That it was. Along with other notorious examples of discrimination against Japanese immigrants, it served as a painful reminder to the Japanese of their failure to gain social acceptance in the new order. Ignoring their own unequal treatment of other Asians, the Japanese nursed bitter grievance over the apparent hypocrisy of Wilsonian idealism. In most accounts of the Paris Peace Conference, the defeat of the racial equality clause receives only passing attention. But for many Japanese it became the prism through which they viewed the new order, and it assumed symbolic importance in justifying Japan's subsequent attack on that order. In 1946, the Showa emperor, Hirohito, cited it first in a document he wrote explaining the causes of the Pacific War: "If we ask the reason for this war, it lies in the contents of the peace treaty signed at the end of the First World War. The racial equality proposal demanded by Japan was not accepted by the powers. The discriminatory sentiment between the white and the yellow remains as always. And the rejection of immigrants in California. These were enough to anger the Japanese people."[45]

There was an inherent contradiction in the fact that Japan was espousing racial equality while maintaining domination over other Asians. But it was probably no greater contradiction than it was for those Western colonial powers who embraced the principle of self-determination while clinging to their empires. For the Japanese, "racial equality" meant "great power equality."[46] The rejection signaled failure to achieve a principal goal that drove modern Japan, that is, the status of a first-rank country.

The Versailles Conference left a residue of alienation over the treatment that Japan had received, and dissension over Japanese policies grew among younger Japanese, especially among a striking number of the future generation of Japanese leaders. At Versailles there were in the delegation future prime ministers and foreign ministers who were deeply resentful of the outcome. They believed that their elders' unpreparedness and deference to the other powers had weakened Japan's status and that a broad reform of the Foreign Ministry bureaucracy was essential.[47] More portentous in its implications for the future, they recoiled from the disposition to accept Wilsonianism as the inevitable trend of the future. The shrewd young Yoshida Shigeru observed that despite "the pious experiment" Wilson had proposed, power politics in the end carried the day. It did not escape his notice, as John Dower put it, that "imperialism had been condemned in principle, but colonial territories other than those of a defeated Germany continued to exist."[48]

THE WASHINGTON TREATY SYSTEM

Wilson's vision of a comprehensive peace settlement to usher in a new international order was shattered by the U.S. Senate's rejection of the Versailles Treaty and of U.S. membership in the League. Despite this failure, Wilsonian principles survived in a postwar U.S. initiative to establish a new regional order in Asia. Two years after Versailles, the United States convened the Washington Conference of 1921–1922 to provide a new set of principles and institutions to guide the workings of the international system in East Asia. Designed to replace the imperialist order, the Washington Treaty System embodied America's evolving policies in the region. This system provided the guidelines for a new order that prevailed for the decade of the 1920s.

Since the turn of the century, U.S. policy in the region had taken shape under successive administrations in the form of several broad principles that would define its goals in East Asia for the remainder of the century. First, the United States would preserve free-trade patterns in the region so that it would be open to U.S. trade and investment, the principles of "the Open Door" as first enunciated by Secretary of State John Hay. Second, in accordance with the views of Theodore Roosevelt, the United States would maintain a stable balance of power in which no other country would become so strong as to dominate the region. And third, in the spirit of Wilsonian ideals of self-determination, the United States would promote the evolution of democratic politics as the surest way to preserve a peaceful region.

The United States sought to stabilize the international order in East Asia according to these broad principles and thus regarded Japanese policies as a challenge to all three. Although they did not label it as such, the stability the Americans sought entailed a containment policy to forestall further Japanese expansion in Northeast Asia. Japan's rising military power since the Russo-Japanese War, along with Japanese unilateralism during World War I, had provoked U.S. distrust of Japanese power and purpose. Although there had been a change of administrations, and Wilson had been repudiated by the refusal of the U.S. Senate to join the League, Americans of both parties were determined to restrain Japanese expansion. The new Warren G. Harding administration was, if anything, more determined than Wilson to curb Japanese power. Republicans, no less than Democrats, were hostile to Japanese ambitions. The chairman of the Senate Foreign

Relations Committee, Henry Cabot Lodge, characterized Japan's success in hanging on to Shandong as "one of the blackest things in the history of diplomacy" and added that Japan represented "the coming danger of the world."[49]

After Versailles, the most immediate and pressing issue of U.S.-Japan rivalry in the Pacific was an emergent naval arms race. Distrust of Japanese intentions pervaded U.S. naval circles. In 1910, Admiral Alfred T. Mahan, whose 1890 book *The Influence of Sea Power on History* had attracted as much attention in Japan as in the United States, identified Japan as "the problem state of Asia." U.S. naval planners were concerned over the weakness and vulnerability of the U.S. position in Asia. In the face of Japan's growing power, the United States needed a fleet strong enough to prevail over the Japanese Navy in the western Pacific. Defeating the Japanese battle fleet would depend upon greatly strengthening bases and defenses in Hawaii, Guam, and the Philippines. U.S. naval planners were especially conscious of the vulnerability of the Philippines, 7,000 miles from the West Coast of the United States and almost 5,000 miles from Hawaii.[50]

During the Great War, the United States had begun an ambitious naval building program designed to bring it preeminence. The program provoked the suspicion of Japan (as well as Britain) and led to the Diet's approval of the Imperial Navy's cherished but immensely costly "eight-eight fleet plan," that is, the plan to construct eight dreadnought battleships and eight modern armored cruisers. These plans augured a dangerous, economically draining arms race among the world's three greatest naval powers. For Japanese naval planners, the object was mastery in the western Pacific. By 1920 in Britain, Japan, and the United States, there was a growing inclination to find ways to stave off a ruinous arms race. The new secretary of state, Charles Evans Hughes, called for a conference in Washington to deal with the issues raised by the incipient U.S.-Japan rivalry. Stability required linking a political arrangement with a naval settlement.

Determined to resolve the naval issue, Hughes opened the Washington Conference with a surprise call for a dramatic and comprehensive naval arms limitation agreement. He sought to initiate what Robert Kaufman called "the first extended effort to limit arms in the history of the United States."[51] Since the turn of the century, the Americans had grown interested in the concept of arms limitation and disarmament. Wilson included it among his Fourteen Points and in the League Covenant. The concept appealed to Hughes as a means to restrain Japan's naval power. Budgetary pressures in Congress were making continuation of the ambitious naval construction program problematic. Moreover, U.S. opinion was inclined to believe that an arms race could lead to conflict.[52] Hughes approached international affairs with characteristic American legalism and moralism. As Kaufman observed,

> He assumed that rationality would triumph in international affairs, that reasonable men could always agree to compromise, that nature guarantees progress. He also discounted the importance of power in international politics. As Hughes saw it, reason and enlightened self-interest, not force, ensured order. As Secretary of State, he would promote arbitration, conciliation, mediation, and the codification of international law in the expectation that these measures would contribute slowly but surely to the evolution of a harmonious order among individuals and nations.[53]

The Americans held that since their interests spanned the Atlantic as well as the Pacific, they were justified in having a substantially larger fleet than Japan. The British argued that since their interests remained global, they too must have a larger navy. In contrast, Japan's interests were regional and limited to the western Pacific. The Naval Arms Limitation Treaty would allow a 5:5:3:1.75:1.75 ratio in capital ships among the United States, Britain, Japan, France, and Italy, respectively. Limits on capital ships for Britain and the United States would be 525,000 tons, and for Japan 315,000 tons. In addition, Britain and the United States were permitted 135,000 tons for aircraft carrier construction and Japan 81,000 tons. To reassure Japan of its security in the western Pacific, the United States and Britain agreed not to fortify their possessions east of Singapore or west of Hawaii. In other words, the United States would not fortify the Philippines.

The old framework of international relations, in the American estimation, had not only failed to impede Japanese expansion, it had seemed to provide the opportunity for it. American impatience with the mores of the imperialist system had been growing since the turn of the century. Hughes was intent on ending the Anglo-Japanese Alliance, which was up for renewal. The Americans opposed the alliance because they believed the Japanese were using it as a cover for expansion. British Foreign Secretary Lord Curzon, in contrast, wanted to maintain the alliance in order "to keep a watch upon [Japan's] movements in China . . . and to exercise a moderating influence on her policy generally."[54] Within the British Foreign Ministry, however, the predominant view was that Britain could not restrain Japan alone and that therefore it was better to work with the Americans.

In the aftermath of the Twenty-One Demands of 1915, by which Japan sought to establish its domination over the weak Chinese government, British disillusionment with the alliance was rife. The British ambassador in Tokyo, Conyngham Greene, observed in 1916, "Today we have come to know that Japan—the real Japan—is a frankly opportunist, not to say, selfish, country, of very moderate importance compared with the giants of the Great War, but with a very exaggerated opinion of her role in the universe."[55] The following year he concluded that "the present hollow friendship cannot be continued and must in due course be resolved into some relation at once less intimate and more genuine; and that we might well try to bring in America on our side to redress the balance in the Far East."[56] The British therefore gave notice to the Japanese in the spring of 1921 that renewal of their alliance was unlikely. The prospect of isolation alarmed the Japanese cabinet on the eve of the Washington Conference. It began to look, as one Japanese delegate put it, like "an attempt to oppress the non-Anglo-Saxon races, especially the colored races, by the two English-speaking countries, Britain and the United States."[57]

In pressing for the termination of the Anglo-Japanese Alliance, the Americans wanted to make clear that the old imperialist order was passing. The alliance typified the particularistic agreements among the powers that needed to be replaced by universalist principles. In place of the alliances, secret understandings, and dependence on the balance of power, the Americans preferred an open declaration of principles that would be binding on all the powers. The upshot was collective agreement at the conference to replace earlier binational security agreements, specifically the Anglo-Japanese Alliance, with a new Four Power Treaty among Japan, the United States, Britain, and France stating simply that the powers would consult with each other should any threat arise to peace in the Pacific. It was, said one U.S. diplomat who helped to draw it up, "general and harmless."[58]

In addition to the arms race, the other critical issue to be dealt with was Japan's role on the continent and the future of a weak and disunited China. The new rules of the game with respect to the continent were spelled out in a Nine Power Treaty, which Secretary Hughes said was to be "a substitute for all prior statements and agreements" concerning China.[59] This treaty upheld equal commercial opportunity and committed the signatories to maintaining "the sovereignty, the independence, and the territorial integrity of China." This general framework of international agreement, rather than the particularistic, bilateral agreements that had been negotiated at China's expense during the imperialist order, would now govern the powers' activities in China. The new international system in East Asia would replace the old balance-of-power politics, and the bilateral agreements among the powers at China's expense, with a proclamation of the self-determination of peoples and the preservation of China's territorial integrity. The American Open Door policy was now given multilateral sanction. There would be no further dismemberment of a weak and divided China, and no attempt to take new advantage of its political weakness. The new order did not change the colonial status quo or the unequal treaties in China. Japan's positions in Korea and Manchuria were tacitly recognized, but there was to be no new territorial seizure. Political change was to be peaceful and evolutionary. Japan agreed to return the sovereignty of Shandong to China while retaining economic rights on the peninsula, and to withdraw its forces sent to the Russian Far East at the end of the war.

In contrast to the Versailles Treaty, the treaties negotiated at Washington passed the Senate with only a single negative vote. In the United States, there was a general sense of satisfaction and self-congratulation that the issues of East Asia had been successfully resolved and Japanese ambition contained. The young Franklin Roosevelt, who had served in the Wilson administration as assistant secretary of the navy, wrote in a 1923 magazine article that Japan and the United States "have not a single valid reason, and won't have as far as we can look ahead, for fighting each other."[60]

Such optimism, however, was misplaced. Within Japan there was a residue of bitterness and alienation. Japan's quest for status was unfulfilled in the view of too many Japanese leaders. When the U.S. Congress passed the Immigration Act of 1924, which in effect singled out the Japanese for no further immigration to the United States, it was one more reminder that Japan had not yet achieved the status that had been its goal since 1868. Secretary of State Hughes correctly warned Congress that if the bill was passed, "the Japanese . . . unquestionably would regard [it] as fixing a stigma upon them." In addition, he said, it "would largely undo the work of the Washington Conference."[61] Nonetheless, the bill passed both houses of Congress overwhelmingly. It undoubtedly fixed the impression among many Japanese leaders that the international system was not going to realize their national interests.

The Japanese were less concerned with the welfare of the migrants than they were with the implications for Japanese status and self-esteem. The Japanese, after all, had themselves never been hospitable to immigrants— and still are not. The point was rather how the Western powers and the Western people regarded Japan and the Japanese people. In the United

States and elsewhere in the West, this point was often overlooked or dismissed. Franklin Roosevelt believed that racial mixing was unhealthy and that restriction of Japanese immigration was morally justifiable so long as it was reciprocal. In his 1923 article, he wrote: "I do not believe that the American people now or in the future will insist upon the right or privilege of entry into an oriental country to such an extent as to threaten racial purity or to jeopardize the land-owning prerogatives of citizenship. I think I may sincerely claim for American public opinion an adherence to the Golden Rule."[62] It was certainly true that the Japanese did not want Americans migrating to Japan, intermarrying, buying land, and seeking citizenship. Nevertheless, Japanese resentment of the West's racial prejudice was filtered through their strong feelings of honor and status.

When Congress singled out the Japanese for exclusion, the infringement of Japanese honor was not only angrily denounced by nationalists, it was also deeply wounding and embittering to Japanese statesmen trying to promote bilateral relations. The industrialist Shibusawa Eiichi called the Immigration Act of 1924 a "scar on the national honor." Kaneko Kentarō, a Harvard graduate and friend of the Roosevelts, resigned as president of the America-Japan Society, regarding the act as "a great insult to Japanese national honor." Nitobe Inazō, a graduate of Johns Hopkins University, who was married to an American woman and who served as undersecretary-general of the League of Nations, resolved not to visit the United States unless the act was revised.[63]

Rising states present a special challenge to a system. If they are to be satisfied to remain in the system, it is necessary to accommodate their interests. As one writer observed, "The status quo powers must exhibit empathy, fairness, and a genuine concern not to offend the prestige and national honor of the rising power."[64] This the Anglo-American powers had not done. They failed to reach out to, much less to understand, this proud but highly vulnerable and insecure new power. The psychic wound inflicted at the time Japan entered the modern international system was repeatedly reopened by the experiences it had in the international system.

JAPANESE ACCOMMODATION: SHIDEHARA DIPLOMACY

Japan's postwar leaders strategically signaled their readiness to trim Japan's continental aspirations, accept the disappearance of the former structure of imperialist diplomacy, and participate in a redefinition of mutual relations among the powers. Japanese acceptance of the radically revised rules and norms was embodied in the policies of Shidehara Kijurō, a skilled and seasoned diplomat, "the first career diplomat recruited by means of civil service examination to serve as foreign minister."[65] He was ambassador to Washington during the conference and then served in five cabinets as foreign minister (1924–1927 and 1929–1931).

"Shidehara diplomacy" steered Japanese foreign policy toward the American vision of a liberal capitalist world order that emphasized economic interdependence. Shidehara believed that Japan's interests were best served by cooperation with the United States, which was Japan's largest source of capital and best trading customer, purchasing 40 percent of Japan's exports in the 1920s. He therefore held that Japan should abstain from aggressive pursuit of its political interests in China and instead concentrate on economic advancement in China in the framework of the international agreement. U.S. policymakers were pleased. Foreign Minister Uchida Kosai observed in familiar phrases that the trends of the world "demonstrate that nations are joining one another in abandoning exclusionist selfishness [and] promoting international cooperation."[66] Despite the political turmoil in China, Shidehara, mindful of the serious damage that Japanese unilateralism had done to Japanese foreign relations during World War I, resolved to adhere to a policy of nonintervention and instead develop Japan's economic interests. For the most part, he resisted intervention in Chinese domestic politics.

Although adapting to the international system was a fundamental, recurring characteristic of Japanese foreign policy, at the same time, inherent in this approach was always the presumption that Japan would adapt in ways that would serve its own interests. Shidehara favored adhering to the new American order, but he nonetheless was determined to aggressively pursue Japanese economic interests in China. Historians almost invariably portray him as a moderate, pro-Western liberal for his adherence to the Washington accords, but it should be emphasized that his reputation for moderation benefits from the contrast with the belligerent policies of the militarists who followed him in the 1930s.[67]

In actuality, Shidehara was aggressive and relentless, obdurate and uncompromising, in his pursuit of economic advantage at the expense of both the Chinese and cooperation with the powers. His assertiveness of economic self-interest in some respects prefigured the approach of Japan's post–World War II economic nationalism. Shidehara, who married into the Iwasaki family, which controlled the Mitsubishi interests, was determined to pursue Japan's commercial interests in an all-out way. A prominent military figure in the General Staff explained the policy in terms of an economic realism that would resonate with later policy in the 1960s. Japanese policy, he said in 1923, was to "substitute economic conquest for military invasion, financial influence for military control, and achieve our goals under the slogans of co-prosperity and co-existence, friendship, and cooperation."[68]

Shidehara's diplomacy, as summed up by the historian Hata Ikuhiko, adhered to three fundamental principles, which in hindsight appear "liberal," although they were carried out with considerable firmness in the pursuit of Japanese economic interest. First, Shidehara was committed to international collaboration with the League of Nations and the other newly established institutions. Second, he practiced an economic diplomacy that served Japanese industrial interests in China, confident that Japan could thus expand its power on the continent without resorting to excessive military and political pressure. Third, he adhered to a policy of nonintervention in China's domestic affairs, accepting the likelihood of a stable and unified nationalist government as compatible with Japanese economic interests.[69] These three fundamental principles amounted to acceptance of the new framework and characterized the major themes of Japanese foreign policy during the decade following the Washington Conference.

Shidehara's accommodation to the new principles of the Washington treaties did not mean that he was prepared to surrender Japanese interests. The recurrent Japanese pattern of accommodation to the forces of the international environment meant neither resisting nor surrendering to change. Shidehara would press Japanese concerns with the Chinese. In the face of Chinese demands for an increase in their minimal tariffs, which would help provide the revenue needed to strengthen the central government, Shidehara adhered to an uncompromising attitude. When the other powers were prepared to grant increases, and when his own staff supported the increases as a way of moderating Chinese behavior and increasing cooperation with the powers, Shidehara adopted a tough stance that blocked progress on even small steps toward greater Chinese tariff autonomy.[70] The success of the Washington System depended upon an evolutionary transformation of China, but Shidehara was unwilling to ease the imperialist fetters on China fast enough to keep pace with the rising tide of Chinese nationalist demands. One authority has summed up his approach by observing that "although in agreement in appearance with Great Power ambitions for a new national integrity in China, the foreign minister was forced to ignore or cover up the extent of Japanese designs for expansion."[71]

Shidehara's aggressive "economic diplomacy" might have stood the test of time if the times had been better. Indeed, in 1928 the Japanese military commanders of the Kwantung Army, the unit assigned to protect Japanese interests in Manchuria, attempted to create an uprising that would have provided the pretext for seizure of Manchuria. Extremist elements in the Kwantung Army arranged the bombing of the train carrying Chang Tso-lin, a Manchurian warlord. Their expectation that this act would create disorder and give a pretext for expanded control of Manchuria failed to materialize. Japanese leaders at this point were clearly not prepared to break from the pattern of cooperation with the powers prescribed by the Washington System. But three years later an entirely different attitude prevailed, in great part because of the changed international environment.

The Weakness of the Washington System

The Washington System was a house built on sand. It lasted through the favorable environment of the 1920s, but it could not weather the international turbulence that began to stir at the end of the decade. It failed to endure and enhance international security because the United States, after establishing the system, ultimately failed to support it, much less give it credible leadership. For an international system to endure it must be secured by the readiness to apply the force necessary to sustain it in the face of inevitable challenges. The Americans had created a system, but it was by no means clear that they would be willing to underwrite it with the determination to stay the course and the commitment necessary to uphold it if its fundamental principles were put in jeopardy.

The Washington System lacked stable footing from the outset. The agreements reached at Washington weakened American ability to enforce them, even had the United States possessed the will. There was, in short, an inherent contradiction in the Washington accords. "For the first time," Robert Kaufman aptly pointed out, "the United States had undertaken formal commitment by treaty to uphold the territorial integrity of China, just as the naval settlement made its enforcement out of the question." That is, the ratios of capital ships agreed upon, together with the pledge not to fortify their holdings east of Singapore and west of Hawaii, ensured that Japanese naval power was dominant in the western Pacific. As a consequence, the United States would find it difficult to threaten military intervention if Japan should further encroach on Chinese sovereignty. The United States would lack credibility to threaten military sanctions to influence Japanese actions in China. Whether Secretary Hughes was aware of the contradiction is unclear, but, as Kaufman wrote, "the Washington Conference created a dangerous gap between force and diplomacy."[72]

Most likely, Hughes "believed that the same factors that had brought Japan to conclude the Washington treaties could also be relied on to persuade it to keep them." That is, Japan had agreed to the naval treaty because its leaders "had become convinced they did not have the resources [necessary] in the face of a determined American opposition." But a decade later, this determined opposition was no longer credible. It was not even apparent. Ultimately, then, in the absence of U.S. ability and determination, "the stability of the settlement reached at Washington depended on the forbearance and success of the Japanese moderates. Equally, it depended on the political stability of China."[73]

Reflecting on the origins of World War II in Asia, Dean Acheson observed at the outset of his memoirs that one of his predecessors as secretary of state, Charles Evans Hughes, had made a "major mistake" at the Washington Conference, and the Japanese "were not long in taking advantage of it." By limiting naval armaments and agreeing to the prohibitions on island fortifications, the United States had ceded Japan military supremacy in the northwestern Pacific.[74]

The Washington System, as its first serious historians, Harold and Margaret Sprout, concluded, "fostered illusory hopes," failed to "nail down details [and] to police performance," and depended too much on "simple good will."[75] Founded on idealism, the Washington System had inadequate enforcement powers and instead depended on voluntary abstention from the use of force. It relied on the hopeful expectation that peaceful commercial competition would replace armed rivalries. As Akira Iriye observed, "It was more a state of mind than an explicit mechanism; it expressed the powers' willingness to cooperate with one another in maintaining stability in the region."[76]

The Americans were eager to assert principles growing out of their own domestic experience as universal, and assumed they could rely on the suasion of public opinion to enforce them, while making crystal clear that the United States would undertake no commitment to the use of force to underwrite them. In assuring the Senate that the Four Power Treaty would keep the peace in the Pacific, President Harding had said: "The four-power treaty contains no war commitment. . . . There is no commitment to armed force, no alliance, no written or moral obligation to join in defense." Accordingly, the Senate, in ratifying it, stipulated that it entailed no U.S. commitment to the use of force to maintain the peace. Signing the treaty, Harding announced that it achieved the protection of the Philippines and that any aggression in the Pacific would be deterred by "the odiousness of perfidy or infamy" that the court of world opinion would render.[77]

The belief that American principles were so incontrovertible as to be self-enforcing through the moral suasion of world opinion was evident in other cases, too, most notably in the Kellogg-Briand Pact signed at Paris in 1928, which called for renunciation of all war and for settlement of all disputes by peaceful means. The pact had its origins in a proposal by French Foreign Minister Aristide Briand that had stipulated that France and the United States never go to war against each other. The French hoped thereby to assure that, should France and Germany become embroiled in conflict, the Americans would not retaliate against France no matter how much the French infringed on U.S. neutral rights. Americans loved the notion, the more so as Secretary of State Frank Kellogg sought to inoculate it by widening it into a general harmless declaration that nearly every nation, including Japan, eventually signed. The United States quickly made clear, as did other countries, that the pact, which "had large popular support and was politically irresistible," had no practical consequences.[78] Supposing some other nation does break this treaty—Why should we interest ourselves in it? asked Senator Thomas J. Walsh from Montana. "There is not a bit of reason," replied the secretary of state.[79] Senator Carter Glass of Virginia announced to his colleagues that he intended to vote for the pact, and yet he said, "But I am not willing that anybody in Virginia shall think that I am simple enough to suppose that it is worth a postage stamp in the direction of accomplishing a permanent peace."[80]

CHAPTER SIX

JAPAN'S ABORTIVE NEW ORDER

The Washington System was a regional subsystem of a fragile and flawed post-1919 global order. Many of the same weaknesses that undermined the global system also eroded the foundations of order in East Asia. The economic devastation and territorial dislocation that European civilization had suffered in the war brought a halt to the integrative trends of the pre-1914 era, when the mobility of capital, goods, and people had reached hitherto unprecedented levels. When the United States emerged as the world's major power and the great creditor nation after World War I, it faced the task of providing leadership for the new order. But the Americans were unprepared to meet the obligations of great-power leadership. Neither in security nor in economic policy were they willing to underwrite the new order that they had proclaimed. Rather, disillusioned with their experience of international politics, Americans retreated from the high ideals Wilson had set for his nation's world role.

There were other flaws in the post-1919 global system. The Soviet Union refused to enter into the international order, instead offering an ideology radically at odds with its prevailing norms. German resentment of the postwar settlement was palpable. The order was inherently unstable. The Great Depression opened fissures in international society, and this, along with economic blocs and a trend toward autarky, destroyed the hopes of making progress in improving the relations among nations. As Robert Gilpin wrote:

> With no one to enforce the rules and manage the system states resorted to nationalistic "beggar-my-neighbor policies" and economic order broke

down. The social purposes and national interests of the Great Powers had changed, and their economic policies had become increasingly divergent as a result of both domestic and international developments. Domestic welfare goals and national rivalries became more important than international norms; this made cooperation impossible.[1]

By the end of the 1920s, the cooperative framework of the Washington System had severely deteriorated.

For an international system to be stable and enduring, the most powerful states must be satisfied with the existing territorial, political, and economic framework. They must be committed to upholding the status quo, particularly its governing institutions and norms, through their prestige and their willingness to use force to preserve it. As the distribution of power changes among the major states, the legitimacy of the rules and institutions must continue to be widely accepted. Legitimacy implies, as Kissinger observed with regard to the Concert of Europe, "the acceptance of the framework of the international order by all the major powers, at least to the extent that no state is so dissatisfied that, like Germany after the Treaty of Versailles, it expresses its dissatisfaction in a revolutionary foreign policy."[2]

Like all new orders, the Washington System involved great-power transitions. British influence in East Asia was in relative decline; U.S. world power was emergent; and Japan was a rapidly rising state in the region. Rising powers test the stability and equilibrium of a system. As they become stronger and richer, they expect to exercise a greater influence commensurate with their new capabilities. If this is denied them, if they are not accommodated, they may turn revisionist. They may be tempted by opportunities offered them where obstacles are surmountable to expand their access to new territories or new sources of raw materials or markets or the lure of intangible gains in prestige, leadership, and security. Depending on many factors, including the degree of their alienation, the nature of their domestic politics, and the willingness and skill of the other powers to cope with this dissatisfaction, the rising power may be prepared to seek the overthrow of the existing system. In the 1930s, Japan reached this point. Japanese Foreign Minister Hirota Kōki observed in the Diet, on February 22, 1934, that Japan would undertake responsibility for creating a new regional order. "The path of a rising nation," he said, "is always strewn with problems. . . . Japan, serving as the only cornerstone for the edifice of peace in East Asia, bears the entire burden of its responsibilities."[3]

Japanese revisionism might never have seen the light of day had the framework of international order not been so fragile. After all, it was a minority sentiment in the aftermath of the Washington Conference, when the dominant Japanese opinion was that its interests could be pursued within the newly established order. Not only did the Great Depression erode the propositions upon which order had been established, the Anglo-American powers that had created the system undermined it—first, by abandoning its liberal tenets in favor of protectionist measures; second, by retreating behind regional blocs; and third, by signaling their unwillingness to commit the resources necessary to enforce the Washington System when Japan threatened to flout its principles.

Japan's ill-fated breakout from the Washington System was the outcome of many converging developments at the beginning of the 1930s. There was, first of all, the rise of Chinese nationalism and its dangerous implications for Japanese interests on the continent. With the Nationalist campaign to unify China and revise the unequal treaties, Japan faced the possibility that it might be compelled to retreat from the position it had achieved on the continent over the previous two generations. Second, the gradual deterioration of the Japanese economy during the 1920s accelerated into the ruinous effects of the Great Depression, which intensified the tensions of a society that had been driven to achieve military and industrial power more rapidly than any other society in history. Third, the loss of coherence in the Japanese political system, the lack of a strong center, helped to remove the cautious realism that had hitherto characterized Japanese political leadership in its dealings with the other great powers. It left political leadership incapable of managing the rising nationalism and the conspiracies of right-wing activists.

Fundamentally, however, it was the inherent weakness of the Washington System itself, the breakdown of order and the growing anarchy within the system, that opened the way for the Japanese leadership to break with it. Wilson had intended to replace the balance-of-power politics of imperialism with a liberal order, but the vestiges of the old imperialist system were everywhere present. The British empire was still in place, the Americans were still in the Philippines, and the French and the Dutch, along with the Japanese, clung to their holdings. In spite of the Nine Power Treaty's intoning of the principles of self-determination and territorial integrity, imperialism was still alive. Treaty ports, tariff control, and extraterritoriality continued in China. Japan's conservative leaders had always been skeptical of the claims of liberalism to serve as a basis of international order. As the weakness of the Anglo-American commitment to it became apparent, Japan's leaders could hardly be expected to resist a return to the principles and practices with which they were most comfortable.

ORIGINS OF JAPANESE REVISIONISM

In creating the Washington System, the Americans wished to roll back Japan's wartime gains and stabilize the status quo. The system provoked a breakdown in the broad consensus among the Japanese policy elite about foreign policy aims that had lasted for the two generations that Japan had been part of the international system. In short, it compelled Japanese elite policymakers to choose between accommodation to a transformed international system now heavily influenced by U.S. interests and values, on the one hand, and resistance to this new status quo, on the other. A fundamental division arose over definitions of Japan's goals and interests and over the assessment of the capabilities of Japanese power. Both the accommodationist and the revisionist views lay within the Japanese realist tradition. The former was a defensive realism, content with the security provided by the Washington System and the belief that only by working within it could Japanese interests be secured. The latter, however, saw the system as stacked against Japan's legitimate aspirations and as compromising its security. In a sense, it was not a disagreement over whether Japan should be satisfied or dissatisfied with the existing distribution of international spoils so much as it was a disagreement over whether Japan had the capacity to alter the status quo in Japan's favor.

In the 1920s, Japanese foreign policy accepted the international framework. So long as the new system appeared stable and was upheld by the United States and Britain, most of the Japanese leaders of that decade were disposed to move with the trends and accommodate to the system's norms and loosely written rules. They were alarmed by the hostility that Japanese unilateralism had aroused in the Anglo-American powers. Japan had been further isolated during the Great War as a result of the new Soviet regime's repudiation of treaties with Japan previously negotiated by the tsarist government. Cooperation with the Anglo-American powers therefore was desirable in that it positioned Japan with the international forces resisting Soviet communism. The Washington System offered sufficient opportunity to pursue Japan's interests within its framework. The accommodationists believed the system adequately protected Japanese security while still giving them room to pursue Japan's national interest. They felt cooperation with the Western powers was compatible with the expansion of Japanese economic interests in China.

Although proponents of the mainstream accommodationist view believed that Japan had received important concessions in the Washington Conference, a significant segment of the Japanese leadership remained unpersuaded. Within Japan there was a latent opposition to the Washington System among these revisionists, who felt Japan should press for changes in the international system to serve its growing power and prestige. They were deeply alienated by the limits and restrictions that the new order put upon Japan and felt Japan had a deep and implacable grievance against the United States and Britain, powers that had come earlier on the international scene and acquired their imperial domains but who now denied Japan its empire in East Asia. They were determined to challenge the status quo and revise the framework set in place at Washington.

In the face of the changes in Japan's external environment in the 1920s, it was not surprising that this latent opposition gained strength in its advocacy of a foreign policy change that would have Japan press its advantage in East Asia, seek to control and shape its external environment, and attempt to restructure the system in accordance with its own security and economic interests. The most influential Japanese ideologue opposing the Washington System and advocating a change in the interwar period was Konoe Fumimaro. His views and leadership mirror the rise of revisionism. Of noble lineage, he cut an imposing figure in Japanese politics, rising to serve as prime minister through most of the four years leading up to Pearl Harbor. It was during his term that Japan blundered into war with China, which led to his enunciation of a national policy of establishing "a new order in Asia." Although he resigned two months before Pearl Harbor, he presided over the fateful events, including the signing of the Tripartite Pact that led to war with the United States.

Konoe is an intriguing figure. In contrast to the single-minded, willful, resolute militarists and ultra-nationalists ordinarily associated with the rise of a Japanese form of fascism in the 1930s, he was cerebral and conflicted, alternately impulsive and vacillating, a nationalist with a residual admiration of Western civilization. Some observers have attributed his brittle and vacillating character to an aristocratic, pampered upbringing. Heir to headship of "the most prestigious and highest ranking noble house in the realm," Konoe had all the status and privilege that this extraordinarily elitest society could confer.[4] His father had been president of the upper chamber of the Diet, the House of Peers, a position that Konoe himself also held in the early 1930s. He took a seat in the House of Peers while still a student at Kyoto Imperial University, where he was exposed to a mixture of nationalist and socialist philosophy, and in 1919 he was designated as a member of the Japanese delegation to the Paris Peace Conference.

On the eve of the peace conference, the twenty-seven-year-old Konoe wrote an essay roundly denouncing Wilsonianism and the emerging new U.S-led order as a freezing of the status quo that worked to the great disadvantage of Japan and other late-developing nations, including Germany and Italy. Published in December 1918 in a prominent nationalist journal, his article, entitled "Reject the Anglo-American Peace Principles," set forth a revisionist argument to which he clung all the way to the outbreak of the Pacific War.[5]

Konoe addressed the impending transformation of the international system in 1918 with a notably sophisticated but cynical realism. Dismissing the euphoria for democratic politics and the prospect of lasting peace as naïve, he brought to bear a view grounded in power politics and a hard-headed definition of Japanese national interest. The young Konoe divided the world into the "have countries" (*moteru kuni*) and the "have-not countries" (*motozaru kuni*). The latter was reference not to the undeveloped countries of the world, but rather to the later-developing countries of Germany, Italy, and Japan. That is, he divided the powers into those that possessed large landed holdings, rich with resources, and those that, because they arrived late on the international scene, lacked such extensive territory and resources. The former, he argued, were determined to entrench the status quo and keep the have-not countries in a subordinate and dependent role.

Konoe scorned the gap between U.S. rhetoric and reality. The high-minded ideals of democracy, peace, and justice that the victors proclaimed and that were sweeping the world, including Japan, he wrote, should be understood not in the abstract but rather as a mask of Anglo-American self-interest in preserving the status quo. America's self-proclaimed universalism was no more than an ideology of Western imperialism and, in fact, contravened international justice: "As the colonial history of England and France attests, they long ago occupied the less civilized regions of the world, made them into colonies, and had no scruples about monopolizing them for their own profit. Therefore, not only Germany but all late developing countries were in the position of having no land to seize and being unable to find any room for expansion."[6] Konoe was not alone in this view. Even in the West, as the British historian E. H. Carr tartly observed, the English-speaking peoples became known on the European continent as "masters in the art of concealing their selfish national interests in the guise of the general good." Carr added that "this kind of hypocrisy is a special and characteristic peculiarity of the Anglo-Saxon mind."[7]

The Anglo-American powers, Konoe concluded, were acting on cold and calculated power considerations. Whatever their liberal ideologies, they were in reality seeking to preserve the status quo, which would perpetuate an unjust apportionment of land and resources and pit the have countries against the have-not countries. Under such unequal circumstances, resistance to the new order was not immoral. Nor was advocating peace a moral cause when it was a means of preserving an unjust apportionment of the world's limited resources. This new order condemned late-developing countries such as Japan "to remain forever subordinate to the advanced nations." Unless something was done to allow Japan "equal access to the markets and natural resources of the colonial areas," Japan would be forced to "destroy the status quo for the sake of self-preservation."[8]

The views of the young Konoe bespoke the breakdown of the broad consensus that had guided Japanese foreign policy since the Meiji Restoration. Among Japanese leaders there was a growing gulf between those who continued to favor pursuit of Japanese interests in cooperation with the powers and those who believed it would now be necessary for Japan to assert its own will more forcefully, lest the powers constrain Japan's continued pursuit of its interests.

Like so many young Japanese over the past century and a half, Konoe's views of the West were an unstable mix of attraction and repulsion. His biographer Oka Yoshitake observed that his intimacy with the throne instilled in him a commitment to the *kokutai,* the emperor-centered national polity, which entailed preservation of national unity over pursuit of private interest and a destiny of Asian leadership abroad. Nevertheless, even in the writings of so committed a nationalist, one finds embedded the deep cultural ambivalence that characterized so much of modern Japanese thought. Curiously, very soon after he wrote this essay asserting Japanese opposition to the Anglo-American order, Konoe published another article expressing admiration for life in the West and a corresponding revulsion of traditional Japanese culture and lifestyle:

> Should I be asked what I am unhappy about in our country, I would readily answer that "everything I see and hear makes me unhappy," not to mention the mundane matters of food, clothing, and residence; every-

thing is bound by tradition, imperfection, and artificiality. I think they need reform from top to bottom. . . . I sorely miss life in the West where I could put on my shoes as soon as I got out of bed in the morning. Back in Japan, I had to wear a kimono, because I frequently attended banquets and other functions where one had to sit or kneel on *tatami*. Our half-Japanese and half-Western life strains us. Without that duality our life would be much better.[9]

The implication that the Japanese needed to reform their society to make it more like the West reveals the same deep cultural ambivalence found among so many other prominent Japanese. This ambivalence did not keep them from being nationalist—in fact, it contributed to their nationalism. Acquisition of power, leadership in Asia, and the higher place to which they would bring Japan in the international hierarchy of prestige were a means of overcoming such uncertainty about their own heritage.

Konoe's rejection of Wilsonian proposals for a new international order prefigured a strong undercurrent of Japanese opposition to the Washington System. As Mochizuki Kotarō, a Diet member and well-known journalist, wrote in disgust, "Our empire has lost everything and gained nothing, and only the expense of building warships is spared."[10] These revisionists pointed out that in addition to ending the Anglo-Japanese alliance, the conference agreements had forced Japan to abandon an ambitious naval building plan, imposing naval limitations that put naval strength far below what many military figures felt necessary. Moreover, the agreements obliged Japan to withdraw its troops from Siberia, where they had been dispatched as part of an Allied expedition at the end of the Great War, and required the return of Shandong to China. Tōgō Shigenori, who later served as foreign minister in the Tōjō cabinet, described it as a "second Triple Intervention," referring to the humiliation after the Sino-Japanese War when the three Western powers had compelled Japan to return the newly acquired Liaotung Peninsula to China.[11]

Given the strength of this bitter opposition, it was apparent that Japan was never fully assimilated into the new order. Perhaps this was an impossible task so far as the hard-liners were concerned. They felt no lasting Japanese stake in the stability of the Washington System. Initially, they demanded changes within the existing order, but their grievances were so far-reaching that they could find little to reassure them. Hegemony in East Asia, they believed, properly belonged to Japan. A balance of power that constrained Japan from pursuing this goal was unacceptable. The revisionists' goal was an East Asian order in which Japan was the acknowledged leader, one in which Japan determined the formal institutional arrangements as well as the informal rules of the system. And as opportunities presented themselves, they increasingly favored overthrow of the Washington System.

No likely diplomatic agreement or adjustments to the Washington System could reassure such implacable opposition. As Kissinger observed, "Whenever there exists a power which considers the international order or the manner of legitimizing it oppressive, relations between it and other powers will be revolutionary. In such cases, it is not the adjustment of differences within a given system which will be at issue, but the system itself. . . . The distinguishing feature of a revolutionary power is not that it feels threatened . . . but that nothing can reassure it."[12] Japanese animosity toward the Washington System was apparent from the very start. Both at the Paris Peace Conference and even more clearly at the Washington Conference, as it became apparent that the new order was intended to change fundamentally the rules of the game in East Asia and to contain Japanese power, Japanese revisionist opposition began to gather strength. Though this opposition remained a minority position through the 1920s, it made Japan potentially a revolutionary power.

Within the navy senior command, there was a deep split between those who agreed with civilian leaders of the government that Japan could not compete with the United States in an all-out naval building program, on one side, and those who increasingly viewed conflict with the United States as inevitable and demanded the right to build to parity, on the other side. The Japanese naval delegation at the Washington Conference divided bitterly over the agreement in what Asada Sadao usefully termed "the battle of the two Katōs."[13] The two Katōs—who were not related—occupied leading positions in the navy and adopted sharply divergent positions that epitomized this fundamental division of views over foreign policy.

Naval Minister Katō Tomosaburō concluded that it was in the best interests of Japan to accept the U.S. proposals for naval limitations rather than face an escalating arms race. Lacking the resources and industrial power to compete with the Americans, he said, Japan must be content with "a peacetime armament commensurate with its national strength."[14] Furthermore, because the Americans agreed not to fortify their bases in the western Pacific, Japan was left secure in East Asian waters. Yamamoto Isoroku, the naval officer who later led the attack on Pearl Harbor, viewed the Washington naval agreement with satisfaction. "The 5:5:3 ratio," he held, "works just fine for us; it is a treaty to restrict the other parties."[15] In the accommodationist view of these men, the likelihood of conflict with the Americans was reduced.

But the naval minister's young chief aide at the Washington Conference, Katō Kanji, representing junior, hard-line naval officers, found the U.S. proposals an affront to Japanese prestige and interests, which he believed required at least a 10:7 ratio with the U.S. Navy. On the day that the Japanese delegation accepted the 5:5:3 ratio, the junior Katō railed against the agreement: "As far as I am concerned, war with America starts now. We'll take revenge on her. We will!"[16] Following the Washington Conference, the junior Katō emerged as leader of an "anti-treaty faction" in the naval command. Narrow and ethnocentric in his views, Katō Kanji regarded the naval arms agreement as another humiliating unequal treaty dictated by the Americans that "deprived the Imperial Navy of its supremacy in the Far East."

For the anti-treaty faction, the Americans' superior industrial economy was not a reason for accommodation. On the contrary, it showed that in the event of conflict the United States could quickly turn its industry to arms production and out-build Japanese strength in the western Pacific. Therefore, they concluded, Japan must maintain a large and unconstrained peacetime armament. The views of the anti-treaty faction were reflected in the Navy General Staff. The General Staff's belief in the inevitability of U.S.-Japan conflict was apparent in the revised national defense policy of 1923: "The United States, following a policy of economic invasion in China, menaces the position of our Empire and threatens to exceed the limits of our endurance. . . . The long-standing embroilments, rooted in economic problems and racial prejudice are extremely difficult to solve. . . . Such being the Asiatic policy of the United States, sooner or later a clash with our Empire will become inevitable."[17]

To such irreconcilable opposition, policies of constructive engagement were probably bound to be futile, for, as Kissinger observed, "It is the essence of a revolutionary power that it possesses the courage of its convictions, that it is willing, indeed eager, to push its principles to their ultimate conclusion." The anti-treaty faction steadily gained influence within the navy. The senior Katō died of cancer in 1923, whereas the junior Katō was appointed commander-in-chief of the Combined Fleet in 1926. To revisionists like Katō Kanji, diplomatic solutions were not likely to succeed. Attempts to respond to specific grievances would not satisfy those who held unlimited objectives. Rather, the revisionists increasingly cited the principles to which they adhered—principles that were fundamentally opposed to the norms and mores of the status quo. In such revolutionary situations, "diplomacy is replaced either by war or by an armaments race," Kissinger wrote.[18] Indeed, the anti-treaty faction began preparing early for what was expected to be a second naval arms limitation conference directed at extending the Washington accords to auxiliary vessels, including cruisers, destroyers, and submarines.

Katō Kanji and a growing number of naval officers viewed naval arms limitation as synonymous with U.S. oppression of Japan. If the "cancer" of the Washington System could be excised, Katō declared in a 1934 speech at a conference of senior naval leaders, "the morale and self-confidence of our navy would be so bolstered that we could count on certain victory over our hypothetical enemy, no matter how overwhelming the physical odds against us." The impetuous Katō's speeches in the 1920s and early 1930s were emotional tirades marked by assertions of Japanese spiritual superiority over westernism, capitalism, and materialism, which he identified with the Washington System—and increasingly with the domestic Japanese political order that accommodated to that system.[19]

The revisionist sentiment in the navy was matched by similar views in the army, although the army's revisionism had different origins. It grew out of the army's emerging strategic thought. The lessons of the Russo-Japanese War, and even more World War I, taught that warfare in the twentieth century would require mobilization of the total resources of the nation and the possession of a strong, secure, self-sufficient industrial base to ensure that a nation was not vulnerable to external wartime economic pressures. Japan must have comprehensive plans to begin mobilizing all its human and material resources for the anticipated conflict. There could be no more extreme example of the adherence to the principle of der Primat der Aussenpolitik than the total-war planners. In their view, all aspects of domestic society had to be subject to the demands of the competitive international system. Studies in the Army Ministry further concluded, as Michael Barnhart wrote, that "neither the home islands nor the empire in Formosa, Korea, and southern Sakhalin could provide resources sufficient for waging modern war. The control of richer territories, such as China, was imperative."[20] Japan must have a fully mobilized homeland and an autarkic regional base in preparation for protracted conflict.

The leading proponent of total-war thought was General Ishiwara Kanji, who studied in Germany for three years and came under the powerful influence of one of Ranke's disciples, the military historian Hans Delbrück. It would not be surprising, as Jack Snyder observed, that he would be "attracted to Leopold von Ranke's views on the *Primat der Aussenpolitik*."[21] Total-war thought became the point of departure of a significant group of army leaders who, focusing on the importance of Manchuria to Japan's future industrial and military power, began to assert a revisionist position toward the obligations Japan had undertaken at Washington. They expressed mounting impatience with Shidehara diplomacy's commitment to respect the Nine Power Treaty's principles and to adhere to a policy of noninterference in the Chinese domestic political situation. Spreading disorder within China, on the one hand, and the Kuomintang's campaign during the 1920s to unify China, including Manchuria and Mongolia, and to abolish the unequal treaties and foreign rights, on the other hand, constituted an increasing challenge for Shidehara's hands-off policies. Moreover, Japanese leaders began to realize that neither Great Britain nor the United States was inclined to back up the Nine Power Treaty principles with force.

General Tanaka Giichi, whose opportunist policies had surfaced during World War I, was the proponent of a "positive China policy" that stood in contrast to Shidehara's stance. Fundamentally, this policy favored sending troops to protect Japanese interests when incidents rose to jeopardize them. It also favored the "separation of Manchuria and Mongolia" from China proper and insisted on maintaining a special position there to prevent the extension of the Kuomintang's Nationalist campaign.[22] In 1925, Tanaka assumed the presidency of the Seiyūkai, the political party that opposed Shidehara's Minseitō (Kenseikai) party. Two years later, when Tanaka's party came to power, he assumed the prime ministership, bringing Japan a step closer to the possibility of challenging the existing policies of adherence to the Nine Power Treaty principles of noninterference.

It was Tanaka's enunciation of this new foreign policy that encouraged the leaders of Japanese forces in Manchuria to plot strategies for separating Manchuria and strengthening the Japanese hold on the region. In 1928, a Kwantung Army staff officer carried out the assassination of the Chinese warlord in the region, expecting that it would set in motion a chain of events leading to Japanese seizure of Manchuria. But the army was not ready to act, and despite the assassination, Chinese control was maintained. The displeasure of the emperor over the incident forced Tanaka's resignation in 1929. The Minseitō returned to power and Shidehara to the foreign ministership. But the incident prefigured growing sentiment in the army to flout Shidehara's reinstituted principles of cooperation with the Washington Treaty accords. A clique of "total-war" officers was gaining adherents in the army, and they were committed to a program of autarky that would ensure economic self-sufficiency. They believed that separating Manchuria from China could be the first step toward establishing Japan as an empire with "the economic capacity to meet even the United States on equal terms."[23] It was Ishiwara, a key leader of this clique, who led the new—and this time successful—plot to seize Manchuria in 1931.

By the end of the 1920s, revisionism was gaining strength among influential elites. Within the naval command, the division between the accommodationists and revisionists grew more bitter. In preparation for the London Conference, convened in 1930 to extend the naval limitations to auxiliary ships, a study conducted within the navy reaffirmed the still dominant view that cooperation with the Anglo-American powers was in Japan's interest. It concluded: "Since Japan's national strength in relation to the Anglo-American power is vastly inferior, it would be to our advantage to keep them tied down to the capital ship ratio of 10:10:6, even though Japan was assigned an inferior strength. . . . Vis-à-vis great industrial powers like the United States and Britain, the utmost effort must be made to avoid a war whose outcome would be decided by an all-out contest of national strength."[24] The report further argued that this ratio was sufficient to deter the United States from "obstructing" Japanese policy in China.

Nevertheless, the opposition led by Katō Kanji, now chief of the Navy General Staff, was vociferous in its determination "never to repeat the mistake of the Washington Conference," Katō said, especially since Japan's auxiliary strength was already over 70 percent that of the United States. Honorific nationalism permitted no compromises. No diplomatic agreement would satisfy Katō and his colleagues, for their argument was now reaching the emotional level of principle rather than specific terms: Japan had every right to parity, and anything less—even 70 percent—was already a concession that infringed Japanese honor. "The real issue at stake," Katō asserted, "is no longer our naval power per se but our *national prestige and credibility.*" At the London Conference, even though a compromise was negotiated that gave Japan a de facto 70 percent ratio until the next conference, the opposition was implacable. (Although Japan was accorded parity in submarine strength, it was at a figure substantially below Japan's existing strength.) When the London Treaty was signed in April 1930, the enraged Katō exploded: "It is as if Japan were bound hand and foot and thrown into jail by the Anglo-American powers."[25]

The conflict within the navy, having become a matter of national honor, broke into the open. Prime Minister Hamaguchi Osachi, who favored cooperation with the Anglo-American powers, was publicly excoriated for having compromised Japan's national security and for having trammeled the independent judgment of the naval command for the sake of a spurious friendship with the Anglo-American powers. On November 14, 1930, presaging an era of what a *New York Times* correspondent called "government by assassination," a young ultra-nationalist stepped from a crowd of well-wishers in Tokyo Station and shot Hamaguchi as he was preparing to board a train. Eighteen months later, junior naval officers broke into Prime Minister Inukai Tsuyoshi's residence and assassinated him, bringing down the last party government.

THE ERODING FOUNDATIONS OF ORDER

Western historiography on the origins of the Pacific War has focused on Japan's internal politics, especially the increased influence of the military in the domestic political order following the Manchurian Incident, as the source of Japan's aggressive foreign policy in the 1930s. As Michael Mandelbaum observed, "The Western historical reconstruction of the origins of World War II has placed the blame on Japan's internal politics, which are generally considered to have produced an aggressive foreign policy that culminated in the December 1941 attack. An 'inside-out' explanation of Japanese behavior gained wide acceptance after the war."[26]

Only rarely is this interpretation challenged. Rejecting the view that Japanese foreign and defense policies were the result of conspiracy and irrational acts of radicals, James Crowley went against the historiographical tide when he wrote in 1966: "Japan's foreign policy in the 1930's may not necessarily be adequately or accurately explained in terms of military incidents, political assassinations . . . army factionalism, . . . thoughts and deeds of right-wing ideologues, zealous junior officers, conspiratorial field commanders, and subordinate staff officers who manipulated the ministers of state as if they were Bunraku puppets."[27] Indeed, as the influence of the political parties receded, the military and the bureaucracy gained the upper hand because they had complementary strategies to deal with the national crisis. Total-war planners committed to mobilizing the economy joined with "reform bureaucrats" who were advocating a state industrial policy and a managed economy as a strategy for surviving the depression. The collapse of the international economy and the descent into beggar-thy-neighbor policies became the bridge by which bureaucrats joined with total-war planners to recognize that the demands of foreign policy required the transformation of the domestic political-economic structure. This change in the domestic political order, a shift in power from the political parties to the military and bureaucratic elites, was intimately tied to the changing international environment. As Akira Iriye concluded, "In the final analysis, the failure of the major powers to develop a recognizable framework of international relations, after they had destroyed the old system of imperialist diplomacy, provided the setting of the Far Eastern crisis."[28] The international system changed at the end of the 1920s. The underlying assumptions of the Washington System eroded, tipping the balance of forces within Japan and providing the conditions for the ascendancy of revisionist sentiment. The changing international opportunities and pressures brought about a significant shift in the domestic political coalitions.

In Japan, the legitimacy of the existing international order was eroding. Diplomatic adjustments were beside the point. The system itself was the issue. It was a revolutionary situation, for it was the fundamental principles underlying the status quo that were being called into question. Events outside of Japan made this moment a turning point and ensured that the Washington System and Shidehara diplomacy lost their domestic legitimization. The liberal international order was collapsing. It never had worked well. In 1930, Shigemitsu Mamoru, soon to be appointed Japanese minister to Beijing, reported that cooperation among the powers to deal with Chinese affairs had broken down. He said, "Japan must cope with East Asian matters on its own responsibility and at its own risk."[29]

Two scholars, Peter Duus and Daniel Okimoto, observing that "many studies of Japanese fascism have placed overriding emphasis on domestic factors, even in explaining Japan's foreign policy" suggested that this emphasis on an inside-out approach provides an inaccurate picture:

To what extent were domestic developments contingent upon and determined by external context and the international environment? Just as the shape of the world in the mid-nineteenth century helped to determine Japan's internal politics then, did not the shape of the world in the 1920s and 1930s shape Japanese domestic politics? . . . It seems to us that an understanding of the 1930s requires much wider and more systematic analysis of the international system than has been done so far. . . . There are gaping holes in our knowledge of how the external environment affected pre-war Japan. There is a growing body of theoretical literature in the field of international relations which can be usefully tested on the case of prewar Japan.[30]

Indeed, the economic internationalism upon which the Washington System depended was everywhere weakening. As Duus later wrote, "The rules of the old order were being abandoned, even by the Anglo-American powers that had established them. The gold standard was giving way to managed currencies, free trade was being supplanted by rising tariffs and trade quotas, and open economic borders were being pushed aside by the creation of exclusive economic blocs."[31] To the Japanese leaders, ever sensitive to the apparent current of events, the formation of economic blocs appeared to be the wave of the future. The Washington System relied on the hopeful expectation that peaceful commercial competition would replace armed rivalries. It turned out to be heavily dependent on economic performance, and when "the great storage battery of the North American economy . . . ran dry, the new order of the 1920s disintegrated."[32] Japanese exports to the United States fell by over 40 percent from 1929 to 1930. In June 1930, Congress enacted the Smoot-Hawley tariff, which raised duties on Japanese imports by an average of 23 percent. The continuing contraction of world trade for a Japan whose well-being was so dependent on trade had reached crisis proportions. Japanese overall exports to the world declined 43 percent by value between 1929 and 1931.[33]

The increasing anarchy in the international system provided strong incentives for Japan to improve its power position. In a truly momentous change for the Japanese, the British, who had advocated free trade since the opening of Japan, abandoned their time-honored commitment to the gold standard and its venerable commitment to international liberalism, instead turning the empire into a closed unit by adopting a system of trade preferences among the Commonwealth Countries. The French had their empire. German economic policies were designed to create a dependent economic sphere in Central Europe and an inflationary policy to stimulate exports. The Soviets had closed Russia's borders. For Japan's leaders, with their embedded realist attitude, the logic of anarchy was clear and irresistible.

The Breakout

The fate of the Washington Treaty System was decided in Manchuria. The Chinese today call it *dongbei,* the Northeast. To the world it was

Manchuria, the region to the north of the Great Wall, homeland of the frontier people who ruled China during its final imperial dynasty from 1644 to 1912. For Japan it was a target of opportunity. Sparsely populated, rich in resources, strategically important as a buffer to Soviet influence, Manchuria represented to the Japanese a legitimate opportunity because of the 100,000 deaths suffered in the Russo-Japanese War. The spacious plains of Manchuria encompassed an area four times larger than the cramped Japanese home islands. It was an area one and a half times the size of Texas. Here the Japanese found the resources that the home islands lacked. Manchuria had always been important to Japanese strategists as the imperialist era unfolded. But its importance grew as they absorbed the thinking of total-war strategy and as their own industrial base shifted from light to heavy industry.

With the tacit consent of members of the Army General Staff, field grade officers of the Kwantung Army provoked an incident in Manchuria on the night of September 18, 1931. A small explosion on the tracks of the Japanese railway outside of Mukden provided sufficient pretext for attacking Chinese troops and expanding Japanese control until all of Manchuria was conquered. Sadako Ogata, in her study of the Manchurian Incident, made clear how sensitive both Japanese civilian and military leaders were to the potential reactions of the powers. The British, especially Foreign Minister Sir John Simon, were seen as fundamentally sympathetic to Japan because of their own colonial holdings, including Hong Kong and India. The Kwantung Army, the Japanese unit responsible for protecting Japanese concessions in Manchuria, concluded in its "Situational Analysis" that the United States was "not likely to plunge into war with Japan."[34] The Americans were preoccupied with the problems of the economic depression; they lacked naval strength due to the naval treaties and their neglect to build even to allowed limits; and so long as the open door for American business to participate in Manchuria remained, the Americans would not see their interests as so jeopardized as to warrant anything more than an expression of disapproval.

The judgment of the military was soon proved correct. Not only did the Americans not intervene in the seizure of Manchuria and the establishment of the puppet state of Manchukuo, the United States did not impose economic sanctions. Washington was divided and indecisive. While giving lip-service to the Washington System principles, the Americans were not prepared to take any decisive action to support them. President Herbert Hoover did not believe that American interests outside of the Western

Hemisphere were sufficient to risk war. He told his cabinet, "Neither our obligation to China, nor our own interest, nor our dignity requires us to go to war." Hoover allowed that he "would fight for the continental United States as far as anybody, but he would not fight for Asia."[35] He worried about the dangers of an arms race, and he was content to rely on the force of public opinion to moderate Japanese policy.

Moreover, in 1932, the U.S. Navy had only built up to 65 percent of treaty strength, whereas the Japanese were at 95 percent. Between 1930 and 1933, Congress failed to authorize the construction of a single new warship.[36] Secretary of State Henry Stimson, whose policies were fated to be linked both to the beginning and the catastrophic end of Japan's effort to create a new order—as secretary of war in 1945 he was centrally involved in the decisionmaking on the use of the atomic bomb—briefly considered imposing sanctions, but Hoover was not prepared to consider this course. Stimson then fell back on what he himself later characterized as "bluff."[37] The United States would not "recognize any treaty or agreement" that infringed the Nine Power Treaty with its provisions for maintaining the territorial integrity of China, the principle of self-determination, and the Open Door. Moreover, if Japan violated the treaty, the United States would not consider itself bound by the Naval Disarmament Treaty agreed on at Washington in 1922. He was, he later recalled, waving an unloaded pistol. If the sea powers had undertaken a concerted action to resist Japan's action, it might have moderated Japan's subsequent behavior. Stimson approached the British to try to construct a common front to uphold the Nine Power Treaty, but he was rebuffed.

Stanley Hornbeck, chief of the State Department's Far Eastern Division—who, as Michael Barnhart wrote, "unlike many of his generation . . . believed that resoluteness and power, not treaties outlawing war and limiting arms, were central to the maintenance of peace"—urged the government to put economic pressure on Japan. It was necessary, Hornbeck said, to "either put up, or shut up." By being unwilling to take concrete measures, and instead adopting a "flabby and impotent" response, the United States would have to reconcile itself to an expansionist Japan.[38] It is, of course, questionable how effective economic pressure would have been at this point. Even Hornbeck believed that the League would have to take the initiative in applying sanctions. In 1931–1932, however, there was not the will in the League or in the United States to do so.

The fundamental weakness of the international order was now laid bare. The mistake had been inherent in the Washington accords. The dangerous gap between stated principles and the will to act embedded in the Washington System was now apparent. The system had been founded more on submission to legitimizing principles and on confidence in self-restraint than on safeguards against aggression. Theodore Roosevelt's view of two decades earlier had proved prescient. "The open door policy in China," he had observed, "was an excellent thing, and I hope it will be a good thing in the future, so far as it can be maintained by general diplomatic agreement; but as has been proved by the whole history of Manchuria, alike under Russia and under Japan, the open door policy, as a matter of fact, completely disappears as soon as a powerful nation determines to disregard it and is willing to run the risk of war rather than forego its intention."[39]

It was a critical moment. The Japanese military now drew confidence from its success and from the lack of effective resistance on the part of the powers. Ogata later concluded that, although concern over Chinese intentions and the ambition of Japanese nationalists in and out of the military were important, "the absence of international opposition with teeth was the overall factor that helped the Japanese military feel free to advance in Manchuria. . . . So long as international opposition contained elements of indecisiveness, ambiguity, or sympathy, Japan found herself possessed of a safe margin within which to consolidate and expand her control." The Manchurian Incident showed Japanese leaders just how weak the Washington System was. "The legacy of the Manchurian Affair was the discovery of this margin between nominal international disapproval and effective international opposition," said Ogata. Once this discovery was made, it "drove [Japanese] foreign policy toward adventurism."[40]

The Japanese military was driven more by a rational, cost-benefit analysis than by ideological fervor. Much has been written about the influence of the ideology of national socialism on the military as an explanation for Japan's continental expansion. But historians have probably exaggerated the role of ideology. Instead, it was the opportunistic pursuit of power evident throughout the modern period that drove Japanese military leaders. On the basis of a study of the Manchurian Incident, Iriye concluded:

> The lack of ideology strikes one as characteristic of the Japanese military. It has become customary [for historians] to talk of . . . the Kwantung Army's anti-capitalist "socialism," young officers' ultranationalism, and other manifestations of "Japanese fascism." Yet what emerges . . . is an almost total absence of ideology as a driving force behind military action. The Kwantung Army and the Tokyo military seem to have believed that

their acts were logical expressions of a rational strategy, designed to carry out what to them was a legitimate goal of national policy. There was little room for moralizing, sentimentalizing, or emotionalism. Even the often alleged strain of anti-Western pan-Asianism was never more than an after-thought, or at most a result, not a cause of, military action. Force and the use of force as a necessary means of obtaining a coldly calculated goal, rather than adherence to a vaguely defined doctrine, characterized the military's behavior.[41]

After the success of the Manchurian Incident and after it became apparent that the Washington System could muster no credible opposition to Japan's flouting of its principles, revisionist sentiment gained a growing ascendancy among Japan's leadership. Rather than meet Japanese violation of the Nine Power Treaty with a determined opposition, the Western powers turned to the League of Nations, pinning their hopes for settlement of the Manchurian issue on a commission of inquiry to be headed by Lord Lytton of Britain. It was to consist of representatives from the United States (even though it was not a League member), France, Germany, and Italy. Although a founding member of the League occupying one of the five permanent seats on its council, Japan had not made a great commitment to the workings of the League because it was doubtful that the League would serve Japan's interests. Japan's indifference was apparent from the fact that it had contributed a relatively low level of personnel to the League's secretariat by the end of the 1920s: Japan contributed 5 members, whereas Italy contributed 23; France 100; Switzerland 126; and Britain 143.[42]

In part because there were few genuine Japanese internationalists, Japan did a poor job of defending itself at the League and in the court of world public opinion. In the course of his investigation of the Manchurian Incident, Lord Lytton wrote to his wife from Shanghai: "The Chinese are so articulate—they talk beautiful English and French and can express themselves clearly. With the Japanese it was a surgical operation to extract each word." The Japanese were ill-prepared to make their case because they "had educated their people to a high level in many fields but had been insistent on educating their bureaucrats in their imperial universities where 'internationalism'—and clarity of expression—had somehow been neglected."[43]

Contrary to the common interpretation, the Lytton Commission report was not a condemnation of Japanese action in Manchuria. The commissioners were at pains to recognize Japan's rights and interests in Manchuria, the misgovernment of warlord rule in Manchuria, and the general absence of law and order in China proper. Lytton tried to find a middle ground for constructive peace. The British Foreign Office believed that the report, on balance, favored the Japanese side. "What the Commissioners wanted to recommend," historian Ian Nish wrote, "was to ignore 'Manchukuo,' revert to the position on 18 September 1931, make Kuomintang China in Nanking the suzerain power but give Manchuria a degree of local autonomy in which Japan's treaty rights would be fully respected."[44]

Given the weakness of internationalism on the Japanese side and the balance of forces in Japanese domestic politics, Lytton's efforts were foredoomed. The nuances of the report were lost on the Japanese Foreign Ministry. The military continued to expand hostilities in north China and Shanghai. As a compromise acceptable to both the military and the Foreign Ministry, Matsuoka Yōsuke was sent to Geneva to lead the Japanese delegation in the League's debate on the commission's report. The unstable Matsuoka was a poor choice. He epitomized the now unbridled revisionism. When the seasoned diplomat Yoshida Shigeru, who was angered at Matsuoka's impetuousness, encountered Matsuoka in Tokyo on the eve of the latter's departure for Geneva, he told him, "You should go to an insane asylum, douse your head in water, and only leave when you have cooled off."[45]

At Geneva, Matsuoka compared Japan to the crucified Christ, saying its just cause would one day be universally acknowledged. He undermined any opportunities to probe conciliatory approaches in the League council, which was Japan's best hope. The Manchurian issue was subsequently referred to the Assembly, where the small countries exercised their influence in a report that was firmer than the Lytton Commission's and condemned Japan for violations. The resolution was adopted by 42 votes to 1, Japan opposing and Siam abstaining. Tokyo then ordered Matsuoka to announce Japan's withdrawal from the League. At home, few openly opposed withdrawal. A fragile blossom to begin with, internationalism in Japan was dead.

With Japanese withdrawal from the League in 1933, the end of the Washington System was at hand. In preliminary talks regarding further naval arms limitations in 1934 in London, the Japanese delegation, led by Rear Admiral Yamamoto Isoroku, demanded parity with the United States, knowing that this would be rejected. The Japanese Navy, because it had built up to treaty strength, now held a total naval tonnage ratio of 10 to 8 in relation to the United States, and it intended to expand its building plans dramatically. "Japan now prepared to strike out on a new, ambitious, and dangerous course of naval autonomy," wrote David C. Evans and Mark R.

Peattie in a later analysis of the events. "The prime symbols of that determination were the monster battleships *Yamato* and *Musashi*," which were "the two largest, most powerful battleships ever built." The planning, construction, and even launching of these ships were surrounded by a curtain of secrecy that kept British and U.S. naval intelligence in the dark.[46] In December 1934, Japan announced its renunciation of the naval arms limitation treaties.

PURSUIT OF REGIONAL HEGEMONY

In modern history the United States is the only power to have achieved hegemony in its region. But other powers, including Japan, have pursued the goal. In fact, U.S. regional hegemony in the Western Hemisphere served as a justification, if not a model, for Japan's ambition. In the uncertainty accompanying the crumbling of an international order, strategic concerns and security objectives now resumed a paramount role in determining Japanese foreign policy. In contrast to the first phase of Japanese imperialism (1895–1918), when imperialism had constituted a recognizable system with its own rules and mores among the imperial powers, Japan's external environment now seemed anarchic and devoid of rules or enforcers. Japanese leaders were drawn to German geopolitical thinking, which maintained that "the world would come to be divided into a few blocs, each under a dominant power," wrote Iriye. He continued: "In this process of 'global redivision,' the powers would engage in a deathly struggle for supremacy. Each great power would have to acquire more resources, mobilize its people, and drive out other nations' economic and political influences from the region under its control."[47]

The leadership now spoke of an "Asian Monroe Doctrine," declaring Japan's determination to take responsibility for order in Asia. The doyen of Japanese diplomats, Ishii Kikujirō, summarized his country's agenda in 1933 in an address to the Council on Foreign Relations in New York. Japan, he said, was motivated by "equality and security" and "activated by the same principle incorporated in the Monroe Doctrine."[48] Japanese had long held an ambition for regional leadership, and their singular success in building their military and industrial power continually fed this ambition. Now that Japan had broken out of the Western-imposed East Asian order, realization of this goal was in sight, and the Japanese felt a sense of elation.

There was more to Japan's ambition than the clear-cut goals of political and economic autonomy in East Asia, however. There was also the nebulous but deeply felt pursuit of cultural autonomy that hearkened back to the psychic wound inflicted at the outset of Japan's entry into the international system. This wound had festered in the years since as Japan had striven and struggled for status and stature in a system that was made and dominated by Western powers. Kamei Katsuichirō, the prominent writer, confided in 1942 that "the war we are engaged in at this moment is aimed outwardly at the destruction of the British and American forces. But internally it is a kind of basic therapy aimed at curing the psychological malaise . . . brought about by modern culture."[49] The Japanese would create their own international order instead of simply submitting to a Western conceived and dominated one. "We are aiming," declared an army spokesman, "to put an end to seventy years' dependence on Britain and America, commercially and economically."[50] More than political and economic autonomy, Japan sought cultural autonomy.

The world Japan had entered in the mid-nineteenth century had required the country to give up its cultural autonomy. Japan's all-out commitment to pursuing national power had entailed a sweeping rejection of the Japanese heritage. Now, at last, it seemed that the Japanese were to be masters of their own fate. They would no longer simply adapt to the trends as they found them. They would lead Asia. They would create its order. Prewar Japan's most eminent political scientist, Rōyama Masamichi, wrote on the eve of Pearl Harbor, in terms that bespoke Japanese pride in the new feeling of independence: "For the first time since the 'opening' of the country in the Meiji era, Japan now possesses a national policy really her own, Japan is truly 'supported by her own feet.' . . . The Japan of today with such a policy of her own is vastly different from the Japan of yesterday which, without any such policy, was simply accommodating herself as best she could to the general world trends."[51]

Although Japan's leaders demonstrated rampant chauvinism, there were widely diverging views of priorities for Japan's future course. The period was marked by terrorism, uprisings, and assassinations. Within the military services there were deep and bitter conflicts over strategy. In choosing to abandon its customary circumspection and to withdraw from the Washington System, Japan set formidable requirements for the nation's defense. An uprising in the army in February 1936, which aimed at the overthrow of the civilian government, revealed the depth of disagreements within the government over the future. To maintain the strategic posture demanded by its "Asian Monroe Doctrine" and by the commitment to

Manchukuo, Japan needed military power sufficient for three major tasks: defeating the Soviet Army, whose strength on the borders of Manchuria had been vastly augmented; compelling the Chinese government to accept Japan's position in Manchuria and northern China; and securing the home islands against the U.S. fleet.[52] These three strategic objectives required a military capability Japan was never able to achieve. The Meiji leaders would have been appalled at the incautious ways in which the new leaders made policy commitments that exceeded the nation's capacities.

There were advocates of total-war planning who, recognizing Japan's unpreparedness, foresaw a long, calculated plan of industrial development. They cautioned against precipitous action and advocated a carefully executed long-term strategy. But owing to the fragmented nature of decision-making, Japan never had a grand strategy. "A grand strategy," Evans and Peattie wrote, "ideally harnesses all the resources of a nation—military, political, economic, and diplomatic—to achieve national policy objectives." From the Russo-Japanese War onward, Japan possessed only "a set of perceived threats, nebulous ambitions, and a keen ability to exploit a strategic opening."[53] Too many Japanese leaders believed that, however difficult the task, Japan's rule of Asia was assured by a half-century of success at surmounting daunting challenges. The Japanese character and spirit had proved its mettle before.

THE NEW ORDER

It was a mark of the times that, in the summer of 1937, elder statesmen turned to Konoe Fumimaro to become prime minister. Two decades earlier, when he had written his revisionist essay asserting that "we must overcome the principles of peace based on the maintenance of the status quo and work out new principles of international peace from our own perspective," his had been a minority view. Now, his revolutionary goals were mainstream. Konoe had clung consistently to the view that the post–World War I system had maintained an inequitable distribution of natural resources favoring richly endowed nations such as the United States and the British empire. Shortly after assuming the presidency of the House of Peers in 1933, he had written of the implacable hostility he felt for an unjust international order that denied Japan fair access to the world's resources:

A distribution of land can hardly be called reasonable when it confines some nations with growing populations and a capacity for expansion within narrow territory, while other sparsely populated nations enjoy vast territories and abundant resources. . . . No nation dissatisfied with the present state of the world will tolerate that. . . . Europeans and Americans condemn the Japanese actions in Manchuria and Mongolia in the name of world peace. They criticize us by invoking the Covenant of the League of Nations and the Kellogg-Briand Pact, and some even call us, the Japanese, the public enemy of peace and humanity. It is, in fact, the Europeans and Americans who are the unmovable block to world peace. They are in no position to judge us.[54]

When Japan had tried to increase its territories, he argued, it had been compelled to defend itself like an accused before his judge. The hypocrisy of such a peace structure could no longer be tolerated. Britain and the United States were trying to contain Japan's legitimate aspirations on the continent. Unless something was done to allow Japan "equal access to the markets and natural resources of the colonial empires," he said, Japan would be forced to "destroy the status quo for the sake of self-preservation." It was time for a worldwide "new deal."

By 1937 when he became prime minister, Prince Konoe was a widely respected figure. Tall, handsome, and gallant, he was cut from a different cloth than Japan's usual colorless leaders. Just forty-five, he was extraordinarily young for a Japanese leader. He seemed a figure of destiny who could guide the nation through the uncharted waters into which it was now launched. At ease with the emperor, respected by the military and bureaucratic elites who were now ascendant, he was welcomed as a national unity figure. Yet, when all was said and done, it became clear that he was not a good choice, for he lacked the discretion and strength of character required for managing the extraordinary challenges of the time. Konoe was an enigmatic figure who often seemed to lack a clear compass for his actions. He appeared self-possessed, but he proved erratic and inwardly uncertain. He gravitated toward the self-confident right wing and then regretted their decisions. He was alternately assertive and weak-willed; faced with difficulty, he was quickly inclined to give up and withdraw. Repeatedly his aides had to encourage him, revive his spirits, and dissuade him from resignation in the face of difficulty. He proved a tragically weak and ineffectual leader for the most tumultuous times the nation had ever experienced. It was during Konoe's first term as prime minister (June 1937–January 1939) that Japan stumbled into full-scale war with China, and during his second term (July 1940–October 1941) that the fateful steps were taken toward Pearl Harbor.

Only weeks after the formation of Konoe's first cabinet in the summer of 1937, owing in considerable part to Konoe's ineptness, a minor skirmish between Chinese and Japanese troops stationed in the area of the Marco Polo Bridge outside of Peking led to all-out conflict with the Kuomintang regime. This incident, on July 7, 1937, whose details are still shrouded in mystery, might have been settled quickly except that China's leader, Chiang Kai-shek, under pressure from his generals to resist further Japanese expansion, reacted swiftly by dispatching four divisions to north China. Konoe, determined to follow his own foreign policy prescriptions favoring a free hand on the continent, responded with an ill-advised sword-rattling statement that only bolstered Chinese determination to resist further Japanese encroachment.

Hopes of reaching a local settlement evaporated. In contrast to the Manchurian Incident of six years earlier, it was not a conflict the Army General Staff wanted. The total-war planners were acutely aware that it would take considerably more time for Japan to develop the kind of industrial structure needed to prepare for an all-out war. To them it was critical to avoid hostilities and concentrate on a fully coordinated effort to develop Japan's economy. But after abandoning the principles of the Washington System and creating an atmosphere dominated by ultra-nationalist goals and a readiness to resort to military solutions, the government was ill-prepared to restrain itself.

Konoe, losing control over the rush of events, blamed Chinese disregard of Japan's legitimate rights and interests and concluded that Japanese soldiers would be obliged to "punish" the Chinese. Fighting grew savage and spread to Shanghai and up the Yangtze River. Unspeakable atrocities committed against Chinese citizens, especially the fateful pillaging and rape and massacre of many tens of thousands at Nanjing in early 1938, left a lasting outrage against the invaders. The extremes of nationalist indoctrination in the Japanese military that produced a contempt for the Chinese people and a rage at Chinese resistance, together with the breakdown of military discipline, contributed to the ferocity and brutality of Japanese troops during a six-week paroxysm of violence. The savagery and staggering loss of life in the wartime Chinese capital made the Nanjing Massacre "the single most notorious Japanese atrocity during the entire Asian-Pacific War."[55]

The die cast, the Japanese leadership pushed ahead with supreme nerve and blind faith, justifying their goals with pan-Asian slogans. They held out the promise of a Greater East Asia Coprosperity Sphere from which all vestiges of Western imperialism would be erased. On November 3, 1938, Konoe declared that Japan's goal was to create "a new order for ensuring permanent stability in East Asia." Dismissing Chiang Kai-shek and the Nationalists as a local regime, he implied that Japan would find a Chinese government willing to cooperate in this goal and that Japan, Manchukuo, and China would work together to establish the new order. When Washington protested the infringement of the Open Door, Foreign Minister Arita Hachirō responded that such "concepts and principles" were no longer relevant.[56]

The Lack of Legitimacy

Having proclaimed a new order, the Japanese now had to produce their own "concepts and principles," Arita said. They had to find some universal message to rally Asians to the cause of a new order. They needed to legitimize their territorial expansion and explain the principles, norms, and values that would govern it. Moreover, they needed to define the structure of the new system—the institutions that would govern it. Every successful international system must rest on a deeply persuasive ideology, a set of values that will command respect and justify the exercise of raw power required to maintain the order.

Accustomed to their own inward-looking, particularistic expressions of nationalism, the Japanese found this no easy task. A legitimating ideology had to be hastily constructed after the fact, for Japan had hitherto justified its Asian goals more in terms of its own national destiny than in the service of a liberated Asia. From the beginning, it was a poorly contrived and artificial effort. Their German and Italian allies were already talking about creation of a new order. The Japanese term for "new order," *shinchitsujō*, was taken from the German. In the recent past, Japanese elites had been skillful at inventing traditions. To promote nationalism, they had manipulated and reworked ideas, institutions, and cultural symbols from the past to form an ideology that would serve present purposes yet still resonate with the basic values and sentiments on which the Japanese social system rested. Could they now somehow rework their Japanese national ideology to make it appealing to other Asians?

The task of creating a new international order in Asia was a goal for which the Japanese were unprepared. Formulating an ideology that would complement Japanese nationalism, unite all Asians, and legitimize a Japanese-led order was peculiarly challenging. For one thing, the task was carried out under the pressures and distractions of wartime conditions. For another, Japan's foreign policy had never been driven by ideals. There were those ideologues outside of government who wished that it had been; they proposed ideals—most often ones that stressed an Asian ideology that would make common cause with other Asian countries in resisting Western imperialism. But Japan's leaders were driven by the nationalist goals of the Meiji Restoration, which prioritized, above all else, the acquisition of military and economic power sufficient to overtake the West. The Japanese never had sought to universalize their experience. Rather, their belief was in the utter uniqueness of their character and their civilization.[57]

This search for a legitimating ideology spread to the military. The views of Lieutenant General Doihara Kenji, who was negotiating with Kuomintang leaders to establish a new pro-Japanese regime, were typical. Japan, he said, needed to "establish an ideology that can be a basis of the realization of Sino-Japanese cooperation." At a time when "democratic civilization" had "lost its progressive character" and the "objective trends of the world" showed that Western liberalism was "bankrupt," Japan would give the world "a new order." He exhorted Japanese intellectuals to become "cultural warriors" and create an ideology that would ensure the progress of Japan.[58]

Konoe had a reputation for acute intelligence and surrounded himself with many of the nation's leading intellectuals. Just prior to his acceptance of national leadership, he had been instrumental in the establishment of the most imposing group of political thinkers ever assembled in the nation's history. The fundamental purpose of this group, known as the Showa Research Association, was to serve as Konoe's brain trust and develop a grand strategy. There was a certain desperation in their task, an intensity and urgency that drove their deliberations, for it was a time of confusion and tumult both at home and abroad.[59] More than at any time since the Meiji Restoration, Japan's future course was indeterminate and uncertain, but Konoe's advisers were convinced they were moving in accord with vast historical forces. As Takahashi Kamekichi, one of the leading thinkers of the Showa Research Association, wrote in early 1937, "the direction of world trends" was clear: Liberalism was crumbling. Japan's breakout from the Washington System was in accord with the collapse of the Versailles order in Europe. Regionalism, economic nationalism, and managed economies were the wave of the future.[4]

The most influential intellectual in the creation of an ideology was Miki Kiyoshi, a leading member of the Showa Research Association. He believed that the task for the Japanese was to transform Japanese culture so that it acquired "universal characteristics" (*sekaisei*) and transcended European culture.[61] Miki, who served as an adviser and speechwriter for Konoe, argued that liberalism had been "reduced to its final extremity" and could no longer command credibility as a universal ideology. Communism, an offshoot of Western liberalism, by pitting itself against liberal democracy, was showing itself to be a destructive and divisive force. European ideologies were engaged in a suicidal struggle, and Japan and Asia had to transcend these Western dead-ends. Reflecting on the outbreak of conflict with China, Miki wrote: "We must do something which will link this incident with the unification of Asia." Japan must convince China to join in a common struggle to expel Western imperialism from Asia.[62]

Miki and other members of Konoe's brain trust drafted a document that attempted to provide a legitimating ideology. *Shin Nippon no shisō genri* (The Principles of Thought for a New Japan) declared that "action in world history always begins with one race," and that because Japan had demonstrated unique gifts for absorbing and combining foreign influences, for adopting Western technology while maintaining a unique national society, it had a "moral mission to lead Asia." It could create a cooperative order based on social solidarity that would contrast with the atomism of Western society, with its selfish emphasis on individualist values. Indeed, a new kind of social solidarity could be achieved that would eliminate the evils of capitalism, class struggle, and bureaucratization: "Classes will cease being classes and become [incorporated into] an occupational order within a higher whole; and this occupational order will be considered functional and not stratified." Miki's thinking reflected the influence of European fascism. "The mission of the East Asian cooperative body (*kyōdōtai*) is to create a 'new East Asian culture' of world significance, as Hellenistic culture was, on the basis of the cooperation of all races in East Asia."[63]

EMULATING FASCIST INSTITUTIONS

Japan's pattern of adapting the character of its domestic political-economic structure to match the modus operandi of the international environment helps explain how fascism in Japan could be achieved without a break from the earlier system. In contrast to the rise of fascism in other states, in Japan there was no putsch, no overthrow of the constitution establishing a new political order. Rather, fascism was instituted "from above." The existing elites perceived a fundamental change in the external environment and undertook a restructuring of domestic institutions to meet that change.

In the 1930s, Japan entered upon an institutional revolution as its leaders now emulated fascist institutions, concentrating political and economic power at home to ensure the success of its new foreign policies. Although this institutional revolution ultimately fell short of its transformational goals, it nevertheless represented a major reshaping of Japanese political and economic institutions. Right-wing nationalist groups spewed forth a torrent of traditionalistic nationalism, but at the heart of government, the military and civilian bureaucrats once again looked abroad for models of institutional innovation—this time to examples of government intervention in the economy in the fascist governments. In his study of prewar labor relations, Sheldon Garon observed that "historians have tended to take the nativist rhetoric of Japanese authoritarianism at face value. They thus overlook the profound impact of Nazi models on contemporary Japanese policies."[64] Japan's leaders were once again taking their cues from the international system.

The Great Depression and the Manchurian Incident brought the army's total-war planners into common cause with civilian bureaucrats who wanted increased state intervention in the economy. Both saw the need for strict economic controls and for centralization to achieve policy integration. A series of laws designed to give government authority to exercise administrative guidance of key industries led to tight state controls over petroleum, automobiles, steel, machine tools, aircraft, shipbuilding, and many other industries. The goal was to establish "state capitalism" and shift the economy from "profit orientation" to "production orientation."

Members of Konoe's brain trust advanced two policies for his grand strategy: first, the outlines of an East Asian Order, or what they called "an East Asian cooperative body"; and second, to support this new international system, an ambitious plan for the creation of "a new political and economic order" at home. Konoe's intellectual adviser, the eminent political scientist Rōyama Masamichi, articulated this link between foreign policy and domestic infrastructure. Japan, he said, had "always adjusted to changed circumstances by creating a new political system." In the 1920s, when Japan was adjusting to international liberalism, "political parties had become possible when linked to a definite international foreign policy." A liberal order with party politics was appropriate, he wrote, when linked as it was to cooperative diplomacy with the Anglo-American powers. Now, however, world trends required the creation of a regional bloc, and a New East Asian Order required a new order at home. "The theory and the policies for building the East Asian cooperative body," he concluded, must "call forth a new [domestic] order for the Japanese nation and the Japanese people." The welfare and destiny of the Japanese nation would be served by the adoption of totalitarian institutions like those at work in Nazi Germany.[65]

The task, Konoe's elite advisers convinced him, was to establish a totalitarian state with a single vanguard party to mobilize the masses and reorganize the economy into cartels under government supervision. The military also insisted that pursuit of Japan's international interests required elimination of the diffusion of power in the Japanese political-economic system. In the summer of 1940, Konoe appointed a blue-ribbon committee representative of different elites to deliberate preparations for the new order. On October 12, all political parties were dissolved and replaced by the Imperial Rule Assistance Association. Konoe, however, lacked the power and the will to overcome resistance from diverse elites seeking to preserve their own prerogatives. Although it was intended as a mass political party similar to those of the European fascist states—the nucleus of a new political structure— the Imperial Rule Assistance Association never fulfilled this function. Local leaders and conservatives in the old-line ministries resisted a surrender of their power to the new organization. The giant financial cliques known as *zaibatsu* and business leaders likewise resisted government controls. Like the abortive Japanese regional order, the drive to create a new domestic political and economic structure fell well short of its goals. In the rush of events, Japan's efforts to reorganize its political economy foundered. Ironically, it was not until after the war, when the U.S. Occupation eliminated many of the elites, that the bureaucrats achieved the power they had earlier sought to complete the institutional transformation and to drive policy.

DEBATING "TWO REPUGNANT ALTERNATIVES"

Neither abroad nor at home did Japan's leaders have clear goals, strategies, or plans for realizing the new order. Rather, in characteristic fashion, they were moving with opportunism, improvising, and adjusting to events. As Nazi victories multiplied, it appeared to Konoe and to many other Japanese leaders that fascism was about to triumph in Europe and that "Japan must not miss the bus." As Holland and France fell and the defeat of England seemed imminent, opportunism ruled the day. The U.S. ambassador in Tokyo, Joseph Grew, reported that the Japanese were "unashamedly and frankly opportunist."[66] Once again, as in World War I, it seemed that Japan had "a heaven-sent gift." It could seize the opportunity offered by the preoccupation of the powers with events in Europe to expand its territory.

This bold opportunism was epitomized in the reckless policies of Konoe's foreign minister, the irascible and unstable Matsuoka Yōsuke. By the spring of 1940, the Japanese Navy General Staff had concluded that America's crash naval building program undertaken at the end of the 1930s would result in its achievement of naval hegemony in the Pacific by 1942. Japan, they believed, needed access to the oil of the Dutch East Indies in order to cope with U.S. power. Matsuoka set out to resolve the impasse by a swift demarche. In the autumn of 1940, he signed the Tripartite Pact with Germany and Italy. The signatories pledged to aid one another if attacked by a power not currently involved in the European war or the fighting in China. Matsuoka thereby hoped to isolate the United States and dissuade it from conflict with Japan, thus opening the way for Japan to seize the European colonies in Southeast Asia, grasp the resources it needed for self-sufficiency, and cut off Chinese supply lines. Furthermore, to free his northern flank, Matsuoka signed a neutrality pact with the Soviet Union in April 1941. As a result, when Hitler attacked Russia in June the Manchurian border seemed secure.

However, Matsuoka disastrously misread world trends. The U.S. reaction to the Tripartite Pact was unexpectedly strong. The opportunism that drove Matsuoka to link Japan's fate with the fascist powers in Europe also turned the United States from its isolationist impulses. Belatedly, the Americans were reawakening to the value of the Washington System's norms. The East Asian Order that they had established and then abandoned was beginning to appear essential to U.S. security interests. As a result of the Tripartite Pact, U.S. leaders now saw the conflicts in Asia and Europe as linked and perceived the specter of confronting hostile hegemonies in both regions. President Franklin D. Roosevelt forbade any further shipment of scrap iron to Japan, and after Japanese troops entered Indochina, he embargoed oil. Japan was vulnerable to American coercion, being dependent on the United States for 80 percent of its fuel needs, 60 percent of its machine tools, 93 percent of its copper, and 75 percent of its scrap iron. Japan's resources were more and more stretched. The country had a gross national product (GNP) of $6 billion and a per capita income of $86. Nearly 50 percent of the government's annual budget went to military expenditures. Courting conflict with the United States, a country at least eight times more wealthy, was perilous. Japan had the choice of maintaining good relations with the Americans or establishing a self-sufficient empire.

At the heart of the emerging conflict was a clash between America's liberal internationalism and Japan's vision of its mission in East Asia. Negotiations between Secretary of State Cordell Hull and the Japanese ambassador Nomura Kichisaburō foundered in a morass of confusion and ineptness. Hull made clear that the United States was not prepared to accept a Japanese order, or even to compromise with the status quo. Instead he told Nomura, in effect, that the principles underlying the Washington System must be restored: respect for the territorial integrity and sovereignty of all nations, noninterference in internal affairs, equal commercial opportunity, and nondisturbance of the status quo in the Pacific by other than peaceful means. To Japanese leaders imbued with pervasive nationalist sentiment, this was unthinkable and tantamount to reducing Japan to a second-class power. As Christopher Thorne has observed, "Where only step-by-step, practical bargaining might just conceivably have succeeded, Hull based his approach in 1941 on sweeping general principles, admirable in themselves, but inappropriate if the aim were to secure a *modus vivendi*."[67] Still, it is doubtful that negotiations could have succeeded in any case at this juncture—given the diametrically opposed views taken by the two sides.

The ideological battle lines between the U.S. and Japanese conceptions of the regional order were further sharpened in the summer of 1941, when Roosevelt and Churchill, meeting in Newfoundland, issued the Atlantic Charter, which in virtually all its provisions clashed with Japanese intentions. Not only did it include the principles Hull had enunciated to Nomura, it also included the additional Wilsonian principle of collective security. Japan's leading newspaper, the *Asahi*, interpreted the charter as a declaration of "a system of world domination on the basis of Anglo-American world views." The choice was either to return to the framework of the Washington System or to plunge ahead.[68] There was no mistaking that the Americans were now insisting that improvement of relations depended upon a Japanese commitment to withdraw from China. In his final note to the Japanese on November 26, Hull insisted that if trade and the flow of oil were to be restored, Japan must accept the Open Door and "withdraw all military, naval, air, and police forces from China and Indochina." Although the Americans were ambiguous about whether this demand also included withdrawal from Manchuria, there could be little doubt, in light of the U.S. nonrecognition policy, that ultimately it would be part of the American expectation.[69]

On the face of it, Japan's decision for war appears to fly in the face of realism. To declare war on a power with no less than eight times the material power might seem a rash and reckless act. Yet, in analyzing the circumstances under which a state may decide to attempt a change in the international order, and the way in which the elite perceives the relative costs and benefits and the price it is willing to pay, one has to take account of the historically formed perceptions of the leadership.[70] As Kissinger observed, "No nation will submit to a settlement, however well-balanced and however 'secure,' which seems to totally deny its vision of itself."[71] The U.S. insistence on Japan's withdrawal from China was completely at odds with the vision that Japanese leaders had of Japan's place in the world. The loss of status and prestige was such a blow to the national self-image that the leaders believed the demands jeopardized Japan's survival.[72]

Repeatedly in the fall of 1941, both as war minister and then as prime minister, General Tōjō characterized U.S. demands as unjustly depriving Japan of its position on the continent, even jeopardizing the Korean colony. It was, he said, a return to "little Japan before the Manchurian incident."[73] Seen in this light, the decision for war was less a reckless, irrational gamble than a choice between two equally "repugnant alternatives": war with a nation of vastly greater wealth and power, or return to an international order that would not only require relinquishment of an empire but the destruction of what had come to constitute the nation's very self-image.[74]

Memories were strong of the Russo-Japanese War, when Japan had taken on a great power and succeeded with the aid of mediation in reaching a great victory. Therefore, rather than turn back, Japanese leaders were prepared to take risks. "Nothing ventured, nothing gained," Matsuoka had earlier concluded. "We should take decisive action."[75] The Navy General Staff pressed for war, arguing that oil reserves were limited and that U.S. naval strength was only increasing. Ultimately, this reasoning was accepted. The president of the Privy Council explained to the emperor a month before Pearl Harbor,

It is impossible from the standpoint of our self-preservation to accept all of the American demands. . . . If we miss the present opportunity to go to war, we will have to submit to American dictation. Therefore, I recognize that it is inevitable that we must decide to start a war against the United States. I will put my trust in what I have been told: namely that things will go well in the early part of the war; and that although we will experience increasing difficulties as the war progresses, there is some prospect of success.[76]

Fatalism was in the air. And the new prime minister, General Tōjō, concluded: "Sometimes people have to shut their eyes and take the plunge."[77] As Nobutaka Ike observed in his study of the Japanese decision, "It is easier to make decisions in the face of uncertainty if one is fatalist."[78]

And so the Japanese leaders took their country into a war that could not be won. After decades of sowing the winds of nationalism among the Japanese people, the elites were now reaping the whirlwind. Their decisions were reached in an atmosphere of shrill sentiment and narrowed debate. The course of events seemed to take on its own momentum. A gnawing fear beset Japanese leaders that time was beginning to work against Japan and that preemptive war must be launched while the advantage was still on their side. Oblivious to the ultimate scope and intensity of the conflict on which they embarked and its implications for their civilization, they plunged ahead with blind faith and desperation. "It is a common mistake in going to war," Thucydides observed, "to begin at the wrong end, to act first, and wait for a disaster to discuss the matter."[79]

Unwilling to submit to Hull's terms, which they regarded as an ultimatum, Japan's leaders determined to undertake a bold and crippling blow to the main U.S. battle force in the Pacific. A surprise strike would give the Japanese time to sweep through Southeast Asia, consolidate their control, and seize the resources necessary for total war. The strategy was a gamble worthy of its mastermind, Admiral Yamamoto Isoroku, commander-in-chief of the fleet. Yamamoto, however, had deep misgivings about prolonged conflict with a power whose superior resources, strategic reserves, and latent energies he knew from many years of study and service in the United States. "If I am told to fight regardless of the consequences," he said, "I shall run wild for the first six months or a year, but I have utterly no confidence for the second or third years."[80]

THE ABORTIVE ORDER

Japan did run wild in the first months of the war, conquering more territory in a shorter time than any nation in history.[81] The Japanese sweep through Southeast Asia destroyed the remaining underpinnings of Western imperial power in East Asia. Colonial governments in Hong Kong, Malaya, Singapore, the Dutch East Indies, the Philippines, French Indochina, and Burma yielded to Japanese forces in rapid succession. By the end of 1942, Japan had established dominion over 350 million people, a population three-quarters the size of the British empire, in a vast area from the Solomon Islands in the mid-Pacific to the borders of India and from the rainforests of New Guinea to the icy shores of the Aleutians.

Immediately following Pearl Harbor, the Japanese government announced that the war would be called the Great East Asian War, "because it is a war for the construction of a new order in East Asia" and entailed the "liberation of East Asian peoples from the aggression of America and Britain."[82] And in the beginning, many Asian leaders were exhilarated by Japanese liberation. The Washington System had declared the self-determination of peoples and an end to the old balance-of-power agreements at the expense of Asian countries, but it had not ended imperialism. Only in January 1943, as part of their effort to ensure Chinese morale, did Britain and the United States declare an end to their extraterritorial and other treaty privileges in China.

Japan's anticolonialism, however, soon had a hollow ring, for the Japanese themselves were a colonial power and not disposed to relinquish their holdings. Moreover, Japan was not a wealthy country that could offer generous "public goods" to underwrite its regional order. On the contrary, occupied territories would have to support the liberators. In sum, as Iriye wrote, "It is indicative of the superficiality of the whole concept [of a new order] that the Japanese failed almost completely to devise a coherent scheme for Southeast Asia and the southwestern Pacific. On the eve of Pearl Harbor, there was virtually no blueprint for the administration and development of the region. . . . The lofty calls for a new Asian order concealed a huge intellectual void."[83]

Even as the imminent Japanese expansion into the far reaches of Asia loomed and Chinese resistance quickened, Japanese leaders continued to formulate an ideology that would overcome, or at least appeal to, Asian nationalism. The navy organized a task force to try to provide ideas. Appeal to the notions of the benevolence of the Japanese emperor and "traditional chauvinism," they recognized, had little appeal outside of Japan. "Don't we have," asked one naval officer, "any 'slogan' comparable with the universality of America's democracy?" The task force was charged with working out ideological explanations that could be included in the imperial declaration of war. A task force adviser was perplexed: "I would like the concept of the Greater East Asian Co-Prosperity Sphere clarified here and now. . . . The theory is full of contradictions. . . . [It] is not a reality, nor is it capable of becoming so. We are deceiving the world."[84]

Events were moving fast, and there was no time to resolve the mounting confusion over ideology. Japanese leaders plunged ahead at any cost. In November 1941, the cabinet-military liaison conference concluded that Japan's purpose in the occupied areas was to "acquire speedily raw materials for national defense and to enable the forces of occupation to be self-sufficient." The first priority for the new order, then, would be to contribute to the military and strategic needs of Japan. As Prime Minister Tōjō told the Privy Council, all of East Asia must be made "to unite with Japan and contribute their respective resources to Japan."[85] Concrete plans for the new order would have to wait. In fact, as Hata Ikuhiko wrote, when Japan acquired new territories it followed a

> ruthless policy of local plunder, reminiscent of early Spanish colonial policy. Land was seized for the settlement of Japanese immigrants in Manchuria; on the Chinese mainland businesses and enterprises were confiscated; and Japanese forces fighting in China and later in the Pacific lived off the land. . . . In modern history there has been no other instance of a foreign expeditionary force's adopting a policy of local self-sufficiency from the very outset. It was a glaring demonstration of the enormous disparities between slogans and realities.[86]

In the early months of the war after the attack on Pearl Harbor, Japanese bureaucrats began working to flesh out the concept of the new order. As a substitute for transcendental, universal ideals, they adopted Japan's domestic social values of respect for status—its "confidence in hierarchy"—as a basis of international order. Japanese diplomats found a phrase to reflect this basis: "Every nation must be enabled to find its proper place in the world." It was this principle of observing a just ranking that the Anglo-American powers were accused of violating. On the day of the attack on Pearl Harbor, Japanese diplomats handed to Secretary of State Cordell Hull a memorandum breaking off negotiations and declaring:

> It is the immutable policy of the Japanese Government to insure the stability of East Asia and to promote world peace and thereby to enable all nations to find each its proper place in the world. . . . It is a fact of history that the countries of East Asia for the past hundred years or more have been compelled to observe the status quo under the Anglo-American policy of imperialistic exploitation and to sacrifice themselves to the prosperity of the two nations. The Japanese Government cannot tolerate the perpetuation of such a situation since it directly runs counter to Japan's policy to enable all nations to enjoy each its proper place in the world.[87]

As the "leading race" of Asia, the memorandum said the Japanese would create a Coprosperity Sphere with a division of labor: Each people would perform economic functions that suited their inherent capabilities. Nationalist writings often contained themes of pan-Asianism and liberation of Asians from Western imperialism, but a report produced by Japanese bureaucrats privately described the goal of the new order as creation of "an economic structure which would ensure the permanent subordination of all other peoples and nations of Asia to Japan." The report, completed by mid-1943, was a massive guide for policymakers and administrators, and clearly not for public consumption. Entitled *Global Policy with the Yamato Race as Nucleus,* it expressed, as John Dower aptly wrote, "a long range vision of Japan's projected global 'new order'—a grand view most harried officials simply had no time to articulate."[88] Even when given time to work out plans for the order, Japanese leaders came up with a scheme not so different from the reality the Japanese military was imposing under the exigencies of warfare. The oppressive rule of international law governing independent states would be replaced by a harmonious regional collectivity based on moral and familial ideals modeled by Japan.

Japan had a national mission to organize other peoples while preserving its own purity. Although local customs and traditions would be respected so long as they did not conflict with Japanese interests, the supremacy of Japanese culture was unquestioned. "In this scheme," wrote Dower:

> Japan was the towering metropole, the overwhelmingly dominant hub of the great autarkic bloc. All currency and finance would naturally be tied to the yen. All major transportation and communication networks,

whether on land or by sea or air, were to center on Japan and be controlled by Tokyo. All war-related industrial production, energy sources, and strategic materials would likewise be centralized and controlled by Japan, and, in general, Japan would be responsible for the production of high quality manufactures and finished products in the heavy-industry sector. While Japan would provide capital and technical know-how for the development of light industry (generally for local consumption) throughout the Co-Prosperity Sphere, most countries would remain in their familiar roles as producers of raw materials and semi-finished goods.

This vertical division of labor, the report said, would benefit all Asians, but its ultimate goal was to create "an inseparable economic relationship between the Yamato race, the leader of the East Asia Cooperative Body, and other member peoples, whereby our country will hold the key to the very existence of all the races of East Asia."[89]

In the face of diminishing prospects of Japanese victory in the war effort, Tokyo began to soften the emphasis on Japanese hegemony in the new order and to stress voluntary cooperation among Asian nations. The Japanese were especially concerned with overcoming Chinese resistance and gaining the full support of Wang Ching-wei, who had broken with Chiang Kai-shek and was prepared to establish collaboration with the Japanese if it was on the basis of alliance rather than subordination. In November 1943, a Great East Asia Conference was convened in Tokyo that gathered leaders from among Japan's Asian friends and allies. It is ironic, but indicative of the weakness of the appeal of Japanese ideals, that the declaration drawn up by the Japanese Foreign Ministry and issued at the conference was directly patterned after the Atlantic Charter. Foreign Minister Shigemitsu Mamoru, driven by the deterioration of the war effort, now insisted on a set of universalistic principles.[90] In contrast to earlier stress on Japanese hegemony, it emphasized the achievement of mutual autonomy and independence, open access to raw materials, and cooperation to achieve economic development.

The Japanese aspiration to create their own regional order depended primarily on raw power. Trying to create a new order while they were at war, their resources stretched to the limit, the Japanese were unable to offer the public goods required to bring them lasting support from the Asian states they sought to govern. Although recognizing that the cause was lost, the Japanese Army by 1944 clung desperately to the hope of a "decisive battle" for the homeland so bloody and costly that the enemy would accept a negotiated end to hostilities—one that would avert an occupation, leave the military intact, and allow Japan to rise again. Only after the atomic bombs fell on Hiroshima and Nagasaki and the Soviet Union entered the war against Japan did the emperor intervene and insist that fighting cease.

CHAPTER SEVEN

THE COLD WAR OPPORTUNITY

T he world had never seen the kind of preponderant power that the United States exercised at the end of World War II. "The United States," said Winston Churchill in 1945, "stand at this moment at the summit of the world."[1] America had unchallenged power and wealth. Unlike other major powers, its homeland remained untouched by the ravages of war. Seven and a half million American service personnel were deployed abroad. The U.S. Navy patrolled the oceans of the world. Its scientists had unlocked the explosive power in the heart of matter. Its industrial base produced 40 percent of the world's output and a third of the world's exports. Its treasury garnered two-thirds of the world's gold reserves.

Despite its preponderant power, the task that the United States faced of creating a new order was daunting, for World War II had been a global conflict. It had been fought not only in Europe but in the Middle East and Asia as well. Where World War I had ended in a negotiated peace, in this war the defeated powers, Germany and Japan, had surrendered unconditionally and awaited the occupation and reforms that would be imposed by the United States and its Allies. Regional issues would be much more directly involved in the postwar settlement. This time, re-creating world order meant dealing with Asia in a much more comprehensive fashion. The future of China, Japan, Korea, and European colonies in Asia had to be determined. The war hastened the unraveling of Western colonialism. During the war, Franklin Roosevelt observed to a journalist, "It almost seems that the Japs were a necessary evil in order to break down the old colonial system."[2] The Philippines gained their independence as promised in 1946; India in 1947; Burma and Ceylon in 1948; Indonesia in 1949; and Malaya in 1957.

World War II produced two major settlements—two sharply divergent organizations of the international system.[3] Although they became intertwined, they had different origins. Both had profound implications for the postwar course of Japan and Asia. There was, first, a Liberal Democratic order that the United States had planned during the war. It was based on a vision of a postwar world inspired by Wilsonian goals of democratic government, free trade, collective security, and the rule of law. This was the order that gave birth to the Bretton Woods system for promoting international trade and economic development and the establishment of a multitude of new institutions, including the International Monetary Fund (IMF), the World Bank, and the General Agreement on Tariffs and Trade (GATT). It also produced the United Nations. This Liberal Democratic vision guided the planning of postsurrender Japan and resulted in sweeping reforms in Japan during the first two years of the U.S. Occupation. These U.S.-imposed reforms were designed to transform Japanese institutions and values to conform with the new vision of the postwar international order.

The other post–World War II settlement, which draws the greater attention because of the perilous political struggle that it entailed, was the Cold War order, which began after hopes of U.S.-Soviet cooperation in postwar planning at the Yalta Conference evaporated. Relations between the two victorious powers deteriorated into a forty-year standoff in which the United States and its Allies organized a system to contain Soviet military and geopolitical intentions. In Asia, the Cold War, which began with the Chinese Revolution and the Korean War, divided the region into a bipolar system and fundamentally altered U.S. policy in the region. The United States was compelled to build a security system in Asia and reorient its policy toward Japan's future. Instead of demilitarization and reform, U.S. policy now sought to rebuild Japan as its principal Pacific ally in the Cold War.

Writing of the moment of Japanese surrender on August 15, 1945, a *New York Herald Tribune* correspondent recorded, "Japan, paying for her desperate throw of the dice at Pearl Harbor, passed from the ranks of the major powers at 9:05 a.m. today."[4] Unconditional surrender, occupation, and demilitarization appeared to mark an end to Japan's status as one of the traditional great powers, but as it later turned out, this reordering of the international system afforded a defeated and outcast Japan an unexpected opportunity to restore its position as a major power. After World

War II, Japan's techniques of adapting to the international system were refined to a high order of skill. By brilliantly adapting to both the Liberal Democratic order and to the Cold War system, Japan focused its efforts single-mindedly on economic growth and rose again in a new form. The Liberal Democratic order provided Japan with the free-trade regime within which it could prosper, while the Cold War order offered the benefits of America's security guarantee.

Stanley Hoffmann has observed that international relations theory tends to concentrate its study on the powerful. More attention should be paid, he suggested, to the strategies of the weak in defending their interests.[5] Occupied Japan was weak and vulnerable, and yet it had a strategy. The Japanese were fortunate to have a postwar prime minister who understood the possibilities and how to exploit them. Yoshida Shigeru was a master of the lessons of Japan's strategic culture. The Liberal Democratic order established an international free-trade regime that Japan was able to exploit by creating a national system of political economy. Japan developed industrial policies and a distinctive set of institutions to take advantage of this new international system. Pursuing policies of economic nationalism within a free-trade order would not ordinarily have been tolerated, but because the United States was locked in a life-or-death struggle with the Communist bloc and gave priority to Japanese economic recovery and to the health of its security alliance with Japan, the strategy succeeded. During the Cold War, the paradigm of a pragmatic and opportunistic adaptation to the international order first established by the Meiji Restoration once again became the focus of national policy.

The unique Cold War foreign policy of Japan is best characterized as "mercantile realism." After the U.S. Occupation ended in 1952, Japan's postwar leaders fashioned a strategy to rise as a great economic power by once again reorganizing itself internally to succeed externally. Postwar Japan withdrew from international politics and became, in effect, a military protectorate of the United States. For decades it had no role in international strategic affairs as ordinarily defined. Avoiding the Sturm und Drang of Realpolitik, Japan often seemed to behave more like an international trading firm than a nation-state.

What is notable, however, is that the traditional strategic principles and patterns of Japanese foreign policy were embedded in this new behavior. The postwar conservative political leaders who survived despite the Occupation's radical reforms revived the prewar purpose of achieving national power, but they focused sharply on economic and industrial goals. The realist pursuit of national power, the drive for status and recognition in the world, the swift adaptation and skillful accommodation to the workings of a new international order, the pursuit of economic autonomy, the absence of ideological commitment, the inclination for alliance with the ascendant power, and the obsession to equal the advanced Western industrial nations all were reconfigured in the formulation of a new and unique foreign policy.

THE FAILED YALTA SYSTEM

Even before the United States entered the war, Americans were thinking of how the postwar world should be organized. At Newfoundland in August 1941, President Roosevelt and Prime Minister Churchill had announced their peace aims in the Atlantic Charter. Its declaration of territorial integrity, self-determination, collective security, and free-trade principles echoed Wilsonian ideals. The wording was sometimes muffled by the need to compromise with British hopes to maintain its imperial status, but the U.S. administration was beginning to draw lessons from the breakdown of international order in the 1930s. The Great Depression, fascism, and war were the result of closed and coercive economic blocs, economic nationalism, and the consequent stifling of free trade. Accordingly, the Atlantic Charter announced that the two powers would "endeavor, with due respect for their existing obligations, to further the enjoyment by all States, great or small, victor or vanquished, of access, on equal terms, to the trade and to the raw materials of the world which are needed for their economic prosperity." Recognizing that war had originated too in the crisis of capitalism during the depression, they further declared the need to organize the international economy so as to promote domestic economic stability and social welfare.

As the war drew to a close in 1944, the Americans, with British cooperation, convened the Bretton Woods Conference to flesh out the principles announced in the Atlantic Charter. The historic moment was at hand to realize the American liberal dream of an order of what political scientist David Calleo described as "vigorously prosperous democracies, enjoying security from military aggression, permitting the free movement of goods, money, and enterprise among themselves, and promoting the rapid development and integration of those nations whom liberal progress had left behind."[6] This pursuit was more than idealism. An open trading system would serve U.S. interests. Free trade has always been the ideology of the strong. U.S. economic interests required unimpeded access to the world's resources and markets.

Under determined U.S. leadership, the decades after the war were marked by an unprecedented growth of world trade. Japan, whose attempt to create an autarkic regime had ended in national catastrophe, profited more than any other country from this growth of world trade. "The international environment of the 1960s," a leading conservative theorist observed, "looked as though heaven (*ten*) had created it for Japan's economic growth."[7] Moreover, the provisions in the Bretton Woods system that protected domestic autonomy allowed Japan to pursue a highly successful export growth strategy while at the same time creating a set of domestic institutions that mitigated the intrusive effects of the free-trade order.

Roosevelt's approach to international security bore some resemblance to Wilson's in that he also proposed a collective security organization, the United Nations, but he coupled it with a concert of power based on U.S.-Soviet cooperation. He seems to have been convinced of the need and the possibility of working successfully with Stalin in the management of the postwar world. As John Ruggie observed, "Bipolarity was lacking from FDR's vocabulary." FDR attempted to "engage" the Soviet Union by involving it, so far as possible, in the workings of the new multilateral institutions.[8]

Roosevelt's conviction that the two powers must cooperate persisted despite the difficulty of working with the Soviet Union. Washington attempted, according to John Lewis Gaddis, "to construct a new world economic order without first resolving the deep political differences which divided the United States and the Soviet Union."[9] The Bretton Woods system was intended to include both capitalist and socialist countries. The Russians attended the Bretton Woods meetings but chose not to participate in the system that it established. Stalin was unwilling to allow international scrutiny of his economy or to give up its autarkic dimensions. At the Dumbarton Oaks meetings, where planning for the United Nations was undertaken in 1944, Soviet suspicions of the U.S.-conceived organization grew. Roosevelt sought both to create a universal framework worthy of U.S. ideals and, at the same time, to engage the Russians in a stable postwar security order. It was his notion that the "four policeman"—the United States, the Soviet Union, Britain, and China—would form a concert of power that would be the basis of permanent membership in the Security Council.

Roosevelt pursued regional settlements in Eastern Europe and East

Asia based on U.S.-Soviet cooperation. Stalin, FDR, and Churchill met at Yalta on the Black Sea in February 1945, just months after the Bretton Woods and Dumbarton Oaks meetings, and reached momentous agreements, sometimes referred to as the Yalta system, which recognized Russian and U.S. spheres of influence in the postwar world. The Yalta system envisioned a new regional order in East Asia to fill the vacuum created by the collapse of the Japanese empire. The British still hoped to reassert their colonial position, but the war had drastically weakened the British position, and the Americans had little sympathy for the reestablishment of European colonial holdings in Asia. The Soviets hoped to renew their influence in the Far East, but the Pacific War had brought an extension of U.S. power into the region that was unprecedented.

Prior to Pearl Harbor, the U.S. role in East Asia had been limited, and the rhetoric of the U.S. Open Door policy had always exceeded the ability and readiness to use force to achieve it. But the wartime effort had inevitably elicited a commitment to the outcome of the conflict that implied a long-term involvement in the fate of the region. Nothing symbolized this enhanced U.S. commitment to the future of Asia in more certain and far-reaching terms than the U.S. policy of requiring unconditional Japanese surrender. The United States was determined not only to end Japanese imperialism, but also to eradicate any possibility of its recrudescence. Throughout the war, the Americans had planned for a postsurrender transformation of Japanese society and politics. Nothing in earlier U.S. relations with Asia had entailed anything approaching such an open-ended commitment to the region.

At Yalta, American thinking about East Asia had three fundamental tenets. First, U.S. leaders hoped that the wartime accommodation with Russia could provide the basis for a postwar order that would permit agreement on issues relating to the future of Japan, China, and Korea. Postulating a U.S.-Soviet modus vivendi in the region, FDR envisioned two spheres of influence. The United States, as the dominant power in the Pacific, would exercise the greatest influence over postwar Japan's future, while the Soviet Union would reestablish its earlier influence in Northeast Asia. Second, between their two spheres of influence was a gray area. The two powers would cooperate in trying to stabilize China and facilitate its emergence as a sovereign nation and as an essential participant in a new regional equilibrium. The Americans hoped that China would become a democratic power inclined toward the United States, and that the Russians could be induced to support the Kuomintang government of Chiang Kai-shek. The details of Korea's fate were left vague, although the implication was that it would not be ready for self-government and that some form of trusteeship would need to be worked out. Third, the former European colonies in Asia would join the Philippines in achieving independence and developing Western-style parliamentary democratic governments. Churchill intended that Britain should retain its colonial position in Southeast Asia, but he received no encouragement from Roosevelt on the matter.

Given his attitude toward British aspirations, Roosevelt was surprisingly willing to accommodate Stalin's imperial aims. Roosevelt's wish that Russia enter the Pacific War undoubtedly made him amenable to the Soviet ambition to return to positions held by its tsarist predecessors. Pressed by FDR to commit to enter the war against Japan, Stalin replied, according to David Kennedy, that "it would be difficult for him . . . to explain to the Soviet people why Russia was entering the war against Japan, . . . a country with which they had no great trouble." But, he added unctuously, if certain "political conditions were met, the people would understand . . . and it would be very much easier to explain the decision."[10] The two leaders secretly agreed, excluding Churchill from their meeting, that Russia should receive not only the Kuriles and southern Sakhalin but also a lease for a military base at Port Arthur, access to a free port in Dalian, and the right to manage the major railways in Manchuria. China would retain sovereignty in these northeastern provinces but would not be told of the concessions made to the Soviets until later. In short, FDR promised Stalin a position of influence comparable to what Russia had exercised in Manchuria prior to the Russo-Japanese War.

Roosevelt promised Stalin the old Russian sphere of influence in the Chinese Northeast, but ironically, on returning to Washington, he assured Congress:

The Yalta Conference ought to spell the end of the system of unilateral action, the exclusive alliances, the spheres of influence, the balances of power, and all the other expedients that have been tried for centuries— and have always failed. We propose to substitute for all these, a universal organization in which all peace-loving Nations will finally have a chance to join. I am confident that the Congress and the American people will accept the results of this Conference as the beginnings of a permanent structure of peace.[11]

There was much roseate optimism about the future. Walter Lippmann in his 1944 book *U.S. War Aims* argued that a lasting peace would depend on regional systems of security, with U.S.-British and Soviet orbits. The Soviets should be persuaded to adhere to democratic practice in their orbit and, with such universal values flourishing, peace would have a moral basis.[12]

Roosevelt unfortunately was basing the new order on unrealistic hopes, and it was in Northeast Asia that those hopes would be most decisively dashed. He was persuaded that he would be able to do business with Stalin because the Russian leader had "something else in him besides this revolutionist Bolshevist thing," which he believed was evident from Stalin's early study for the priesthood. "I think," said FDR, "that something entered into his nature of the way in which a Christian gentleman should behave."[13]

It proved impossible to extend the U.S.-Soviet wartime accommodation. As U.S.-Soviet relations deteriorated, President Harry S. Truman from the start of his administration quickly abandoned FDR's engagement of the Soviet Union. U.S.-Soviet relations frayed over disagreements in Eastern Europe and the Middle East. The implications of the so-called Truman Doctrine and the enunciation of the Marshall Plan in 1947 were summed up in the July issue of *Foreign Affairs*, when George Kennan, the director of the State Department's policy planning staff, wrote that the United States must adopt a "policy of firm containment designed to confront the Russians with unalterable counterforce at every point where they show signs of encroaching upon the interests of a peaceful and stable world."[14] The descent into a bipolar standoff in Europe was confirmed in the creation of the North Atlantic Treaty Organization (NATO) in April 1949.

The U.S.-Soviet falling out soon extended to Asian issues. The Yalta system envisioned in East Asia was particularly fragile. Part of the reason was Soviet aims. Another reason was the civil war in China. Over the objections of Churchill and Stalin, Roosevelt had accorded China the status of a major power that would serve as a foundation of the regional order, but that country's domestic politics were still unresolved, and the nation was still struggling for institutional viability. Although the Soviets initially agreed to support the Nationalists and encourage Mao Zedong to join in a coalition government, both Stalin and the Americans were misguided in their expectation that the bitter enemies could be reconciled. Moreover, the divided occupation of the Korean Peninsula also ended in conflict. In 1948–1949, the Russians and the Americans withdrew their troops from the Korean Peninsula, leaving its fate in the hands of the Syngman Rhee regime in the South and the Kim Il Sung regime in the North. In a carelessly worded speech the following year, Secretary of State Dean Acheson excluded South Korea from the U.S. "defensive perimeter."[15]

The civil war in China soon proved intractable to U.S. influence. Seizing the opportunity provided by a war-weakened Nationalist government, the Communists scored repeated military successes. When the victorious Chinese Communists sought a guarantee of their security in an alliance with the Russians, the Yalta vision was no longer viable. In January 1950, as they concluded their Sino-Soviet treaty, Mao asked Stalin if it would not go against the decisions of the Yalta Conference. Stalin replied to the pleased Chinese leader: "True, it does—and to hell with it! Once we have taken up the position that the treaties must be changed, we must go all the way. It is true that for us this entails certain inconveniences, and we will have to struggle with the Americans. But we are already reconciled to that."[16] In June 1950, when the Korean War erupted, the Yalta system was a dead letter. What had been envisioned as a gray area between the Russian and U.S. spheres of influence now was absorbed into the Soviet sphere.

The assumption at Yalta was that Japan would be occupied and thoroughly demilitarized, that its leadership would be tried and purged, and that its entire capacity for national strength would be permanently crippled. In 1948, as the Cold War loomed in Asia, however, the Occupation reversed course, ending two years of sweeping reforms of Japanese society and politics and embarking on a policy of promoting Japanese recovery as the anchor of an emerging new Pacific strategy in the Cold War.

PAX AMERICANA IN JAPAN

In his seminal essay analyzing the way in which the international system can shape domestic institutions, Peter Gourevitch observed, "The clearest form of external influence on domestic politics is outright invasion and occupation."[17] There is no better example than postwar Japan. Never in the history of any modern nation has there been a greater external impact on a nation's domestic institutions than what Japan experienced following its surrender. The international system dealt its ultimate blow to Japan's century-long pursuit of power, primacy, and autonomy. As the emperor intoned laconically in his surrender rescript to his people: "The war situation has developed not necessarily to our advantage, while the trends of the world [*sekai no taisei*] have all turned against our interest."[18] The country was an international outcast, occupied by enemy forces for the first time in its history.

The U.S. Occupation reflected, successively, both of the postwar settlements. The first two years, 1945–1947, represented the reformist phase of the Occupation and were the product of the Liberal Democratic order and its wartime planning. The second phase of the Occupation, 1948–1952, focused on the economic recovery and rehabilitation and was shaped by the emerging Cold War international order.

The Liberal Democratic principles that inspired American thinking about the postwar international order were also of course the basis of U.S. planning for the remaking of postwar Japan. Wherever Americans exercised influence, they sought to implant these values and ideals. Nowhere else was this missionary zeal so unrestrained as in postwar Japan. America's wartime adversary, physically and spiritually devastated, occupied and defeated for the first time in its history, lay open to the influence of the victors. The occupation of Japan represented the very culmination of American liberalism. There was a certain irony that General Douglas MacArthur, the mastermind of the Occupation, was associated with the right wing of the political spectrum in the United States. But his adherence to the liberal credo was testimony to the depth of American faith in the universal claims of its values and institutions. Most of the Americans who participated in the Occupation lacked any clear understanding of Japan's history and culture. They did not consider this an insurmountable barrier, however, because they believed that American values and institutions were of universal validity and that the mission of the Occupation was therefore to instill these values and to build these institutions in Japan.

To the Americans, the whole modern system in Japan had become distorted; because it had not developed along the lines that it had developed in the United States, it was somehow abnormal, unhealthy, and premodern. The United States, whatever its faults, was the most modern of all nations, and since it was assumed that all societies had to develop along more or less the same lines, it was also assumed that changes in Japanese society should be modeled after U.S. institutions. As MacArthur wrote in *Life* magazine in 1947, the values and institutions that came out of the American experience "are no longer peculiarly American, but now belong to the entire human race."[19]

Determined to strip Japan of militarism and the capacity to wage war, the Americans set out to revolutionize the Japanese political structure and society and to erase all vestiges of nationalist doctrine. The occupation forces purged the military and political elites and conducted war crimes trials that held Japanese leaders responsible for crimes against humanity and conspiracy to commit aggression. In nearly every way imaginable, the Occupation sought to ensure that the Japanese state would not be motivated by its traditional pursuit of national power. In one glaring omission, however, the occupation forces left almost the entire civilian bureaucracy intact to run the day-to day business of government. This serious shortcoming of occupation policy ultimately allowed the conservative elite the foothold it needed to retain its old dominance. Although MacArthur imposed a democratic system and a new constitution that provided for popular sovereignty, the bureaucracy preserved remarkable strength of continuity from prewar days and became the major power in postwar Japanese politics.

In a further momentous decision, MacArthur chose to retain the imperial institution and to absolve the emperor of any war responsibility. His decision to keep the emperor as a constitutional monarch served to maintain political stability and to sanction and facilitate reform, but it also left a clouded and ambiguous public sense of responsibility for the war. If the sovereign himself was not even compelled to abdicate and accept responsibility for the disastrous happenings, could his subjects be expected to engage in deep self-reflection? Leaving the elite bureaucracy and the emperor in place constituted two major omissions in U.S. occupation policy, and these omissions diluted the democratic intentions of the Americans and provided the conditions for a conservative resurgence once the Occupation ended.

The Occupation's hastily written and extravagant constitution included among its many liberal provisions an article renouncing rearmament and the right to use force in the conduct of foreign affairs. Article 9, inspired by MacArthur, mirrored the utopian idealism of the time. It provided that "the Japanese people forever renounce war as a sovereign right" and declared that "land, sea, and air forces, as well as other war potential, will never be maintained." Japan, the preamble of the constitution stated, would rely for its security on the peace-loving peoples of the world. The education system would aim to contribute to "the peace of the world and the welfare of humanity by building a democratic and cultural state." The Occupation likewise set out to democratize the economy by breaking up the trusts (*zaibatsu*), redistributing land, and instituting far-reaching labor union rights. The results were mixed. Land reform was an unmistakable success, while trust busting and labor reforms fell well short of their goals. Nevertheless, by 1947 MacArthur felt that the work of reform was nearly complete and surprised reporters and the U.S. government in Washington by suggesting that it was time to plan the end of the Occupation. But before his plans could materialize, the tension between the Soviet Union and the United States and the growing power of the Chinese Communist movement led key U.S. planners to rethink the objectives of the Occupation.

THE EMERGING COLD WAR STRUCTURE IN ASIA

It was the triumph of the Communists in the Chinese Revolution in October 1949 and the outbreak of the Korean War the following June that brought Asia fully into the Cold War. But well before these decisive events, growing tensions with the Soviet Union had impelled a rethinking of the Occupation's objectives. Concern over Japan's vulnerability had been rising for several years and had already prompted a fundamental change in occupation policy. In February 1948, shortly after authoring his famous *Foreign Affairs* article advocating a strategic doctrine of containment, George Kennan made a trip to Japan. Washington soon came to view Japan as a central part of this containment doctrine.

Kennan was concerned that should a peace treaty be negotiated at that time, Japan might soon gravitate—through subversion, intimidation, or domestic radical sentiment—into the Soviet orbit. Given its educated workforce and the consequent industrial potential of its people, Japan represented a prize for whichever side might co-opt it. "Our primary goal," Kennan reasoned, must be to insure that U.S. security "must never again be threatened by the mobilization against us of the complete industrial area [in the Far East] as it was during the second world war." The danger was that the Occupation, in its zeal to demilitarize Japan, would leave it an easy target for Soviet co-optation. The policy planning staff in the State Department concluded that "Japan cannot possess an independent destiny. It can function only as an American or Soviet satellite."[20] Kennan recommended that the purpose of the Occupation be fundamentally revised: "No further reform legislation should be pressed. The emphasis should shift from reform to economic recovery. . . . Precedence should be given . . . to the task of bringing the Japanese into a position where they would be better able to shoulder the burdens of independence."[21] Kennan further explained:

> With the Russians in occupation of North Korea, [Japan] was semi-surrounded by the military positions of the Soviet Union. Yet no provision

of any sort had been made. It was simply madness to think of abandoning Japan to her own devices in the situation then prevailing. She had been totally disarmed and demilitarized. . . . In addition to this, Japan's central police establishment had been destroyed. She had no effective means of combating the communist penetration. . . . In the face of this situation the nature of the Occupational policies pursued up to that time by General MacArthur's headquarters seemed on cursory examination to be such that if they had been devised for the specific purpose of rendering Japanese society vulnerable to communist political pressures and paving the way for a communist takeover, they could scarcely have been other than what they were.

Kennan's recommendations were subsequently accepted by the National Security Council and given presidential approval. Kennan later identified his role in revising policy toward Japan as, "after the Marshall Plan, the most significant, constructive contribution I was ever able to make in government."[22]

Accordingly, a marked shift in occupation policy ensued. Known wryly in Japan as "the reverse course," it was marked by a notable retreat from the idealism and the utopianism of the early Occupation. The entire emphasis of the Occupation shifted from reform to recovery. Along with growing concern about the Japanese left wing's strength, the Occupation aimed to stabilize and stimulate the economy. The precarious economic conditions in Japan aroused concern that the Communists and socialists might succeed in winning a mass following and that Japan would be rendered susceptible to Russian political pressures. In February 1949, the Detroit banker Joseph Dodge was brought to Japan as a financial adviser to the Occupation for the purpose of reviving the Japanese economy. By recommending a balanced national budget and establishing an official exchange rate, Dodge sought to curb inflation and to attract foreign investment. Later in the year, planners in Washington also began to devote attention to providing Japan with foreign markets and sources of raw materials. With Chinese Communist success assured, Washington wanted to deflect Japanese trade with China; the favored area for Japanese economic expansion, from Washington's point of view, now became Southeast Asia.

As the Yalta vision of the future structure of East Asia dimmed and the conflicting aims of the United States and the Soviet Union became unbridgeable, U.S. leaders scrambled to build an alternative system for this vast region into which the war had brought a widening U.S. commitment.

The Americans were initially intent on limiting U.S. commitments in Asia. Secretary of State Dean Acheson's January 1950 speech, in which he discussed the U.S. "defensive perimeter" in the western Pacific and seemed to exclude South Korea and Taiwan, has been blamed for encouraging a North Korean invasion. But in reality, congressional agitation for withdrawal of U.S. combat forces from South Korea following the 1948 elections was a more impressive key to U.S. intentions.

The outbreak of the Korean War in June 1950 was the decisive event that precipitated the Cold War order in East Asia. The North Korean invasion led Washington to a series of decisions that put in place a new security structure in East Asia.[23] In Washington, Japan came to be seen as the ultimate goal of the conflict—the key to the balance of power in Asia.

In the changed international context, the United States viewed the conclusion of a peace treaty with Japan as more about ensuring a Cold War alliance with Japan than about liquidating the legacies of World War II. John Foster Dulles, the Republicans' leading expert on foreign policy, had been brought to Washington as Acheson's consultant on the treaty. This gesture at bipartisanship helped to build a domestic consensus on Asia policy. Dulles's role in creating the new Cold War security structure was critical. He was determined to conclude a peace treaty that would ensure Japanese engagement with the West. Dulles said, "The lessons of Versailles should be remembered. . . . We must not make the same mistake with Japan."[24] Co-opting a beleaguered Japan and keeping the Japanese left wing from coming to power were both critical to the American vision of its own interests. Pentagon planners were beginning to consider the need for long-term bases in Japan and even Japanese rearmament. Okinawa and the great naval facilities at Yokosuka south of Tokyo were now seen as indispensable to the evolving strategy.

Washington's first inclination was to counter the Sino-Soviet bloc by establishing a balance of power through a comprehensive treaty structure for the Pacific akin to NATO. In 1950, Republican Congressman Jacob Javits from New York proposed legislation to create a counterpart to NATO in the Pacific. In the spring, the State Department began planning a Pacific Pact that would provide a collective security blanket for U.S. allies in the region. The pact would allow U.S. troops to remain in Japan and encourage Japan to undertake limited rearmament while at the same time reassuring Japan's former adversaries, including Australia, New Zealand, and the Philippines, that such rearmament would not threaten them.[25] The purpose was to facilitate Japanese rearmament but to keep it under international control. Such an alliance, permitted under Article 51 of the UN Charter, would internationalize Japanese forces, Dulles reasoned, and thereby "ease reconciliation with the present . . . Constitution."[26]

Dulles was strongly committed to creating a multilateral Pacific Pact because it would permit Japanese rearmament while providing ongoing constraints on the former enemy. In this way, all other Pacific nations could be assured that Japanese nationalism was bridled. As he explained to MacArthur in December 1950, "This would provide a framework with which a Japanese force, if developed, could have an international status rather than a purely national status."[27] Dulles envisioned inclusion of the island nations of Australia, New Zealand, the Philippines, Japan, perhaps Indonesia, and the United States. Japan's military would be woven into a multilateral organization, as Germany's was in NATO.

But multilateralism of the kind that created NATO was not possible in Asia. Both in Japan and among the other countries that Dulles hoped to include in the Pacific Pact, the resistance to the creation of such an organization was strong. Historical, geographical, and political forces all militated against multilateralism. The Japanese pacifism and demilitarized state structure that the Occupation had established made Japanese inclusion difficult. In Australia, New Zealand, and the Philippines, where memories of Japanese imperialism were still fresh, the governments were strongly opposed to a liberal peace treaty with Japan and to the rearming of Japan. They were also opposed to policies that would restore Japan as an economic competitor in Southeast Asia. They insisted that if U.S. policy was to be reoriented in this way they must have security guarantees. Dulles needed the cooperation of these allies for the new strategic position Japan was to occupy in U.S. Asian policy, but the Pacific nations resisted his scheme for a Pacific NATO, as did the Japanese prime minister.

At this key juncture, Washington was forced to build a security structure markedly different from its containment strategy in Europe. With the possibility of a single blanket organization similar to NATO foreclosed by the resistance of the nations in the region, especially Japan itself, the United States negotiated a series of singular agreements. As described by one informed observer, the treaty system established by the United States in the Pacific was "piecemeal and jerry-built." It was a patchwork affair, cobbled together without an effort to create a cohesive and integrated system.[28]

On the eve of the 1951 San Francisco conference, which was held to conclude both a peace treaty and a security treaty with Japan, the United States negotiated a bilateral security treaty with the Philippines and a tripartite mutual defense pact among Australia, New Zealand, and the United States (ANZUS). Bilateral security pacts were signed with South Korea in 1953 and the following year with the Nationalist government on Taiwan. In 1954, key Southeast Asian countries were brought together in the Southeast Asia Treaty Organization (SEATO). Although it entailed multiple signatories, SEATO was not a multilateralized collective self-defense organization like NATO; it simply prescribed consultations in the event of outside attack. These many security treaties bound the United States to each ally, but they did not bind all the allies among themselves. What later came to be referred to as the "hub-and-spokes alliance structure" contrasted sharply with the integrated NATO structure established under U.S. leadership in Europe.

Amidst all of this patchwork, what was remarkable was the reversal of Japan's role. In five years' time, it was transformed from bitter wartime enemy to the lynchpin, the key ally, in the new U.S. security structure in Cold War Asia. This transformation confronted Japan with fundamental choices as to how to respond to the emerging structure of relations in which it would be asked to assume an active role. And it also provided an opportunity for Japan to accommodate to the new world order in a fashion that would begin to allow it to restore its status as a major power.

YOSHIDA SHIGERU AND JAPAN'S RESPONSE

One of the most surprising and important developments of postwar Japan was the resilience of the conservative elite. As in the case of the Meiji Restoration, so in the "American revolution" in Japan, members of the old ruling class reemerged. Despite the revolutionary reforms that the Americans imposed during the early years of the Occupation, conservative leaders, values, and institutional practices survived the upheaval and served as central features of postwar Japanese politics and foreign policy. The postwar political order, then, was not as radically new as many observers thought at the time. In largely sparing the civilian bureaucratic elite from the purge, the Americans permitted an unexpected continuity of a key part of the prewar conservative hierarchy. Oblivious to the potential power of an independent bureaucratic elite, which in the prewar period had drafted over 90 percent of the legislation submitted to the Diet, the occupation forces kept the bureaucracy intact to run the day-to-day business of government.

Seasoned bureaucrats emerged in a dominant position in the postwar order. In addition to their traditional power base in the ministries, these veterans of the prewar conservative establishment moved into leadership positions in postwar political parties and provided a continuity of both personnel and purpose. Despite the fact that the postwar political regime was, in many respects, quite distinct from its predecessor, the values of the prewar state thereby survived in a new setting. The significance of this development was profound. This survival of conservative leadership resulted in the continuation of the strategic principles and logic of Japan's prewar approach to the international system.

Among the surviving conservatives, the key figure in shaping postwar politics and the conception of national purpose was Yoshida Shigeru, who was prime minister for most of the first decade of the postwar period and who served concurrently as foreign minister during much of this time. Yoshida is one of the most important figures in modern Japanese history. Japan has not been known for its great leaders. The political culture does much to discourage the emergence of a strong charismatic individual leader. But Yoshida was an exception.

Leaders like Yoshida had rarely been seen since the Meiji oligarchs had passed from the scene. Shrewd and arrogant, brilliant and abrasive, scion of a prominent family, he rose through the ranks of the prewar Foreign Ministry, serving during the 1930s as ambassador first to Italy and then to Great Britain. Devoted to the imperial cause, Yoshida believed it was best pursued by accommodation to the Anglo-American powers and "making use of" those powers for the benefit of Japan. During the 1930s, he had often been appalled by Japanese international relations—not by the goals of Japanese imperialism but by the way they were implemented, which he believed needlessly affronted the Anglo-American powers. During the war, his opposition to the militarists landed him in the custody of the Kempeitai, the military police, who held him under arrest for ten weeks after they discovered he was behind a secret but abortive attempt to bring about an early end to the war.

Although Yoshida was at heart a conservative, an elitist, and a nationalist, his wartime opposition to the militarists made him acceptable to the Occupation as a leader of postwar Japan. His appointment as prime minister was sanctioned by the Occupation in May 1946, following the first postwar election. Despite his enmity toward the militarists, Yoshida was neither a liberal nor a democrat. He was a realist and nationalist, determined to preserve as much as possible of the old imperial order and to set Japan on a path that would restore the nation as a great power. In the desolation and despair of the postwar days, when Japan was an international pariah and the nation's fortunes were at the lowest point in history, Yoshida succeeded in putting together a sense of national purpose that guided the country for the next four decades. It far outlived his own career, in part because he installed a powerful group of followers in the conservative ruling party and in the bureaucracy to carry on his policies in the decades after he left office.

Yoshida's influence also endured because of his extraordinary skill in perceiving world trends and in using them to Japan's special advantage. Yoshida epitomized Japan's strategy of adaptiveness to the changed international system and brought to this tactic a special skill and memorable brilliance. In circumstances that required the utmost deftness, he more than any other modern Japanese statesman possessed the tactical insight to make the best of the desperate situation.

Yoshida embodied some of the extraordinary qualities of statecraft that Machiavelli had counseled in his treatise on the art of politics. He had a keen sense of the potential benefits that Japan might garner from the changes then taking place in international politics. When he formed his first cabinet in the spring of 1946, Yoshida observed to a colleague that "history provides examples of winning by diplomacy after losing in war" (*sensō de makete gaikō de katta rekishi wa aru*).[29] That is, a defeated nation, by exploiting the shifting relations among world powers, could contain the damage incurred in defeat and instead win the peace. Yoshida was a keen student of diplomatic history; he may have been likening himself to Talleyrand, the French foreign minister who had gone to the Congress of Vienna in 1815 to win back with diplomatic skill what France had lost in the disastrous Napoleonic wars.[30] Already in 1946, when he became prime minister, tensions between the Americans and Soviets were apparent, and Yoshida sensed that disputes between victors over the postwar settlement might be used to Japan's advantage. In fact, the Cold War offered just such an opportunity.

In the immediate postwar period, Yoshida's primary concern in foreign affairs was to restore Japan's reputation and gain acceptance by the international community. This goal entailed convincing world opinion that Japan had changed and that the Japanese people were indeed committed to a new, peaceful course. Yoshida determined that Japan should associate itself as closely as practicable with the United States, the new hegemonic power. But doing so did not mean sacrificing the national interest to the U.S. purpose. On the contrary, as he said half seriously, "Just as the United

States was once a colony of Great Britain but is now the stronger of the two, if Japan becomes a colony of the United States, it will also eventually become the stronger."[31] In other words, Japan could look to its long-range interests by assuming for the time being a subordinate role within the U.S. international order.

As the Americans began to regard Japan as the key to the future balance of power in Asia, Japanese leaders had to determine how to respond to the emerging Cold War structure and the American expectation that Japan should now actively join in providing for its own security and contributing to the containment of Communist power in the region. Negotiating an end to the Occupation compelled Yoshida to formulate in much greater detail and sophistication the nature of Japan's postwar national purpose. He knew that in the changed international environment, the United States was unlikely to relinquish its military position in Japan in the near future. If Japan were to gain its independence—that is, an end to the Occupation— any time soon, it would be necessary to offer the Americans continued access to bases inside Japan. Therefore, in May 1950, Yoshida dispatched his protégé, Ikeda Hayato, to Washington to offer bases in exchange for an early return to sovereignty. In the course of the negotiations that transpired over the next several years, Yoshida worked out a brilliant strategy— what we may in retrospect call a Yoshida Doctrine[32]—that served for the next several decades.

The critical moment for the determination of Japan's postwar strategy arrived in 1950, when the Korean conflict crystallized the structure of the new order. The U.S.-Soviet rivalry presented both dangers and opportunities to Japan. The dangers were that Japan would be drawn into Cold War politics, expend its limited and precious resources on remilitarization, and postpone the full economic and social recovery of its people. On the positive side, however, Yoshida knew that the Cold War made Japan strategically important to the United States. He recognized that the Americans were no longer intent on reforming Japan but instead rehabilitating it to serve its interests in the global struggle with the Soviet bloc. Transforming Japan into a democratic political economy was no longer a priority. U.S. policy toward Japan, in short, was now a piece in a much larger puzzle. Japan was an asset that was essential to U.S. foreign policy strategy.

"The future of the world," Dulles repeatedly asserted, "depends largely on whether the Soviet Union will be able to get control over Western Germany and Japan by means short of war. . . . The world balance of power would be profoundly altered."[33] The situation gave Yoshida bargaining leverage. He reasoned that Japan could make minimal concessions of passive cooperation with the United States in return for an early end to the Occupation, a long-term guarantee of Japan's national security, and an opportunity to concentrate on all-out economic recovery.

The United States now purposed to draw Japan into a regional defense system and to remilitarize it for the Cold War. As Vice President Richard Nixon publicly admitted in 1953, U.S. leaders came to feel that imposition of Article 9 and the disarmament of Japan were "mistakes." When Dulles came to Tokyo in June 1950 to negotiate a peace treaty and the end of the Occupation, he urged Japanese rearmament. In this and subsequent meetings, Dulles sought to undo the MacArthur constitution by establishing a large Japanese military force. He broached the concept of the Pacific Pact. Yoshida refused to accede to these demands. This option of integration with neighboring Asian nations was not attractive to him because of his sense of nationalism. In marked contrast to his contemporary Chancellor Konrad Adenauer in Germany, who sought to resolve the "German question" and the fear of German rearmament by integrating West Germany into NATO, Yoshida had no interest in a regional alliance. Nor did he attempt to deal with war guilt by taking the initiative in reaching out to former victims of wartime aggression. Whereas Adenauer proposed reparations to Israel, Yoshida was interested in reparations only to the extent that they might pave the way for development of trade relations. Ōtake Hideo wrote that "unlike Adenauer . . . Yoshida never desired cultural or political integration of Japan with the West or with neighboring Asian nations. Although he was eager for international economic integration, he wished to maintain a distinctive cultural identity for the Japanese people."[34]

Seizing the opportunity for what Professor Nagai Yōnosuke termed "blackmail by the weak," Yoshida refused to accede to U.S. demands.[35] He established his bargaining position with Dulles by making light of Japan's security problems and intimating that Japan could protect itself through its own devices by being democratic and peaceful and by relying on the protection of world opinion. After all, he argued, Japan had a constitution that, inspired by U.S. ideals and the lessons of defeat, renounced arms, and the Japanese people were determined to uphold it and to adhere to a new course in world affairs.

Yoshida's "puckish" and bravado performance left Dulles (in the words of a colleague) "flabbergasted," embittered, and feeling "very much like Alice in Wonderland."[36] In succeeding meetings, Yoshida negotiated from this position. He skillfully argued that rearmament would impoverish Japan and create the kind of social unrest that the Communists wanted. We now know that through backdoor channels he was even prevailing on Japan Socialist Party leaders to whip up anti-rearmament demonstrations and campaigns during Dulles's visits to Tokyo.[37] Allusion to the prospect of a leftist government coming to power became a convenient pretext for holding to his position and dissuading the Americans from putting undue pressure on Japan to rearm. Yoshida further pointed out to Dulles the fears that other Asian countries had of a revived Japanese military. He even enlisted the support of MacArthur, who obligingly told Dulles that Japan should remain a nonmilitary nation and instead contribute to the free world through its industrial production.[38] The transformation of Japan into an industrial power, needless to say, was precisely what Yoshida sought. Yoshida's firmness spared Japanese military involvement in the Korean War and allowed it instead to profit enormously from procurement orders. Yoshida privately called the resulting stimulus to the economy "a gift of the gods."[39] More such gifts appeared over the next decades.

In the protracted negotiations with Dulles, Yoshida made minimal concessions; he consented to U.S. bases on Japanese soil and a limited rearmament, which was sufficient to gain Dulles's agreement to a peace treaty and to a post-Occupation guarantee of Japanese security. Yoshida grudgingly agreed to upgrade the National Police Reserve, which MacArthur had established in July 1950 with 75,000 men, to the status of National Security Force in January 1952 with 110,000 men. Yoshida's manipulation of both domestic politics and U.S. pressure was shrewd and cynical. At every step of the negotiations, Yoshida invoked the strength of left-wing and pacifist sentiment as a means of tempering U.S. pressure for rearmament. Moreover, he was keenly aware of apprehension in the United States, as well as in Europe and Asia, about rearmament possibly going too far and reawakening militarism. The potential of a nationalist revival, on the one hand, and a left-wing takeover, on the other, served as a brake on U.S. demands.

Above all, it was Yoshida's cynical use of the U.S.-imposed constitution that served as his best shield. A comment that he made to a young aide, Miyazawa Kiichi, is highly revealing of his method. Miyazawa, who later became a prime minister and a durable political leader, recorded in his memoir that Yoshida told him: "The day [for rearmament] will come naturally when our livelihood recovers. It may sound devious (*zurui*), but let the Americans handle [our security] until then. It is indeed our Heaven-bestowed good fortune that the Constitution bans arms. If the Americans complain, the Constitution gives us a perfect justification. The politicians who want to amend it are fools."[40] Yoshida was convinced that the Cold

War would require the United States to maintain its presence in Japan, which alone would be sufficient to deter a Soviet attack. He would therefore give exclusive priority to pursuing Japanese economic recovery and maintaining political stability and would defer indefinitely the task of preparing the Japanese people for a return to the hard realities of international politics.

Those who theorize about the structure of international politics are sometimes faulted for failing to give sufficient significance to human agency—to the difference that the individual can make. The Meiji leadership group, with its remarkable sensitivity to the workings of the international system and its formulation of a strategy to accommodate to it, is an example of the importance of individuals. Yoshida is another extraordinary example of an individual who made a big difference. There was nothing inevitable about his choices. Although American power and influence in Japan were immense, Yoshida had room for maneuver. As Iokibe Makoto has emphasized, other conservatives who might have been leaders in this era would have made different choices.[41] They sharply disagreed with him and strongly favored rearmament and a tighter alliance with the United States. Many of them were deeply sympathetic with the course of action the Americans were pressing.

Ashida Hitoshi best exemplified this position. An exponent of cooperation with the Anglo-American powers in the 1920s and an opponent of militarism in the 1930s, he maintained his liberal stance through the dark days of the 1940s. In the postwar period, he chaired the Constitution Review Committee in the Diet, where, as he later explained, he inserted amendments to Article 9 designed to allow for self-defense and for participation in UN peacekeeping forces. When the defense issue surfaced in 1950 with the outbreak of the Korean War, Ashida grew increasingly agitated, writing in his diary one month after the war started: "I think the Japanese today are truly foolish and cowardly. There are fools who think the [Korean] incident is a war that concerns third parties with no relation to them."[42] In December, he wrote, "It is impermissible for Japan alone to adopt the attitude of a bystander. Japan today is in urgent need of unifying its national purpose. . . . The government should explain to the people that Japan is on the brink of danger and that the Japanese people must resolve to defend the country by their own efforts."[43] In January 1951, likeminded conservatives issued a declaration asserting that "the Japanese are not a cowardly people who will rely on the occupation powers to preserve their stability and security while standing by with arms folded and without shedding a drop of blood."[44]

Yoshida rejected such admonitions from his fellow conservatives. He also had to contend with a strong and vocal left wing, which demanded that Japan adopt a neutral stance in the Cold War; that no post-Occupation U.S. bases remain on Japanese soil; that a comprehensive peace treaty, including the Soviet Union and China as well as the United States and its allies, be signed; and that no amendment of the constitution to allow rearmament be contemplated.

Between these two widely divergent views—on the one hand, the conservatives, supporting rearmament, and on the other, the progressives, inalterably opposed to it—were a sizable number of conservatives who backed Yoshida. Reflecting deeply on the lessons of defeat, they had come to believe that postwar Japan could best pursue its national interest by concentrating on building industrial strength so as to become a powerful trading state. A remarkably revealing anecdote about Ōkita Saburō, postwar Japan's leading economic planner—who, significantly, also served as foreign minister in the 1970s—illustrates how the war influenced postwar foreign policy choices. In the spring of 1945, as the last months of the war were unfolding, Ōkita visited an old friend who was an engineering professor at Tokyo Imperial University. Knowing that the war was already lost, the two men fell to talking about the lessons learned and about Japan's postwar prospects. The engineer recorded in his diary that Ōkita felt that all was not lost if Japan could draw the proper lesson from its tragic experience, namely, that "Japan, poorly endowed with natural resources, must shape its future around precision engineering." In other words, Ōkita believed that Japan must concentrate its energies on taking imported raw materials and fashioning them into high-quality products for export:

> Ōkita made himself comfortable and we spoke for a long time. He told me this story from around 1882 which an Englishman—it might have been Bagehot—used to tell as a warning to the people of his time. A poor warrior wanted to buy a splendid suit of armor but had no money, so he cut down on the amount of food he ate and little by little saved enough to buy a fine suit of armor. A war broke out and courageously he left to fight, but because his body had become so weak from his years of semi-starvation, he could not bear the weight of his armor and was soon slain by the enemy. This was just what happened to Japan. He did not think that a defeated Japan would be allowed to rearm at all, but this would probably be a blessing in disguise. I completely agreed with what he said. I will actually be happy if rearmament is completely prohibited. An army in uniform is

not the only sort of army. Scientific technology and fighting spirit under a business suit will be our underground army.[45]

As it turned out, the postwar international system provided Japan with extraordinary opportunities for a newly focused national purpose: building Japan into a great economic power. Defeat had utterly discredited a military strategy for gaining access to the raw materials and markets that were essential to national strength. Building Japan's industrial strength early in the twentieth century had been intended to restore Japan's national independence, but industrialization had only increased Japan's reliance on the external world. Devoid of the raw materials required for modern industry, Japan had to import them; it had to export finished goods to pay for them. Overcoming the resulting vulnerability and restoring its independence and self-mastery became a paramount objective. Japan fought the Pacific War to reestablish its economic autonomy, but its paucity of resources created a deep dependence on foreign markets and a profound vulnerability that military power had failed to overcome.

It was Yoshida's exceptional judgment that enabled him to begin to weave these many strands of domestic opinion together with international trends to form a coherent strategy. With the heavy hand of the military now removed from control of national policy, the economic bureaucrats and their industrial partners were free to pursue Japan's security interests on their own terms. The emerging bipolar structure of the international system meant that the original American concept of a Liberal Democratic order, based on free trade and multilateral institutions to manage the international political economy, was applied to a more limited area than the worldwide system originally envisioned at the time of the Bretton Woods Conference. Instead, the concept came to provide greater cohesion to the Western bloc in the Cold War struggle. Moreover, the Cold War increased America's willingness to provide a wide range of "public goods" to strengthen the Western bloc that it led.

THE YOSHIDA DOCTRINE AND THE SAN FRANCISCO PEACE TREATY

At this critical moment, as the structure of the new international system in East Asia emerged, Yoshida made fundamental choices that set Japan on its course for the remainder of the Cold War period. His resistance to U.S.

pressure for Japanese remilitarization carried a price. On September 8, 1951, the same day that the San Francisco Peace Treaty was signed, a security treaty was also signed between Japan and the United States that was highly unequal. It preserved many of the occupation prerogatives of the U.S. military and in effect made Japan a military satellite of the United States. In addition to granting bases to the United States, it gave the United States the right to intervene to quell domestic disorder in Japan, the right to project military power from bases in Japan against a third country without consulting Japan, and an indefinite time period for the treaty. In addition, the United States insisted on extraterritorial legal rights for its military and dependents. At the same time, to ensure Senate passage of the treaty, Yoshida was compelled to recognize Taiwan as the legitimate government of China and thus to forswear normal relations with the mainland government.

U.S. pressure on Japan to participate actively in its alliance system was unrelenting. Shortly after the peace and security treaties were signed in October 1951, Congress passed the Mutual Security Assistance (MSA) Act, which was designed "to consolidate the American alliance system through the supply of weapons and equipment, participation of allied officers in training programs in the United States, and the overall coordination of military strategies."[46] The efforts of the Americans to persuade Japan to participate in this more intimate military relationship called forth another bravado performance by Yoshida in which he sought to gain the economic benefits of the relationship while avoiding the strategic obligations.

The United States pressed Japan to accept military aid for a threefold expansion of its forces from the 110,000-man National Security Force to an army of 350,000. Yoshida knew that increasing the size of the army, besides being controversial at home, would hasten the moment when the United States would press Japan to dispatch it for overseas conflict in the Cold War. He was instinctively hostile to participation in the arrangement, but he also knew that Japan nonetheless needed the aid for economic development and reconstruction that the Americans held out. Japanese business leaders wanted further economic aid for reconstruction, acquisition of advanced technology, and improved industrial competitiveness. These business leaders, along with the Ministry of International Trade and Industry (MITI), also advocated building an arms export industry in Japan. Yoshida and Ministry of Finance (MOF) bureaucrats were, however, leery of building a defense industry for export. A military-industrial complex not only could ensnare Japan in external military affairs but would also impose budgetary demands.

Yoshida again set out to contain U.S. pressure for military obligations and to use MSA aid for economic reconstruction and development. He concentrated on diverting the bulk of MSA support into commercial purposes and, at the same time, acquiring advanced technology that could be spun off for commercial purposes, principally through licensed coproduction of U.S. weapons. "Thus, with help from the Americans, Japan's defense bureaucracy and the arms industry became subordinate to the economic bureaucracy and civilian producers."[47] Professor Nagai Yōnosuke sees this as a turning point: If Japan had moved toward a military-industrial complex in tandem with the Americans, he said, "there would have been no Japanese economic miracle."[48] Given the enormous pressure that Dulles and the U.S. government brought to bear, however, Yoshida had to expand the National Security Force in order to preserve a satisfactory relationship with the United States. Nonetheless, his finely honed sense of national purpose once again succeeded in limiting Japan's obligations. It was to become a pattern for the future postwar decades of U.S.-Japan relations: Japan would respond to U.S. pressure with the minimum concessions necessary to maintain the alliance relationship, invoking the constitution to justify the minimalist approach.

The MSA agreement that Japan and the United States signed in March 1954, while acknowledging (as in the security treaty) that "Japan will itself increasingly assume responsibility for its own defense," at the same time emphasized that "Japan can only contribute to the extent permitted by its general economic conditions." It also acknowledged that "the present Agreement will be implemented by each Government in accordance with the constitutional provisions of the respective countries." At the signing ceremonies, Okazaki Katsuo, the Japanese foreign minister, explained: "There are no new and separate military duties. Overseas service and so on for Japan's internal security force will not arise."[49] Japan was able to direct substantial MSA assistance into economic development, helping to overcome the economic stagnation that set in as the Korean War ended.

In the same month that the MSA agreement was signed, the Japanese government, complying with the demands brought by Washington, introduced legislation to reorganize and to expand the armed forces, including an air force. Even while providing the legal basis of Japan's subsequent military organization, Yoshida was able to temper U.S. demands in significant ways. In 1954, the Defense Agency was established with responsibility for ground, maritime, and air self-defense forces with a total of 152,000 men— substantially less than half of what the United States had demanded.

Facing the strong likelihood of continued U.S. pressure to expand its military and contribute to the Cold War struggle, Yoshida proceeded to erect new barriers against such demands. Article 9 had to be interpreted in such a way as to preempt U.S. pressure. The government was advised by an elite bureaucratic agency, the Cabinet Legislation Bureau (CLB), on the legal aspects and ultimately the constitutionality of prospective legislation.[50] Yoshida personally supervised the drafting of a new interpretation of Article 9 that would permit possession of a military with only "the minimum necessary" for self-defense in the event of an invasion. Moreover, according to this interpretation, the Self-Defense Forces (SDF) could not be sent abroad or participate in any collective defense arrangements. For the remainder of the Cold War, the CLB adhered unswervingly to this interpretation.

Since the Japanese Supreme Court steadfastly declined to be drawn into political controversy by ruling on issues involving the constitutionality of the Self-Defense Forces, Yoshida's narrow interpretation of the constitution, defended by the CLB, endured for nearly four decades. That is, from 1954, when the Self-Defense Forces were organized under U.S. pressure, until the end of the Cold War, it was the fixed policy of the Japanese government that the constitution did not permit participation in collective defense arrangements or deployment of the SDF abroad. Thus, for example, during the Vietnam conflict, when the United States pressed its South Korean ally to dispatch over 300,000 men to participate, the Japanese government, insisting on its constitutional prohibition, avoided deployment while benefiting from the procurement orders that the war produced. Yoshida, of course, had compelling reasons for his stance. He knew that acquiescence to U.S. demands would be deeply divisive at home and arouse opposition throughout Asia. But the fundamental reason for his choice was the conviction that Japan must not allow involvement in the Cold War to impede its economic recovery.

So narrow and self-centered was Japan's sense of national purpose that U.S. Ambassador to Japan John Allison concluded in 1954 that "Japan has no basic convictions for or against the free world." The Americans reluctantly accepted the fact that the ideals of the Western alliance and of the Liberal Democratic vision of world order held little persuasive power for the Japanese leadership. Dulles, once again frustrated by Yoshida's intransigence on the rearmament issue, confessed himself "grievously disappointed" that there was neither "revival of the spirit of sacrifice and discipline" nor a "great national spirit."[51] As

Yoshida's aide, Miyazawa Kiichi, put it years later: Japan would conduct a "value-free diplomacy."[52]

In December 1954, Yoshida fell from power. In one sense, it was the end of an extraordinary era, for Yoshida had dominated domestic politics during the formative postwar decade. In another sense, as we shall see, the era was not over. Yoshida's influence continued for several more decades. He was forced into retirement by his conservative opponents, political nationalists who chafed at his economics-first policies and his refusal to forge an independent foreign policy. They governed from 1955 to 1960 with a wholly different approach. They wanted to revise the constitution, to carry out a forthright rearmament, to negotiate a more equal security treaty with the United States, and generally to pursue a more autonomous and independent course.

The agenda of Yoshida's conservative opponents, which could have succeeded in 1950 if Yoshida had supported it, encountered great obstacles in the latter half of the 1950s. The left wing of the Japan Socialist Party (JSP) was now firmly in control of the party and passionately committed to an ideological defense of the constitution and a neutralist foreign policy. In addition, Yoshida, now out of power, sabotaged the efforts to achieve an independent foreign policy stance by raising doubts in Washington about his successor's negotiations with the Soviet Union to achieve a peace treaty. With a Japanese conservative government in power that was bent on revising the constitution, Washington had an opportunity to achieve the kind of response on rearmament that it had long sought, but at the same time it was suspicious of Tokyo's independent course. In any case, the JSP had gained sufficient strength in the Diet to oppose the conservatives, and its hold on public opinion through the support of the media, intellectuals, and the unions made constitutional revision virtually impossible.

The United States and Japan did, however, move to revise and update their security treaty. Kishi Nobusuke, an anti-Yoshida conservative who served as prime minister from 1957 to 1960, wanted to eliminate the unequal aspects of the existing treaty, including the clause permitting U.S. intervention in domestic disturbances. He wanted a voice in the deployment of U.S. forces stationed in Japan, and he wanted a fixed term for the treaty and an explicit guarantee of U.S. protection in case of an attack on Japan. Kishi, who had served in the Tōjō cabinet and had been indicted as a war criminal during the Occupation, aroused widespread distrust among Japanese. The JSP mounted fierce public opposition to ratification of the new security treaty, which was nevertheless signed in 1960. Ratification was rammed through the Diet, and the issue provoked the greatest mass demonstrations in Japanese history. As the final deliberations in the Diet were completed, hundreds of thousands of protesters gathered in front of the building and 6 million workers went on strike. When final ratifications were exchanged at the foreign minister's residence, beer crates were stacked by the fence so that the U.S. ambassador could escape student activists, if necessary, by scaling the fence and running across neighboring gardens to a waiting limousine. Although such a humiliating conclusion to the ceremonies was avoided, the 1960 security treaty crisis did result in the cancellation of a visit from President Dwight D. Eisenhower. Prime Minister Kishi resigned, and the conservatives retreated to Yoshida's economics-first strategy.

This tumultuous reaction to raising the divisive issues of rearmament gave a long-term advantage to the Yoshida strategy. The demonstrations of 1960 showed the strength of popular opposition to rearming. If conservatives continued to raise the issue of rebuilding Japan's military, they would subject the country to prolonged turmoil. For the next two decades, Japan's leaders shelved these divisive issues to avoid weakening the nation's political stability. The conservatives, who in 1955 were all joined in a newly formed Liberal Democratic Party (LDP), turned again to the Yoshida wing of the party, which was now acknowledged as the mainstream. For the remainder of the Cold War, excepting the Nakasone administration (1982–1987), the LDP was dominated by the Yoshida wing.

The Costs of the Yoshida Doctrine

The realism of Japan's conservative elite brought many successes, but they came at a high cost in national self-respect. Yoshida's strategy was deftly executed. To assume a role of "subordinate dependence" on the United States worked beyond all realistic expectation. All-out concentration on policies of economic realism proved a viable means of restoring Japan's role as a great power, but this approach exacted a great toll on Japan's national pride and amour propre. To acquiesce in a role of dependence and subordination to the United States in its security policy, Japan sacrificed a good measure of international respect.

Later, in the 1960s, when his policies were hardening into a long-term national strategy, Yoshida felt cause for regret. He wrote to a colleague that

"the renewal of national strength and development of political independence require that Japan possess a military force as a matter of national
honor," and he confessed to "deep feelings of responsibility over the present situation on the national defense issue."[53] In 1963, he wrote in his book
Sekai to Nippon (Japan and the World):

> In my recent travels, I have met with leaders of other countries who have
> recovered from war and are contributing to world peace and prosperity. I
> feel Japan should be contributing too. For an independent Japan, which is
> among the first rank of countries in economics, technology, and learning,
> to continue to be dependent on another country is a deformity (*katawa*) of
> the state. . . . For Japan, a member of the United Nations and expecting its
> benefits, to avoid support of its peacekeeping mechanisms is selfish be-
> havior. This is unacceptable in international society. I myself cannot es-
> cape responsibility for the use of the Constitution as a pretext (*tatemae*) for
> this way of conducting national policy.[54]

There was a deep irony in the course that Yoshida set for the nation. On
the one hand, he was a patriot in the traditional sense. He was married to
the granddaughter of the prominent early Meiji leader Ōkubo Toshimichi
and therefore had strong ties to the goals and values of the Meiji Restoration. Yoshida's strategic approach to the international system was very
much in the tradition of the Restoration. An opportunist in the large
sense, his commitment was to establishing Japan's position in the world by
accommodating to the existing international order and adapting to its
structure in a way that would serve Japan's interests. This approach carried
its risks. Where the Meiji leaders had risked Japan's cultural identity by emulating all the institutions of the West and accepting rather than resisting
the mores of the imperialist system, Yoshida risked Japan's integrity and
self-respect by sacrificing all semblance of political independence in the interest of the more practical goal of economic recovery.

After he left office and began to reflect on his legacy, Yoshida seems to
have had second thoughts. Perhaps he was chagrined at the cynicism and
sheer opportunism of his approach. When his biographer and scholarly
admirer Kōsaka Masataka identified his policies with a strategy of "neo-
mercantilism," Yoshida flatly rejected such a characterization of his purpose.[55] For Yoshida to disown a neo-mercantilist strategy was akin to Karl
Marx's famous *je ne suis pas marxiste*. In the last years of his life, Yoshida acknowledged this approach as "selfish" and demeaning, a "deformity" that

called into question Japanese integrity. Most likely, Yoshida's inbred nationalism was repelled by the politically and diplomatically passive Japan implied by his policies. As he saw his successors settling comfortably into an indefinite dependence on the U.S. security guarantee, he came to see the price of a neo-mercantilist strategy and acknowledged his own responsibility for the path taken.

Japan once again suffered a deep psychic wound as a result of its opportunism. As in Meiji, Japan's opportunistic adaptation to the international order created an intense need for a cultural identity that would restore national pride. Dower wrote:

> Yoshida came to play a symbolic role that was especially galling to a staunch patriot, for the rigid conformity to U.S. Cold War policy . . . reinforced the impression that the San Francisco System really amounted to a form of "subordinate independence" within the new postwar American imperium. As it turned out, this anomalous status provided the circumstances under which Japan proceeded on a course of economic nationalism that brought unimagined material prosperity within a few decades—but at an enduring psychological and ideological cost. Japan's ultimate role as a "great" nation— always the proud Yoshida's goal—remained cabined and contorted by the constrictions of this dependent independence. As a consequence, the international respect for Japan which Yoshida so passionately sought has remained qualified and condescending.[56]

Yoshida may have thought of his strategy as short term. Once economic recovery was achieved, Japan would "naturally" rearm. Resistance to Dulles and U.S. pressure was tactical, an effort to avoid entanglement in the Cold War and give Japan the opportunity to recover from defeat. Perhaps he did not think he was authoring a doctrine. However that may be, as the years of the Cold War system stretched out, his successors took his tactical approach and made it doctrine. They elaborated it into grand strategy that reverberated for many years to come.

CHAPTER EIGHT

THE YOSHIDA DOCTRINE AS GRAND STRATEGY

The choices Yoshida made at the beginning of the Cold War set Japan's foreign policy course for the next forty years. For the duration of the Cold War order, his policies formed the starting point of a new, but at the same time characteristically Japanese, approach to the international system. Yoshida's policies were greatly elaborated by his successors over the next several decades into a fullblown national strategy. Not since the Meiji period had Japan possessed such a coherent, integrated, and purposeful set of policies designed to secure its long-term interests.

For a defeated and pariah nation to find a way to rebuild its national power was not an easy undertaking. The lessons of history were writ deep on the psyche of the national mind. The searing experiences of defeat and occupation demonstrated the futility of pursuing autonomy and great-power status through military means. The postwar elite knew that it must seek a new path for rebuilding Japan. Although it was new, the strategy they chose bore familiar characteristics of earlier patterns and approaches. It involved adapting to the Liberal Democratic international order that the Americans created at the end of World War II as well as to the subsequent Cold War order superimposed on it. In addition, it involved managing complex and unprecedented domestic politics, which were now much more intrusive on policymaking than in earlier periods. It was also another opportunity for Japan to exercise the *Primat der Aussenpolitik*.

Despite his firm denial of having authored a foreign policy "doctrine," Yoshida's name became associated with Japan's unique Cold War foreign policy. Three fundamental tenets marked Yoshida's tactical approach in response to U.S. pressure to rearm and play a more active role in the Cold War struggle:

1. Japan's economic rehabilitation must be the prime national goal. Political-economic cooperation with the United States was necessary for this purpose.
2. Japan should remain lightly armed and avoid involvement in international political-strategic issues. The Self-Defense Forces would not be deployed abroad. Japan would not participate in collective defense arrangements. Not only would this low military posture free the energies of its people for productive industrial development, it would prevent divisive domestic political struggles.
3. To gain a long-term guarantee of its own security, Japan would provide bases for the U.S. Army, Navy, and Air Force.

This policy of shunning international political-military commitments while concentrating on economic growth was elaborated by Yoshida's successors. Because of its effectiveness in dealing with the international as well as the domestic political environment, the Yoshida Doctrine proved much more durable than its author anticipated. As Japanese economic recovery gave way to high economic growth, the doctrine took on a life of its own. At home, it served to maintain a balance among widely diverse views on foreign policy. It was a political compromise between the pacifism of opposition groups and the security concerns of the right-wing conservatives. Ultimately, it was expanded beyond the strategy Yoshida had intended to restore Japanese status in the world.

Under two prime ministers, Ikeda Hayato (1960–1964) and Satō Eisaku (1964–1972), both of whom had been closely associated with Yoshida, the Yoshida Doctrine was consolidated into both a national consensus and a more systematic strategy. What had been for Yoshida a means of recovery from the war was developed into an enduring strategy of pursuing Japanese interests in the unique circumstances of the Cold War international order. Working within the constraints of both their domestic political opposition and their dependence on the U.S. alliance, the postwar foreign policy elite rebuilt Japan's security by maximizing its economic and technological strength. After 1960 and for the remainder of the Cold War, with the exception only of the administration of Nakasone Yasuhiro (1982–1987), the LDP held faithfully to the economics-first policies of Yoshida.

The result was an exclusive concentration on policies of economic nationalism—policies on which the LDP, the bureaucracy, the political opposition, and the populace generally could achieve substantial agreement. In this way, the appeal of the political Left was steadily co-opted, and the nation settled down to a long period of single-minded pursuit of high economic growth. This growth continued for the remainder of the Cold War. A broad national consensus in favor of a mercantilist role in international affairs prevailed in the mainstream of the political, bureaucratic, and business elites as a policy best suited to Japanese national interests.

ADAPTING THE DOMESTIC STRUCTURE

The key figure in building Yoshida's policies into a national consensus for economic growth was his understudy, Ikeda Hayato, who became prime minister in 1960. Coming to power shortly after the mass demonstrations of opposition to the security treaty, Ikeda turned the nation's attention away from divisive political issues and focused it on improving the nation's livelihood. The 1960 demonstrations chastened the conservative elite, especially those political nationalists who had hoped to strengthen Japan's international role by building its political and military influence. The spectacle of crowds of hundreds of thousands surrounding the Diet and a fiercely divided legislature inside indicated that if conservatives continued to raise the issue of rebuilding Japan's military, they would subject the country to prolonged turmoil and probably be driven from power. Accordingly, for the next two decades, the Yoshida wing of the party, which was acknowledged to be the LDP "mainstream," shelved these divisive issues. It accommodated the right wing by maintaining a stable alliance with the United States, and it propitiated the left wing by limiting rearmament and concentrating on economic growth policies that would improve living standards.

This shrewd accommodation of the domestic political front worked so well that Professor Igarashi Takeshi has referred to it as a "domestic foreign-policy system."[1] Ikeda, who had been Yoshida's key economic adviser and finance minister, reestablished domestic tranquillity by concentrating on policies of managed economic growth. Working with economic bureaucrats in MOF, MITI, and the Economic Planning Agency, Ikeda formulated a plan for doubling the national income within a decade. This plan, which had its origins in the Kishi administration but had been sidetracked by the priority given to the security treaty, was part of a systematic and well-coordinated effort to formulate policies that would steer clear of ideology, raise living standards, and improve social overhead capital. Almost imperceptibly, the appeal of the political Left was co-opted. Ikeda's policies served to unify the nation and to convince most of the leaders of the ruling party that it could best consolidate and legitimate its hold on the electorate by adhering to the policies of economic growth that Yoshida had initiated. Nakamura Takafusa, a leading economic historian, later wrote that "Ikeda was the single most important figure in Japan's rapid growth. He should be remembered as the man who pulled together a national consensus for economic growth and who strove for the realization of the goal."[2]

The effort to provide domestic support for foreign policy went beyond the harmonization of domestic political conflict. The conservative elite skillfully adjusted the entire domestic institutional infrastructure to support the emerging foreign policy. The process was more complex and more innovative than the Meiji emulation of Western laws and institutions had been. In this case, postwar Japanese leaders shaped a set of distinctive and unique economic institutions to take advantage of the unprecedented opportunities to expand Japan's international trade. Acknowledging the deep roots of this opportunism, a Japanese vice minister of international trade and industry observed, "Japan has usually considered the international economic order as a given condition and looked for ways in which to use it."[3]

Many countries have enacted change in their domestic system to accommodate change in the international system. What was different about the Japanese response to the post–World War II system was the greater complexity of Japan's strategic response. This complexity was a result of the unique circumstances of the era: Japan's junior position in the U.S.-Japan alliance, the greater intrusiveness of domestic opinion on the policy process, the existence of domestic institutions imposed from outside, and the subsequent conjunction of both the Liberal Democratic vision and the Cold War bipolarity in the making of the international structure.

The Occupation imposed institutions on Japan to fit the Liberal Democratic vision of order, but Japan now proceeded to adapt these institutions to the opportunities that were at hand. Bureaucrats, steeped in the experience of the prewar and wartime efforts to mobilize the economy, formulated a coherent set of policies and institutions to pursue rapid economic growth. Step by step, as the Occupation came to a close, strategically minded economic bureaucrats began to organize Japan's institutions and policies in a fashion that would allow Japan to succeed in the international economic order. The roots of their thinking lay far back in their past—namely, in the Meiji period's reaction to the challenge that Western economic power presented in the nineteenth century, which in turn stemmed from even earlier times.

A JAPANESE FORM OF CAPITALISM

The Meiji leaders never accepted the liberal economic paradigm as appropriate for Japan. While quickly adapting to the demands of the international system, they began slowly to devise their own course for industrial development. They were eclectic in their approach, selecting bits and pieces from Western models.[4] Yoshida, who deeply admired the Meiji leaders' strategic choices and followed in their tradition, recalled their care in avoiding dependence on foreign capital: "Japan's leaders in the Meiji era were above all realists. Thus, fearing that the importation of foreign capital would permit alien interests to obtain control of the nation's economy, they prohibited the introduction of such funds. But at the same time they saw no danger in employing foreigners for the purpose of acquiring foreign knowledge, and this was encouraged."[5]

Drawing on their own practical experience in the domain governments of the late Tokugawa period and also on the affirming theories of the German Historical School of Economics, the Meiji leaders formed their own strategy for a late-developing capitalism. They put the needs of the state for security and social solidarity at the center of the economic system and rejected classical economic theories based on individual consumer and producer and the efficiency of free exchange between them. The government fostered industries, including munitions, shipbuilding, shipping, railways, iron and steel, heavy engineering, and machine tools, that it saw as being in the national interest. Moreover, it promoted policies that would shield society from the disruptive effects of the market.

Subsequently, in response to the exigencies of the Great Depression and the Pacific War, the Japanese defined a more elaborate set of developmentalist institutions that would speed the growth process and increase industrial productive efficiency. Government intervention sharply increased. The wartime experience profoundly influenced many of the central features of the postwar economy. Over the course of a century, through remarkable statecraft and a shrewd pragmatism, Japan devised its own particular mix of policies and institutions to promote industrialization. It was generally distrustful of self-regulating markets, instead setting great store on maintaining social cohesion in the coordinated pursuit of a singular national purpose.

The Cold War system provided Japan with the opportunity to bring to fruition its own form of capitalism. Almost unnoticed, the bureaucracy created the Ministry of International Trade and Industry in 1949 with a charge to strengthen Japan's competitive ability in the export market, promote technological change, and enforce efficient use of resources through mergers and various kinds of collusive arrangements among the largest firms. In the same year, the Foreign Exchange and Foreign Trade Control Law gave the new ministry its first and most important tool to influence corporate decisions: the power to allocate all foreign exchange. If they were to grow and compete, Japanese firms had to import raw materials and foreign technology. MITI used the new law to influence the growth rate of various industries and their capacity to acquire new technology.

Enactment of the Foreign Capital Law in 1950, the next step in constructing the high-growth system, gave MITI the power to limit, restrict, and control foreign investment, ownership, and participation in management of business ventures in Japan. Next, in 1951, the Ministry of Finance, together with MITI, established the Japan Development Bank, with access to a huge investment pool known as the Fiscal Investment and Loan Plan (FILP), the nation's postal savings system. The system was a favorite place for individuals to save because their accounts were tax exempt. FILP thus amassed savings four times the size of the world's largest commercial bank. It became "the single most important financial instrument for Japan's economic development,"[76] especially since MITI used it to provide low-cost capital to industries it favored for long-term growth.

At the same time, MOF was ensuring the availability of capital. By insulating the domestic capital market from the international capital market, it could ration and guide the flow of capital to large firms in industries such as steel, shipbuilding, automobiles, electronics, and chemicals that were adopting new technology and were central to increasing productivity and exports. Government policies directed cheap and plentiful capital to the lead industries, and new laws prodded their development. Tax, monetary, and fiscal policies were all marshaled to minimize the long-term risks of adopting new technology and boldly expanding productive capacity. The state was the guarantor.

Laws to prod development of critical industries were enacted. In addition to allocating credit, the government used many other potent tools of industrial policy, including imposing high tariffs to protect industries critical to the growth strategy, establishing import quotas, reforming the tax system to favor growth, and giving direct and indirect subsidies to key industries. Finally, as the Occupation ended, MITI had the U.S.-inspired Anti-Monopoly Law revised and watered down so as to relax restrictions on cartels, interlocking directorates, mergers, and various forms of collusive behavior. By 1971, thirty-six manufacturing cartels had been sanctioned by industry-specific laws. At the same time, the government severely limited imports of foreign manufactured products through stringent quota and tariff policies, as well as through inspection procedures, product standards, and a formidable array of other nontariff barriers.

In the 1930s, the total-war strategists in the military had laid out plans to mobilize every aspect of the Japanese society and economy to meet the competitive imperative of the external environment. These plans were never fully realized during wartime, but ironically, the bureaucracy resurrected this totalist strategy in the postwar period and focused it wholly on economic growth. Quasi-wartime controls were implemented to close off the financial system to the rest of the world; economic strategy was devised with a military tactical sense that was often reflected in the terminology used. As two Japanese economists who worked for the government described it, "The banks and economic bureaucracy functioned as a general staff behind the battlefield in this second 'total war' called high economic growth."[7] MOF officials likened their tight regulatory controls over Japanese banks to "the escort of a convoy of ships by a warship."[8]

Won over to a consensus about how to proceed to bolster the national economy, the Japanese people concentrated their efforts on saving rather than consumption; as the same two economists put it, "rapid growth became a 'war to be won,' the first total war in Japanese history for which all of the nation's resources were mobilized voluntarily."[9] A diplomat reminisced in 1979: "The [mighty battleship] Yamato and the [fighter airplane] Zeros—forerunner of the postwar Japanese technology—are still very much alive, so it is said among us Japanese, in mammoth tankers, excellent automotive engines, etc., which Japan turns out by the thousands and millions. Thus they have served our nation in a manner never foreseen in their heyday."[10]

In this way, Japan made its way in the post–World War II world by relentlessly pursuing its own narrowly defined self-interest. Regaining its prewar level by 1954–1955, the economy then maintained an astonishing rate of growth, averaging over 10 percent for each of the next fifteen years.

The high-growth period from 1950 to the oil shock of 1973 saw the flowering of postwar Japanese capitalism. A strong public opinion supporting growth as the overriding national purpose served to mute political conflict. Business and government worked hand-in-glove to formulate long-term goals and policies. As a political movement, labor had little say about policy, and it was effectively co-opted in any case by the success of economic expansion and by such features of the employment system as lifetime employment and company unions. Although double-digit annual growth increases disappeared after the oil shocks of the 1970s, the economy recovered, adjusted to the new conditions, and resumed annual growth at a healthy but more moderate pace.

This postwar Japanese capitalism has been characterized by one economist as a "bridled capitalism." Rather than giving market forces free rein, the system consisted of "policies and institutions, reflecting a shared ideology of 'catching up with the West,' [which] effectively performed the role of a bridle."[11] The conservative elites in government and business guided the economy. Market forces were made more vigorous through incentives to encourage more saving, more rapid acquisition of new technologies, and more risk-taking so that firms would become more productive, efficient, and competitive.

AMERICAN FORBEARANCE

Relying on the U.S. preoccupation with the Cold War to provide Japan with security and an open market, Japan intensified its bureaucratic controls and strengthened its mercantilist policies. Adherents to the Yoshida strategy determined to profit from the international order even while flouting its liberal norms. The conjunction of the liberal trading order and the Cold War gave Japan the opportunity to access the U.S. market while at the same time enjoying American tolerance of their own illiberal institutions at home. These institutions would not have been tolerated in the Liberal Democratic order that the Americans originally envisioned, but the fact of the Cold War elicited American forbearance.

More than any other country, Japan was the beneficiary of the postwar international order. For more than twenty-five years after the end of the war, Japan operated in extraordinary and uniquely favorable political-economic circumstances. In contrast to every other major power, Japan was spared the psychological and material costs of participating in international politics.

Until the end of the 1960s, Japan benefited from a special relationship with the United States under which the latter sponsored Japanese recovery and development. The United States kept its market open to Japan's goods while allowing Japan to severely limit access to its own economy. The expanding world trade that the United States was promoting through the IMF and GATT permitted a vigorous expansion of Japanese manufactured goods and the ready purchase of abundant and cheap raw materials.

Cut off from Western industrial contacts during the war years, Japanese engineers and technicians were eager to close the technological gap. The Japanese skill in emulation was about to see its greatest successes. "The quiet visitor taking notes and photographing everything is a much derided stereotype of the Japanese businessman abroad," wrote Thomas Rohlen, "yet it was precisely such seemingly enigmatic visitors who upon returning home, applied their carefully gathered information to produce technological advancement."[12] Japan had easy access to new, inexpensive, highly efficient Western technology, which it imported in large quantities. According to Richard Samuels:

> Between 1951 and 1984 . . . more than forty thousand separate contracts were signed by Japanese firms to acquire foreign technology; over that thirty-four-year period Japan paid $17 billion in royalties—a small fraction of *annual* US R&D costs. With nylon from DuPont, nuclear power from General Electric and Westinghouse, the transistor from Bell Laboratories, and the television tubes from Corning, US technology licenses were "the technological basis for nearly all of Japan's modern industries."[13]

In order to strengthen its allies in the Cold War, the United States was willing to subordinate its short-term economic interests. It thus provided U.S. markets, technology, and aid to them, singling out Japan for special treatment. As one U.S. government official wrote in 1952:

> The most highly industrialized country in the Far East must remain outside the Soviet orbit if there is to be a free Asia, and to this end U.S. policy should be directed by whatsoever means are necessary, military or economic, to assist in the establishment of political tranquillity and economic betterment in all of free Asia, . . . and until it is clear that Japan can stand firmly on its own feet, the United States must of necessity lend support, even to the extent of providing an unrestricted market for such Japanese goods as American consumers find attractive.[14]

The international economic policy of the United States, the economist Marina Whitman observed, was "primarily a stepchild of our national security objectives."[15] The Kennedy and Johnson administrations continued to give priority to Japanese economic development as a means to ensure Japan's stability. In 1964, the State Department, with the aid of the embassy in Tokyo, drafted a secret policy paper on the future of Japan that urged support of Japan's economic goals and recommended "firm Executive Branch resistance of American industry demands for curtailment of Japanese imports."[16]

There is a considerable literature on the institutions Japan created to pursue high economic growth. Many of these studies of Japanese developmentalism—that is, the accumulation of institutions and policies formulated by Japan's enlightened bureaucrats to promote rapid economic growth—praise it as a viable alternative to classical liberal political-economic theory. Once again, this "inside-out" approach gives little heed to the unique external environment of these policies. The Japanese model succeeded not simply through the brilliant strategic planning of its bureaucrat-intellectuals, although there was plenty of that, but also through uniquely favorable international conditions. Japan's ability to pursue developmentalist policies with such success in the postwar era was in great part contingent on the special circumstances of the Cold War. In Stephen Krasner's words, "Developmentalism has been tolerated by the existing international order, or more accurately slipped under the door, as a result of American security and ideological concerns which allowed, even sometimes tacitly encouraged, departures from classic liberal principles."[17] Indeed, Japan framed its postwar developmentalism with this uniquely favorable international environment in mind. It was the crowning achievement of the characteristic approach of adapting domestic institutions to the external order.

THE NUCLEAR ISSUE

By the end of the Ikeda administration in 1964, the Yoshida Doctrine was deeply embedded in the Japanese political system. In the 1950s, MOF had blocked attempts to build the defense sector as an export industry, and it continually limited increases in the defense budget. China's nuclear experiments and the proposed Nuclear Nonproliferation Treaty (NPT) prompted further elaboration of the strategy. Yoshida's protégé Satō Eisaku, who served as prime minister for eight years (1964–1972), longer than any other individual in Japanese history, dealt with the thorny issues of the nuclear option. In 1968, the United States and the Soviet Union proposed a nonproliferation agreement to the United Nations Disarmament Commission. It was later approved by the UN General Assembly and took effect in 1970. The NPT prohibited all nuclear testing and established a worldwide network of monitoring stations. The issue of ratification of the NPT held implications not only for Japan's status as a great power but also for its commercial and technological advantage.

Moreover, it raised highly sensitive issues of national identity, with a vocal sector of the public on the Left embracing the antinuclear movement. Postwar progressive ideology proclaimed Japan a nation transformed by its experience of war, atomic bombings, and defeat, a nation dedicated to showing the way to a new world in which nations would exist free of weapons and war. Either way, to both the Left and the Right, it was a nationalist issue. On the Right, political conservatives, especially, were reluctant to close the door to Japan's inclusion among the nuclear powers. They believed exclusion from the "nuclear club" would relegate Japan permanently to second-class status as a power. Fukuda Takeo, the LDP's secretary general, raised a public storm of protest from the progressive parties and their supporters when he said on December 14, 1967, that "the majority of the Liberal Democrats see the need to outgrow the 'nuclear allergy.'"[18]

China conducted its first nuclear weapons test in October 1964. Shortly afterward, in January 1965, Prime Minister Satō, meeting with President Lyndon Johnson, said that he felt that if the Chinese Communists had nuclear weapons, the Japanese should also have them. He acknowledged, however, that the majority of the Japanese were dead set against possession.[19] A year later, after the NPT draft was circulated, Satō commissioned a secret study of Japanese nuclear policy. The study concluded that its civilian nuclear power program provided the option of pursuing nuclear weapons, but that it ought not to be exercised in light of both public and international opinion. Reluctantly, with divided hearts, the conservatives concluded that Japan would forego the nuclear option.

In 1967, Satō announced the Three Non-Nuclear Principles, pledging that Japan "will not manufacture or possess nuclear weapons or allow their introduction into this country," and the Diet subsequently formalized them in a resolution. Lest the principles be regarded as unconditional, Satō clarified matters in a Diet speech in 1968. He outlined the four pillars of Japan's nonnuclear policy: (1) reliance on the U.S. umbrella; (2) the three nonnuclear principles; (3) promotion of worldwide disarmament; and (4) development

of nuclear energy for peaceful purposes. Although he later received the Nobel Peace Prize, in part for this pledge, Satō was privately cynical, referring
to the Three Non-Nuclear Principles in a conference with the U.S. ambassador as "nonsense."[20] In secret protocols, the Japanese government gave
the U.S. military permission to keep nuclear weapons in Okinawa after its
reversion to Japan in 1972 and to "transit" through Japan planes and ships
carrying nuclear weapons. Critics responded by subsequently labeling the
policy the "Two-and-a-Half Non-Nuclear Principles."

An internal Foreign Ministry document in 1969 concluded: "For the
time being, we will maintain the policy of not possessing nuclear weapons.
However, regardless of joining the NPT or not, we will keep the economic
and technical potential for the production of nuclear weapons, while seeing to it that Japan will not be interfered with in this regard."[21] Therefore,
although Japan signed the NPT in 1970, it delayed ratification for six years
while negotiating maximum leeway for its civilian nuclear power program
with the International Atomic Energy Agency (IAEA). Japan, by calling attention to the provision allowing withdrawal from the agreement with
three months' notice should "extraordinary events" require it, signaled that
it would keep open the option and in the meantime press ahead with research. For the time being at least, Japan was satisfied that, as a second report commissioned by Satō put it, "the days are gone when the possession
of nuclear weapons is a prerequisite for superpower status."[22]

Yet not all Japanese leaders agreed. Throughout these deliberations,
Japanese conservative leaders nursed painful heartburn over the forfeiture
of the prestige that possession of nuclear weapons would confer. They regarded possession of nuclear weapons as an attribute of international
prestige and of rank in the international hierarchy.[23] For a country whose
sensitivity to status had always been keen, this factor was not easily laid
aside. In December 1971, shortly after he retired as head of MITI,
Miyazawa Kiichi reminded other countries that Japan retained the option
of rearmament, telling an interviewer:

> Recent events have been influenced by distinctions between "first-rate" and
> "second-rate" nations, using nuclear capabilities and atomic stockpiles as
> yardsticks. . . . If the major nations of the world who have nuclear capabil-
> ities try to be too assertive and push Japan around too much and too far,
> they may run the risk of opening up what they most want to avoid. There
> is already a body of opinion in Japan which feels that dependence on the
> US nuclear umbrella is basically incompatible with our national sovereignty.
> When the coming generations assume a greater role in the society, they may

want to choose the lesser of two evils and opt to build their own umbrella instead of renting their neighbor's, if only to satisfy their desire to be their own masters. This may become likelier as time passes and memories of Hiroshima and Nagasaki recede.[24]

Japanese leaders were keenly sensitive to the way in which acquisition of nuclear weapons had enhanced China's status in Western eyes and to westerners' persistent distrust of Japan's potential for return to militarist policies. In 1970, as director of the Defense Agency, Nakasone Yasuhiro dissected in cold, analytical terms the power politics at work:

> Both the 1963 partial nuclear test ban treaty and the current nuclear non-proliferation treaty are primarily designed—even if covertly—to preempt, or rather deter, both Japan and West Germany from acquiring nuclear arms and thereby undermining the basis of US-Soviet nuclear hegemony. China opted for "going nuclear without pants." Japan, on the other hand, has remained non-nuclear, preferring to be decently dressed. Only history will be able to determine who was wiser. Whether wise or foolish, Japan should not forget . . . that nuclear arms policies tacitly are a reflection of a US-Soviet agreement regarding their respective share of the trophies of World War II.[25]

Accordingly, Japan gave precedence to economic and technological interests, insisting that IAEA inspection procedures not obstruct the efficient development of the power industry or permit leaks of industrial secrets. The NPT negotiations demonstrated that in the most profound security issue of the time, Japan was increasingly defining its grand national strategy in the context of long-term economic interests. In Korea and China, however, the suspicion persisted that Japan remained intent on developing its ability to become a nuclear power.

OTHER ADDITIONS TO THE YOSHIDA DOCTRINE

In addition to the Three Non-Nuclear Principles, there were other important additions to the Yoshida Doctrine. In 1970, the Mutual Security Treaty was again open to reconsideration, and with U.S. intervention in Vietnam stirring domestic opposition, particularly among Japanese students, care had to be taken to defuse the kind of domestic turmoil that had roiled Japan in 1960. To preserve Japan's low posture in international politics, Satō formulated the policy of the Three Principles of Arms Exports, which provided that Japan would not allow the export of arms to countries in the Communist bloc, to countries covered by UN resolutions on arms embargoes, or to countries involved or likely to be involved in armed conflicts. This policy enshrined the position that MOF had consistently held, namely that Japan should resist the temptation to build a powerful military-industrial complex. Subsequently, the cabinet of Prime Minister Miki Takeo (1974–1976) extended this ban on weapons exports to all countries and defined "arms" to include not only military equipment but also the parts and fittings used in this equipment. In 1969, the Diet passed a resolution limiting Japan's activities in outer space to peaceful and nonmilitary purposes.

As a further corollary to the Yoshida Doctrine, constraining defense expenditures to less than 1 percent of the GNP became a practice in the 1960s, although it did not become official government policy until adoption of the National Defense Program Outline in 1976. The government explained its formulation of security policy as "an exclusively defensive defense." Troops and weapons would have no offensive capacity, nor would Japan maintain any ability to project power abroad. Thus, jets would have no capability for bombing or midair refueling. An aircraft carrier was out of the question.

Even as Japan resisted developing its military, U.S. pressure on Japan to take on a share of the security burden in the region increased during the 1970s. Especially during the Nixon administration, Americans pushed the issue of Japan's role in the collective security of Asia in connection with the possible return of Okinawa. The Nixon Doctrine of 1969 declared that the United States would depend on its Asian allies to assume more responsibility for containing communism in the region. But the Japanese were adamant. Direct involvement in a regional security organization, said Ōhira Masayoshi, who served as foreign minister from 1962–1964 and 1972–1974, was "impossible."[26] While South Korea dispatched more than 300,000 troops to fight alongside the Americans in Vietnam, the Japanese avoided direct military involvement. Instead, the Japanese economy battened on procurement orders for the U.S. military in Southeast Asia. Japanese leaders constantly used interpretation of the constitution as a shield against U.S. pressure to participate in collective security undertakings. So long as the Cold War standoff with the Soviet Union continued, Japanese leaders were confident that the United States would not abandon Japan.

When President Ronald Reagan took office in January 1981 and rallied U.S. allies for a tougher stand in the Cold War, including an arms buildup,

Japanese bureaucrats felt the need to shore up the Yoshida Doctrine. The issue that made Japan particularly vulnerable to pressure was the provision in the UN Charter authorizing all nations to engage in collective self-defense. Article 51 held that "nothing in the present Charter shall impair the inherent right of individual or collective defense." To forestall U.S. pressure for a more forthright contribution to the Cold War effort, the Cabinet Legislation Bureau (CLB) brought the constitutional prohibition and its public support into a more resolute stance. This elite and influential administrative agency, shrouded in secrecy and little noticed during the Cold War, epitomized the policy autonomy that bureaucrats possessed. The CLB reviewed all proposed legislation and rules for consistency with the Japanese constitution and legal precedents. Ministers and lawmakers acceded to its interpretation and the precedents that its rulings created. The Japanese Supreme Court rarely overturned its rulings. The CLB's interpretation of the constitution was deferred to throughout the Cold War years, and as such it became, as Richard Samuels put it, "a powerful break on major policy change."[27] Its interpretation of Article 9 in 1954 stated that Japan could possess only "the minimum necessary force" for the exercise of self-defense for the homeland. For the duration of the Cold War, the CLB bureaucrats adhered to these constraints.

The Yoshida school prime ministers found the CLB interpretation most convenient. It gave them cover. Shortly after the election of Reagan, the CLB, in May 1981, expanded its tightly worded proscription on collective self-defense. The new wording said:

> Since it is a sovereign state, Japan has the right of collective self-defense under international law. The Japanese government nevertheless takes the view that the exercise of the right of self-defense as authorized under Article 9 of the Constitution is confined to the minimum necessary level for the defense of the country. The government believes that the exercise of the right of collective self-defense exceeds that limit and is not, therefore, permissible under the Constitution.[28]

Such a minimalist interpretation of what the constitution permitted was a political rather than a legal interpretation. It was the final building block in the institutionalization of the Yoshida Doctrine's grand strategy for steering Japan through the multiple foreign and domestic challenges of the postwar period.

THE TRIUMPH OF ECONOMIC REALISM

As Japan's industrial and financial power grew, it could have become a great military power. Many, perhaps most, foreign observers expected this to happen. Herman Kahn, in his book *The Emerging Japanese Superstate* (1970), which was widely read because it called attention to the potential military implications of Japan's resurgence, concluded that the "Japanese will almost inevitably feel that Japan has the right and duty to achieve full superpower status and that this means possessing a substantial nuclear establishment."[29] Mao Zedong and Zhou Enlai feared that Japan was on the verge of resuming a militarist course.[30] After all, modern Japan had always been motivated by the pursuit of power and status. In the face of such expectations, Japan's persistent low posture was puzzling. Generally, foreign observers explained this persistent political passivity as the result of the trauma of defeat, the nuclear allergy, and a deeply divided public. They underestimated the authority that Japan's economic organs now exercised in the postwar state. What was rarely recognized was that Japanese realism was as strong as ever. It was simply being exercised in a different fashion.

In the postwar era, the Japanese realist pursuit of maximizing power was now concentrated on economic competition. The instruments of power were no longer armed forces, military bases, vast armaments, and territorial control, but instead productive efficiency, market control, trade surplus, strong currency, foreign exchange reserves, advanced technology, foreign direct investment, and foreign aid. The trading state had replaced the armed state. Among Japanese leaders there was a growing conviction that, in the nuclear age, military power carried less advantage than it had formerly in the calculus of state power. They were convinced that economic competition was becoming more important in international relations than military competition. Military conflict among major states was less likely than in the past. The nationalist politician Ishihara Shintarō asserted that "economic warfare is the basis for existence in the free world. . . The twenty-first century will be a century of economic warfare. . . . There is no hope for the United States." Power was determined more by wealth and technology than by territorial control and military capability. "We are going to have a totally new configuration in the balance of power in the world," concluded the chairman of Sony, Morita Akio. "The time will never again come when America will regain its strength in industry."[31]

Japan's strategy was to build the economy through international trade.

This export-led strategy was not new, but it was pursued with more single-mindedness vigor than ever before in the postwar period. It entailed nurturing and building comparative advantage in industries that held the most promise for export-led growth. Because Japan was resource poor, it also entailed limiting imports so far as possible to primary products (raw materials, fuel, and food) and exporting manufactured goods. Japan would become a processing trade nation. By adopting new Western technology as rapidly as possible, it would strive to produce and export increasing quantities of more technologically advanced, internationally competitive products. Japan rode the tide of an unparalleled period of expanding world trade. Japanese exports increased nearly 25-fold between 1955 and 1970. Over a longer period, from 1955 to 1987, exports achieved an astonishing 114-fold increase.[32]

Japan's rise as an international investor was dramatic evidence of its growing economic power. Surplus savings so great that they could no longer be absorbed at home were exported to the rest of the world. Year after year during the 1980s, Japan amassed trade and current account surpluses. Japan's net external assets rose from $10.9 billion in 1981 to $383 billion a decade later. By 1990, Japan had become the largest net creditor in the world, "the greatest creditor nation the world has ever known." In 1970, the cumulative value of Japanese overseas investments was $3.6 billion; in 1980, it was $160 billion; and in 1991, $2.0 trillion.[33]

A fundamental part of this emerging strategy was the nurturing of technological supremacy. It therefore became a vital element of this national security strategy to maintain an autonomous industrial capacity to prevent penetration of Japanese markets by foreign manufactured goods and foreign investment in key areas of fundamental technological strength. Strategic, high-technology, high-value-added industries were targeted for development. To dominate these industries, Japanese strategy was "to pursue *relative* gains in terms of market share, rather than *absolute* gains in terms of profits."[34] As economist Edward Lincoln wrote, "Japan's pattern of trade on imports has been and remains very peculiar when compared to those of other countries—a peculiarity that cannot be explained through standard economic factors. Japan does indeed exhibit an aversion to manufactured imports and avoids the two-way trade in many manufactured products that characterizes the trade of other nations."[35]

Japan's dependence on raw material imports and its consequent strategy gave it the world's most skewed import-export balance. While in other industrial countries, manufactured goods made up 50 to 65 percent of total imports, they made up just 30 percent of Japan's imports in the mid-1970s.

At the same time, 95 percent of Japan's exports were manufactured goods. Japan achieved extraordinary success in preventing foreign direct investment; only 1 percent of Japan's assets in the 1980s were foreign owned.[36] It was rightly observed that "Japanese strategists have been more willing to accept U.S. military on their soil than they have U.S. bankers or manufacturers."[37] In the calculus of economic realism, other advanced industrial economies posed a threat to Japan. To protect its independent technological capability, Japan had to nurture and aggressively defend its leading industries.

Economic power was used to resolve foreign policy issues. Japan's mounting trade surplus, the closed nature of the economy, and the free ride it took on the international system provoked resentment and anger abroad. During the 1970s, when Americans began to complain that Japan was taking advantage of the U.S. guarantee of Japanese security, the Japanese offered an economic solution. In 1978, to defuse the growing criticism of Japan as a "free rider," the Japanese government began to contribute to the expense of maintaining U.S. bases in Japan. Privately, the conservatives cynically referred to this as a "sympathy budget" (*omoiyari yōsan*), implying a certain disdain for the complaints. Soon, it was providing nearly $5 billion annually to defray a substantial cost of the bases. In addition, Japan increased its contribution to international organizations, including the Asian Development Bank, the United Nations, the World Bank, and the IMF.

Japan also promised to vastly increase its foreign aid, and its official development assistance (ODA) became a principal tool of foreign policy. By the end of the 1980s, Japan was not only the world's greatest creditor nation, it was also the world's largest aid donor. Nearly two-thirds of this aid went to Asian countries, amounting to six or seven times the sum of annual U.S. aid to the region. Japanese ODA was targeted for strategic commercial purposes. Instead of focusing on single infrastructure projects—a dam, a harbor development, or a highway, for example—the strategy of the Japanese government became more proactive and comprehensive, more attentive to the development of structural complementarities with the Japanese economy.

Economic realism dictated the pursuit of regional hegemony by new means. The Asian bloc that Japan had once sought to create by military force, it now would constitute through its economic power. Japan moved swiftly and adeptly to seize leadership in Asia's economic dynamism. The most important development was the Plaza Hotel Accord of 1985 and the sharp rise in the value of the yen. At the Plaza summit, the Group of

Seven agreed to increase the value of the yen from 260 yen to 180 yen to the dollar. This international agreement made it profitable to shift production and assembly of many Japanese manufactures to other Asian countries that had lower wage scales. Thereafter, the yen continued to rise, making offshore manufacturing increasingly attractive. The task of formulating a comprehensive and coordinated approach to Asia through economic policies fit the postwar inclination of the Japanese state, with its strength in economic institutions, capacity for bureaucratic planning and coordination, and ability to fine-tune policies to enhance market forces. Japan offered other Asian countries a persuasive set of economic inducements to follow its leadership: foreign aid, commercial loans, technology transfer, direct investment, and preferential access to the Japanese market.

Economic realism did not preclude the potential importance of military power. Japanese economic planners believed that if they maintained a strong technological and industrial base, Japan could be transformed into a military power should that become necessary in the future. The option would be there. Two American analysts of this Japanese thinking observed: "A state with a powerful technological and industrial base is capable of transforming itself from a military pygmy into a military giant within a short span of time, whereas states with large militaries that allow their industrial and technological base to wither find themselves in a more difficult predicament."[38] The example of America's rapid transformation in the early 1940s was persuasive. Although the United States in 1939 produced only a quarter as many military aircraft as Germany, two years later it was producing well over twice as many.

A particularly interesting formulation of Japan's grand strategy was offered by the brilliant political thinker Nagai Yōnosuke. Setting forth a concept of the "moratorium world" and of Japan as a "moratorium state," he held that the merchant role suited Japan's strategic needs in the emerging international structure.[39] Nagai argued that world politics was in a state of transition as it went from the traditional international order (the Westphalian system), in which the status of nation-states was established according to their military power, to what he called a Kantian peaceful world order, in which the security of states would be preserved by collective international arrangements. This transition stage was marked by a nuclear standoff or parity between the superpowers, which had created a power moratorium in the world. As a consequence, military power counted for less in determining the hierarchy of nations, while international economic strength and technological know-how counted for more. In this moratorium world, there was no longer a single agreed-on measure of status among nations: One state might have great military power; another might have great economic strength. It was not necessary to the status of a state that it possess both attributes. Therefore, the incongruity between Japan's economic power and military weakness was not anomalous, he wrote, but rather reflected the changing nature of international competition. The expectation that Japan must maintain a military establishment consistent with its economic capability represented a projection onto the international community of a drive in Western society to achieve consistency in personal status. The Japanese, however, were accustomed to inconsistency of status: In the Tokugawa system, samurai had political-military power and prestige, while the merchants had economic power. Moreover, among the samurai there was a complex allocation of different roles. Among the feudal lords, for example, the outer daimyo were given great territorial domains but no place in the central government, whereas the hereditary daimyo had administrative power but little territory. The purpose of this complex system, Nagai said, was "to prevent the centralization of power by the drive to achieve consistency of status, which is a weakness of all men." What was necessary for the advancement of human society, he added, was the "globalization of the Tokugawa system." This Tokugawa system had kept the peace in Japan for two and a half centuries before the intrusion of the Western international system.

Japan's strategy, Nagai wrote, ought to be to persevere as a moratorium state, adhere to its peace constitution, and "maintain the inconsistency in its status as a lightly armed, non-nuclear economic power." Strategic planning should concentrate on developing the most sophisticated technology and the ability to convert it to military use should the need arise. Should the United States increase its pressure on Japan regarding trade issues, or should the Soviet Union build its military power in the Far East, Japan could threaten a nationalist response: revision of the constitution, conversion of its industry and technology to military use, development of nuclear weapons, and so on. This potential threat gave Japan the leverage to withstand foreign pressures and preserve its moratorium status. Nagai was convinced that, as Japan's grand strategy, "the Yoshida Doctrine will be permanent" (*eien de aru*).[40]

The elites were growing confident in the strategy that cast Japan as a modern-day Venetian trading state. In a series of essays, later gathered into a widely read book entitled *Japan as a Merchant Nation,* a leading economic bureaucrat articulated for a popular audience the strategy by which Japan would pursue its security interests.[41] MITI's vice minister for international affairs, Amaya Naohiro, drew analogies from Japanese history to illustrate the role of a merchant nation, which he said the Japanese people must pursue relentlessly. He likened the contemporary international system to Tokugawa Japan, when society was divided into four functional classes: samurai, peasants, artisans, and merchants. The United States and the Soviet Union were playing the roles of samurai, whereas Japan, basing itself on commerce and industry, was like the prosperous but unarmed Tokugawa merchants; third-world countries were the artisans and peasants. Amaya urged the Japanese to show the shrewdness and self-discipline of the merchant princes of the feudal period, whose adroit maneuvering in the midst of a samurai-dominated society allowed them to prosper. What was required was to be unabashedly opportunistic, to stay the course, and to put aside the samurai's pride of principle.

> For a merchant to prosper in samurai society, it is necessary to have superb information-gathering ability, planning ability, intuition, diplomatic skill, and at times ability to be a sycophant. . . . From now on if Japan chooses to live as a merchant nation in international society, I think it is important that it pursue wholeheartedly the way of the merchant. When necessary, it must beg for oil from the producing nations, sometimes it must grovel on bended knee before the samurai.[42]

The Tokugawa merchant was not above using his wealth to gain his way, and Amaya counseled that Japan similarly must be prepared to buy solutions to its political problems: "When money can help, it is important to have the gumption to put up large sums."[43]

By the 1970s, both in Japan and—equally important for Japanese self-esteem—abroad, it was readily acknowledged that Japan had advanced to the front rank as a global economic power. Soon it overtook the Soviet economy. In 1972, Japan surpassed England, and soon after, West Germany, to become the free world's second-largest economy. The century-long catch-up drive was reaching its goal. The distinguished Kyoto University anthropologist Umesao Tado wrote in 1967 that though Europe was still enjoyable for sightseeing, it was no longer useful as a model for innovation. "The relative decline in status of the European countries in the postwar world," he wrote, was evident in that the Japanese were "either moving shoulder to shoulder with Europe or already . . . out in front." He concluded that the "Japanese today cannot fail to perceive the bankruptcy of Europe."[44] Japan now set its sights on overtaking the U.S. economy. After the humiliation of the Vietnam War, the Watergate crisis, the seizure of U.S. hostages in Iran, and, above all, the Japanese conquest of the U.S. automobile industry, success seemed inevitable.

Confidence mounted that Japan was overtaking the West in technological capacity. A survey conducted by the government's Economic Planning Agency in 1985 found that among Japan's 1,600 leading firms, 90 percent believed that they had caught up with or surpassed the technological capacity of U.S. firms. A U.S. government study in 1990 warned that Japan led the United States in five of twelve emerging technologies and was gaining rapidly in five others.[45] In Japan, the growing trade frictions with the United States were often dismissed as sour grapes. "Americans," observed Ōgura Kazuo, one of Japan's senior diplomats, in 1991, "simply don't want to recognize that Japan has won the economic race against the West."[46] One exception was the Harvard sociologist Ezra Vogel, who in 1979 published his book *Japan as Number One*.[47] Arguing that Japan had outdone other countries in its skillful organization of a modern industrial society, Vogel's book became a runaway best-seller in Japan. The Japanese had been striving for over a century to hear this judgment.

The Japanese attributed their success to the unique characteristics of the Japanese people and their culture. They had mastered the skills of organizing a modern industrial society with greater success than any other people. Their historically formed institutions, with their stress on harmony and collective values, had proved more productive and competitive than those elsewhere. More than one writer drew this irresistible conclusion. The widely read economist Iida Tsuneo wrote: "Is it not possible that Japan may be quite different from other countries? Is it not possible that Japan may be quite superior to other countries?"[48] Japan's pursuit of rank in international society had not been extinguished by defeat in World War II.

By 1980, national pride in the status Japan had achieved was palpable. One of the most striking examples of the persistence of this rank consciousness is found in the quasi-official *Study of the Japanese National Character,* conducted at five-year intervals since 1953. Among the questions asked in this periodic survey was, "Compared to Westerners, do you think, in a word, the Japanese are superior? Or do you think they are inferior?" For Japan this was a natural question, given the strength of rank consciousness and the historic goal of catching up to and overtaking the West. In 1953, in response to the question, only 20 percent answered that the Japanese were superior. In 1983, 53 percent answered that the Japanese were superior.[49]

ECONOMIC REALISM AND
THE TROUBLED SPIRIT OF POSTWAR JAPAN

Yet, despite having caught up economically with the advanced nations, many Japanese still were not satisfied. Whatever material progress Japan had made, whatever theorists said about economic and technological power being the wave of the future, Japan remained dependent on the United States for its security. This dependence, together with a heavy reliance on the U.S. market to absorb nearly 40 percent of Japan's exports, made Japan constantly vulnerable to U.S. pressure.

Throughout the modern period, the realism and opportunism that characterized the foreign policy of the Japanese conservative elite has been deeply unsettling to the formation of Japanese identity. Surrender and occupation made the psychic wound first inflicted during the Meiji period a thousand times more painful. Japan was a nation broken in spirit by a conflict that had cost it every vestige of empire and nearly 3 million lives, including the first victims of the atomic age. It was an international outcast, occupied by foreign soldiers for the first time in its history. Japan had suffered more than a shattering military defeat. Japanese pride of identity, which had come to depend more on the exercise of power than on its historical cultural achievements, was wholly undermined by defeat. The approach of the Occupation drove home this point. Once again, the Japanese had to contend with the challenge of Anglo-American liberal values and their claim to universal legitimacy. In this view, Japanese fascism was the enemy of civilization and justified the policy of unconditional surrender. The Japanese system was deemed so reprehensible and immoral that it must be totally defeated and reconstructed. The Occupation reforms pushed the destruction of Japanese identity to the limit—and perhaps beyond.[50]

Many Japanese wholeheartedly accepted this searing indictment of their own civilization. They embraced the universalist pretensions of the new institutions established by the Occupation. Defeat and occupation left a radical legacy of pacifism in domestic politics that mounted the greatest challenge yet to Japanese values because it came from the Japanese themselves. The postwar generation of Japanese progressives accepted the judgment of the Tokyo trials. They looked at their own country, as the conservative theorist Murakami Yasusuke lamented, through the eyes of international liberalism.[51] This self-inflicted wound was more pervasive and persistent than the westernism of many Japanese had been in the early Meiji period. As a result, Japan's collective identity in the postwar period was far more uncertain and contentious than it had been in the prewar period.

Postwar Japan was deeply divided. Most of the articulate sectors of the population were sympathetic with the progressive cause. The media, writers, teachers, students, labor leaders, and white-collar workers favored the new values of social reform, democracy, and pacifism. In the face of such a strong progressive tide, it was remarkable that the conservatives were able to cling to power. The key to their success was an alliance with the bureaucracy, which the Occupation left intact and that provided a strong basis for the conservatives' staying power. Despite the wrenching changes imposed by the Occupation, seasoned bureaucrats, such as Yoshida, were left largely unscathed and in a dominant position in the political system. They provided the foundation for a strong holdover of conservative values.

Because the electorate was so deeply divided, the mainstream, Yoshida school conservatives, avoiding outright confrontation between opposing views, focused on building a strong consensus behind the popular goal of economic growth, meanwhile adopting the language of pacifism. Publicly they took the position of supporting the imposed constitutional order: They proclaimed Japan a nation transformed by its experience of war, atomic bombings, and defeat, dedicated now to showing the way to a new world in which nations would exist free of weapons and not resort to war. This was the face of Japan that the conservative leadership showed to the world: It was the ideology taught in the schools; it was the rationale offered internationally for Japanese foreign policy; it served to legitimate the abstention from collective security arrangements, even while Japan depended on the international order for its growing prosperity; and it was the stuff of UN speeches by Japanese prime ministers.

The view of Japan as a pacifist nation, fervently held by the progressives, was cynically used by the postwar conservative leadership to dampen domestic confrontation. It served as a pretext for their strategy of concentrating exclusively on the goals of economic nationalism. Every country has its share of sophistry in its foreign policy rationales, but in the case of Japanese conservative leaders, the gap between pretense and reality was extreme. As the longtime MITI bureaucrat Amaya Naohiro wrote in 1989, "Postwar Japan defined itself as a cultural state holding the principles of liberalism, democracy and peace, but these were only our avowed principles (*tatemae*); our actual sentiments (*honne*) were the pouring of all our strength into economic growth."[52] Another economic bureaucrat, Sakakibara Eisuke, likewise observed that "the savvy of the conservatives in keeping avowed principles and actual sentiments separate and maneuvering so as to avoid confrontation [with the progressives] was highly effective on one level, enabling the Liberal Democratic Party to remain in power for close to four decades," but contributed to a "poverty of public discourse and to political cynicism and apathy."[53]

For a time it had appeared that a genuine two-party system, with the LDP and JSP alternating in power, would dominate Japanese politics. But the JSP consumed itself in fractious internecine warfare (ideological battles in which the public gradually lost interest) while the LDP, following the traditional pragmatic bent of Japanese conservatism, steadily co-opted the opposition's issues. The meaningful competition for power was fought out among factions within the LDP, which was dominated for the most part by adherents to the Yoshida strategy. Over time, the JSP largely acquiesced in the LDP's one-party rule in return for a share of the pork barrel and behind-the-scenes consultation. A tacit agreement between the two parties assured that divisive issues of constitutional revision and substantial military spending would be laid aside and priority given to economic growth and social welfare. The conservative mainstream of the LDP actually found the Socialists' advocacy of the pacifist neutrality useful, for they helped keep the Americans, with their demands for greater Japanese involvement in the Cold War, at bay.

As economic bureaucrat Sakakibara wrote in 1993, "Yoshida's strategy of countering foreign demands by taking refuge in public opinion was adopted by his successors, so that until very recently, Tokyo's most important weapon in negotiations with Washington was the Japanese public's continued belief in left-wing ideals."[54] In a remarkably candid 1994 interview with a *New York Times* correspondent, Takeshita Noboru, the powerful LDP tactician and former prime minister (1988–1989), admitted that there had been a tacit understanding between the conservatives and the progressives. "There was a sort of burden sharing between us," Takeshita said. "If I were to use a pejorative adjective, I'd call it a cunning diplomacy."[55] The London *Economist* later rightly described what appeared on the surface to be a fierce ideological struggle between the conservatives and the Socialists as "in reality . . . more [a] carefully scripted charade than any serious conflict of ideology."[56]

Japan's use of a narrow interpretation of the constitution to limit positive commitments to the Cold War effort in Asia is an example of how powers in the international system find "clever ways to gain power at the expense of their rivals."[57] The sharp-tongued former foreign minister, Sonoda Sunao, revealed the cynicism that lay behind the conservative elite's approach to U.S. efforts to enlist Japanese cooperation in maintaining Asian security. Recalling Prime Minister Satō and his proclamation of Japan's Three Non-Nuclear Principles, Sonoda explained: "The Americans were always asking us to do this or do that, to take over part of the burden of their Far Eastern policies. But all their efforts were sabotaged by one Japanese cabinet after another. That's why Satō Eisaku got the Nobel Peace Prize. He got it for his accumulated achievements in the field of sabotage. I suppose he is the only Prime Minister ever to have got the Nobel Peace Prize for sabotage."[58]

A genuine pacifism implies willingness to sacrifice for the observance of pacifist principles, but cooperating with U.S. military power and taking maximum advantage of it called into question Japanese motives. Murakami Yasusuke, one of Japan's leading social scientists, who was deeply respected by conservatives, observed in 1990: "In a sense the Japanese became a nation of hypocrites, proclaiming adherence to the concept of unarmed neutrality but at the same time quite willing to enjoy the fruits of the economic prosperity made possible by the Pax Americana. The Yoshida doctrine, we might say, ended up sapping the intellectual integrity of Japanese pacifism."[59]

The strategy of adapting opportunistically to the structure of the Cold War system while exploiting the advantages of the free-trade order proved to be remarkably successful, but it was bought at a high price. It was demeaning to rely wholly on another nation for security.[60] After surrender and occupation, Japan inevitably would have been dependent on the United States. But to prolong this dependence indefinitely as a matter of policy required suppression of national pride and self-respect.

The shocking suicide of the great postwar novelist Mishima Yukio drew the nation's attention to the loss of its samurai spirit. Mishima went to Self-Defense Forces headquarters and harangued a battalion of SDF cadets on November 25, 1970. He appealed to them to join the battle "in the name of the emperor against a postwar democracy that had deprived Japan of its army and robbed the nation of its soul," in the words of cultural critic John Nathan.[61] When the cadets began to hoot and jeer, the novelist, only forty-five, went inside and committed hara-kiri. Chalmers Johnson, reflecting on this event, wrote that Mishima's effort to revive the "withered soul" of Japan, while viewed at the time as an aberrant act, nonetheless remained in the minds of many Japanese "an exemplary metaphor for Japan's frustrations with its dependent foreign policy."[62]

Once again, as they had before, Japan's leaders were willing to risk Japanese identity in the pursuit of national power. Just as the Meiji leaders had been willing to swallow cultural pride and borrow massively from an alien civilization, so Japan's postwar leaders were willing to live under a foreign-imposed constitution, tolerate the continuing presence of U.S. bases on their soil, and defer to U.S. domination of many aspects of their foreign policy. Yoshida's biographer, Kōsaka Masataka, frequently observed that the greatest challenge of the Yoshida strategy was maintaining national morale: "A trading nation does not go to war," he wrote. "Neither does it make supreme efforts to bring peace. It simply takes advantage of international relations created by stronger nations." To survive as a trading nation, Japan had to manage its crisis of spirit. All trading nations, Kōsaka wrote, face this crisis, because they stand for no fixed principles but simply adapt to whatever the situation requires: "This, however, tends to weaken the self-confidence and identity of the persons engaged in the operation. They gradually come to lose sight of what they really value and even who they really are."[63]

Postwar Japan's most durable political leader, Miyazawa Kiichi, who held office as prime minister, MITI minister, and MOF minister, among other positions, was the most consistent adherent of the Yoshida Doctrine. For him, Japan had to remain an exception to the normal pattern of nation-states. Miyazawa, who as a young bureaucrat was an aide to Yoshida, tenaciously defended a passive international role for Japan by insisting that the constitution made Japan a "special state" and precluded it from normal participation in international politics. In creating a "peace state," he wrote in 1984, "the Japanese people have gambled their future in a great experiment, the first of its kind in human history." Accordingly, Japan could not justify any point of view other than its own self-interest. Japan's foreign policy, Miyazawa told an interviewer in 1980, "precludes all value judgments. It is a pretense of a foreign policy. The only value judgments we can make are determining what is in Japan's interest. Since there are no real value judgments possible we cannot say anything." When challenged politically, Japan could only defer. "All we can do when we are hit on the head is pull back. We watch the world situation and follow the trends," Miyazawa said.[64] Here was certainly one of the clearest statements of the opportunist and adaptive impulses that pervaded Japanese foreign policy for decades. Miyazawa's view underlined the bleak spiritual stance inherent in neo-mercantilism.

Japan's goal was to avoid an independent political position in international affairs. The foreign affairs commentator Matsuoka Hideo wrote in 1980 that Japan should avoid becoming entangled in international disputes by deliberately "missing the boat." When international disputes arose, Japan should always "go to the end of the line" and wait quietly, unnoticed, while other nations stepped forward to declare their positions on controversial issues. He called this passive and reactive policy a "diplomacy of cowardice" (*okubyō gaikō*), but it served Japan's interests by maintaining good relations with other countries and thus preserving its global access to markets and raw materials. "No matter where or what kind of dispute or war arises," he concluded, "Japan must stand aloof and uninvolved."[65] In a 1985 essay, Kōsaka Masataka, probably the most representative intellectual spokesman for the LDP mainstream, recognized that this opportunistic international behavior created "a serious identity problem for the nation" but nevertheless urged that Japan, in its own long-term interests, continue to adhere to the Yoshida Doctrine and "preserve an indomitable spiritual strength without having any clear-cut and explicit principles."[66]

Japan had indeed caught up with Western economies, but its achievement was at a considerable cost. The opportunistic way in which it had often pursued its goals left many Japanese people without a clear sense of their own national purpose. The novelist Ōe Kenzaburō chose in his 1994 Nobel Prize speech, entitled "Japan, the Ambiguous," to dwell on his nation's lack of moral direction. He recalled how the great Meiji novelist Natsume Sōseki had explored Japan's demeaning dependence on the Western cultural model and how it deprived the Japanese of any sense of integrated selfhood. Sōseki had said that integrity would be impossible "until the day came when feeble Japan could stand shoulder to shoulder financially with the greatest powers of Europe." The integrity that a sense of cultural autonomy and independence might have provided was, unfortunately, Ōe observed, never regained:

> Sōseki's gloomy judgments were prophetic in every way but one: he could never have known that the day would come when Japan would be able to "stand shoulder to shoulder financially with the greatest powers of Europe." That day *has* come, but without the beneficial effect that Sōseki imagined it would have. . . . The spiritual deficit has become more acute. True, Japan has modernized, but at the cost of an ugly war which it started in China and which left neighboring Asian countries devastated. Japan itself was reduced to a smoldering ruin; Tokyo was razed to the ground,

and a worse fate befell Hiroshima and Nagasaki. Still, modernization continued with the postwar reconstruction and the subsequent period of rapid economic growth; but these have, in effect, led to a deeper kind of decline, a state of outright spiritual poverty. In this sense, Sōseki was correct, frighteningly correct.

. . . If Japan is to find a way out of its current predicament—by which I mean its lack of any moral direction—then it must do so by establishing a sense of morality that can be shared with Western nations but that, for its own purposes, is founded firmly on the traditions of Japan's premodern period. Only then will Japan be able to shed its "black sheep" image and play an appropriate role in the world community.[67]

Indeed, Western critics saw Japan as an outlier that seemed to adhere to no universally accepted principles. The Dutch journalist Karel van Wolferen reached the harsh judgment that

the most crucial factor determining Japan's socio-political reality . . . is the near absence of any idea that there can be truths, rules, principles, or morals that always apply, no matter what the circumstances. . . . Concepts of independent, universal truths or immutable religious beliefs, transcending the world reality of social dictates and the decrees of power-holders have of course found their way into Japan, but they have never taken root in any surviving world-view.[68]

This disparagement of Japanese culture cut to the quick. It was such views that Murakami Yasusuke had in mind when, with more than a little acerbity, he observed that "Western critiques of Japanese culture have also often noted a lack of principles; a situational, two-faced lack of morals; and untrustworthiness. But it is impossible that the culture of a country comprising more than 100 million people, which is a first-rank economic power and, in international comparison, safe and stable, should be merely unprincipled and full of contradictions—regardless of whether one likes the culture or not."[69] A distinguished conservative intellectual, Murakami believed that modern Japanese history could demonstrate cultural values of universal applicability that would be particularly valuable to the later-developing countries of the world. He brought his views to bear in the Nakasone administration that came to power in the 1980s.

NAKASONE'S FAILURE: THE LIMITS OF THE SYSTEM

As grand strategy, the Yoshida Doctrine guided the country's fortunes smoothly and shrewdly to achieve long-term goals; however, it left the country unprepared to deal with the political consequences of its newly acquired national economic power, and it ignored the latent issues of wounded national pride caused by the subordinate role Japan adopted in the U.S.-dominated world system.

Unexpectedly, the conservatives opposing the Yoshida Doctrine found an opportunity to attempt to overturn the national strategy. Owing to a deadlock within the LDP, Nakasone Yasuhiro, a longtime conservative critic of the Yoshida strategy, was chosen to become prime minister. During his five-year term as prime minister (1982–1987), he made a bold and ambitious attempt to reorient Japanese national purpose and to define a new and broader national interest. Nakasone was the first anti-mainstream conservative to become prime minister since Kishi in the 1950s. He had long been known as a hawkish advocate of autonomous defense, and he favored termination of the security treaty and the conclusion of a "genuine" alliance with the United States on the basis of equality. Moreover, he wanted Japan to establish, as he put it, "a constitution independently drawn up by the Japanese people." Decades after the signing of the San Francisco Peace Treaty, Nakasone remained unhappy with the choices Japan had made at that time. He wrote in 1982:

> In hindsight one could argue that Prime Minister Yoshida's strategy represented in its own way, a rational decision. By leaving Japan's defense to another country, he was able to reduce the defense burden, allowing the country to concentrate on rebuilding its devastated economy and reconstructing a stable democratic nation. Yet I cannot help but wonder, even now, about what might have happened had Japan made a different choice at that critical juncture. Ever since . . . I have made it one of my political goals to transcend the so-called San Francisco system.[70]

Nakasone wanted to do something that had never been done before in modern Japan. He sought an internally generated sense of national purpose. Rather than adapting to international trends, he would lay out a self-determined course for the nation. Instead of taking an opportunistic approach to foreign affairs, Japan would have its own ideals. It would provide a model for other countries instead of emulating others. Although it had been subject to the values of international liberalism for a century and a half, Japan would now provide a message of universal significance from its own history. He believed that all of these unprecedented changes in Japan's approach to the international system were now appropriate because Japan's position in the system was changing. Japan was no longer a developing nation following after the advanced industrial countries. Its moment to mount the stage of world leadership was at hand. As Nakasone wrote on the eve of assuming the prime ministership, "The first necessity is a change in our thinking. Having 'caught up,' we must now expect others to try to catch up with us. We must seek out a new path for ourselves and open it up ourselves."[71]

Nakasone had in mind a new "grand design" to supplant the Yoshida strategy and to transform the role Japan had adopted since it entered the international state system in the nineteenth century. With the bureaucracy and the mainstream of the LDP largely still tied to the Yoshida Doctrine, Nakasone repeatedly attempted an end run around them by appointing commissions and advisory panels to highlight his pet proposals and bring forth predetermined policy recommendations. His vision owed much to a brain trust brought together in the 1970s by the late Prime Minister Ōhira Masayoshi.[72] It was undoubtedly the most impressive assemblage of the nation's intellectual leaders since Konoe's ill-fated Showa Research Association had tried to plan Japan's role in the late 1930s. Out of this extraordinary mobilization of political, business, and academic leaders came a neoconservative agenda for remaking Japan.

The "neoconservative" movement had the goal of replacing the conservatism of the late developer—the policies and consensus of catch-up modernization—that had guided Japanese foreign and domestic policies in the postwar decades with a new conservatism that focused on Japanese leadership. The term also referred to the many common themes shared with the Reagan and Thatcher neoconservative movements, which were ascendant at the time. These emphasized small government, deregulation, greater reliance on market forces, and a more strident confrontation with the Soviet bloc. Japanese neoconservatism, however, differed markedly from its analogues in the United States and England in that it came at the end of a century-long struggle to overtake those same industrial nations. The Ōhira Research Groups argued that having achieved the purpose for which it was built, the structure of government controls should be relaxed. All of the technology that could be borrowed from the West had already been borrowed. In most fields, Japan had reached the frontier. The case for bureaucratic guidance had been persuasive when Japan was still behind and the industrial future was clear, but its effectiveness had disappeared when Japan had caught up.

Neoconservatism not only stressed the end of Japan's followership, it proclaimed the beginning of a new era in which the Japanese would be more culturally self-reliant. For more than a century, Japan had denigrated its own heritage by acknowledging the superiority of Western culture, but its success in overtaking the West and in producing superior manufactures had awakened a worldwide interest in Japanese culture. "Japanese culture," an Ōhira group concluded, "is no longer simply the possession of the Japanese."[73] In this new era, the Japanese would not only return to their own cultural values but also share them with a universal audience.

Nakasone set out to transform the pragmatic, opportunistic, and reactive pattern of Japan's policies. Japan had to set forth its own self-generated objectives and principles. Through a series of high-profile foreign trips, he sought to use the diplomatic responsibilities of his office to undo the impression of a politically passive Japan. Though often more rhetoric than reality, these diplomatic activities gave Japanese foreign policy a more activist cast.

Immediately after taking office, Nakasone made an unprecedented trip to Seoul and approved a long-term loan that explicitly linked Korean military spending to the strategic defense of Japan. Subsequently, in a memorable visit to Washington in January 1983, he made a series of bold public statements on strategic issues that bespoke a new, proactive role in the alliance. In a departure from the Yoshida Doctrine's Three Principles of Arms Exports, he announced approval of the transfer of purely military technology to the United States. Then, in a Washington news conference, he unleashed a series of rhetorical flourishes that implied a readiness to undertake strategic commitments that far exceeded Japan's capacity. Japan would aim for "complete and full control" of its straits controlling the Sea of Japan "so that there should be no passage of Soviet submarines and other naval activities in time of emergency." Warming to his topic, he asserted that Japan should act like "a big aircraft carrier" (ōkina koku bokan)— his interpreter, sharing the hyperbole of the moment, used the colorful phrase "an unsinkable aircraft carrier" (fuchin kubō)—to prevent the penetration of Soviet backfire bombers into Japanese airspace. Nakasone declared an end to taboos on discussion of constitutional revision of Article 9. His bravado performance delighted Reagan and began a warm relationship that suited the needs of both leaders.

Next, at his first G-7 summit meeting, held in Williamsburg, Virginia, in

May 1983, buoyed by the rising tide of interest in his leadership, Nakasone supported Reagan's determination to confront the Soviet's installation of SS-20 nuclear missiles in Europe and Asia. Boldly aligning Japan with the West, he asserted that "security is indivisible." The summit's commemorative photograph, showing the handsome Japanese leader standing tall between Reagan and Thatcher and chatting affably, was warmly received by the Japanese public. Flying back to Tokyo after leaving Williamsburg, Nakasone wrote exultantly in his diary:

> This must be the beginning of a new era in our diplomacy. Departing from the traditional, reactive (*hito no kaoiro ukagau*), wait-and-see (*hiyorimi*), opportunistic (*rikōteki*) style, I behaved broad-mindedly and led the meeting with my own strategy and with my goals of [promoting] the interests of the free world and Japan. I believe that I made the boldest diplomatic move in the postwar world next to Yoshida's peace settlement [in 1951]. [Japan] has not been, thus far, able to make good use of its capability as an economic major power from the standpoint of international politics. I made 100 percent use of it. It is the true value of politics. . . . This new emergence of Japan in international politics must be maintained, and this status must not be curtailed or abandoned. Such will be the single most important qualification for Japanese leaders from now on.[74]

Nakasone sought a defense buildup to support his new stance. Despite MOF's determination to reduce the government's budget deficit, he instituted annual increases of 5–7 percent in defense spending, recalling in his diary that the first time he ordered the director of the Budget Bureau to make such an increase, the bureaucrat's face "twitched and turned pale."[75] He determined to break through the limitation on defense spending that stipulated expenditures of only 1 percent of GNP. A commission he appointed to consider the issue brought forth a recommendation in 1986 to lift this limitation, but when faction leaders and MOF resisted, he was only able to achieve a level of 1.004 percent of GNP. This frustration of his purpose by the entrenched political interests was repeated in the course of his many attempts to change the national strategy.

Nakasone argued the need for sweeping institutional reforms to prepare Japan for its new role as a leader in the international system. During his five years in office, he pressed for change on many domestic fronts. The century-long pursuit of equality with the West had left its mark on all of Japan's institutions, which had been designed to promote a uniform and disciplined national effort to achieve this goal. They had also been designed to insulate Japan from direct influence by foreign companies and individuals. To play the new role of an international leader, Japan's economic, social, and educational institutions had to be made more open, flexible, tolerant of diversity, and responsive to the international expectations associated with Japan's new status.

Nakasone and his advisers in fact believed that Japan must leave behind many aspects of the distinctive Japanese model of capitalism. These were institutions of economic nationalism that from a Western perspective constituted an illiberal way of conducting affairs: government industrial policy, cartels and other forms of collusion, a closed distribution system, enterprise groups (*keiretsu*), forced placement of government debt, noncompetitive public-sector procurement, import restrictions, tax preferences, and encouragement of savings to promote exports. Having caught up in so many areas, it was no longer in Japan's interest to maintain these policies. They had worked brilliantly in facilitating Japan's industrial takeoff, but they had outlived their usefulness and now served to protect weak and inefficient industries. In addition, they were the focus of mounting foreign criticism of unfair, beggar-thy-neighbor strategies.

In 1985, Nakasone appointed an advisory group, chaired by the former governor of the Bank of Tokyo, Maekawa Haruo, to recommend measures to deal with growing trade surpluses. The Maekawa Report the following year recommended restructuring the economy, removing protectionist barriers to trade, increasing imports, changing preferential tax treatment for savings, and reforming the distribution system that kept consumer prices high. This proposal to loosen the reins on the economic structure and to shift to a leadership role in the global economy proved frustratingly difficult to implement, however, because of vested interests, persistent official preference for pursuing national autonomy, and the success that traditional policies had earlier achieved. Nakasone eventually had to admit that restructuring the economy was a long-term goal that he could not achieve in his term.

Reform of the education system, another of Nakasone's priorities, likewise proved difficult. Nakasone and his advisers believed that during the long years of catching up with the West, the school system had become so highly centralized and rigid, so intent on rote memory work and test scores, so focused on meeting company hiring policies and providing a mass-produced supply of workers for Japanese industry, that creativity and diversity had been stifled. Furthermore, they believed that these were qualities that Japan would need in the future. Standardization and regulation of education had become a deadweight inhibiting the development of the more diverse and creative workforce that would benefit the economy in the twenty-first century.

In 1987, an education council appointed by Nakasone recommended changes to liberalize the rigid system. These changes included introducing greater latitude into school curricula and establishing a wider range of criteria for judging achievement than simple test scores. What the council wanted to encourage was greater individuality and creativity so that Japan could generate its own ideas about how to succeed as an international leader in the future. Nakasone and his advisers also wanted the schools to take the lead in the internationalization of Japan. They wanted to open the schools to international influences, remove obstacles to hiring foreign teachers and enrolling foreign students, improve foreign-language instruction, and enhance Japanese understanding of other cultures. The desired product of a reformed education would be a newly self-confident Japanese populace—an educated Japanese citizenry at home in the world, not clinging to other Japanese when abroad, but rather communicating easily with foreigners and understanding their mores. Once again, however, efforts at reform were undermined by long-ingrained habits of mind and bureaucratic defenses, this time in the Education Ministry.

Nakasone had a keen grasp of the role that attitudes toward history can play in forming a people's self-image and enabling them to embark on great undertakings. Midway through his term, in a noteworthy address to an LDP seminar at Karuizawa in 1985, he stressed the need to overcome the negative identity of the postwar period:

So that Japan may progress toward becoming an international state (*kokusai kokka*), it is important that Japan once again reconsider its identity. In the prewar period Japan had the emperor state view of history. After we lost the war, the Pacific War view of history emerged; it is also called the Tokyo [War Crimes] Tribunal view of history. The allied countries, acting on their own, made [international] laws, made Japan the defendant, and in the name of civilization, in the name of peace and humanity, judged Japan. History will have to make the final judgment of the justice of those procedures and judgments. . . . However, the view that emerged in Japan at that time was that Japan was bad in everything. It was a kind of self-flagellating trend of thinking. Even now it still remains. . . . I am opposed to this kind of thinking. . . . It is the establishment of the people's image that counts. From this standpoint, it is necessary to establish Japan's identity by judging the past achievements of Japan in terms of the universal nature of world history.[76]

Convinced that self-confidence must begin with an appreciation of traditional institutions, Nakasone attempted to take a symbolic step in this direction at the Yasukuni Shrine, the Shinto shrine honoring the spirits of the war dead in the modern era. Going back to Yoshida, prime ministers had visited the shrine in an official capacity during the autumn festival, but not on August 15, the day commemorating the end of World War II. Following the constitutional provision for separation of religion and the state, they had visited only as private persons, not in an official capacity, on that date. Families of the war dead, a powerful LDP constituency, had long lobbied for restoration of the shrine's prewar status. Nakasone appointed a private advisory panel to deal with this constitutional issue, and once the panel gave its approval, he became the first prime minister to offer his prayers at the shrine in his official capacity on the day commemorating the end of the war. His official visit, on August 15, 1985, evoked such vehement protests in China and Korea that he absented himself from the shrine a year later. Although he hoped to balance a revived nationalism with a healthy respect for the traditions of other peoples, the effort fell short. At the end of his term, Nakasone, brooding about the persistent international distrust, concluded, "I think a century must pass before the suspicion and distrust of our neighbors will dissipate."[77]

Despite an extraordinary effort at self-generated reforms, Nakasone's agenda was largely unrealized. The dominant view held that the performance of Western-style institutions in Japan demonstrated their durability and worth. There was fierce resistance from the bureaucracy and the mainstream conservatives. Nakasone's failure is especially significant because it demonstrated the limits of the Japanese system.[78] So strong and embedded was the Japanese trait of dependence on the external structure to provide the motivation for change in Japanese politics and society that Nakasone's determination to fashion a self-generated new direction ultimately failed. So long as the Cold War international structure persisted, it would be difficult to change a foreign policy and an institutional structure that had been so successful in exploiting that order. The balance of power in Japanese politics still tilted toward the adherents of the Yoshida strategy. Nakasone left office in 1987 with a wry remark that the outcome of his effort to transform Japan's international role was "yet to be seen."[79] It would take the stimulus of powerful external events—the collapse of the Cold War system—to prod Japan to reform its foreign policy and its domestic institutions. Japan would undertake fundamental change only when a new order in East Asia stimulated it to do so.

CHAPTER NINE

THE POST–COLD WAR INTERVAL IN EAST ASIA

The dissolution of the Cold War order came suddenly, unanticipated and stunning in its precipitous ending. The Soviet empire and its ideological underpinnings collapsed not as a result of defeat on the battlefield but through a massive implosion of the Soviet system. Rarely in history had the components of world order changed so abruptly. The end of bipolarity unmistakably signaled a vast shift in the international distribution of power. It also marked the extinction of Soviet communism and the triumph of Western capitalist democracies. More than previous hegemonic conflicts, the Cold War was a conflict of two systems, two ideologies. Liberal political and democratic principles triumphed, although for a time it appeared that another competitive system might arise.

At the end of the Cold War, Japanese state-led capitalism briefly challenged the vision of an international order led by the United States and dedicated to the expansion of free trade and democracy. The efflorescence of Japanese capitalism in the 1980s, which excited both admiration and anxiety, initially led to the conclusion that Japan more than any other country stood to capitalize on the post–Cold War conditions. There was a widespread belief that Japan had succeeded in developing a superior economic system, one that had not only caught up with the other advanced economies but was now prepared to lead a new international system modeled on the trading state.

Japan rode on the waves of liberalism's triumph without adopting its principles. It stood on the side of the West, but its ruling elite, on the whole, shared little passion for the ideals of liberalism. The superior economic performance of Japanese capitalism in the aftermath of World War II drew worldwide attention, achieving new levels of economic competitiveness based not on classic liberal norms but instead on distinctive Japanese organizing principles. Japan's leaders had constructed a system of illiberal institutions that had outperformed the Western capitalist democracies. The success of Japan's unique industrial policies, and its socially and culturally embedded institutions of capitalism, appeared to foretell a new era of economic and technological competition among the great powers.

Samuel Huntington wrote in 1991 that the United States was justifiably "obsessed with Japan for the same reason that it was once obsessed with the Soviet Union. It sees that country as a major threat to its primacy in the crucial arena of power. . . . An economic cold war is developing between the United States and Japan, and Americans have good reason to be concerned about the consequences of doing poorly in that competition."[1] Japan represented a new kind of power. As the political economist Robert Gilpin wrote at the time: "Western liberal societies find Japanese economic success particularly threatening because it is the first non-Western and nonliberal society to outcompete them. Whereas Western economies are based on belief in the superior efficiency of the free market and individualism, the market and the individual in Japan are not relatively autonomous but are deeply embedded in a powerful nonliberal culture and social system."[2]

Yet instead of marking the beginning of Japan's preeminence, the end of the Cold War system unexpectedly led to the disruption of the Japanese system. Much of the expectation that Japan would become the new international leader ignored the extent to which Japan's historical advance depended on adjusting to the international order rather than creating it. Japan's success in the Cold War had benefited from the unique conditions of the bipolar order, which had allowed it to profit from the free-trade order while flouting its liberal principles. Japan's reversal of fortunes has usually been explained as arising from the mismanagement of the economy. Yet on a deeper level, the major changes in Japan's external environment, and the consequent uncertainty about the structure of the future international order, caused profound problems and led to a paralysis in policymaking. Collapse of the bipolar international system fundamentally disoriented the Japanese grand strategy and domestic political economy. Exposed to the new post–Cold War conditions, the Japanese challenge faded.

In contrast, the U.S. economy, buoyed by technological breakthroughs and adapting swiftly to the tides of economic internationalization, began to enjoy sustained high performance. The other major powers faced a resurgent America as its wealth and power grew steadily during the 1990s. The United States became a singular superpower and for the third time in the twentieth century confronted the task of re-creating the international order. No state had so dominated its times since the Roman or Chinese empires. The U.S. defense budget was larger than the next nine largest military budgets combined.[3] The historian Paul Kennedy, whose best-selling book *The Rise and Fall of the Great Powers* (1987) had forecast a U.S. decline, was awed by the "spectacular" resurgence of U.S. power and wealth and the global reach of its influence. He wrote in the *Financial Times* in 2002:

> Nothing has ever existed like this disparity of power; nothing. I have returned to all of the comparative defence spending and military personnel statistics over the past 500 years that I compiled in *The Rise and Fall of the Great Powers,* and no other nation comes close. . . . Charlemagne's empire was merely western Europe in its reach. The Roman empire stretched further afield, but there was another empire in Persia, and a larger one in China. There is, therefore, no comparison.[4]

French Foreign Minister Hubert Vedrine concluded that the United States had outdone its own superpower status of the twentieth century: "U.S. supremacy today extends to the economy, currency, military areas, lifestyle, language and the products of mass culture that inundate the world, forming thought and fascinating even the enemies of the United States."[5]

The dramatic events of 1989–1991 that saw the demise of the Soviet Union destroyed only part of the post–World War II international system. The bipolar order disappeared, while the Liberal Democratic order remained intact. In contrast to U.S. leaders in 1918 and 1945, however, the U.S. leaders of 1989–1991 offered no new formulations of how to re-create the world order. The United States itself was unprepared for the sudden, unexpected end of the old order. There was no Woodrow Wilson, no Franklin Roosevelt, no U.S. president with a vision of new international institutions. Nor was there even a strategist like George Kennan in the government to provide a new concept of international security. It was not until the terrorist attacks of September 11, 2001, against the World Trade Center and the Pentagon that a new grand strategy began to take shape.

For the first decade after the end of the Cold War, the Americans were convinced that their original plans for world order in the aftermath of World War II were still valid. As John Ikenberry wrote,

> After past great wars, the old international order tended to be destroyed and discredited, and the way opened for sweeping negotiations over the basic rule and principles of postwar order. After 1989–1991, Western leaders were more likely to argue that international order was working quite well. Western policy toward the Soviet Union had been vindicated, and the organization of relations among the industrial democracies remained stable and cooperative.[6]

Lacking new goals, a new concept or paradigm of international order, the United States was content with the institutions of the Liberal Democratic order that had been established at the end of World War II and prior to the onset of the Cold War. In the summer of 1989, Francis Fukuyama's essay "The End of History" proclaimed that, having defeated the forces of fascism and communism in the twentieth century, the West had triumphed in grand historical terms. Fukuyama declared that the United States and its allies had achieved "the end point of mankind's ideological evolution and the universalization of Western liberal democracy." There were, at last, no ideological competitors. "The triumph of the West, of the Western ideal," he wrote, "is evident . . . in the total exhaustion of viable alternatives to Western liberalism."[7]

Many American and European observers were essentially of the same mind. The respected international relations theorist John Ruggie, for example, concluded that no new paradigm was likely to emerge in the foreseeable future: "In this ambiguous context, [we should return] to the animating ideas America's leaders had in mind for the post [World War II] era, before the advent, and during the early days, of bipolarity. . . . A central task for American foreign policy analysts and practitioners, then, is to adapt this ideational and institutional legacy to the new, post–cold war international landscape."[8] The international institutions that had been created at the end of the war had to be extended to the far reaches of the old Soviet empire.

The fact that the U.S. economy demonstrated superior performance throughout the 1990s, while the socialist model had collapsed and the Japan model stagnated, seemed to confer legitimacy on American capitalism as a model of universal applicability. In the United States and in the international financial institutions that the United States dominated, the belief that following a liberal, market-driven economy was the most efficient way to promote growth under the new conditions of globalization came to be called "the Washington consensus."

Although American power was now preeminent in the world, it was not clear how this would affect regional order in Asia. In the 1990s, Asia entered what we might call an interregnum,[9] a period of flux when the shape of a new order was not yet apparent. Cold War stability gave way to a new uncertainty. The demise of the Soviet Union, the growing strength of the Chinese economy, and the stagnation of the Japanese political economy combined to create what at first appeared to be a different strategic environment in East Asia. The uncertainty in the region was a result of the fact that the end of the Cold War in Asia was less decisive than in Europe. Although the Cold War paradigm that had heretofore controlled the configuration of the regional order had weakened, it did not wholly disappear. Important remnants of the Cold War remained. Korea remained divided. Taiwan's future was unresolved. Japan and Russia still were without a peace treaty, owing to the territorial dispute over the southern Kurile Islands. Governments that were at least nominally Communist held on to power in China and Vietnam as well as in North Korea. The U.S. security structure in the region designed for the Cold War remained. Efforts to build multilateral institutions where none had previously existed produced new but fragile organizations.

Soviet power and influence in Asia had disappeared, but the future structure of the regional system remained indeterminate, without coordinates or hierarchies. The fragility of the existing constellation of power in the region was apparent, but there were no clear signs of how the regional structure would be refashioned. In part, this interregnum was a result of the uncertainty of the American role and purpose. The United States had yet to formulate a new strategic vision for the region, preferring to adhere to Cold War strategies, including a continuation of the U.S. security blanket for Asia, with modest amendments. The United States was a sort of "regent" of this interregnum, the temporary stand-in, maintaining order for the time being.

The U.S. Pacific Command, headquartered in Honolulu, maintained the security of the region west from Hawaii across the Pacific and around to the Indian Ocean. Of the Pacific Command's 300,000 personnel, a third were forward deployed in Japan and Korea. Bilateral security treaties that had been designed for the Cold War—treaties with Japan, South Korea,

Australia, the Philippines, and Thailand—remained in force. The United States clung to this bilateral alliance structure and, so long as Cold War issues persisted, showed little interest in exerting its energies on behalf of new multilateral institutions or a new regional structure. While the United States used its power to maintain the status quo, the region's other powers—China, Russia, and Japan—were each preoccupied with domestic problems. Russia had to recover from the collapse of its old order and make the transition from a command economy. China was still an emerging power of uncertain purpose, preoccupied with the staggering tasks of nation-building and economic development. And Japan experienced a tide of troubles that began with economic stagnation and spread to political confusion and a loss of social cohesion.

THE PREDICAMENT OF POST–COLD WAR JAPAN

The reversal of Japanese fortunes during this period was startling. As the 1990s began, it soon became apparent that the economic boom in the latter half of the 1980s had created a bubble of alarming proportions. After the rapid appreciation of the yen after the Plaza Accord—its value doubled against the dollar—the government, fearing economic recession, resorted to monetary stimulus by lowering interest rates and strongly encouraging banks to lend. A massive asset price inflation resulted in the tripling of stock prices and urban real-estate prices. Alarmed at the heights that asset inflation reached, the Ministry of Finance attempted to ease their price level, but once the bubble burst, asset prices collapsed and economic stagnation set in. Unemployment reached postwar highs. Business failures were widespread. Banks held portfolios of nonperforming loans. Macroeconomic policy oscillated clumsily between stimulus and tax increases.

It might have been possible to blame the tide of troubles that swept over Japan in the 1990s simply on economic policy errors, except that it soon became apparent that the troubles had deeper sources than economic mismanagement. This "lost decade" revealed pervasive problems in the Japanese system that pointed to widespread institutional fatigue, social malaise, and loss of national purpose. Added to the policy mistakes was a plethora of corruption scandals among elite bureaucrats, often involving unethical and illegal relations between business firms and politicians. Always a pillar of the Japanese system, the bureaucracy suffered incalculable damage to its image of integrity and competence. Moreover, this official malfeasance called attention to the lack of transparency that characterized the central role of the bureaucracy in Japan's developmentalist system. Bureaucratic leadership, efficient when long-term strategy and national purpose were set, lost its effectiveness.

Lacking purposeful leadership, the political system foundered in confusion and drift. Policies and institutions that had functioned so well in the Cold War days became outmoded. The political system, predicated on the Cold War order, was beset by confusion and bewildering party realignments. The era of stable one-party rule ended in 1993, when the LDP lost power for the first time since its founding in 1955. Its uninterrupted thirty-eight-year rule, unequaled among major powers in the postwar era, had enabled the Japanese elite to pursue long-term policy goals. Although it returned to power a year later, the LDP now depended on coalition support from other parties. Its hold on power was now tenuous. It was forced to strike shameless compromises with other parties; and, amidst drift and gridlock, voter identification with the LDP, or any party, dwindled. Japan experienced a shocking loss of social cohesion during this period. The tradition of lifetime employment weakened, young people became alienated, and the older generations seemed confused and disoriented. The times cried out for leadership, but the political class evinced a peculiar pattern of passivity, indecisiveness, and incapacity in dealing with the nation's problems. In the first post–Cold War decade, Japan had nine prime ministers.

Japan was living in the in-between times. The international political economy was suddenly in the throes of profound change. Among the world's regions, Asia experienced the greatest uncertainty. The regional interregnum offered no clear paradigm to which Japan might relate to reshape the character and purpose of its institutions. The ill-defined future was reflected in immobilism in Japanese politics. Uncertain what shape the new paradigm would ultimately take, Japan's conservative leaders floundered, unable to discern from the indeterminate trends a clear new direction for the nation. The late Professor Kōsaka Masataka explained: "Consensus is obtained without great difficulty when the nature of the task is clear. Often, for instance, the Japanese have been good at adapting to strong, decisive pressures from outside. But when the situation is blurred they are in trouble."[10] It was not coincidental that Japan was suffering from drift and immobilism at a time when the tectonic plates of the international system itself were shifting and the nature of the international system was uncertain. Japan's characteristic adaptive approach lost its power to shape decisive responses when there was no clearly defined system to adapt to.

Japan's external environment in the post–Cold War era was changing in such fundamental ways that leadership was deeply conflicted over how to respond. First, the developmentalist institutions that characterized Japan's capitalist economy confronted a new phase of global capitalism for which they were clearly unsuited. The nature of capitalism itself and the technological paradigm underlying it were entering a new and unprecedented phase. Second, the end of the Cold War eroded the effectiveness of the Yoshida Doctrine as a national strategy and disrupted the internal political order that had been formed to support it. Third, Japan confronted a radically transformed regional environment. Since the beginning of its modern history 150 years earlier, Japan had grown accustomed to a weak and passive Asia that it could comfortably expect to dominate. Only in the post–Cold War decade did it become apparent that the regional order had vastly changed. The conspicuous dynamism and change in its immediate external environment meant that Japan's relations with its Asian neighbors became a new, more complex and demanding challenge for which little in its previous history had prepared it. Each transition in the international system that modern Japan had faced for the past century and a half presented difficult challenges to which the nation skillfully adjusted. But the post–Cold War system remained uncertain and fluid. It as yet offered no clear image of the future to which Japan could adapt.

THE CRISIS OF JAPANESE CAPITALISM

The transformation of the international economy in the 1990s represented one of the most extreme changes in Japan's external environment. The end of the Cold War removed the constraints on economic globalization that the autarkic policies of Communist governments had posed. National economies were increasingly linked through trade, financial flows, and foreign direct investment by multinational firms as the U.S. government, the new World Trade Organization, and the European Union promoted further market liberalization. A new technological paradigm bringing a revolution in communications and information fueled these developments. This globalization of capitalism, as one economic historian described it, brought a host of intertwined developments:

The digital revolution changed many dimensions of advanced capitalist societies in fundamental ways; the world economy became substantially more interdependent because trade and the cross-border flows of information, technology, and capital are larger than ever; competition grew more intense than ever because of both reduced impediments to trade and a large excess capacity in many markets of manufactured products; and to maintain or increase competitiveness, the largest firms and financial institutions merged at an accelerating pace within and across national boundaries.[11]

Japan's severe economic setbacks and the change in the international economy created a crisis for its developmental capitalism. Its unexpected economic decline after the Cold War posed the difficult question of whether, faced with the new conditions of technological revolution and economic internationalization and the need to restore the nation's economic competitiveness, the Japanese must now abandon the distinctive institutions of Japanese capitalism that had served them so well, or would be able to retain and adapt these institutions and preserve social cohesion. This new phase of capitalism coincided with the end of Japan's own long struggle to catch up with the advanced industrial economies and consequently aggravated the already difficult challenge of transitioning to a more mature capitalist economy. Efforts to reform during the Nakasone years had failed despite the fact that the prime minister and his advisers had recognized that many of the developmentalist institutions had outlived their effectiveness and had to be replaced by more open arrangements. But the demands of reform ran counter to Japan's longtime historical experience, and given the apparent successful performance of the Japanese economy through the 1980s, their proposals were a tough sell. As the Cold War came to an end, Japan still had not come to grips with the issues of transforming its "catchup" institutional structure.

The radical deterioration of Japan's economic fortunes in the 1990s gave rise to prolonged political struggles and debates over future policy. Three distinct views surfaced in this ongoing national debate: the convergence view, the conservative view, and the view that sought a third way.[12] First, there were those who believed that Japan should move toward an Anglo-American model of capitalism for one or more of several reasons: Either market forces would triumph and bring about convergence, the Japanese would choose to emulate the institutions that were outperforming their own, or a new set of internationally negotiated rules and institutions would require Japan to change. As the competitive disadvantage of Japan's nonliberal form of capitalism became evident to them, many Japanese regarded the distinctive socially and culturally embedded institutions of their economic system as no longer assets and demanded sweeping change in the modus operandi of their economic system. To reformers convinced of the superior efficiency of the Anglo-American model of liberal capitalism, the globalization of capitalism in the post–Cold War era, together with Japan's achievement of a mature capitalist economy, called for far-reaching changes—for an unfettering of the economy to free it from many of the state-centered controls that had accumulated over more than a century. The prominent business leader Ushio Jirō was convinced that Japan should "emulate the United Kingdom and the United States, where the economy is robust because of small government."[13] To satisfy the expectations of its people, and to stave off a declining standard of living, Japan needed to make the transition from a producer-oriented economy to a consumer-oriented economy. It would have to restructure its nationally managed capitalism in order to keep pace with economic internationalization and interdependence. Excessive regulation was a principal target of reformist criticism.

Reformers saw the increasing interdependence of globalized capitalism as evident in total trade, the range of products traded, cross-border capital flows, international joint ventures, and technology transfers. Information flowed through cyberspace in massive amounts. Facilitated by the new technology, investors could respond virtually instantaneously to new conditions. Daily international capital flows by the mid-1990s exceeded $1 trillion. Competition grew more intense as tariff and nontariff barriers were reduced and developing economies produced more competitive products.

Japanese institutions proved less responsive to market signals. This is not surprising, since the institutions had been formulated in the first place to promote the cooperative relations that markets tend to diminish. American capitalism permitted easier termination of employment and established market-determined wages, but generally at the cost of greater income disparity and social friction. Liberal economies were able to move swiftly to allocate capital to the new firms and industries that were at the forefront of the technical innovation. The greater transparencies of firms in the market-based economies better suited the conditions of the information and communications revolution.

Faced with fierce resistance from vested interests, Japan's reformers were slow to achieve results. The prominent economist Nakatani Iwao, a deeply frustrated reformer, consoled himself by recalling that it was a matter of national style for Japan to observe historical trends and move with the tide. He acknowledged in a 1996 book how ineffective Japan had been in carrying out deregulation and reform of its economy. He attributed inaction to institutional obstacles and the complacency of the people, and he ruled out the notion that self-generated sources of change could emerge to alter Japanese politics and culture. Yet Nakatani nonetheless concluded that Japan would ultimately change. He wrote:

> When we [Japanese] carefully perceive the change in the times (*jidai no henka*), the change in history (*rekishi no henka*), the change in the surrounding environment (*kankyō no henka*), when we perceive all aspects of these changes, and when we precisely grasp the direction of these changes, then an overwhelming number of Japanese will correctly understand the meaning of the historical turning point facing present day Japan and will begin to move in the correct direction[,] and the reform of Japan will take place with unexpected rapidity.[14]

And yet, there was a strong and stubborn conservative view in this national debate over the future of Japan's economic structure. The forces resisting change were formidable. Labor fought to protect its institutionally embedded entitlements; agriculture and business interests that had been shielded from foreign competition demanded continued protection; and the bureaucracy clung to its vested power. Those opposed to the convergence view argued that whatever the difficulties caused by the bubble, Japan had evolved the institutions and policies that best fit its historical preference for cooperative and harmonious social relations. They argued that cooperation between government and business, among firms, and between management and employees reflected the values, norms, and ideology of Japanese society.

There was a strong element of national pride in preserving these institutions. Developmentalism was a Japanese form of capitalism, an achievement of modern Japan that came out of the adaptation of Japan's own civilization to the tasks of industrialization. Japan had achieved catchup not by mechanically imitating the West and producing a superficial civilization, but rather by progressing along an independent Japanese course determined by Japanese values. Moreover, many conservatives believed that once political stability returned and the effects of the bubble were overcome, Japanese values would prove superior; that is, cooperation and social cohesion would ultimately be more effective over the long term in promoting growth and efficiency. Although many of the distinctive developmentalist institutions, such as lifetime employment, showed strains under the economic pressures that emerged after the Cold War, the core characteristics of Japanese capitalism remained largely intact. The longtime experience of late development was historically embedded and secured by thick networks of human relations. The veteran economic bureaucrat Sakakibara Eisuke argued that Japan should "rise above the oppression of mega competition" and "aim for the future" based on "Japan's own identities," without destroying cooperative institutions through outright liberalization.[15]

Finally, there was a third view in this debate that took a position between the previous two and argued for a hybrid outcome. It recognized that Japan would inexorably be shaped by the new forces of globalization, that it would have to bend to the power of market forces, global competition, and interdependence as well as to the strength of ordinary consumers' demands for change. But at the same time, it was also aware of the tenacity of Japanese institutions and national preferences. Nemoto Jirō, who headed one of the major business federations, was one who favored a "third way"—a new way of "minimizing unemployment and sustaining growth with neither the disparity of income seen in the United Kingdom and the United States nor the burden of overly generous social welfare programs of Germany."[16]

Japan's historic proclivity to emulate the best practices while at the same time evolving its own distinct institutions seemed to favor this third way. It was still difficult to discern when the world economy would stabilize and under what parameters, and no one could ultimately know how the implications of information and communications technology would play out. Japan could not easily adapt to a moving target. It could move incrementally, however, and eventually, if national decline were to be staved off, it would have to reorganize its political and economic system to respond to the external pressures for change. By its nature, the process of realigning institutions to accommodate the shift in the international economy would be a longer evolutionary process than the process of making the necessary changes in Japan's security relations, where the demands could be more immediately and urgently felt.

The struggle among these three alternative responses to the globalization of capitalism continued during the 1990s before the Japanese found the right mix of continuity and change. The period severely tested Japan's abilities to adapt, emulate, and innovate.

THE UNRAVELING OF THE YOSHIDA DOCTRINE

During the Cold War there had been a direct and causal relationship between the prevailing character and modus operandi of the international system and the political character of Japan's domestic regime.[17] The Cold War anchored Japanese politics for more than four decades, offering Japan ample time to adapt to its constraints and opportunities. That the nation's domestic political system was so intimately tied to its Cold War foreign policy led Professor Igarashi Takeshi to call it a "domestic foreign policy system."[18] Once the bipolar system disappeared, the impact on both the Yoshida strategy and the internal political order (sometimes called "the 1955 system," for the year that it took firm root) was bound to be profoundly disruptive.

Just how unprepared the Japanese system was for the new environment soon became clear. A series of crises in Japan's external relations in the 1990s forced its leadership to acknowledge that the strategies effective in the Cold War were no longer viable. These crises threatened goals that had been given top priority, especially the preservation of the U.S. alliance and the respect and reputation of Japan in the world. The Persian Gulf conflict, which broke out in 1990 when Iraq invaded Kuwait, was the first great international crisis of the post–Cold War period. When the United States organized an international coalition to restore peace under a United Nations resolution, pressure mounted on Japan, as a great economic power dependent on the Middle East for two-thirds of its energy, to take an active part in supporting the coalition. Japan was thrown into a period of prolonged political turmoil. It lacked both political consensus on how to respond and a legal framework that would enable it to proceed. Decades of withdrawal from international politics immobilized the Japanese political scene. Foreign policy issues that had been pointedly and purposefully evaded for decades now had to be confronted. The most fundamental issue was whether the constitution permitted collective security. The Cabinet Legislation Bureau, long the guardian of the Yoshida Doctrine, adamantly insisted that dispatch of SDF troops to join the coalition in any form was constitutionally prohibited. The CLB held to the narrowest possible interpretation, refusing to approve even a Defense Agency proposal to send transport planes to rescue refugees and holding that overseas flights could only be for training purposes.[19]

The government's confused efforts to offer even minimal personnel in support of the coalition proved a shameful spectacle of disarray. Japan initially promised a medical team of a hundred specialists, but less than twenty volunteers could be found. After a brief stint in the region, even they returned home. Tokyo also pledged that Japanese civilian aircraft and ships would transport food, water, and medical supplies, but airlines and longshoremen recoiled from involvement in the hostilities and the pledge was never fulfilled. The Americans, no longer restrained by the priorities of the Cold War, expressed outrage at Japan's reluctance to join the coalition. The U.S. House of Representatives angrily approved a resolution to begin withdrawing U.S. troops from Japan. Eventually, in response to U.S. pressure, Japan's political leaders decided that rather than sending personnel, they would make a $13 billion contribution to support the coalition. The sizable sum, however, was belittled in many foreign quarters as "checkbook diplomacy" and treated as a failure to become truly engaged in meeting the responsibilities of a country so deeply dependent on the stability of the international system. It was the first major sign that, in the changed context, economic power alone would not achieve Japan's foreign policy interests. The harsh international criticism and the spectacle of political disarray in full view of the world community proved a traumatic experience that shook the foundations of the Yoshida Doctrine and the domestic order. The Kyoto University political scientist Nakanishi Hiroshi wrote that "it was the experience of the Gulf War, which was so humiliating in the eyes of the majority of Japanese, that dealt the most serious blow to the 1955 system."[20]

The storm of international criticism that greeted Japan's grudging support of the UN-sanctioned coalition stunned Japanese politicians and opened deep fissures in the conservative elite. Many conservatives believed that Japan must adhere to its established policies regardless of the foreign criticism. The veteran LDP leader Miyazawa Kiichi, who assumed the prime ministership in the wake of the Gulf crisis, stoutly opposed sending SDF troops or even logistical help, saying, "We must clearly state that we cannot change the Japanese Constitution at this time. Even if other countries say that having such a constitution is outrageous, we must maintain the position that we decided on this and it's not for others to interfere."[21]

Other conservative leaders, however, perceived the need to adapt to the changed international environment. Inoki Masamichi, former head of the National Defense Academy, said the time had come to stop resorting to "the devious (*zurui*) measure of using the Constitution as pretext" for avoiding responsibilities in the international community.[22] Former prime minister Nakasone, reflecting on the shambles of Japan's international position, concluded that the Gulf War experience demonstrated that the Yoshida strategy no longer had credibility in the world and that it was necessary to reeducate the Japanese people to wean them from the politics of "prevarication" (*gomakashi*).[23]

Ozawa Ichirō, a blunt and forceful young LDP leader, convinced that continued adherence to a mercantilist foreign policy risked weakening the U.S. alliance and increasing Japan's international isolation, set forth a reform agenda reminiscent of Nakasone's plans. Although of a younger generation, he had risen to leadership in the LDP as a protégé of some of its most powerful and corrupt old-guard leaders. Nevertheless, possessed of the quintessential characteristics of the elite tradition—its realism, pragmatism, and sensitivity to changing trends—Ozawa recognized that the national interest made it imperative for Japan to change its policies and undertake fundamental reforms of its political system in order to adapt to a changing international order. He frequently expressed an admiration for the progenitors of Japan's conservative tradition—the Meiji leaders who, although privileged members of the old samurai elite, perceived the challenge of Western imperial power to the national interest and launched the pragmatic reforms that began Japan's modern history.

Ozawa was the most influential of the younger politicians who were dismayed by Japan's domestic disarray during the Gulf War. He was unhappy with the decision to simply provide financial support for the war, and he felt that to continue in such an irresponsible path was to risk isolation. Japan, he said, "must do things normally, in the same way as everyone else."[24] Japanese exceptionalism was no longer viable. Japan must become a "normal country" (*futsū no kuni*). Ozawa dismissed the government's long-standing constitutional interpretation prohibiting overseas deployment of troops as the characteristic "prevarication" of the Yoshida strategy, which he said had made Japan selfish and money grubbing. The nation, he said, had ignored the cost of maintaining the international peace and freedom on which the Japanese economy depended.[25]

Calculating that the Yoshida Doctrine was no longer viable, Ozawa tied his political fortunes to leading the movement for fundamental change of Japan's international role, with all the domestic political and economic changes that would entail. An LDP study group that he chaired concluded that "Japan is being asked to shift from a passive stance of mainly enjoying the benefits of a global system to an active stance of assisting in the building of a new order."[26]

Sensing that he was riding an emergent trend, Ozawa published a book in the spring of 1993 setting forth a plan for a sweeping institutional transformation to make Japan a "normal country." His book, *Nihon kaizō keikaku,* sold nearly a million copies and was published in translation a year later as *Blueprint for a New Japan.*[27] Ozawa argued that Yoshida's purpose had been misunderstood. Reluctance to remilitarize in the 1950s was intended to permit recovery from the wartime ravages, not to become a permanent mercantilist foreign policy. The end of the Cold War, he asserted, made it imperative to adopt an activist international role or risk weakening the U.S. alliance and international isolation. He advocated electoral reform to encourage the development of genuine two-party politics and debate over the nation's future course. Deference to the bureaucracy and the Cabinet Legislation Bureau to determine foreign policy was no longer acceptable.

In the wake of the debacle of the Gulf War, Ozawa was instrumental in engineering the first significant departure from the Yoshida Doctrine. Stung by the foreign criticism of its failure to aid the UN coalition, the Diet passed the United Nations Peacekeeping Operations Cooperation Bill on June 15, 1992. The legislation ended the ban on sending the Self-Defense Forces abroad. It limited troop deployment to logistical and humanitarian support for United Nations missions, monitoring elections, and providing aid in civil administration. Under a compromise required to gain the support of small opposition parties, a section of the law regarding SDF involvement in armed UN missions—such as monitoring cease-fires, disarming combatants, and patrolling buffer zones—was frozen for the time being.

Although the legislation came too late to permit participation in the Persian Gulf coalition, in September 1992 the government dispatched a contingent of 700 personnel to join the UN peacekeeping mission intended to end the long civil war in Cambodia. It was the first time since 1945 that Japanese troops had been deployed abroad. After the success of the Cambodian mission, Japan dispatched forces abroad in a noncombat capacity as part of several UN peacekeeping activities, sending them to Mozambique (1993), Zaire (1994), the Golan Heights (1996), and East Timor (2002).

The Gulf War awakened the Japanese to the realization that they were navigating in new and uncharted waters. Subsequent crises in Japan's immediate region provided more evidence to Japanese policymakers that its strategy had to change. Mounting tensions on the Korean Peninsula began to demand Japanese engagement and soon became the most immediate and compelling influence in undermining the Yoshida Doctrine.

During the Cold War, Japan had remained determinedly disengaged from many security issues, and among these was the struggle between the two Korean states. The Chōsen Sōren, the pro–North Korean organization in Japan, was given wide latitude to send large sums of financial support to Pyongyang. Japanese trade with the Democratic People's Republic of Korea (DPRK) was not carefully monitored, and manufactured parts essential for weapons, especially missiles, had found their way to North Korea without great difficulty. It was no secret that North Korean spies operated within Japan and spy ships worked the coastal waters. Suspicions that Japanese citizens had been abducted and taken back to North Korea were not vigorously pursued. Japan's left-wing parties were openly sympathetic to the DPRK, although well aware of the spiraling misery of its society. The Japan Socialist Party maintained ties to the North Korean Workers Party. The conservatives turned a blind eye to the Cold War division on the peninsula, often seeming to do little more to support the Republic of Korea (ROK) than was required to satisfy the United States.

Normalization of relations with the ROK in 1965 and the payment of reparations were largely in response to U.S. pressure. Likewise, it was only with strong encouragement from the United States that Japan would acknowledge that the security of the ROK was, as the Satō-Nixon communiqué stated in 1969, "essential to Japan's own security." On these grounds, President Chun Doo Hwan in 1982 requested a grant of $6 billion in credits from Japan in recognition of the contribution that the ROK's huge defense burden was making to Japanese security. Nakasone, determined to impress President Reagan and reverse the policies of the Yoshida Doctrine, made an unprecedented trip to Seoul in January 1983 to approve a long-term government loan of $4 billion, which he and the Koreans explicitly linked to the strategic defense of Japan. Nakasone's efforts to demonstrate support for the ROK during the Cold War was an exception to the rule; benign neglect of the struggle on the peninsula was the more common approach among the mainstream conservatives.

Mainstream LDP toleration of the DPRK foreign policy stance was most apparent in the last days of the Cold War. In 1990, Kanemaru Shin, the most powerful figure in the LDP, led a bizarre initiative to North Korea to try to normalize relations with Pyongyang without consulting Seoul or Washington. Kanemaru met alone with Kim Il Sung. The latter, furious with the Russians, who had just normalized ties with Seoul, allegedly told Kanemaru that the "yellow skins" must stick together against the "white skins."[28] Kanemaru reportedly emerged from the meeting with tears in his eyes, convinced of Kim's sincerity. In what turned out to be an astonishing aberration, Kanemaru proceeded to make the kind of profuse apology for past Japanese sins that South Koreans had long demanded but never heard. Further, he indicated readiness to provide reparations to the DPRK—not only for the colonial period, but also, inexplicably, for the abnormal relations in the postwar period. Seoul was at once in an uproar, Washington was stunned, and in Tokyo the Foreign Ministry was deeply embarrassed. One interpretation of Kanemaru's démarche suggests that he hoped to receive kickbacks for his faction from North Korea and from North Korean firms operating in Japan once the huge payments of compensation to the DPRK were under way. However that may be, the uproar provoked by the proposals led to their swift abandonment. Still, the incident fed South Korean suspicions of Japanese duplicity and was interpreted as evidence of a two-Koreas policy designed to perpetuate the division on the peninsula.

The end of superpower rivalry changed the context of the Korean problem. Issues dividing the peninsula were no longer tethered to the global conflict. Both states of the divided Korea, when they were fully integrated into the Cold War framework, lacked autonomy to pursue policies independent from their superpower patrons. Both states had enjoyed the protection and aid of their patrons. The end of great-power conflict, however, led directly to North Korea's political isolation and economic decline. Russia terminated its strategic ties with the DPRK, and China made clear its disapproval of the DPRK's autarkic path. Both Russia and China opened normal relations with the ROK and promoted a brisk trade with the South. To offset its growing vulnerabilities, North Korea increased its determination to develop nuclear weapons and missile technology as equalizers and bargaining chips.

In 1993, the DPRK provoked a crisis by its decision to withdraw from the Nuclear Nonproliferation Treaty. When a showdown between North Korea and the United States over its nuclear weapons program made war appear imminent, the U.S. command in Japan requested Japanese backup assistance in the event of conflict. Japanese officials were unable to respond to the request. Once again, Japan's inability to meet the expectations of the new era was evident. Citing the great Japanese stake in dealing with the proliferation issue in its immediate region, the United States asked the Japanese government to contribute fuel and material for U.S. forces, to provide ships and planes for sweeping mines and gathering intelligence, and to cut off financial flows to North Korea. Japanese officials equivocated. Jimmy Carter's trip to North Korea in the summer of 1994 led to an agreement that defused the crisis, but U.S. Secretary of Defense William Perry later said that if conflict had ensued and U.S. forces had not had access to Japanese bases and backup assistance, "It would have been the end of the alliance."[29]

Partly as a result of U.S. dissatisfaction with Japan's response to the Gulf War and to the confrontation with North Korea, and partly as a result of China's assertiveness in the Taiwan Strait crisis in March 1996—as well as Japan's increased appreciation of the value of the alliance—Tokyo agreed in 1997 to a revision of the Guidelines for U.S.-Japan Defense Cooperation. These revised guidelines provided for a modestly increased role for Japan in the event of a regional crisis and sought to draw Japan into a tighter, more integrated, and therefore more effective operational alliance. The guidelines provided for U.S.-Japan cooperation in support areas such as mine-sweeping, economic sanctions, and access to Japanese airfields and ports.

Further threats to Japan from the North Korean regime increased Japanese vulnerability and led Japan to approve new security measures that steadily eroded the Yoshida Doctrine. The most alarming event for the Japanese government was the launching of a North Korean three-stage ballistic missile over Japan on August 31, 1998. Although evidently not a military weapon but a failed effort to test a ballistic missile, it roused Japanese anger. Japanese leaders realized that DPRK missiles with the potential to be nuclear armed constituted the most significant threat to Japanese security since 1945. Japan responded by announcing its decision to develop its own surveillance satellite system.

Putting up its own spy satellites represented a departure from the policy framed decades earlier as part of the Yoshida Doctrine not to participate in activities that could be construed as the militarization of space. In addition, the North Korean missile prompted the Japanese government to cooperate with the United States on ballistic missile defense, which implied that it would dilute prohibitions on the export of military technology and even participate in collective defense—reversing policies that had been sacrosanct during the Cold War. Instead of shunning interference with North Korean activities, Japan showed greater willingness to consider modest measures of defense cooperation between Japan and South Korea. The government adopted a plan to stem the financial support received from North Koreans and to exercise tighter surveillance over the sale of products that could contribute to DPRK weaponry. In 2001, the Japanese Maritime Self-Defense Force sank a North Korean spy ship in the first use of military force by Japan since the end of the Pacific War. Policymakers rethought Japan's self-binding rules of engagement and openly discussed the development of its military capabilities, including power projection. The North Korean admission in 2002 that it had abducted Japanese citizens in the past became a deeply emotional public issue in Japan. In sum, DPRK brinkmanship and belligerence stirred a new and potent security consciousness in and out of government.

Even more significant, North Korean actions confirmed Japanese dependence on the U.S. alliance. The terrorist attacks on the United States on September 11, 2001, led to an assertive use of U.S. power in a war on terrorism that put new expectations on Japan for alliance support even outside of the region. The administration of Prime Minister Koizumi Junichirō reluctantly realized that it could only expect to rely on U.S. support in dealing with the North Korean threat if Japan responded satisfactorily to U.S. requests for assistance in the U.S. war on terrorism. Memories of the Gulf War experience, together with the realization that Japan needed to bolster the alliance, led Japan into further expansion of its SDF activities.

In response, the Japanese provided offshore, rear-area, noncombat logistical support for the UN-sanctioned coalition action against the Taliban regime in Afghanistan, deploying Aegis-equipped destroyers and tankers to shuttle fuel to coalition navies in the Indian Ocean. Following the U.S. attack on Iraq in 2003, the Japanese government approved deployment of a small contingent of ground troops to Iraq to provide humanitarian assistance, giving symbolic support to the U.S.-led attack. Though still limited and circumscribed, these were the first military deployments Japan had ever made in support of the United States. Cautiously, incrementally, at times almost imperceptibly, Japan began to respond to the new strategic conditions of the post–Cold War era. The parameters of debate about security expanded. Issues of collective security, constitutional revision, rules of engagement for military units, power-projection capabilities, and even the nuclear option, which had long been taboo in the public arena, were now raised for debate. Although Japan was moving slowly away from the Yoshida Doctrine, however, it still had no new strategy to replace it.

In short, the grand strategy of Japanese foreign policy that had held sway for the second half of the twentieth century began to unravel. But in addition, the end of the Cold War also radically transformed the context of Japanese domestic politics. A political system established in 1955 and organically tied to the international order was bound to be undermined by a fundamental change in that order. The principles that defined the two major parties founded in 1955, the LDP and the JSP, were largely shaped by the bipolar standoff in international politics. Japan was entering a new era that sooner or later would render the old political alignments outmoded.

In the summer of 1993, the Japanese political world experienced a stunning upheaval. Ozawa played a critical role in bringing down the 1955 system. Forming his own faction of dissidents (and later organizing his own party), he joined forces with opposition groups to end the LDP's thirty-eight-year one-party rule. For the first time since 1955, the LDP lacked a majority necessary to form a government. The proximate causes of this debacle were a series of scandals involving LDP leaders and their failure to deliver on promises of political reform legislation. But more fundamentally, the primary motivating force was change in the international system. Fallout from the Persian Gulf War gave impetus to the events leading to domestic political turmoil. Subsequently, the LDP was able to return to power, but only by joining with other parties whose own agendas differed. This development precluded the possibility of a strong, clear policy direction for the nation.

With the collapse of international communism, the left-right axis in Japan's domestic politics weakened. In a cynical maneuver, the LDP even joined with its longtime nemesis, the Japan Socialist Party, in 1994 in order to form a coalition and return to power. The Socialists, for their part, in exchange for making their leader the new prime minister, disowned their entire Cold War foreign policy agenda. They joined the LDP in a coalition government led by the longtime left-wing Socialist Murayama Tomiichi. Nothing revealed so dramatically the disintegrating Cold War paradigm in Japanese politics as Murayama's abandonment of all his ideological principles at his initial press conference as prime minister. For forty years, the Socialists had opposed the Self-Defense Forces as unconstitutional. They had supported unarmed neutrality, and they had opposed U.S. bases in Japan, the U.S.-Japan alliance, recognition of South Korea, civilian nuclear power, defense of the sea lanes, cabinet ministers' visits to the Yasukuni Shrine, flying of the Rising Sun Flag, singing of the national anthem in schools, and more. Murayama abruptly reversed the party's entire foreign policy agenda.

After Murayama's volte-face, the Socialist Party lost its raison d'être, and in the following years its support dwindled. Defense of the "peace constitution" weakened, and support of the U.S. alliance increased. The influence of unions and sectors of the media that had supported the left-wing progressive position during the Cold War diminished. The 1955 political system was gone. Despite the disappearance of the Cold War paradigm in domestic politics, and despite electoral reforms designed to promote a political system more representative of the conflict of ideals, no new paradigm to organize domestic politics emerged. Shifting coalitions and party realignments left Japanese politics rudderless and adrift. In this confused state, a reactive pattern to new foreign policy challenges emerged: A crisis would beget U.S. expectation of Japanese response, which, following domestic political turmoil, would result in a small step away from the Yoshida Doctrine. Without any internally generated new policy stance, and in response to outside pressures, the Yoshida strategy, by almost imperceptible degrees, began to drift from its old moorings.

A New and Uncertain Environment in Asia

With the end of the Cold War, Japan had experienced a crisis of its capitalist system. Its political system was in disarray, both internally and in its external relations. But in addition, Japan confronted a radically transformed regional environment in an area that as yet offered no clear sense of what its future structure would be. Across the region, an unprecedented economic strength and nationalist vitality was emerging. This new Asia required Japan to accommodate to forces of historical change wholly at odds with the ways that it had related to its neighbors in the past. Engaging this radically changed environment was profoundly disorienting to a Japan accustomed to a weak and backward Asia. In every way, Japan was ill-prepared for these new conditions.

The end of the Cold War revealed a new economic strength in Asia that was bringing about a deep, long-term shift in the global distribution of power.[30] Asian countries were acquiring the wealth and power to shape their regional system and even to influence the character of the world system. In a movement largely masked by the Cold War, the center of gravity of the global economy had begun to shift from the North Atlantic to the Asia Pacific region. The newly prosperous Asian nations, most of which had only recently gained their independence, entered into a phase of rapid economic growth. This quiet transformation was attended by dramatic improvements in living standards, health, and literacy. Asia was beginning to recover the position it had held prior to the Industrial Revolution, when the per capita incomes of many Asian countries had been at or above the world average. With the dissolution of the Soviet empire and the earlier

Chinese abandonment of Maoist Communist ideology in favor of a pragmatic pursuit of economic development, a new dynamic governed the region. These startling changes became apparent in the 1990s as first South Korea, Taiwan, Hong Kong, Singapore, and Thailand began to experience rapid economic development and then as others, most notably China and India, entered a period of high economic growth. These Asian nations became a multipolar group of increasingly strong, prosperous, independent states interacting with one another in diplomatic, strategic, and economic affairs.

After being dominated by the Eurocentric world throughout the modern era, Asia began to come into its own as a distinct and coherent regional state system, increasingly subject to its own internally generated dynamics. Asian states that had only recently been part of a colonial backwater, for two centuries the objects and victims of history's major forces, began to emerge as dynamic and competitive actors. The titanic struggle between the Western and the Communist worlds that had divided the region for four decades overshadowed changes that were taking place in Asia.

Ever since the Industrial Revolution, the Western powers had determined the nature of the norms, rules, and institutions that governed the international order. In many respects, Asia was a subsystem of the Western international system. Throughout the modern history of Asia, the world system had shaped the regional order. Asia was acted upon and simply responded. Now, it was becoming an actor.

With the end of the bipolar world system in 1989, there were new forces at work in Asia. Although remnants of the Cold War system remained, it was a vastly different region than it had been under the Cold War order. The Western age in Asia was at an end. Just as the Treaty of Nanjing in 1842 had marked the beginning of the imperialist order in East Asia, so the reversion of Hong Kong to China in June 1997 symbolized for many the beginning of an era when Asian nations acquired the power to take active roles in the international system and to shape their regional order.

Psychologically Japan was wholly unprepared to deal with the dynamic, new, competitive Asia. Since entering the modern international system a century and a half earlier, it had been accustomed to dealing with a backward and colonized region. As the educator Fukuzawa Yukichi famously wrote in 1885, Japan felt it needed to "escape from the bad company of Asia." There was no time to revive Asia and form a united front against Western imperialism. Instead, Japan had aimed to join the West and treat

Asians as the West treated them. Asia was the arena for Japan to contest Western imperialism and displace it with its own leadership. Japan had its advocates for an Asian cultural identity, but an identification with Asian cultural traditions was always circumscribed by Japan's persistent sense of its own unique political mission. Japan's highest values had been fixed on the achievement of national power.

Even after World War II, when its dreams of an Asian empire were shattered, Japan had failed to develop a new relationship with its own region. Partly this was a result of the immense task of rebuilding the nation's livelihood at home. Partly it was the result of the Cold War, which divided Asian countries and prevented development of new relations. More fundamentally it was the result of the fact that the postwar conservative leadership had no disposition to construct a new relationship with Asia. Yoshida was largely uninterested in such a relationship because it would have required Japan to disown its imperial past and actively reach out to Asia's new leaders through reparations and genuine remorse for the destruction and suffering caused by imperialist rampage.

Such repentance was inconceivable to Yoshida and his protégés. To Yoshida, integration with Asia would be useful if it carried economic benefits, but not if it required disowning the past. Japan's conservative leadership resisted the efforts of John Foster Dulles to engage Japan in collective security agreements with other Asian nations. Professor Ōtake Hideo observed that it was Yoshida's nationalism that led him to reject integration: "Unlike [German Chancellor] Adenauer and Japanese leftist intellectuals, Yoshida never desired cultural or political integration with the West or with neighboring Asian nations. Although he was eager for international economic integration, he wished to maintain a distinctive cultural identity for the Japanese people."[31]

With such attitudes deeply held among the postwar ruling elite, the task of settling accounts for the past was put off for another day. Although many Japanese were extremely self-critical in assessing Japan's wartime role, mainstream conservative leaders failed to deal forthrightly with the issue of Japanese wartime activities in Asia. Only grudgingly and after international outcry did education bureaucrats permit high-school social studies texts to mention the Japanese invasion of China. Repeated international protests forced the dismissal of cabinet ministers who had argued that the colonization of Korea had been legitimate or that the rape of Nanjing was a fabrication. Only reluctantly, when confronted with undeniable evidence, did the government admit that tens of thousands of Asian women had been compelled to serve as "comfort women" to provide sexual services to the Japanese military, or that germ warfare experiments had been conducted extensively in China.

Such continuing resistance to owning up to Japan's past actions made the formal, carefully scripted apologies that Japanese leaders did offer seem insincere and incomplete. Japan's conservative leadership felt little sense of identification with other Asians. Moreover, Tokyo avoided accepting refugees from Southeast Asia. Two decades after the Vietnam conflict was over, as of the end of 1994, Japan had permanently settled fewer than 10,000 of the nearly 1.3 million refugees. Even distant Germany, a slightly smaller country, had accepted more than twice the number of refugees from Indochina as Japan.

Japan remained aloof from Asia and concentrated on investment and production at home and trade with the West. When a remarkable confluence of economic forces in the mid-1980s made it profitable to transfer many Japanese manufactures offshore to other Asian countries, propelling Japan into an unanticipated, deep involvement in Asia, Japan approached Asia with characteristic paternalism. Moving swiftly to seize leadership of the region's economy, Japanese bureaucrats formulated a regional industrial policy quite similar to the one used at home. It involved close business-government cooperation and the coordinated use of private investment, official aid, and trade to help Japanese multinationals build vertically integrated production networks throughout Asia. A 1988 study by the Economic Planning Agency recommended a comprehensive integration of the economies of Asia, with the Japanese bureaucracy serving as the "Asian brain" that would mastermind the development of the region's economy.[32]

Bureaucrats envisioned a kind of benign division of labor that prescribed a lead economy with others ranked hierarchically behind in the order of their economic strength and technical sophistication. The favorite metaphor for this structure was the "flying geese formation." The three-tier division would place Japan at the front, then the newly industrializing economies of South Korea, Hong Kong, Taiwan, and Singapore, and finally the Southeast Asian countries and China.[33] This approach bore a marked resemblance to the regional hierarchy proposed by Japanese imperial planners in the 1930s.

As Japan's economy drew the admiration of the world, the Japanese self-image as the inevitable leader of Asia was bolstered. It confidently projected developmentalist capitalism as a model for the developing states of Asia. But the expectation that Japan could resume the paternalistic role of the mid-nineteenth century was soon confounded. The region proved too dynamic and proactive, the pace of growth too rapid and uneven. Japan's own economic dynamism stalled. It was less able to provide generous amounts of foreign aid and investment, and the model of development that it had promoted was tarnished. The Japanese economy remained the least open of all Asian countries, when "openness" is defined as the ratio of exports or imports to GDP.[34] Other residual features of Japan's illiberal economic regime, including nontariff barriers and resistance to foreign investment, handicapped both Japan's appeal and its aspirations to lead Asian regionalism.

Moreover, Japan lacked legitimacy to become the region's leader. Countries of the region still had memories of Japan's role in World War II. Its subsequent aloofness from the region, and its narrow pursuit of economic self-interest during the Cold War, complicated the task of restoring trust. Owing to the pursuit of the Yoshida strategy, former Ambassador to Thailand Okazaki Hisahiko mused, "Japan forfeited its chance to build up a record as a country deserving of international trust." Even providing economic aid in the region did not help Japan win the confidence of its neighbors. As Okazaki said, "The widespread perception of Japan as a country driven purely by economic motives makes this difficult."[35]

There are complex and contradictory new forces in the region that make for uncertainty about the nature of the future order in Asia. There are both integrative and divisive forces at work. Regional identity and common aspiration struggle against rising nationalism and strategic rivalries. Broadly speaking, there are two possible scenarios of Asia's future over the coming ten to twenty years. One is hopeful, the other disturbing. The first scenario foresees the steady liberalization of Asia resulting in the progressive development of free-market forces, trade, and investment. These developments would knit the countries of the thriving and prosperous region together, bring about the steady development of democratic governments, and encourage multilateral institutions to manage economic issues and resolve political and security issues.

There is evidence that this optimistic scenario could prevail. The collapse of the empires controlled from Europe and the end of Cold War divisions meant that Asia was no longer divided by externally imposed political barriers. Technological progress and improved communications are breaking down the geographical barriers that historically separated one part of Asia from another. Interactions among states in the region—hitherto largely sporadic—are becoming more frequent and intense. Diplomatic, economic, political, and cultural interaction, once constrained by geopolitical forces, are now facilitated by improved transport and communications. Above all, the increasing integration and dynamism of the region is impelled by economic growth, which is contributing to the expansion of interdependence and intraregional flows of trade and investment.

There are also the beginnings of new multilateral institutions that are attempting to bring Asian nations together to deal with common problems. Among these new institutions are the Asia-Pacific Economic Cooperation (APEC) and the offshoots of the Association of Southeast Asian Nations (ASEAN): ASEAN Plus Three, which brings together the Southeast Asian nations with the three Northeast Asian nations of Japan, China, and South Korea, principally to deal with economic issues; and the ASEAN Regional Forum (ARF), a periodic meeting of foreign ministers to discuss security issues.

Despite these hopeful signs, there is another possible scenario for Asia's future. This one projects a turbulent Asia in which power politics overwhelms the forces of liberalization. Alongside the integrative trends lie divisive forces. At the same time that the region is being knit together by trade and improved communications, there are other forces that suggest the possibility of a dangerous and unstable future. Asia lacks a fixed regional structure, a recognized legitimate order, to cope readily with the turbulence of its new dynamism. In this alternative future, strategic rivalries and alliances would be forged to attain strategic objectives. Arms races, border disputes, and nationalism would emerge. It is true that with the states of the region pursuing rapid industrialization, competition for resources—especially new sources of energy—could lead to rivalries and dispute. One is struck by the sheer number of states in Asia, by their cultural, religious, and ethnic antagonisms, and by the ways in which many of them regard others as strategic competitors instead of partners.

It is likely that Asia will eventually acquire a complex multipolar structure. This structure would involve a group of major powers, including China, Japan, Russia, India, and the United States (assuming it remains engaged in Asia), as well as a number of middle-ranking powers. As this structure evolved, Asia could experience the kind of competitive struggles and rivalries that Europe underwent. Compared to the bipolar structure of the Cold War, multipolarity offers more opportunity for instability and is often more prone to conflict. Asia will likely be characterized by sizable power asymmetries. Resources, military power, and productive efficiency will be distributed unevenly. The power structure within the region will change as states grow at different rates because of political, economic, and technological developments. Balances of power may emerge, but maintaining them is an uncertain process. Coalitions can shift, and occasions for miscalculation can increase. In light of the wars and instability that marked the multipolar European state system for centuries, it is reasonable to wonder whether "Europe's past might be Asia's future."[36]

In fact, post–Cold War Asia exhibits much greater complexity than the European state system did throughout its centuries-long history. The diversity of the cultural, religious, and ethnic traditions within Asia is universally recognized as a source of disunity. The wide range in territorial size, population, and stage of economic development adds to the immense complexity of the region. But although cultural differences could give rise to disagreements, they in and of themselves will not likely be the cause of conflict. Rather, it is the collision of national interests that will likely be the source of regional instability.

The outcome of this period of explosive economic growth in the region is uncertain, however, and no one can say which scenario will become reality. What is clear is that the emergent system of increasingly prosperous and ambitious states lacks a settled equilibrium. The region lacks a consensus on the rules and norms that should prevail among them. Moreover, such issues will have to be worked out within the region, as it is unlikely that Asian countries will ever again be satisfied to have them imposed from outside. The Asian states have already reacted against ready acceptance of Western norms.

Asian leaders since 1989 have with increasing frequency asserted alternative values, institutions, and rules of order. These assertions reject Western claims of universalism as dogmatic and legalistic and oppose the "Washington consensus," instead advocating an Asian form of capitalism with a legitimate role for state-led economic growth and, in the cultural sphere, social goals beyond individualism. What this means, of course, is that Asian countries are seeking a greater say in determining the rules and institutions that govern international economic and political affairs. Thus, to be viable, any new international order must take into account the values and interests of these rising states.

The age of full-blown nationalism has arrived in Asia. The sheer number of Asian actors has grown, and this fact alone is likely to make it difficult for them to agree on regional rules and institutions. The rise of mass nationalism will further complicate matters. When the Cold War began, most of these countries were newly liberated colonies. Japan was the only industrial nation in the region, and it was the only one that had experienced a nationalist mobilization of its people. Decolonization, however, completed the modern state system in Asia. During the Cold War, the process of state building—which includes forming a central state structure, extracting resources, organizing a military, establishing mass education, and the like—inevitably promoted nationalism in Asian countries, but it was restrained and muted by the overlay of the ideological conflicts between the superpowers. The end of the Cold War cleared the field for nationalism.

Historically among nation-states, the pursuit of rapid industrialization inevitably leads to the emergence of mass nationalism. Growing literacy and improved communications awaken the masses to national political issues and create pressures for political participation. Leadership is challenged to find ways to incorporate the masses into national political life and to accommodate the tensions and antagonisms of a burgeoning industrial society. Industrialization—especially rapid catch-up industrialization—brings with it social dislocations caused by the movement of people from the country to the city, by the shifts in values and the disturbance of vested interests, by the rise of new and harsher class antagonisms, and by the widening differences between the generations.

Industrialization undermines domestic political equilibrium, yet it is this very stability that successful industrialization requires. Thus, the leaders begin to use nationalism as a tool to maintain social cohesion. A nationalist ideology can legitimate and even exalt the hardships that industrialization inevitably entails. It can justify the effort and self-sacrifice, the high savings rates, and the deferral of consumption that are required. Despite repeated predictions of its demise, nationalism remains the most powerful political emotion in the modern world. Nowhere will it be stronger or more widespread than in Asia, because nowhere else is industrialization proceeding so rapidly.

Moreover, nationalism inevitably spills over into foreign relations. It can be argued that every case of industrialization has led to expansionism. The political scientist Samuel Huntington wrote that in the past, "the external expansion of the U.K. and France, Germany and Japan, the Soviet Union and the United States coincided with phases of intense industrialization and economic development."[37] The number of unresolved border disputes between states in the region at the end of the Cold War was sobering: Besides those that remained between Japan and Russia, Japan and

China, and Japan and South Korea, there were unresolved disputes between Russia and China, China and India, Laos and China, China and Burma, India and Pakistan, Cambodia and Vietnam, China and Vietnam, China and Taiwan, Indonesia and Timor (apparently resolved), Malaysia and the Philippines, and—in the case of the Spratly Islands—among China, Vietnam, the Philippines, Malaysia, and Taiwan together.

Nationalism thrives on different views of the past. For Japan, the arrival of the age of nationalism among its neighbors will be particularly challenging. Especially in China and Korea, nationalism has its roots in the struggle against Japanese imperialism. Koreans recall Japan's "cultural aggression," which required them to take Japanese names, speak Japanese, and worship the emperor. Antipathy for the Japanese became the bedrock of Korean nationalism; celebration of liberation from Japanese rule, on August 15, 1945, is a great patriotic holiday. During the Cold War, aside from trade contacts, Japan and the divided Koreas maintained distant and correct relationships rather than cordial ones. A half-century passed with only limited progress in dealing with the historical legacy of bitterness.

Japan's carefully scripted apologies to Korea for the colonial period were not accepted as sufficient or sincere. The emperor's vague words in 1984 on welcoming the South Korean president suggest why: "It is indeed regrettable," Hirohito said, "that there was an unfortunate past between us for a period of this century, and I believe that it should not be repeated." More forthcoming apologies were offered later, but they were frequently undermined by utterances of Japanese cabinet members insisting that annexation had been "legal" or "beneficial." Japanese textbook accounts of relations between the two countries failed to own up to Japan's colonialism, and the visits of conservative politicians to the Yasukuni Shrine in Tokyo, which memorializes Japan's foreign wars and their heroes, offended Koreans.

A particularly emotional issue arose in the 1990s with revelations of the experiences of "comfort women," tens of thousands of Koreans and others who had been compelled to serve in military brothels for the imperial army. The Japanese government, after initially refusing to acknowledge the revelations, later established a private fund to compensate survivors, but it resisted a United Nations Human Rights Committee's recommendation that it make an official apology and compensation. In addition, the plight of 700,000 Korean residents in Japan, many of whom were brought to Japan during the colonial period to do hard labor, aggravated the relationship. Although some of the more demeaning aspects of their treatment, such as the requirement of periodic fingerprinting, were eased in the 1990s, Korean residents are often excluded from job opportunities in the public sector and are not extended voting rights.[38]

The election of Kim Dae Jung as ROK president in 1998 brought an interlude of courageous leadership that sought to tame the nationalist impulses. Kim set out to repair the breach between South Korea and its closest neighbors. In his inaugural address, he declared his intention to improve relations not only with North Korea, through his so-called sunshine policy, but also with Japan. The Japanese were delighted by his willingness to resist nationalist demagoguery, in contrast to his predecessor, and to seek a new relationship. He at once made good on his intentions by taking conciliatory moves on a range of issues, from the comfort women to the fisheries dispute. Koreans, in turn, were pleased with Japan's decision to send economic aid at a time of critical financial need. Recognizing the importance of economic cooperation, South Korea took steps to encourage greater Japanese investment and loans, particularly for small and medium-sized firms.

Kim's visit to Tokyo in October 1998 stands out as a major event in Japanese-Korean relations. His willingness to address the Japanese in their own tongue delighted them. He met with Akihito, calling him "emperor" rather than *nikkō*, or "Japanese king," a term of little respect that Koreans had used since 1945. Moreover, Kim eased the bans imposed a half-century earlier on Japanese investment and on the importation of Japanese movies, music, magazines, and other popular culture. Addressing the Diet, he accepted a comparatively forthright apology for Japanese colonial rule from Prime Minister Obuchi Keizō and added that "South Korea should also rightly evaluate Japan, in all its changed aspects. And search with hope for future possibilities."[39]

The nationalism of young Koreans and Chinese, however, remains deeply rooted in distrust of Japan. There are also strong anti-Western currents in nationalist ideologies throughout Asia. These ideologies assert the cultural values of these new states over and against Western claims of universalism. Nationalism may or may not lead to territorial expansionism in the new era in Asia, but it is certain to be a powerful force that any stable system must somehow accommodate.

Although there is incipient cooperation among them on economic matters, Asia's new multilateral institutions are weak and indecisive. Asian states have had little experience in the modern international system—other than as its victims—and little experience in leading multilateral international institutions. Asia has had no regional security organization comparable to NATO. As Asia has become more integrated through improved communications and increased intraregional trade and investment, a variety of new multilateral experiments have sprung up to try to fill the vacuum. The rising competitive rivalries and appearance of nationalism could be mitigated by the development of multilateral institutions, but thus far they lack substantial infrastructure and, more significantly, a strong sustaining motivation.

Driven by its economic interests but handicapped by its historic constraints, Japan pursued a cautious, low-key strategy in post–Cold War Asia. As it slowly moved away from the Yoshida strategy under the impetus of economic interests and the new international environment, Japan explored multilateralism in both the economic and security arenas. Multilateralism had many advantages for Japan. Although bilateral relations with the United States remained critical to both Japan's foreign policy position and its domestic political structure, Japanese trade with Asia now exceeded trade with the United States. Japanese foreign direct investment (FDI) in Asia grew much more rapidly than Japanese FDI in North America. Japan's economic surge into Asia after 1985 required more involvement in the region to protect its increased interests. As multilateralism emerged, the U.S.-Japan alliance no longer dominated Japan's foreign relations as thoroughly as it once had. The historical legacy of the Pacific War was still not overcome within the region, but multilateralism provided a cover, a quiet approach to regional relationships that could help to restore Japan's legitimacy and claim to leadership. Engagement in multilateral organizations not only offered a way to respond to foreign suspicions and criticism of its self-absorption, but also a way of overcoming domestic resistance to a more active international role.

Japan approached the new conditions in Asia with caution and circumspection. It was clear that these new conditions would require momentous changes in Japanese strategy. But until the structure of the new order in Asia was clear, Japan would move incrementally. It had to determine how to adjust its distinctive economic institutions to the new Asia. It had to see whether its ally, the United States, would develop a new strategic vision for the region. It had to await the resolution of the divided Korea. And it had to await clearer signals regarding the kind of great power that its neighboring colossus, China, would become.

CHAPTER TEN

JAPAN AND THE RISE OF CHINA

China poses most forcefully the contending visions of the future of Asia: the optimistic view of a prosperous, liberalizing, and peaceful region as opposed to the pessimistic view of a turbulent Asia in which power politics and conflict prevail. On the one hand, the long-anticipated awakening of China from economic backwardness has already convinced many observers that the economic integration and prosperity of East Asia is at hand.[1] On the other hand, history teaches us to regard skeptically the arrival of a new great power on the world scene. It has often disrupted international tranquillity, provoked bitter conflict, and proved the source of great human suffering and tragedy.

Historically, rising powers have challenged the status quo; often, they have eventually sought to revise the rules and institutions of the existing international order. By capturing a growing share of trade in a relatively short time, they tend to give rise to intense economic conflicts. The wars of the twentieth century make the case. The rise of Japan brought Asia the greatest conflict it had ever experienced—as did the rise of Germany in Europe. The potential size of the Chinese colossus, together with these still fresh memories of the destruction and carnage of the past century, have been more than enough to focus the world's attention on China's emergence in our time.

Great-power transitions have been fraught with danger. When mismanaged by the established powers, they can have cataclysmic consequences. The challenge for statesmanship is how to avoid war in the midst of such fundamental shifts in relative power among nations. Often the key issue is whether the status-quo powers make concessions generous enough to satisfy the revisionist power without seeming to appease it or confess weakness.

The interests of Japan and the United States, the two great status-quo powers of the region, will be the ones most challenged by this emergent new power. How they manage this imminent great power transition—singly or together—will tell much of the story of the international relations of the coming decades. Coping with China's emergence will be a great test of the effectiveness and worth of the U.S.-Japan alliance. Although allies, their interests and approaches to this era of uncertainty in the regional system are by no means wholly congruent. They will be challenged to find common policies toward China's ascent.

Triangular relations among China, Japan, and the United States will largely determine the new order in East Asia. Relations among the three nations are of key strategic importance because they are at the heart of the balance of power in Asia. The political scientist Samuel Huntington, when interviewed by a Japanese journalist in Tokyo in 1999, was asked how Japan should pursue its interests in relation to an ascendant China. He responded, "It is in Japan's interest to stay with the U.S. as long as Washington makes clear that it will continue to be a major force and presence in East Asia. When that is over, I would advise the Japanese government to cut a deal with China."[2] If its alliance with the United States faltered, Japan would have to find a way to accommodate Chinese power and still preserve Japan's autonomy.

The importance of these triangular relations is not new. They were at the heart of regional order (and disorder) throughout the twentieth century. When Japan became a continental power early in the century and began its encroachment on a weak and divided China, its relations with the United States were strained. By the time of World War I, the three fundamental principles that would guide U.S. policy in the region throughout the century had already taken shape. The United States was determined to prevent the domination of the region by any one power, to keep the region open to U.S. trade and investment, and to seek the spread of democratic government as the surest way to preserve peace and stability in the region.

Pursuing these principles entailed shifting relations with China and Japan for the remainder of the century. Following the U.S.-led defeat of Japanese imperial power in 1945 and the Communist revolution in China in 1949, the triangular relationship in the second half of the century took on a different dynamic, although the fundamental goals of U.S. policy remained intact. The Americans abandoned their sympathy and support of Chinese nation-building and constructed an alliance with Japan to contain Communist power, compelling a weak and dependent Japan to abjure political relations with the People's Republic. The Nixon opening to China in 1971, however, resulted in two decades of more balanced and amicable relations among the three nations. Joining in a virtual alliance to contain Soviet power in the region, they shared a common purpose. The triangle was equilateral. It was in some respects the best of times.

The post–Cold War environment introduced a new set of dynamics. Disintegration of the Soviet Union undermined the previous sense of common purpose, and despite an increasing economic interdependence, no substitute has been found to provide a stable basis for the triangular relationship. During this interregnum, the order of the region was unstable, and its future unknown. None of the three governments was very steady and purposeful in its policies toward the other two. All were ambivalent and uncertain about the best course to pursue. Relations among the three became complex, intertwined, and interdependent. If Washington made any attempt to engage either Beijing or Tokyo in bilateral discussions, the effort was closely assessed and analyzed by the other. At the same time, Japan and the PRC had their own relations, which Washington had to monitor closely.

Relative power in the 1990s was shifting. The positions of the United States and China improved, whereas Japan's deteriorated. Japan experienced economic stagnation and political gridlock, which diminished its clout and prestige. Modern Japan had never had to deal with a strong China. World attention turned from the Japanese miracle to fascination with China in a way that was psychologically jarring for Japan. For those Japanese who thought about their future strategic role and their aspirations for leadership in Asia, nothing was so disturbing as the rise of China in the 1990s. The potential size of China's economy, the uncertainty about its future power and purpose as a nation, the anti-Japanese nationalism of young Chinese, the potential magnitude of environmental degradation in China, the rising competition between the two countries for resources, and the potential political and social turmoil in China all alarmed the Japanese.

In some ways, the renaissance of U.S. power during the 1990s was as important as China's rise in changing the security environment in the region. The end of the Cold War created the conditions for an emergent strategic competition between the United States and China. China became increasingly critical of the U.S. position in Asia, including its forward presence and bilateral ties. The militaries of both countries looked on the other as a hypothetical enemy. Japanese attitudes about U.S. power in the region were contradictory. At the end of the Cold War, the Japanese wanted the reassurance that the United States would continue to be involved in the region. But once that continued involvement was evident, they were ambivalent. They wanted the United States to be engaged, but they were wary of Washington unilateralism. They wanted consultation, but they were not ready for a dialogue. They wanted China balanced, but they did not want a confrontation. Even so, it was clear that the post–Cold War era contained the seeds of a Sino-Japanese strategic competition for regional leadership.

ENGAGEMENT OF CHINA

Both the United States and its Japanese ally are seeking to engage China in a broad, long-range policy framework that will draw emergent Chinese power into a stable regional order. The policy of "engagement" of the rising power relies on the hope that conflict with the rapidly ascendant power can be avoided and that great-power transitions can be accomplished peacefully. According to this view, China can be drawn into accepting the norms of the global capitalist system as its trade increases, as its interdependence with other states in the system grows, and as its wealth and prosperity grow. A prosperous China will give rise to a strong middle class, which as it seeks power will be a force for democratization. Democracies, in this view, are not inclined to warfare—at least with each other. People free to pursue their own well-being are reluctant to support aggressive behavior. By engaging China and encouraging its economic development, the United States and Japan seek to make it a stakeholder in the status quo.

Engagement will be difficult for Japan and the United States to pursue jointly, however, because their goals, while overlapping, are not wholly consonant. Tokyo and Washington have often been at odds with respect to China, but aligning their policies offers substantial rewards. Japanese and American business interests, with government support, are competing for influence and advantage in the China market, and this competition may dampen the enthusiasm for a cooperative approach on economic issues, but in the long run the interests of both are often best served through cooperative policy initiatives. Parallel approaches also increase the possibility of working together in other areas, such as helping to shape the future of Korea and Taiwan. However, Japan and the United States have different historical memories as well as different perspectives, policy instruments, and strategic stakes, and all of these variables make it unlikely that they will wind up with mutually compatible approaches unless they work at it consciously and steadily.

Broadly speaking, U.S. and Japanese interests regarding China are similar. Both seek a peacefully inclined China as it undergoes the wrenching social and economic changes that industrialization inevitably entails. Both want to encourage a smooth integration of China into the international political and economic systems, even as it builds its national power and becomes more assertive of its interests. Moreover, they seek the establishment of the rule of law in China to facilitate trade and investment. Each country desires to forge a broader relationship with the PRC without abandoning its ties to Taiwan. Japan and the United States agree on the desirability of patience, flexibility, and restraint in the solution of the Taiwan issue. They also seek China's assistance in achieving the peaceful coexistence and eventual unification of the two Koreas. Finally, both would like to have China's cooperation in maintaining peaceful maritime transit in the western Pacific. For both countries, engagement is conditional on the responsiveness of China to these policies.

Although the United States and Japan are both pursuing policies of conditional engagement, they bring different perceptions, approaches, and policy tools to the implementation of engagement. Japan's engagement policy has a number of characteristics that distinguish it from U.S. policy. First, geographical propinquity makes China more immediately dominant in Japan's strategic calculus on a range of issues, including environmental degradation, energy competition, territorial disputes, and potential fallout from political turmoil. Second, the burden of twentieth-century history weighs heavily on Sino-Japanese relations, leaving among older Japanese a legacy of guilt and remorse for the suffering inflicted during their fifteen years of occupation. Japan has often conceded the moral high ground to China in a way that inhibits a self-confident and assertive Japanese policy stand. Third, the unique aspects of the postwar system in Japan, which give its foreign policy a strong economic orientation and weak political leverage, have led Japan to shape its engagement policy largely through the use of development aid. Fourth, Japan's position in the international system as a middle-ranking power allied with the United States inevitably influences the way in which it engages China. Japan does not wish to be held hostage to the alliance in its China policy, and it seeks as much autonomy in this area as is consistent with the maintenance of strong alliance relations. Finally, Japan's strategic culture reinforces the cautious nature of Japanese engagement policy. Japan has a strong tendency to avoid confrontation and to adopt a wait-and-see pragmatism.

As a consequence of recent developments, including a more confrontational Chinese approach to the Taiwan issue and generational change in Japanese domestic politics, Japan's China policy is evolving toward a more political approach. Prior to the end of the Cold War, Japan pursued a China policy that separated economics from politics. Although economic engagement remains the dominant Japanese approach, a recent series of events has contributed to the increasing politicization of the relationship.

In contrast to the cautious pragmatism of the Japanese engagement policy, U.S. policy asserts traditional U.S. goals in East Asia. It opposes the emergence of a dominant regional power, favors free and open trade, and seeks to promote democracy. U.S. engagement policy stems from a global perspective and is exercised through political-military policies and influence in international organizations. The United States is constrained from the use of official aid to Communist countries, including China. (The Export-Import Bank does provide loans and guarantees for U.S. exports and investments in China, however.) Therefore, it depends heavily for its economic influence on the encouragement of private initiative and economic forces and its influence in international financial institutions. The forward deployment of U.S. troops in East Asia, the network of bases and alliances in the region, and the role of the Seventh Fleet in maintaining regional security all give U.S. engagement policy a forceful character, which is reinforced by the promotion of democratic values challenging the legitimacy of the Chinese political system. In effect, the United States is pursuing elements of a containment policy along with engagement. In this assertive stance, American sensitivity to the complex, multifaceted dynamics of the strategic triangle has sometimes been lacking. Successful coordination of engagement policies with Japan will require great sensitivity to the dynamics of Sino-Japanese relations.

Though it is sometimes compared to the relationship between Germany and France, the Sino-Japanese relationship is unique. The relations between China and Japan have long been complex and replete with nuances that U.S. policymakers must constantly have in mind. Historically, Japan sat on the outskirts of the Chinese cultural sphere, sufficiently remote to maintain its own strong sense of cultural identity. In premodern times, Japan, uniquely among East Asian nations, remained aloof from the Sinocentric world order. The Japanese regarded their emperor no less than the Chinese emperor as "the son of heaven." Cultural borrowing from China, once thought to have been stimulated by the irresistible radiance of Chinese culture, is now understood to have been motivated more by Japanese awareness of strategic danger from the continent than by cultural awe. While steadfastly resisting incorporation into the Sinocentric order, Japan also found ways to accommodate to that order and to maintain useful relations with it. In modern times, Japan's more rapid development, together with the institutional backwardness of China, created a scenario that almost inevitably invited Japan to dominate its neighbor, with results that we all know.

It is not easy for Americans to fully understand the geopolitical realities that dominate the Sino-Japanese relationship today. It is even more difficult for Americans to plumb the depths of historical emotions and the complex psychology of the relationship. The historian Akira Iriye neatly summed up the tangled background of feelings this way:

> The Chinese and Japanese have lived as Asian neighbors for nearly two thousand years. Being geographically so close and yet psychologically quite remote, despite their common cultural roots, the two peoples have developed a sense at once of commonality and disparity, interdependence and autonomy, mutual respect and suspicion, attraction and repulsion, and admiration and condescension toward one another. They have talked of their shared heritage and their identity as Asians, but they have not hesitated to seek outside assistance to fight against one another. They have contributed to each other's cultural and modern transformation, but their patterns of development have been vastly dissimilar. Throughout, the fact of their existence and the patterns of their association have been among the most enduring features of the history of East Asia.[3]

THE LEGACY OF JAPAN'S COLD WAR CHINA POLICY

Throughout the postwar period, Japanese political leaders hoped to pursue an independent China policy. They saw Japan's interests vis-à-vis China as distinct from U.S. interests, and they did not trust the instincts of Americans in making China policy. Japan therefore acquiesced to U.S. policy leadership only when it seemed essential to maintaining the fundamental cohesion of the U.S.-Japan alliance.

At the end of the Occupation, Japan's perspective on China was markedly different from that of America's postwar leadership. In desperate economic straits, politically crippled and strategically dependent, Japan hoped to build a new relationship with China on an almost exclusively economic foundation. Sino-Japanese trade was important to both countries. On the eve of the Pacific War, China accounted for 17 percent of Japan's imports and 27 percent of its exports.[4] Prime Minister Yoshida believed that a key element of Japan's recovery lay in restoring trade relations with China, and he pressed for as much leeway in Chinese policy as he could acquire. "I don't care whether China is red or green," he told an American correspondent in 1949, the year of the Chinese Revolution. "China is a natural market, and it has become necessary for Japan to think about markets."[5]

Moreover, Yoshida found U.S. policy toward the Chinese Revolution and the Sino-Soviet alliance misguided. He had spent many years of his early career in the foreign service in prewar China, and he was convinced that Chinese culture and national character would eventually break up the Beijing-Moscow alliance. Americans, he believed, had an imperfect understanding of Chinese society. In his memoirs, published in 1957, he wrote: "America has not reached the point of truly knowing China. It can be said that the policies which America has adopted toward China in the postwar period have been almost a total failure."[6] Similar doubts about Americans' capacity to understand China and about the effectiveness of America's China policies persist among Japanese leaders today.

The roots of postwar Japan's China policy lie in the negotiations that brought an end to the U.S. occupation of Japan in 1951. Shortly after the San Francisco Peace Treaty was signed, while the peace treaty and the mutual security pact were still before the U.S. Senate for approval, Yoshida was pressured to sign a letter that undermined Japan's own policy goals. This was in an atmosphere shaped by the Korean War and the McCarthy investigations. The letter, largely drafted by Secretary of State John Foster Dulles, acknowledged that Japan "desires ultimately to have a full measure of . . . commercial intercourse with China which is Japan's closest neighbor," but it clearly stated that "the Japanese Government has no intention to conclude a bilateral treaty with the Communist regime of China." The Yoshida government was then forced to sign a peace treaty with the Nationalist government on Taiwan, although Yoshida refused to acknowledge the Chiang Kai-shek government as the government of all China. In effect, he maintained a two-Chinas policy.

The Eisenhower administration was of two minds regarding Japan's trade relations with the mainland. Whereas Dulles wanted to isolate the PRC economically, in part as a means of forcing it to break with Moscow and turn to the West, President Eisenhower feared that cutting Japan off from trade with China might drive Japan into the arms of the Communist bloc. Taking advantage of this ambivalence, Japan developed a substantial trade with the PRC during the 1950s and 1960s in spite of its political nonrecognition. So long as Japan adhered to the political conditions imposed by the United States, recognized Taiwan, supported its UN membership, and adhered to strategic restrictions on exports to China, the United States showed little concern. Japan, acting through nongovernmental actors, was free to quietly develop trade ties with China.

The Japanese skillfully exploited the peculiar features of their own political structure to facilitate these ties. Essentially, they established a "division of labor." Mainstream and anti-mainstream elements within the ruling conservative party each tended to look after their own ties to Taiwan and the mainland. They found ways of deploying socialists to work on the China issue when it suited their purpose. The close links between government and business also facilitated the segregation of firms to work the Taiwan or the mainland side of the commercial street.

Private initiatives among competing groups with a variety of motivations often ran ahead of government initiative. The Japanese individuals behind these trade agreements were motivated by past ties with the PRC and by an Asianist philosophy. This philosophy saw Japan's future destiny as linked more closely with China and other Asian countries than with the West and was motivated in part by a deep sense of guilt for the suffering Japan had inflicted on China during the war years.

The absence of a government determination to manage trade resulted in a complex, pluralist trade structure between China and Japan. The complexity was heightened by Taiwan's sensitivity to Japan's trade with the PRC as well as by Beijing's sensitivity to Japan's trade with Taiwan. As Soeya Yoshihide observed, "The Taiwan factor was at times a more potent influence on the development of Japan-China trade than the Washington factor, albeit at a less fundamental level."[77] Although the issues surrounding Japanese trade with the PRC are often characterized as *seikei bunri*—referring to the separation of politics from trade—the reality was that it was highly political. Zhou Enlai, who had spent many years as a student in Japan, played a key role in facilitating the private agreements, and by 1964 Japan had become China's leading trade partner.

So incensed was Taiwan (supported by pro-Taiwan LDP members) by the developing trade ties with the PRC, and by the prospect that Japanese Export-Import Bank credits might be used to facilitate it, that Yoshida, after he left office, traveled to Taipei to reassure the Taiwanese leaders that Japan's economic aid to support the trade would remain wholly private.[8] Conversely, Beijing (supported by pro-Beijing LDP members) expressed its disapproval of the apparent deference to Taiwan. Successive Japanese administrations were repeatedly whiplashed by the strong political currents and compelled to reiterate their pledge of nonintervention in the trade with mainland China, which by 1966 represented more than a quarter of Japan's Asian trade. [9]

THE NIXON OPENING TO CHINA

Nixon's surprise opening to China in 1971 was a severe shock to Japan and especially to its conservative leadership. The Japanese had been assured that no fundamental changes in U.S. relations with China were impending and that they would be consulted should this be undertaken. When the president announced in a television address on July 15 that his national security adviser, Henry Kissinger, had just returned from a secret visit to Beijing, and that he himself would soon also visit China, the Japanese were stunned. Prime Minister Satō learned of the diplomatic breakthrough that would transform the Cold War system in East Asia just three minutes prior to Nixon's announcement.

Nixon had earlier lost respect for Satō, believing he had not fulfilled a promise to restrain textile exports to the United States, and he was determined to end Japan's trade advantages in the U.S. market. A month after his China speech, he delivered a second shock to the Japanese, announcing "new economic policies" that would force a revaluation of the yen. Together, the "Nixon shocks" produced an abrupt psychological distancing between the United States and Japan.

Sino-U.S. rapprochement altered the balance of power in the Cold War and fundamentally changed the political landscape in East Asia. Nixon's surprise opening to China and the fallout from it were more momentous for East Asia, one of Japan's leading diplomatic historians later observed, than the fall of the Berlin Wall in 1989.[10] Nixon and Kissinger hoped to extricate the United States from Vietnam by establishing a new set of relations with the two Communist powers. Initially stunned at the lack of prior consultation, the Japanese hastily moved to normalize relations with the

People's Republic ahead of the United States. Painful memories of the U.S. administration's decision to leave the Japanese in the dark still reverberate in Tokyo. It left a legacy of Japanese wariness over Sino-U.S. relations that remains a significant, although often submerged, element of the complex psychology in the triangular relationship today.

Although Nixon's démarche did not totally change the international system in East Asia, it did revolutionize the way it worked. As Ogata Sadako observed in her study of the normalization process, "No American action left a more profound impact on Japanese foreign policy in the postwar period than the unilateral decision by President Nixon to go to Beijing to seek rapprochement. The impact went far beyond the immediate reaction of sourness or of rushing to move ahead of the United States. It changed the meaning of the U.S.-Japan Security Treaty and forthwith the alliance itself."[11]

Beijing had become increasingly uneasy over Japan's growing strength. If, as the Guam (Nixon) Doctrine of 1969 intimated, the Americans pulled back from Asia, Japan would develop greater autonomy. The Chinese were worried that Japan's growing civilian nuclear power program would give Japan the option of producing nuclear weapons. U.S. Secretary of Defense Melvin Laird had said that the United States might not oppose a nuclear Japan.[12] In fact, Japan's new Defense Agency director, Nakasone Yasuhiro, was openly discussing the need for an autonomous defense, and an unprecedented Defense Agency white paper issued in 1970 declared enigmatically that "in view of the danger of inviting adverse foreign reactions and large-scale war, we will follow the policy of not acquiring nuclear weapons at present."[13]

Nixon and Kissinger played on China's concern over Japan's increasing power. Zhou Enlai raised the possibility of a sudden revival of Japanese militarism with Kissinger in one of their early conversations in Beijing in 1971:

DR. KISSINGER: Mr. Prime Minister, I will give you my frank assessment. . . . If I can begin, according to my habit, with a philosophical point. If I can contrast China with Japan as a society, China by tradition has a universal outlook but Japan has had a tribal outlook.

PRIME MINISTER Zhou: They are more narrow. It is also quite strange. They are an island. Britain too is an island mass.

DR. KISSINGER: They are different because Japan believes that their society is so different that they can adjust to anything and preserve their national essence. Therefore the Japanese are capable of sudden and explosive changes. They went from feudalism to emperor worship in two to three years. They went from emperor worship to democracy in three months.[14]

Nixon was capitalizing on the Chinese wariness of Japan, and this left Zhou suspicious. In his memoirs, Kissinger recalled: "On my first trip to Peking Zhou En-lai accused us of tempting Japan into traditional nationalist paths. It took me some time to convince him that the U.S.-Japan alliance was not directed against China; indeed that the surest way to tempt Japanese nationalism would be to set off a competition for Tokyo's favor between China and the United States."[15] In February 1972, Zhou said to Nixon, "Japan's feathers have grown on its wings and it is about to take off. . . . Can the U.S. control the 'wild horse' of Japan?"[16] Nixon assured Zhou and Mao that the United States intended to maintain the security treaty with Japan; otherwise, Japan would have to build defense capabilities itself.

Nixon and Kissinger convinced the Chinese leadership to see the Mutual Security Treaty in a favorable light, persuading Zhou and Mao that it was targeted at a potential Soviet threat and would serve to contain "Japanese unilateralism." In fact, two years later at one of their meetings, Mao lectured Kissinger on the need to be more attentive to the Japanese, lest a loss of trust lead to the return to unilateralism and nationalism in Japan. Kissinger listened while Mao told him that because of his secret opening to China, "They are afraid of you and you should try to lessen their fear." Kissinger was less impressed by the substance of Mao's advice than he was by the Chinese strategic reversal. "Barely two years after establishing contact," he marveled, "the grizzled revolutionary was giving a tutorial to the American Secretary of State on how to keep America's alliances together. Starting from opposite ends of the ideological spectrum, we had become tacit partners in maintaining the global equilibrium." Kissinger concluded that "the Chinese, indeed, came to stress that US-Japanese relations were more important than US-Chinese relations."[17]

The Cold War order was now configured in a dramatically different way. The end of Sino-U.S. confrontation freed Japan to normalize relations with China, which Prime Minister Tanaka achieved in September 1972, transferring diplomatic recognition from Taiwan to the PRC. In 1978, China and Japan concluded a Treaty of Peace and Friendship. The destruction of the Sino-Soviet alliance and the formation of a virtual U.S.-China-Japan entente radically shifted the power balance in East Asia, undermining the Russian position in the region. For a quarter of a century, the Chinese maintained a benign view of the U.S.-Japan Mutual Security Treaty.

The Japanese reaction to the Nixon opening, however, was ambivalent and conflicted. On the one hand, it portended a new regional stability and opened the way for Japan to develop a new relationship with China—a relationship that had hitherto been frustrated by U.S. wishes. On the other hand, there were deeply troubling aspects to the Nixon opening. There was the sense of betrayal at the way in which it had transpired. Still today, the memory of this "nightmare," as one Japanese diplomat termed Nixon's unilateral action, influences Japanese thinking about the triangular relationship. The fear is that sudden change could well happen again.[18]

The Japanese soon felt even more slighted by the enthusiasm the United States had for its new relations with Beijing. It seemed to them that the U.S. president was placing greater weight on this relationship than on the long-standing ties between the United States and Japan. On August 15, 1971, the anniversary of Japanese surrender and one month after the announcement of his planned visit to China, Nixon announced his "New Economic Policy." It was a second "shock" to the Japanese. Aimed primarily at the mounting Japanese trade surplus, this policy cut the dollar loose from the gold standard, imposed an import surcharge, and forced the upward valuation of the yen. Once again, Prime Minister Satō was given only a few minutes' advance warning. In his announcement, lest there be any doubt who the culprits were, Nixon added that the economic threat that the United States faced was "far more serious than the challenge that we confronted even in the dark days of Pearl Harbor."[19]

The Nixon shocks signaled a Sino-U.S. rapprochement, freeing Japan from the freeze on political relations with the mainland that the Americans had imposed, and led to a normalization of Sino-Japanese relations. But it also changed the dynamics of the U.S.-Japan alliance and began decades of mounting trade antagonisms. Gyohten Toyoo, a prominent finance official, has recalled that Japanese leaders saw the triangle changing to their disadvantage. They felt that the Americans were "playing a kind of China card to Japan" and that "the Nixon administration was thinking about the possibility of using Communist China as a counterweight to Japan in post-Vietnam Asia."[20] Indeed, Nixon appeared to favor a balance of power that would put Japan on its own. In January 1972, he remarked, "I think it will be a safer world and a better world if we have a strong, healthy United States, Europe, Soviet Union, China, Japan, each balancing the other, not playing one against the other, an even balance."[21]

Although the Nixon opening to China bruised Japanese pride, it laid the groundwork for mutual accommodation among the three powers. It led to at least tacit U.S.-Japan-China security cooperation against the Russians. Over the next two decades, a consensus on many issues became tantamount to a triple entente to contain Soviet influence in East Asia. Significantly, during the mid-1970s the Pentagon eliminated planning for the contingency of war with China for the remainder of the Cold War. The changed strategic environment transformed the political climate in Japan and enabled hitherto taboo military cooperation to take place between Japan and the United States, such as joint planning, intelligence sharing, joint exercises, and joint training. This accommodation was surely facilitated by Russia's efforts to play a larger role in Asia. Moscow began building a significant Pacific fleet: It inherited U.S. bases at Cam Ranh Bay; its air force and navy began intruding regularly into Japanese air space and territorial waters; and it staked out a more active strategic presence in the Asian subcontinent as well as in Indochina.

In addition to joining into this virtual alliance against the Russians, Japan and the United States acknowledged that Taiwan was a part of China, and all three powers pledged to work for a peaceful reconciliation. Although China reserved the right to reunify Taiwan by force, and the United States maintained an interest in assisting Taiwan's capacity for self-defense, differences over interpretation of the agreements were generally played down. Beijing accepted America's continued regional security role, including the alliances with Japan and South Korea. Japan and the United States encouraged China's economic reforms and its entry into the World Bank, the Asian Development Bank, and the International Monetary Fund. China was seen to be on the path to political reforms, and the United States soft-pedaled differences with China over issues of human rights. For its part, Japan was not concerned about these issues.

While initially harsh in its treatment of an ally, the Nixon opening helped to create a new and balanced triangular situation, easing Sino-Japanese enmity and leaving the United States in the position of having good relations with both nations. This implicit entente of the three powers from the mid-1970s to the end of the Cold War was an unusual period in a century of triangular relations. For more than fifteen years, until the Tiananmen Incident of 1989, the United States enjoyed close ties with both Japan and China and did not have to choose between them.

Japan's Aid-Based Engagement Policy

At the end of the 1970s, while the United States concentrated on strategic cooperation with China to oppose Soviet power in East Asia, Japanese policymakers quietly set about establishing a very different sort of relationship with China. The government began to use official development assistance (ODA) to shape a policy of engagement. This aid-based policy, complex in its motivations and multifaceted in its perception by both donor and recipient, was based on a long-term view of the development of the bilateral relationship to serve multiple Japanese interests.

The genesis of Japan's aid policy toward China lay in the way reparations for China had been settled after World War II. The 1951 San Francisco Peace Treaty provided for Japan to make war reparations to the countries it had invaded. In light of the Japanese occupation of Chinese territory, which lasted for fifteen years, and the resulting casualties, exceeding 10 million Chinese, the claims against Japan could have been astronomical, severely impairing Japanese economic recovery. In the Japan–Republic of China Peace Treaty signed on April 28, 1952 (the same day that the San Francisco Peace Treaty took effect), Taiwan explicitly renounced the right to demand reparations from Japan. This was probably the result of U.S. pressure, although Chiang Kai-shek recalled in his memoirs that Japan was in such dire economic straits that, "with the Red imperialist forces now intent on grabbing Japan, anything in our policy likely to enfeeble Japan would be counterproductive."[22]

Consequently, in 1972, at the time of the normalization of relations with the PRC, the Japanese argued that since Taiwan, representing China, had renounced the right to reparations, the PRC was not legally entitled to them.[23] For many years Zhou had favored waiving reparations as a way of separating the Japanese people from their government and weakening the pro-Taiwan forces in the Diet. But he was so angered by Japan's "legalistic argument" that he threatened to send the Japanese negotiators home. In the end, intent on the higher goal of cementing a new relationship with Japan and the United States, Zhou and Mao agreed to waive any claim to reparations.[24]

The Chinese later came to regret this decision. Following the rise of Deng Xiaoping in 1977 and his ambitious program of economic modernization, the Chinese desperately needed capital. The PRC had long avoided foreign loans as a matter of principle—the Chinese were determined to be self-reliant and remembered China's bitter history of economic exploitation by foreign powers—but Deng's pragmatic approach changed that disposition.[25]

At this point, Japanese policy underwent a subtle but highly significant transformation. It began with a crisis in economic relations following the first euphoria of Japanese investment in China in 1978. At this time, nearly four dozen contracts for Japanese investment were concluded with the Chinese, including contracts for a gigantic steel plant to be built at Baoshan near Shanghai. This "China fever" among Japanese business interests proved short-lived, however, and the rosy assumptions harbored on both sides proved unreal. The Chinese were forced to suspend and cancel dozens of contracts, including ones for the Baoshan plant, and Japanese business interests protested and made demands for compensation.

At this moment of crisis in their economic relations, Japanese government leaders moved to assert a stronger hand in the relationship. During his October 1978 visit to Japan, Deng indicated receptivity to low-interest Japanese government loans in the form of ODA. The respected and influential Japanese economic commentator Hasegawa Keitaro wrote at the time:

Reading between the lines, many Japanese saw Deng's statement as a request for reparations from Japan for damage caused during World War II. It cannot be denied that many Chinese still desire war reparations from Japan and feel that now is the time to make this demand known, enabling China to extricate itself from its economic difficulties. And yet officially the reparations issue has already been settled. In 1972, at the time of the restoration of Sino-Japanese diplomatic ties, Premier Zhou Enlai resolved it by renouncing China's right to make reparation claims. Naturally even then there was strong opposition within China to Zhou's decision, and it has not yet died out. Economically, payment of reparations by Japan would play a decisive role in helping China overcome its economic crisis. Deng hesitated to make an open request for reparations, however, for it would reflect unfavorably on the earlier decision by Zhou, who is still held in high esteem. The real intent of Deng's statement, therefore, was to signal his difficulties to the Japanese so that they would come forward on their own accord with a reparations offer.[26]

If there was any doubt about Deng's intentions, he was more explicit in later years. Amid rising tensions between the two countries in June 1987,

Deng asserted that Japan had an obligation to assist China's development because, as he put it, "it has the biggest debt to China. In 1972 China did not ask for reparations. Frankly speaking, we harbor dissatisfaction over this point."[27]

The Japanese government formulated a policy of engaging China through economic aid. Prime Minister Ōhira and his foreign minister, Ōkita Saburo, responded to Deng's request, and during their visit to Beijing in December 1979, they announced Japan's first postwar government loans to China. They were disposed to provide substantial economic assistance for a number of reasons. First, they welcomed the political moderation of Deng and his new economic pragmatism as contributing to regional stability. Second, they saw it as an opportunity to advance Japanese economic interests through investment in infrastructure projects that would facilitate trade and encourage Chinese openness to further Japanese investment. And third, they privately thought of this as reparations owed China. By providing grants and low-interest loans, Japan hoped to nurture friendly relations, overcome the animus left from the wartime occupation, draw China into peaceful participation in a stable regional order, and structure an interdependent economic relationship that would benefit Japanese trade and investment and provide some measure of leverage to moderate Chinese policy.

Foreign Minister Ōkita, perhaps Japan's leading postwar strategist of economic development, played a key role in devising Japan's economic engagement policy. He had a deep personal interest in China. Born in Dalian, Manchuria, where his father published a newspaper for the Japanese colonial population, he served as an economic planner for colonial development in the Greater East Asia Ministry during the war.[28] He had assisted China's aluminum and steel industries in Manchuria, and he had served as an economic adviser to the PRC.

The circumstances under which Japanese ODA began, therefore, signaled a tacit understanding on both sides that it was related to the Chinese expectation that Japan was obligated to provide reparations. As a consequence, Japan was willing to overlook the ways in which its aid to China contradicted the guiding principles of its foreign-aid policies and to endure the manner that China adopted in its continuing expectations of this aid as an entitlement.

Japan's new policy of economic engagement of China raised problems with other countries, including the United States. The Americans and Europeans complained that unless aid grants were "untied," Western business interests in China would suffer. The ASEAN countries complained that Japanese aid to China would come at the expense of aid to Southeast Asia. The pro-Taiwan forces in the Diet complained that aid might strengthen the Chinese military. Ōhira therefore announced "three principles" guiding Japan's aid to China: close consultation with the United States in determining its aid policy, implementation of a balanced loan policy in view of the interests of other Asian countries (especially ASEAN), and avoidance of support for China's defense-related industries. How extensively Japan observed these principles is the subject of debate among all parties.

In the two decades after 1979, ODA became the centerpiece of a comprehensive engagement strategy. China became the principal recipient of Japanese ODA, although not always on an annual basis. Unlike other developing nations, whose aid from Japan was negotiated annually, Tokyo extended aid on a multiyear basis to finance projects that China proposed. Total Japanese aid during this period amounted to over $23 billion. Much of it was for large-scale infrastructure projects, including ports, roads, airports, and railways, which proved lucrative for Japanese firms while also promoting the interdependence of the two economies and the integration of China into the world economy. Trade and investment grew substantially. Japan continued as China's leading trade partner, and total trade grew to $66 billion in 1999. At the same time, owing to its reliance on Chinese raw materials, Japan became a net importer after 1986 and ran a $19.5 billion deficit in 1999.

Japanese engagement policy addressed other challenges and opportunities critical to Japan's long-term interests in China. In the 1990s, Japan directed increasing support to environmental and energy projects. Starting in 1993, China became a net importer of oil. China's expanding dependence on imported energy supplies, and the prospect of competing with China for energy sources, prompted ODA support for Chinese projects that explored new domestic sources of energy and greater energy efficiency. Similarly, the prospect of industrial pollution from China led MITI in 1992 to initiate its Green Aid Plan partly based on ODA funds. It sought to support Japanese commercial interests, matching private capital with public funding, while contributing to Chinese efforts to stem massive environmental degradation.

The Burden of History

Japan's economic engagement of China was part of a comprehensive foreign policy strategy toward Asia that took shape in the 1980s. This strategy would serve Japan's economic goals by ensuring access to markets, raw materials, and sources of energy as well as the preservation of good relations with all countries that were key to Japan's economic progress. The effort to foster a friendly interdependence with China was fraught with frustrations. Because the Chinese saw the aid as reparations owed to them, they were not inclined to express gratitude or even to publicize it among the Chinese people. On the contrary, Chinese leaders reminded the Japanese repeatedly of their obligation to make restitution for the wartime damage and destruction. This obligation entailed not only reparations but also apology, self-reflection, and remorse.

The issues of war responsibility have been profoundly divisive among Japanese parties, factions, and generations. Even within the ranks of conservatives there was no consensus on how to address these issues. The rise of popular nationalism in Asia, and the remembrance of Japanese imperialism as a central element of this nationalism, made the interpretation of Japanese history an international issue. Appeals to nationalism were embedded in the contemporary politics of China. As a consequence, the two decades after the signing of the Treaty of Peace and Friendship in 1978, while marked by a substantial expansion of Japanese-Chinese economic relations, also saw a succession of political disputes growing out of Chinese demands for historical self-reflection.

These disputes followed a certain pattern. They were generally occasioned by Chinese anger over an apparent Japanese unwillingness to acknowledge responsibility for wartime damage and atrocities committed in China. Chinese demands for apology were a mixture of genuine anger, intimidation, and manipulation. Typically these disputes resulted in Japanese acquiescence to Chinese demands. But neither in China nor in Japan was there closure. The Japanese government was painfully aware that a failure to stem anti-Japanese sentiment abroad would jeopardize its foreign policy strategy. Therefore, in most of these disputes, Tokyo retreated in the face of Chinese accusations, but critics at home charged appeasement. Opinion in China held that Japan still had "not atoned on the psychological level."[29]

The role of the Japanese Ministry of Education in screening Japanese history textbooks, and especially their interpretation of Japanese imperialism in Asia, was a focal point of these disputes. In 1982, reports in the Japanese press led to charges that the Japanese Ministry of Education was whitewashing Japanese aggression and atrocities committed at Nanjing and elsewhere. As the charges mounted, the ministry authorized the inclusion of considerable additional material on these atrocities in textbooks, resulting in intense criticism from conservatives who resented foreign interference in the writing of national history. These conservatives disputed the more critical interpretations of the national past.[30] Their well-publicized denials, however, only served to renew Chinese criticism.

In 1985, Prime Minister Nakasone's official visit to the Yasukuni Shrine, the national war memorial, occasioned protests in both China and Korea. In the face of these protests, Nakasone promised not to repeat the offense. He was particularly sensitive to the anti-Japanese sentiment among students in China, which he tried to address by increasing the funding for cultural and student exchanges. In fact, owing to the stimulus of Nakasone and others, the number of students from China increased rapidly beginning in the 1980s. Students from the mainland in Japan numbered 501 in 1980, but by 1990 they numbered 18,063, and in 2001 there were 44,041 (by which time they constituted 56 percent of all foreign students in Japan).

National sentiment in both China and Korea was frequently inflamed by the statements of Japanese politicians seeming to justify Japan's imperial past. In most cases, the offending politician, if he was a member of the government, was promptly forced to resign. One notable incident occurred in 1987, when Deng told a visiting Japanese party leader that Japanese politicians should be "more humble" and learn to resist the revival of militarism. An exasperated Japanese vice foreign minister anonymously referred to Deng as a leader who was "above the clouds" and "hard in the head," hinting at senility. The Japanese bureaucrat was soon identified, and the Japanese leadership quickly pacified Chinese anger by compelling him to take early retirement.

Throughout the 1980s and early 1990s, the Japanese repeatedly deferred to such pressure and refrained from joining the West's increasing criticism of China's restraints on political freedom. The Japanese leadership believed that a long-term policy of economic engagement would serve Japan's own economic interests. As the director-general of Asian affairs at the Foreign Ministry, Tanino Sakutarō, explained, "We should remember that a more stable, affluent China will benefit not just itself but all of Asia and in fact the world. We need to avoid reacting emotionally and applying only Western values to each new set of political and social phenomena as it unfolds in China. Instead we should direct our efforts to bringing China into the framework of Asian peace, development, and prosperity."[31] This Asian strategy entailed not only distancing Japan from Western criticism of Chinese human rights violations, but also accepting Chinese criticism of Japanese wartime misdeeds.

The Chinese leadership persistently raised the history issue in circumstances that privately angered many Japanese. The PRC president during the 1990s, Jiang Zemin, was particularly persistent in hectoring the Japanese.[32] In 1995, on the occasion of his first state visit to South Korea, Jiang held a joint press conference with President Kim Young Sam, and the two Asian leaders lectured Japan on adopting, as Jiang said, "a correct view of history." Jiang went on, "We must be vigilant against a Japanese militarist minority. Although a half century has passed since the end of a war between China and Japan, some Japanese politicians still have a wrong historical view." To which Kim added, "We will correct Japan's bad habits."[33]

Many Japanese began to feel that their government had made substantial efforts to apologize for past aggression. They especially emphasized the first imperial visit to China by the emperor and empress in 1992, which had generated protracted concern and controversy in Japan during its planning stages. Despite fears that the visit would inject the imperial institution into politics or result in an incident damaging Sino-Japanese relations, the government went ahead with the visit, hopeful that it would lay the past to rest and help the two countries turn the corner in their bilateral relations. This was not the case.

Although the issue of historical interpretation would seem to be something for Japan and its Asian neighbors alone to resolve, an incident at this time illustrated how it played into the triangular relationship with the United States. As he flew over Fukuoka on the first leg of a trip to the United States in 1997, Jiang Zemin radioed a message to Emperor Akihito by way of the control tower below: "We wish good health to the Emperor, peace to the Japanese people, and prosperity to Japan," he said. In Tokyo, according to the *Asahi*, the Foreign Ministry was pleased at this thoughtful gesture by the Chinese president. However, when Jiang landed in Honolulu, where he stopped en route to Washington, his first official act was to drive to Pearl Harbor and lay a wreath at the Arizona memorial. The mood at the Foreign Ministry abruptly changed: By recalling a war in which Chinese and U.S. soldiers had fought shoulder-to-shoulder against Japanese invaders, Jiang was once again using history to put the Japanese on the defensive in the context of triangular relations.[34]

Their success in compelling the Japanese to hold to a low posture and repeatedly apologize for the past led the Chinese leaders to overplay their hand. A new generation of Japanese politicians was emerging in the 1990s. They had no firsthand recollection of the 1930s and 1940s and had long since tired of the Chinese demands for apology and atonement. Jiang Zemin's visit to Tokyo in November 1998, the first visit of a Chinese head of state to Japan, marked a turning point. Japanese leaders are virtually unanimous in describing it as the pivotal event in rising popular frustration and anger with Chinese criticism. Jiang's hectoring in the presence of the emperor, and his demand that the Japanese provide a written apology for past aggression, exhausted Japanese forbearance.

In part, Japanese exasperation was the result of timing. A month earlier, the new Korean president, Kim Dae Jung, had visited Tokyo. Kim's willingness to address the Japanese in their own tongue, and to ease the bans on Japanese investment and importation of Japanese popular culture, delighted them. Above all, Kim emphasized that "South Korea should also rightly evaluate Japan, in all its changed aspects and search with hope for future possibilities."[35] Kim's magnanimity stood in marked contrast to the confrontational approach of Jiang Zemin, who pointedly told the emperor and other Japanese leaders that China was not yet ready to forgive the past. By making clear his determination to establish a new and positive relationship with Japan, Kim succeeded in attaining an explicit written apology for the past. The Chinese demanded the same kind of written apology but were unwilling to prepare the ground as Kim had. The visit ended on a sour note.

POLITICIZATION OF SINO-JAPANESE RELATIONS

The end of the Cold War removed the strong imperative for China, Japan, and the United States to cooperate in a strategic partnership to contain Soviet power. The disappearance of a common threat to unite them allowed divisive issues to emerge and once again to destabilize the triangular relationship. The massive student demonstrations in Tiananmen Square that occurred in 1989, the same year that the Cold War ended, began a period of persistent tension between the United States and China over human rights and security issues. The brutal suppression of demonstrators in

Tiananmen shocked the world and prompted economic sanctions by the major powers. At the same time, freed of a concern with its northern border, China redirected its attention to Taiwan and other offshore issues—claims to the Senkaku/Diaoyu Islands, the Spratleys, and offshore oil and gas fields—all of which raised the possibility of conflict with U.S. and Japanese interests. This more confrontational approach was dramatized by the Taiwan Strait missile crisis in the spring of 1996, when China fired missiles into waters close to Taiwan to demonstrate displeasure with Taiwan's assertions of greater independence during its first democratic election of a president.

Initially, Tokyo avoided confrontation, allowing the United States to press China on all of these issues. In the aftermath of Tiananmen, Washington's determination to link trade and human rights in its approach to China caused heartburn in Tokyo. The Japanese were unenthusiastic about punishing China with sanctions. Former President Nixon remarked at the time that "anyone who thinks Japan will introduce democracy into China must be smoking paoti."[36] Indeed, Japan resumed its economic engagement with China just a year later, becoming the first of the G-7 nations to abandon the punitive stance. Even when Beijing ignored Tokyo's protests and undertook nuclear testing in 1995, the Japanese only briefly froze grant aid. When visiting Beijing in 1994, Prime Minister Hosokawa Morihiro delighted his interlocutors by declaring that it was wrong to try to impose Western concepts of human rights on other countries. Likewise, Japanese negotiators reached an early agreement with China on World Trade Organization (WTO) accession, leaving it to China's other major trading partners to press Beijing to make concessions that would bring membership.

U.S. trade officials were irked, knowing that Japan had made minimal demands on China to commit to free-market principles and that whatever concessions the United States won would apply to China's other trading partners. U.S. Trade Representative Charlene Barshefsky remarked that "by and large, the Japanese have not contributed to the creation of a commercially meaningful agreement."[37] During the Taiwan Strait crisis, even though missile tests alarmed the Japanese by evoking an image of a militant China projecting its power into the sea lanes, Tokyo remained cautious, expressing only "understanding" of U.S. actions in deploying two aircraft carriers to the Strait. As a Japanese Foreign Ministry spokesman explained, "[Our] position is much more vulnerable than that of the United States, so what we can do or say is very limited."[38]

Japan would have preferred to rely on its economic tools (for example, aid, technical cooperation, investment, and trade) to continue to shape its bilateral relations with China, but with its economy sagging and China's rapidly expanding, those tools were less effective than they had once been. In the post–Cold War strategic environment, Japan became increasingly wary of Beijing's growing assertiveness and conscious of the need to strengthen its alliance with the United States. In 1997, Tokyo agreed to a revision of the Guidelines for U.S.-Japan Defense Cooperation, which provided for an increased role for Japan in the event of a regional crisis. Recognizing that these guidelines could be invoked in the event of a crisis with Taiwan, Chinese leaders became openly critical of the U.S.-Japan alliance.

With the passing of an older generation of "China handlers," Beijing lost most of its effective defenders in Japan. By the late 1990s, the number of old China hands in the LDP with close ties to the Chinese leadership who could be counted on to defend and mend the relationship were sparse. Those who had in the past expressed sympathetic views of China, such as Kono Yōhei or Katō Kōichi, were now on the defensive. Katō provoked loud criticism when he said in a 1998 speech that "Japan, the U.S., and China should construct a triangular relationship and maintain an equal distance from each other."[39] A number of younger generation LDP lawmakers were now openly hostile in demanding an end to Japan's constant deference to Chinese demands. Opinion surveys showed a mounting popular antagonism toward Chinese activities and policies.

At the same time, there was a residual popular sympathy with Taiwan among the Japanese and revived interest in the plight of this former colony. Japan's rule in Taiwan had been conducted with a lighter hand than elsewhere, and Japanese business and political circles had maintained strong ties. This relationship was enhanced by the advent of democratic politics on the island. The president of Japan's National Defense Academy, Nishihara Masashi, in 1999 summed up the growing Japanese affinity for Taiwan: "Their economy is in good shape. They have free elections. There is a sort of respect for Taiwan. We don't hear Taiwanese people criticizing Japanese like the mainland Chinese do. They don't demand apologies for the wartime. We feel more comfortable with people from Taiwan."[40] Japan was the largest exporter to Taiwan, supplying electronic equipment and components to the island's flourishing high-tech industries. Japanese lawmakers had extensive and cordial relations with their Taiwan counterparts.

A crop of new issues between China and Japan symbolized their growing rivalry for regional leadership. China voiced its opposition to Japan's aspiration to join the UN Security Council as a permanent member. It opposed Japanese initiatives for regional economic leadership, such as Japan's proposal for an Asian Monetary Fund. China hosted a regional economic summit in 2002 and proposed a free-trade agreement with the ASEAN countries, a bloc that had once acknowledged Japan as its outside partner.

Periodic incidents involving the unsettled ownership of the Senkaku/Diaoyu Islands, with their rich oil and gas deposits and competition for energy resources, heightened tensions. Beginning in the summer of 2000, Chinese naval research ships were repeatedly sighted roaming Japanese coastal waters without prior notification and without any declared purpose. The press referred to them as "spy ships," and the experience left the Japanese with an increased uneasiness and suspicion of Chinese intentions. After avoiding an expression of strategic concern for the peace and security of Taiwan during the Cold War, in February 2005, in a joint statement with the U.S. government, Japan explicitly made such a statement.[41] At about the same time, in the announcement of its new National Defense Program Outline, Japan for the first time referred to China's growing military strength as a source of "concern." The development of U.S.-Japan cooperation in ballistic missile defense drew a sharp reaction from Beijing.

One of the clearest indications by 2000 that the relationship was changing was the mounting criticism in Japan of its massive aid program to China. The widespread Japanese anger at China's demands for national repentance contributed to increasing public scrutiny and severe criticism from politicians of the huge ODA directed at China. The grudging way in which China viewed this aid led to growing doubts in Japan about its effectiveness in meeting Japanese goals. Viewing the aid as reparations owed China, the Chinese government felt little need to inform its people about this aid and its symbolic value in showing Japan's desire for friendly relations. Nor did it meet Japanese expectations of moderating the buildup of Chinese military spending and the development of nuclear armaments. Japanese critics further pointed out that China itself was giving aid, sometimes to regimes that the Japanese did not support. Finally, the Chinese leadership had gone to great lengths to ensure that the ODA did not permit Japanese business interests to gain a dominant role in their economic development. Why, many Japanese politicians asked, should we aid the buildup of an unfriendly rival? In 2005, Japan announced that it was time for China to "graduate" from ODA assistance and that it would end yen loans by 2008. A Chinese official reportedly found the term "graduation" disparaging, as it implied a teacher-student relationship with Japan. The huge aid program therefore wound down toward a sour ending.

The strategic environment in East Asia at the outset of a new century thus had contributed to a more "normal" relationship between China and Japan in place of the anomalous relationship that had prevailed during the Cold War. Japan could no longer justify its old patronizing view of China as a backward country unable to achieve successful nation-building. Instead, it had to acknowledge that this neighbor, twenty-five times its size and with a population ten times its own, was achieving growth rates comparable to Japan's own high growth in the 1960s.

Indeed, Japanese thinking about China's future was marked by contradictory fears. On the one hand, Japan had cause for concern that China might not be able to cope with the challenges of modernization and that turmoil and disruption, whether political, social, or environmental, next door would inevitably impact Japan. On the other hand, Japan feared the potential success in Chinese modernization, which could result in potentially hegemonic power in the region. Given China's geographically dominant position along East Asia's coastal periphery, as its military power grows it could present an increasing threat to the security of Japan's sea lanes. "At some point after 2020," as one naval strategic authority wrote, "China may be sufficiently emboldened by the modernization of its naval, air, and missile capabilities to threaten obstruction of Japan's seaborne imports for strategic leverage and to satisfy its resource needs in competition with those of Japan."[42]

While many Japanese regarded the prospect of a powerful China with foreboding, the dominant view held that, despite annual double-digit increases in military spending, China's emergence as a potentially threatening regional power was still some time off in the future. China was viewed as making steady progress in modernizing its military, but having started from a low level in its power-projection capabilities. For the time being, at least, the threat posed by Chinese military power was significantly less than the threat that had been posed by Soviet military power in the 1980s.[43] So long as the U.S. alliance remained strong, the military balance would not be in China's favor. Although there was an underlying anxiety in the view of many Japanese experts that political turmoil could provoke a more aggressive Chinese foreign policy, the majority opinion felt that Chinese behavior would be highly constrained by its integration into the world economy.[44]

In the meantime, Japanese economic leaders in business and the bureaucracy belatedly began to invest heavily in China. Although many of

Japan's sunset industries were challenged by China's lower wage structure, leaders of Japan's large world-class businesses, together with the bureaucrats in the Ministry of Economy, Trade and Industry (MITI's successor), convinced of the synergies between the two economies, were determined to promote bilateral economic cooperation.

THE STRATEGIC TRIANGLE

The ebb and flow in the U.S.-China bilateral relationship during the 1990s exacerbated Japanese fears of both entrapment and abandonment in their alliance with the United States. Times of tension between China and the United States alternated with warming relations. After Tiananmen, the Japanese resisted being drawn into U.S. confrontations with China over human rights and over Taiwan. But at the same time, the alliance had to be nurtured lest the United States see it as losing its value. During President Bill Clinton's administration, the Japanese had cause to worry about the strength of the alliance. The administration, as part of its economic renewal agenda, adopted a tough and confrontational approach to its trade problems with Japan while warming up toward Beijing. After confronting China in the Taiwan Strait crisis in 1996, President Clinton later proposed a "strategic partnership" with China. In 1998, he made a nine-day visit to China—longer than any other U.S. president—without stopping in Japan. His visit was closely watched by the Japanese and awakened memories of Nixon's surprise opening to Beijing. Their concern was not allayed when Clinton joined President Jiang in praising China's economic management. In fact, they contrasted it with the Japanese failure to reform its economy and lead the region out of its financial crisis. The George W. Bush administration, in contrast, referred to China as a "strategic competitor" and made a deliberate decision to downplay trade problems with Japan and draw it into a tighter alliance.

In the long term, the alliance is a hedge against an aggressive China dominating the region. The United States and Japan are essentially status-quo powers; it is Beijing that may wish to alter the map, asserting new rules and procedures for governing the framework of power relations. Still, in any calculation of costs and benefits, it appears that for the near term, China's interests lie in accepting the engagement rewards that Japan and the United States hold out to it. The new Chinese leadership is not driven by ideological zeal. Its legitimacy depends on its ability to maintain economic progress, and for this purpose, its cooperation with the United States and its closer neighbors is essential. Future growth prospects require a continued commitment to reform and openness. Beijing recognizes the value of its access to the U.S. and Japanese markets and investors. This recognition has repeatedly moderated the latent nationalism in China policy and its verbal attacks on both U.S. "hegemonism" and Japanese "militarism." China's stake in open world trade and its entry into the World Trade Organization are, at least for the present, encouraging China to commit to multilateral trading rules.

The calculus of many observers in the United States and Japan that development of a market-oriented economy will intensify pressure for pluralistic politics in China is plausible but problematic. It is true that China's growing interdependence with its trading partners, including Taiwan, will likely keep it on a moderate foreign policy course. The legitimacy of its Communist Party leadership rests on strong economic growth. Should growth falter, leaders would have to resort to fostering nationalism, a choice that they have thus far been reluctant to make, perhaps recognizing that the force of nationalism could prove so difficult to control that it could soon boomerang and end in their overthrow. In fact, a weak and divided China unable to cope with the staggering problems of national transformation is a prospect that many Japanese leaders see as more likely and no less dangerous than a strong and overbearing China.

China faces myriad problems that could lead to economic slump and social unrest: a floating population with high unemployment in the cities, the growing gap between rich and poor, weakness in the banking system, inefficiency in the state-owned enterprises, labor unrest, and elements of traditional rebellion. Should economic progress stall and lead to increasing social tensions, the Chinese leadership, lacking any other plausible ideological appeal and facing mounting pressures for wider participation in politics, might reluctantly turn to a strident form of nationalism and a more assertive foreign policy to serve their need for domestic legitimacy. The difficulties of nation-building could lead China down a nationalist path that makes it less susceptible to engagement policies.

Japan seeks as much autonomy in its China policy as is compatible with maintaining the cohesion of its alliance with Washington. Throughout the Cold War period, Japanese leaders saw Japan's interests vis-à-vis China as distinct from U.S. interests and sought to pursue an independent China policy. Sakakibara Eisuke, the veteran economic bureaucrat, writing in May 2004, decried the conservatives who were drawing too close to an all-out pro-American stance, which inclined them to take an ideological position in opposition to the Chinese government. He urged Japanese conservatives to recognize that although there were some advantages to be derived from the U.S. alliance, there was also an important Japanese economic interest to be served by ensuring close ties with China. "What is necessary at present," he concluded, "is a strategically pragmatic approach, namely a pro-U.S. and pro-China line in order to use the China card toward the U.S. and the U.S. card toward China."[45]

A number of forces encourage Beijing and Tokyo to pursue closer collaboration. Their economic interests are in some respects complementary. China needs capital; Japan needs markets. Both depend on trade and require secure lines of communication to key trading partners—most importantly their suppliers of oil. China still accords top priority to the modernization of its economy, and it needs outside help to accomplish this objective. Japan is a prime source of assistance through its exports of capital equipment, flows of investment funds, technology transfers, technical assistance, and help in educating China's human capital. In addition, Japan is counting on exports to China to sustain its economic growth and on imports from China to lower its cost structure.

Many Japanese leaders, as well as Chinese leaders, bridle at displays of unilateralism in U.S. policy and the hubris they often detect in official U.S. pronouncements. U.S. primacy has prompted some Japanese to empathize with China's promotion of "multipolarity"—a euphemism for its desire to check America's preponderance. Moreover, at a time when Europe is swiftly expanding its continental market and groping for common defense and foreign policies, and when North Americans are moving fitfully toward free western hemispheric trade, there are obvious incentives for Sino-Japanese cooperation in pan-Asian initiatives—for example, ASEAN Plus Three. In a world in which borders are arguably less consequential and certainly more porous, both countries are recognizing the need to address certain problems (for example, environmental pollution) together. To date, China's residual need for U.S. (as well as Japanese) help in modernizing its economy, its respect for U.S. military prowess, and its perception that Washington's ambitions are constrained by a host of foreign policy preoccupations all temper its zeal to construct a countervailing coalition. Needless to say, Japanese temptations to play along with Beijing on this score are tempered by a clear-eyed recognition of the larger stakes in Japanese cooperation with the United States.

These considerations notwithstanding, powerful forces complicate

Sino-Japanese relations, exacerbating latent sources of mutual distrust. In the long term, China will want a lowered U.S. military presence in the region. At the same time, the Chinese have no wish to see Japan embark on a strategically independent course or deviate from long-established limitations on its defense policy. Conversely, the Japanese have no desire to see China build a blue-water navy or project power into those areas of Asia where Japan's maritime interests are engaged. Strategically, Tokyo and Beijing share an interest in avoiding, or at least postponing for as long as possible, overt military rivalry. Both are anxious to avoid the diversion of resources that an arms race would provoke.

For the time being, Japan is moving cautiously, gauging the changing power configuration, assessing the prospects of Chinese nation-building and their implications for the region and Japan's place in it. The outcome will heavily affect the security institutions that Japan may be required to develop. The U.S. alliance is essential to this wait-and-see approach, but at the same time Japan's leaders do not want to be hostage to the China policy of the United States. They want to preserve the options that an autonomous policy offers.

CHAPTER ELEVEN

THE PROSPECT OF A
NEW EAST ASIAN ORDER

As the new century dawned, the prospect of a settled new order was clouded. It was a fluid time in global politics. The tempo of change in Asia was especially challenging. Japan had to adapt to a dynamic region of strategic rivalries, arms races, border disputes, competition for resources, and rampant nationalisms, and only fitful progress was being made toward development of effective multilateral institutions to attempt to manage this turbulence. For the time being at least, U.S. military power maintained a semblance of order, and across the spectrum of Japanese opinion, all parties wished to preserve the alliance. The resurgence of the U.S. economy, which the Japanese had written off in the 1980s, and the extent of unipolar U.S. dominance represented a vast shift in the correlation of international power. Always attentive to power transitions, the Japanese gained renewed respect for American influence.

But the United States had its own global agenda. After the terrorist attack on the United States of September 11, 2001, Japan's ally, the guarantor of Japanese security, and the guardian of regional stability, underwent a profound change in its foreign policy. The danger to the international state system posed by the spread of weapons of mass destruction in the hands of shadowy, suicidal groups who could not be deterred by conventional means added a new dimension to the instability and insecurity of the post–Cold War era. The shock of the surprise terrorist attack, and the prospect of still more devastating and difficult-to-detect threats, galvanized a new assertiveness of U.S. power. In meeting this threat, U.S. President George W. Bush implied that the United States would not depend on international law and institutions. Rather, it would use its unrivaled power to deal with the terrorist threat. The administration presided over what John Lewis Gaddis called "the most sweeping redesign of U.S. grand strategy since the presidency of Franklin D. Roosevelt."[1]

The United States' expectations of Japan grew substantially after 9/11. Long-simmering U.S. discontent with "Japan's free ride" burst forth in a new insistence that Japan should assume a greater burden in the alliance. Keenly sensitive to the crisis that had resulted from Japan's failure to respond to these expectations at the time of the first Gulf War and during the Korean nuclear crisis in 1994, Japanese policymakers reluctantly offered support for the new agenda. The Bush administration made clear that alliances were less important than coalitions of willing partners ready to join in meeting the new dangers. Not only did the United States want Japan's participation in the out-of-area campaigns, it wanted a much tighter, proactive cooperation and a realignment of U.S. forces that would integrate Japan into a global strategy for the war on terrorism. The impact of all these developments on Japan was huge.

The war on terrorism foreshadowed profound changes in the way the post–Cold War international system would function and increased the fundamental uncertainty of the interregnum in East Asia. While the contours of the future remained ill-defined, it was difficult for Japan to make firm choices about its foreign policy. What would it take to precipitate the emergence of a clear new regional structure, and what role should Japan play in its formation?

The rise of China as a great power and the purpose to which China would put its new power would be critical determinants of a new East Asian regional order. The future role of the United States in Asia, and the durability of the U.S.-Japan alliance, would also be fundamental to the distribution of power in the region. It is difficult to predict what catalytic event might trigger the emergence of a new international order, but one possibility stands out: resolution of the stand-off on the Korean Peninsula.

THE PIVOTAL ROLE OF KOREA'S FUTURE

The outcome of the Korean issue has the potential to reshape the regional order in fundamental ways. A reunified Korea would force the great powers to deal with a powerful new state with a revised international orientation. It would be a state of considerable strategic importance. Would a unified Korea remain allied with the United States? If so, what would be the reaction of China? If it were nonaligned, could Japan feel secure? A host of questions with critical strategic implications are raised by the possibilities of a reborn Korean state.

Japan has a huge stake in the outcome of unification because it will determine the fundamental nature of its strategic relationship with its closest neighbor. But more is at stake for Japan than its future relations with Korea. So central is the issue of Korean unification to the future structure of international relations in the region that it will bear heavily on Japan's relations with the other major powers whose interests intersect on the Korean Peninsula. Of greatest concern is the future of relations with the United States. How and under what circumstances unification takes place, the role of Japan in the process, and the outcome of unification will profoundly influence the shape of the U.S.-Japan alliance. A postunification U.S.-Korean alliance and a continued U.S. military presence on the peninsula would reassure Japan that a unified Korea would be disposed to improve ties with Japan. The postunification status of U.S. forces in Korea is bound to have ripple effects on the U.S. military presence in Japan, which may end up being reduced and reconfigured—although Japan will likely wish for it to continue.

The course that unification takes will also bear importantly on Japan's relations with China and Russia. A unified Korea that tilted toward China or even stood equidistant between China and Japan would complicate Japan's future strategic position. In the first post–Cold War decade, China developed a significant relationship with Seoul—and it has to be remembered that throughout much of Korea's history prior to the twentieth century, Korea was part of the Sinocentric order. This relationship adds to the complexity of Japanese policymaking. In some respects, it gives Japan an incentive to improve its relations with Russia, which may have a similar interest in diluting China's role in a unified Korea.

As Nishihara Masashi, president of Japan's National Defense Academy, explained in 1996, "Japan seeks a united Korea that is friendly to Tokyo and Washington, that is economically viable and politically open, and that will allow token U.S. presence to remain."[2] A unified Korea that retains nuclear weapons, tilts toward China, refuses to countenance a continued security relationship with the United States that includes some continuing U.S. military presence, and/or is resolutely hostile toward Japan in its vision of the future would represent a major foreign policy defeat for Japan and a critical problem for the nation's future.

In the past, the Japanese have tended to be deeply ambivalent about Korean unification. On the one hand, a strong united Korean state could entail political and economic problems and competition; on the other, a continuation of a divided Korea extends the life of an unpredictable state that presents a security threat. In some respects, because the nature of re-unification has been so uncertain in its implications for Japan's interests, Japanese policymakers have often privately preferred a continuation of the status quo. Given the difficulty of peacefully achieving the kind of united Korea that they favored, most Japanese policymakers quietly concluded that their wisest course was not to hasten unification, but rather to maintain the status quo of a divided Korea for as long as possible. This strategy meant supporting U.S. policies of deterrence, attempting to contain tensions, fostering cordial ties with South Korea, and promoting policies that pursue a gradual reconciliation rather than a rapid and potentially violent reunification.

A failed state unable to serve the minimal needs of its people, the Democratic People's Republic of Korea (DPRK), or North Korea, has regime survival as its first priority and resists reforms and increased external contacts. Its long-term viability is doubtful. A change of its political system may be gradual and evolutionary, or it may come through radical upheaval. Broadly seen, two reunification scenarios are possible: (1) the absorption of North Korea into the Republic of Korea (ROK) as a by-product of Pyong-yang's collapse, owing either to war or to internal implosion, civil discord, or a massive humanitarian crisis; or (2) a gradual movement from North-South confrontation toward successful coexistence, and then to unification through negotiations.

Either of these possibilities could unfold with many variations. The unification of Korea may prove a protracted process. It is possible that North Korea will succeed in muddling through and sustain the status quo of a heavily armed standoff with South Korea, but it is also possible that the two states will succeed in finding a peaceful coexistence. Widely held anticipation among foreign observers in the mid-1990s of a potential North Korean collapse was overdrawn. Foreign observers have often underrated the staying power of the DPRK, which stems from its pervasive nationalist mindset and totalitarian controls, sustained by a century of isolation. Some kind of "grand bargain" that will establish a modus vivendi of the DPRK with its neighbors is possible. Over time, a phased reunification might take place. Still, while a soft landing for the North is plausible, there is also the strong possibility that in the intermediate future reunification may come about through war, through collapse of the DPRK, or through its absorption by the ROK.

Although it has critical interests at stake, Japan labors under multiple constraints that make it difficult to take the lead in resolving the complex issues involved in Korea. Tokyo finds its policy options limited by many historic legacies and complex strategic considerations. The underdeveloped character of Japan's military-strategic institutions, the burden of a long and troubled history of Japanese-Korean relations, and the need to defer to U.S. policy all keep Japan from developing a proactive policy. In keeping with its historic pattern, Japan is therefore more likely to be adaptive, accommodating to the changing circumstances in a cautious and incremental fashion until the outcome is clearer.

Japan's position is delicate. It cannot afford to resist unification. Moreover, in the potential scenarios for unification, Japanese cooperation with the United States is essential. U.S. leadership in resolving strategic issues on the peninsula remains indispensable, although successful U.S. initiatives will require a skillful policy coordination with Japan that takes account of its interests and sensibilities. A collapse of North Korea would immediately draw Japan into uncharted waters. Japan's involvement in coping with the uncertainties and the humanitarian crisis that such a collapse would entail would be unavoidable. Japan would be expected by the international community to provide economic assistance, including giving the long-deferred reparations to the North for the colonial period, to support the growth and prosperity of a unified Korea. At the same time, the Koreans would be highly sensitive to the way in which this assistance was provided and suspicious of any sign that it would give Japan significant long-term influence on the peninsula. The resources that Japan would bring to bear and the role it played would go a long way toward determining an enduring settlement on the peninsula and achieving a stable new order in Northeast Asia.

Resolution of Korea's future would trigger a full-scale rethinking of the role of the United States in Asia. It would require addressing the logic of the U.S.-ROK alliance, the U.S. military presence on the peninsula, and beyond that, the future character of the U.S.-Japan alliance. After the Cold War, the divided Korea was the principal justification for the forward deployment of 100,000 U.S. troops in Japan and Korea. When the issues of a divided Korea are resolved, the pressures to drastically reduce the number of forward-deployed troops will be very strong. Many Koreans, Japanese, and Americans might wonder why there would be any further need for the alliances, let alone forward-deployed U.S. military forces. Much would depend on the perception of China's power and purpose at that time. It is quite possible that nationalist sentiment in Korea would reject a postunification U.S. security role on the peninsula. Some Japanese might consider the unification of Korea as an opportune time to phase out the U.S. military presence in Japan as well. Finally, the United States itself might well consider the settlement of the divided Koreas an opportune time to drastically scale back its security commitments in the region.

On the other hand, a unified Korea might seek a continued security connection with the United States, the most distant of the major powers, as a necessary means of fortifying its independence vis-à-vis its powerful neighbors. The United States might be willing to perpetuate the alliance with Korea, while greatly reducing the base structure and deployments, as a means of supporting a strong ally and helping to forestall a future Korean bid for nuclear weapons. Japan should welcome such a decision, because continued defense links between Washington and Seoul could diminish the lure of possible security ties between Korea and China. Also, even a modest U.S. military presence on the peninsula should help to sustain political support in Japan for some residual U.S. presence, perhaps naval arrangements at Yokosuka. China has traditionally opposed foreign military bases on the Asian mainland. Thus, although China will be wary of a continued U.S. presence, it might conceivably be persuaded to accept a U.S. military role in Korea if it were slimmed down and confined geographically to areas well away from China's border. Even China might eventually conclude that a Korea loosely aligned with the United States would help to both stabilize the peninsula and contain Japanese inclinations for a more independent role. This, too, would depend on the state of U.S.-China relations at that point.

It will be especially important to ensure that a unified Korea is a non-nuclear state. Japan has a huge interest in encouraging this outcome, for despite its long-standing policy and the sentiments of its people, Tokyo would find it difficult to resist acquiring nuclear weapons of its own if a united Korea were to develop them or obtain them from a failed North Korea. North Korean possession of nuclear weapons was characterized in 2003 by Japan's former vice minister of foreign affairs as "a truly nightmarish and totally unacceptable development" that would subject Japan to "an agonizing choice between accepting the position of easy victim of nuclear blackmail or developing its own nuclear capacity, which would trigger internal turmoil in Japan." Such developments would cast a pall over Korean-Japanese relations and complicate the U.S. strategic position in Northeast Asia.[3]

THE UNITED STATES AS A BALANCER
IN A MULTIPOLAR ASIA

A substantial reduction of the U.S. military presence in the region would contribute to the emergence of a multipolar order in East Asia. The United States might do well to become an "engaged balancer," playing a role in Asia somewhat similar to England's historical role in Europe. To maintain the regional balance, in other words, the United States would attempt to stay on better terms with the Asian powers than they were with each other, intervening only if the balance of power seemed in jeopardy.[4]

It would be difficult, however, to serve as a *distant* balancer. U.S. interests in the region are too important, and regional instability is likely to continue in the absence of significant international institutions to maintain an equilibrium. The United States, hampered by the influence that domestic politics has in foreign policymaking, has never been skillful at engaging or re-engaging on a flexible basis. Should the United States substantially disengage from the region, whether from budgetary pressures, trade disillusionments, isolationist sentiment, or preoccupation with terrorism, Japan could face a defining moment. U.S. disengagement would likely in itself exacerbate instability in the region, and Japan would be compelled to rethink its strategic position.

If Chinese regional ascendancy seemed likely, it would be in keeping with Japan's pragmatic traditions to achieve a beneficial relationship with China that ensured Japan's security and replaced the U.S.-Japan alliance. Japan's tradition of realism could lead it to cut a deal with an ascendant China and decide to coexist. The Japanese could achieve a modus vivendi with China that stopped short of bandwagoning—a choice that might be unavoidable for smaller regional states. As it did historically in the Sinocentric world, Japan could preserve its political independence and its own autonomous system. It could reserve the option of militarization to keep the pressures of Chinese regional hegemony from becoming stifling. Because of the threat that Japan could easily convert its civilian technologies to weapons production, including the nuclear option, some such Japanese grand bargain with Chinese regional hegemony is conceivable.

However, if the United States remains deeply engaged in East Asia and committed to maintaining a balance of power, a continuation of the U.S.-Japan alliance in a more symmetrical arrangement seems likely. America's long-term engagement in Asia is required to protect U.S. economic interests. There is legitimate concern in Washington that East Asia might create its own economic bloc that would include preferential trade arrangements and a regional monetary fund. Indeed, incipient moves to establish an Asian free-trade area have surfaced against the backdrop of APEC's weakness. In light of European and U.S. efforts to accelerate economic integration in their own regions, it is not surprising to find that pan-Asian momentum for regional cooperation is picking up. Still, U.S. economic interests would oppose any decision that would exclude the United States from an important role in ensuring that regional trade remains open.

The most challenging task for the United States in the role of an engaged balancer would be the skillful management of the strategic triangle of U.S.-China-Japan relations and especially the growing power of China. Although China is certainly the Asian country with the greatest potential to emerge as a rival of the United States at some future time, it cannot be a realistic military competitor of the United States for decades. In any comparative sense, its nuclear deterrent is limited. Much of its defense equipment is outdated, it has no real Asian allies, its capacity to project power over distance is still modest, and it is well behind in the revolution in military affairs. Though China's economic development has been swift, its leaders face formidable political challenges. Future growth prospects demand a continued commitment to a policy of reform and openness. China's stake in open world trade and its entry into the WTO appear to have reinforced its commitment to multilateral trading rules. China recognizes the value of its access to U.S. markets and investors.

Although Chinese leaders are inclined to caution and moderation and remain focused on near-term problems, in the long run the possibilities are open-ended. In one fashion or another, the rise of China will alter fundamentally the distribution of power in the region in ways that will require changes in the nature and governance of the system. By virtue of its relative size and resources, not to mention its historic traditions, a strengthened China could lay claim to a kind of natural hegemony in the region. If it continues substantial growth and maintains political unity, a modernized China would likely challenge the long-standing commitment of the United States to maintain a balance of power and to prevent any other power from exercising regional hegemony. As its growth continues, China may become less dependent on trade, but it will be able to use the sheer size of its market to influence other nations.

Looking forward to that time when China's natural hegemony might become a reality, the United States will need a new strategy to pursue its goals in the region. The most important of these should be to actively encourage the building of strong multilateral institutions in a region that lacks them. Historically, creating international institutions has served in the long run to further U.S. interests. At some cost to the diplomatic maneuverability of the United States and its visceral preference to exercise its influence through resort to unilateral use of its power, the formation of regional institutions could serve to embed American values of democracy, human rights, and free trade in the region. In this way, the United States could extend its influence even after its power relative to other Asian countries had diminished.

The role of the United States as the most distant of the major powers, as the "regent" in the present regional interregnum, is essential to the prospect of building a framework of international order. The lack of international institutions in Asia, the weaknesses of those that exist, and the inexperience of Asians with multilateralism all offer the opportunity for the United States to use its regental power not only to provide the public goods of security and market access, but also to take a proactive role in building new international institutions for the Asia Pacific.

THE FUTURE OF THE U.S.-JAPAN ALLIANCE

The character and durability of the U.S.-Japan alliance will be a critical determinant of a new order in the region. With the global war on terrorism taking priority, the United States may undertake further initiatives to revise and restructure the alliance in terms of partnership and reciprocity. These initiatives will have an immense influence on Japan's role in the region. In a multipolar Asia in which the Korean issue was resolved and the United States moved toward the role of engaged balancer, the U.S.-Japan alliance, if it survived, would necessarily be markedly different from the one that existed during the Cold War. The Mutual Security Treaty was the price Japan paid to regain its sovereignty; defense cooperation was not a matter of free choice. The alliance was not of Japan's own choosing; rather, it was the result of defeat and occupation. Japan was therefore bound to accept a subordinate role in the alliance. Nevertheless, weakness was turned to Japan's advantage. The United States provided security guarantees, unimpeded access to a huge market, protection of the sea lanes for imported raw materials, a bonanza of economic and technological assistance, and acquiescence in building a highly protected home market. There was little cooperation between the U.S. military stationed in Japan and Japan's Self-Defense Forces—no integration, no joint command, no inter-operability, and limited consultation.

The alliance served to reassure Japan's neighbors that it would not rearm as an independent power. But it also left Japan with the option to return to an independent and sovereign stance if and when the alliance was terminated. That is, in contrast to Germany, which chose to engage itself in a multilateral framework of economic and security obligations, through NATO and the European Union, that would limit its future options and thus reassure its neighbors, Japan resisted any such engagement and instead bound itself in a series of self-abnegating restrictions. While forswearing all military involvements, by choosing to bind itself rather than becoming enmeshed in a web of multilateral institutions Japan preserved its autonomy for future contingencies.[5]

Once the Cold War ended, the terms of the grand bargain that underlay the alliance became outmoded. Even before it ended, in fact, the terms were subject to growing tensions owing to Japan's growing economic strength. Americans resented the unilateral security guarantees, the absence of substantial defense cooperation, and the flouting of liberal trade principles from which Japan drew such obvious advantage.

The anomalous nature of the alliance was evident in the way the allies conceived their relations. The purpose of the alliance was not only to defend but also to restrain Japan. The top U.S. Marine Corps general in Japan, in 1990, told a *Washington Post* correspondent that U.S. troops must remain in Japan at least until the beginning of the twenty-first century, in large part because "no one wants a rearmed, resurgent Japan. So we are a cap in the bottle, if you will."[6] The Japanese chafed at the constant deference to U.S. foreign policy positions and the damage to national pride that such deference—and the presence of garrisoned foreign troops on their soil—inflicted. Resentment provoked by such suppression of nationalism was never far from the surface. In a frequently recounted incident, LDP leader Shiina Etsusaburō in Diet proceedings once referred to the garrisoned U.S. troops as "the watchdogs at the gate" (*banken*) guarding Japan. When another Diet member questioned Shiina about whether it was not rude and insulting to refer to the Americans as "dogs," Shiina, in mock apology, responded, "Excuse me. They are honorable watchdogs at the gate" (*banken-sama*).

In the face of the incongruity apparent in the U.S. provision of security for such an economically powerful competitor, Japanese leaders took steps to defuse U.S. anger. In 1978, the Japanese government, without any legal basis, began paying an increasing amount of the expenditures for maintaining the bases. The director of the Defense Agency, Kanemaru Shin, coined the patronizing term "sympathy budget" (*omoiyari yosan*) to show the government's "consideration" for the U.S. forces. This budget eventually grew to an annual sum of $5 billion. Although it was not used to pay the personnel costs of the U.S. military forces, which would have made them mercenaries, still the Americans took umbrage at the term. During a visit to Japan in 2000, Undersecretary of State Strobe Talbot expressed indignation, telling LDP politicians that the U.S. forces were not in Japan for "charity."[7] Such incidents bespoke the anomalous nature of the grand bargain that underlay the alliance during the Cold War.

If the alliance is to survive, it must achieve a new, efficient, and equitable division of labor that serves the interests of both countries. Japan and the United States view the character and purpose of the alliance in the new era in different ways. The Americans are relatively clear, forthright, and forceful in their vision of its future role. From an American perspective, the alliance should be expanded to maintain regional stability and to serve in the global war on terrorism. Inasmuch as the China-Japan-U.S. triangle provides the core of the regional balance, to close down the alliance with Japan would open up new questions about Japan's strategic posture that would likely jeopardize regional stability. It would throw Tokyo back on its own resources, leading to a substantial increase in its independent force capability and possibly to a strategic rivalry with Beijing. However, it is also conceivable that an independent Japan would be impelled to reach a strategic accommodation with China that would undermine long-term U.S. goals in the Pacific. Thus, even if the issue of Korean reunification is resolved, a U.S.-Japan alliance will be in the U.S. interest for its contribution to regional stability.

A bipartisan report in October 2000 coauthored by Richard Armitage, subsequently deputy secretary of state in the Bush administration, and Joseph Nye, assistant secretary of defense in the Clinton administration, proposed that America's "special relationship" with the United Kingdom should serve as a model for the alliance with Japan. The Armitage Report, as it came to be known, described the alliance as "the keystone of . . . U.S. involvement in Asia" and as "central to America's global security strategy." The report outlined ways in which the alliance could be made much tighter. It emphasized Japan's need to reform its political-economic system in ways that would permit much greater Japanese activism in promoting liberal ideals at home and abroad. It also called for revising the prohibition on Japan's participation in collective self-defense and for lifting limitations on its participation in UN peacekeeping missions. It sought greater integration of roles, missions, and eventually even of forces; the sharing of intelligence and military technology; and a commitment to systems interoperability. In short, it sought a Japan fully committed to a bilateral internationalist agenda.

Subsequently, as deputy secretary of state, Armitage did not hesitate to articulate what the Americans wanted. After the terrorist attacks of September 11, 2001, when Operation Enduring Freedom was organized to take down the Taliban in Afghanistan, Armitage called in the Japanese ambassador to say that the United States expected Japan to "show the flag"; and when the invasion of Iraq began, the United States asked for Japanese "boots on the ground." On many occasions, both Secretary of State Colin Powell and Armitage suggested a U.S. desire for a Japanese constitutional amendment to make an unambiguous commitment to collective defense.

Not surprisingly, the Armitage Report—and its distinctly paternal tone—evoked deep ambivalence among Japanese leaders. They welcomed U.S. attention to the security links with Japan, but they worried about the agenda. Although Great Britain and Japan do have some similarities—the obvious ones being that both are democratic trading nations located off the Eurasian landmass—the dissimilarities are legion. England and the United States share a common political heritage that has evidenced itself in a century of common international aspirations. For Japan's conservatives, however, the Anglo-American political ideals have often been anathema. Democracy is not an indigenous phenomenon that Japan has ever sought to export. The Japanese have not achieved a democratic revolution on their own; it is not in their life's blood. These were not values the Japanese themselves had struggled for and made their own. As the movie director Kurosawa Akira wrote in his autobiography, "The freedom and democracy of the postwar era were not things I had fought for and won; they were granted to me by powers beyond my own."[8]

England, a nuclear power and a permanent member of the UN Security Council, is "partner of first choice" when the United States decides to intervene militarily around the world. British leaders typically enjoy a solid parliamentary majority and are accustomed to asserting a lead in international security issues. Japan, lacking nuclear weapons and permanent membership on the Security Council, still distrusted by its neighbors, in every way the junior partner in the alliance, positioned in a region of far greater uncertainty than England's in Europe, cannot in the foreseeable future hope to share a truly balanced and symmetrical relationship with the United States. The Japanese consequently worry that if Washington uses the model of security cooperation with London as the benchmark for what it expects of Tokyo, Japan will face a host of unwelcome and troubling choices.

Japanese anxiety over U.S. unilateralism grew in the aftermath of 9/11 and the enunciation of the Bush doctrine of preemption. Morimoto Satoshi, a thoughtful adviser to the government on foreign policy and security affairs, expressed the overwhelming Japanese worry: "[There is] the clear emergence of the United States' unilateralism as the sole superpower and the increasing domination and hegemony in its interaction with other countries. . . . We are faced with a difficult challenge: to incorporate U.S. unilateralism into broader trends of multilateralism and regionalism, and persuade it to act in harmony with them."[9] Many Japanese feared that a closer alliance relationship would draw them, as the junior partner, into supporting a U.S. agenda that would deprive them of their autonomous approach and complicate the independent pursuit of their own interests, particularly in Asia.

Despite the proposed sharing of power with Japan that the Armitage Report recommended, the Japanese leaders do not wish to be hostage to the demands of U.S. foreign policy any more than necessary. The model of the special relationship with Great Britain is not persuasive to Tokyo. To regard the relationship with Japan as one that could become like the UK model in the foreseeable future misreads Japan's strategic approach to international affairs and its role in the international system.

The Japanese are indeed wary, as Kissinger put it, of being "invited to share burdens based on concepts devised in Washington and transmitted to Tokyo as received truth."[10] But they lack a long-term vision of their own to communicate. Instead, characteristically, they are disposed to observe the unfolding trends in the international system before making their choices. And yet the alliance remains of the greatest consequence to Japan's future. There is no other potential ally with which Japan can join in the foreseeable future to fortify its security. Having only begun to build a new security structure, Japan finds the U.S. alliance essential for at least the near term. Although there is in Japan a sentiment that favors a deeper involvement in Asia's new multilateral institutions, these institutions remain weak, and engagement of Asia alone is no substitute for the security guarantees and market access that the U.S.-Japan alliance ensures. As one prominent strategist in Japan, cautioning against an "impetuous Asianism," wrote, "It is vital not to damage the bedrock of the bilateral alliance on which the fate of this nation rests."[11] The alliance is a cornerstone not only of Japan's foreign policy but also of its domestic political structure. Any fundamental change in its nature will have ripple effects through the entire Japanese system.

Nevertheless, Japanese conservatives do not share the same foreign policy imperatives as Washington does. They will seek to expand their autonomy even as they do what is required to maintain the alliance. Characteristically, they approach the American vision of the international system with a substantial amount of psychological distance, trying to determine how Japan might best relate to that system to advance its own interests. Japanese leaders are not prepared to say a priori what they want or where they stand. Although they aspire to be more assertive, there is little evidence of success in developing internally generated goals and purpose. In 2002, a senior official of the Foreign Ministry charged with long-range policy planning wrote:

Management of the alliance was simpler under the quasi-wartime conditions of the Cold War era. Now we have to decide what kind of alliance will best serve the current "peacetime" situation. In Japan's case, furthermore, the nation itself is at a turning point. While the Japanese people are groping for a new national image, circumstances are pushing us to articulate once again the character of the nation. As we formulate that image, *we must stop regarding the international environment as a predetermined condition to which we are supposed to respond as deftly as possible.* Instead Japan must aim at becoming a major player in the world, equipped with its own well-formulated vision of an international order that is compatible with its national interests. Japan must decide for itself what has to be done to make that vision reality. For that, I believe the major task is deciding how to make use of the Japan-U.S. alliance to the greatest advantage.[12]

The Japanese want to formulate a new, self-generated strategic vision, gain self-mastery and autonomy, and shape a new self-image, but there is little sign that such goals will readily emerge from domestic sources alone. History suggests that Japanese leaders will more likely take their cues from the unfolding international system.

Japan and the United States historically have had an entirely different experience of the international system. The Americans themselves shaped the international system and brought their values and national experience to its making. For nearly the whole of Japan's modern history, it has acted in a system made by the Anglo-American powers and manifesting their liberal beliefs. While adapting to this reality, Japan did so within a powerful conservative tradition that was embedded in their national life. From this conservative perspective, America's triumphalism since the collapse of communism has not been altogether pleasant. Japan had experienced it before—in 1918 and 1945. Flushed with victory, convinced of the impregnability of their values, the Americans were seen to be self-righteous and intolerant of other cultures. Although Japanese conservatives see no realistic alternative to U.S. military power to maintain international stability, in their heart of hearts they retained a distaste for the dogmatic assertions of international liberalism and its justification for interventionism and unilateralism.

Most of the Japanese elite of the postwar generation remains deeply ambivalent about the view of their history imposed by the Tokyo War Crimes Tribunal. The Greater East Asia War, as conservatives call it, cannot be so easily attributed, they believe, solely to Japanese militarism. It was the West's original intrusion into Asia that led Japan to arm and expand to defend itself. The attack on Pearl Harbor was a desperate act by a Japan driven into a corner by U.S. ultimatums. Other countries had their empires; Britain and the United States did not give up their imperial privileges in China until 1943. The war, they invariably conclude, did succeed in ending Western imperialism.

The war's ending, in their view, was a cruel bombing of a country already looking for a mediated settlement. How is it, many conservatives ask, that the Americans would not apologize for Hiroshima and Nagasaki? They regard the war crimes trials as victor's justice, one-sided and biased in their verdicts. Many conservatives acknowledge that the military may have committed acts in Asia for which the Japanese should apologize, but they bristle at their neighbors' interference in how the Japanese teach their own history. They point out that Chinese leaders themselves have not come to an honest assessment of the crimes committed as a result of the Maoist policies of China's past. Japanese leaders resent the unwillingness of Koreans to acknowledge the positive contributions made by Japanese colonial rule. Through such reasoning, much of the postwar conservative elite harbors resentment toward foreign views of Japan's war guilt.

THE CHANGING NATURE OF ELITE POLITICS

There was no mastermind to meet the challenge of accommodating to Japan's changing post–Cold War environment—no Meiji oligarchs, no Yoshida Shigeru, no political party with a coherent strategic vision or definition of national purpose. Nor were there any transcendent ideals to point the way. Still, there were leaders steeped in the conservative traditions who understood that the end of the old international order would require a change of course. They would take up where Nakasone's effort had failed. Among them, Ozawa Ichirō stands out.

For a time, it appeared Ozawa might fill the role of masterminding the accommodation to a new order. He grasped immediately the implications that the end of the bipolar order would have for Japanese foreign policy and domestic institutions and for the survival of the political class. "We have to change in order to remain the same," he wrote.[13] He offered a sweeping vision of how Japan should adapt to the new era. But the times were too uncertain, the clash of forces in domestic politics too unresolved, the new external order too indeterminate, to bring forth successful new leadership. Ozawa moved boldly, gambling his future in various strategies to shape a new coalition of reform forces, but repeatedly he was frustrated and overwhelmed by the confused and troubled times in Japanese politics. The prime ministership eluded him.

After a succession of eight bland and ineffectual prime ministers in the 1990s, a colorful and determined reformer (with a distinctive Beethoven-style hairdo and a love of opera, Elvis, and heavy metal) won the office in 2001. Koizumi Junichirō had support from LDP rank-and-file members who feared that rising popular frustration would doom their party. With consistent popular appeal, he held the prime ministership for five years, longer than anyone since Satō Eisaku (1964–1972). Although a longtime member of the LDP, with family conservative credentials that included three generations of service in the Diet, he turned on the entrenched interests in his own party, promising to "respect no sacred cows" and to pursue an agenda of deregulation, privatization, democratization, destruction of factional dominance, and constitutional reform.

Koizumi had no grand design as Nakasone had, and he laid out no well-articulated agenda as Ozawa had, but his efforts to bring about reform were more successful than theirs. He was able to capitalize on the public's growing frustration with the economic doldrums, the gridlock in politics, the corruption in the bureaucracy, and the resistance to reform among entrenched interests. A brilliant communicator and a skilled political tactician, he succeeded in building popular support for change and turned in a stunning electoral triumph in 2005. His success demonstrated that elite politics were changing in three fundamental ways that promised to make foreign policymaking more complex and unpredictable: Public opinion is becoming more important, the balance between bureaucrats and politicians is shifting, and generational change is underway.[14]

Despite the continuity of many aspects of elitism, there are unmistakable signs that the democratic elements of the Japanese political system will be more intrusive in foreign policymaking in the future than they were in the past. In most societies, the foreign policy decisions are to a great extent the prerogative of a small number of leaders, and in Japan the elite historically had extraordinary latitude to chart the nation's course in the world. Prior to World War II, decisionmaking was a function of contention and consensus within and among elites. Articulate public opinion sometimes helped to structure their debates, and it could influence the parameters within which policy was made, but the mass mood was led and shaped by the elite and for the most part was amorphous. Moreover, the elite preserved its policymaking autonomy by mobilizing nationalism. The political myth of the emperor system encouraged submission to the authority of the central political institutions of society. The elite still made the critical decisions that were required to compete with other societies. Culture and nationalism legitimated the policy autonomy of the state.

Similarly, after 1945, although the mass mood of war weariness, isolationism, and pacifism set the bounds within which the Yoshida Doctrine was forged, the elites had extraordinary freedom to manage both domestic and foreign policy. Despite the democratic institutions imposed by the Occupation, successive decades of LDP rule only muted the influence of domestic politics on foreign policy. The Diet, ostensibly the highest policymaking body in Japan, provided a buffer for this elite. Working closely with business leaders, conservative politicians and bureaucrats managed Japan's neo-mercantilist foreign policy with little intrusion from public opinion. In the 1990s, however, as Japanese political institutions floundered in the face of the economic and political problems facing the nation, voter identification with the parties dropped precipitously. Voters responded to populist appeals, and fresh, independent, reformist proposals drew much greater support.

A second, related change in elite politics is the increasing influence of professional politicians. Beginning in the 1990s, several factors made the political process more responsive to electoral politics, including a sharp decline in party loyalty among voters; growing disenchantment with backroom politics, corruption, and policy failures; and electoral reforms that encouraged a more issue-oriented politics and the proliferation of voluntaristic organizations. A new breed of young politicians who were more attuned to popular issues took advantage of the disarray in the bureaucracy to seize the initiative. The balance between the bureaucrats and politicians is shifting as the latter gain increased weight in the policy process.

This development is closely but not exclusively related to the unsettled external environment. Bureaucrats are most valuable when there is consensus about long-range policy goals, when precedents are already set, and when the situation requires efficient implementation. Their technocratic expertise was effective in the sheltered environment provided by the U.S. security guarantee during the Cold War. Industrial policy that entailed substantial government involvement in managing the economy and economic foreign policy was the purview of technocrats in the elite ministries and was almost always beyond the reach of public scrutiny. The leading role of the bureaucracy and the remarkable policy autonomy that it possessed were legitimated not only by traditional values but by the meritocratic principles that governed its recruitment.

In the new era, Japan is no longer shielded from the Sturm und Drang of international politics. The drift of international events will mandate policies that encompass political-strategic issues as well as economic ones. This will require a political elite capable of shaping a new definition of Japan's role in the world acceptable to domestic opinion and congruent with the realities of the external environment. The bureaucrats are not disposed to bring about an institutional revolution. They are not prepared to deal with rearmament and alliance politics, constitutional revision, and the reorganization of the political-economic infrastructure. As a new structure of international order takes shape in the region, pressures from the outside to deal with political-strategic issues will mount. Japan will become fully engaged in the international politics of a conflict-prone era and will be compelled to adopt a political role, to make difficult choices, and to develop a greatly expanded strategic policy. In an uncertain context, without an established consensus to unify public opinion and elite goals, bureaucratic authority will be weakened and the technocrats will have to give way, at least in part, to the professional politicians.

Finally, a third change in elite politics is the emergence of a new generation of political leadership. One of the main factors driving Koizumi's initial popularity in 2001 was the generational change under way in the nation's leadership. When Hirohito died in 1989, the same year that the Cold War ended, the Showa period of his reign (1926–1989) came to an end and the new emperor, Akihito, began his reign. The name Akihito chose for the era of his rule was Heisei, a term referring to peace at home and abroad. The new generation of the Heisei era was strongly behind Koizumi's reform agenda. Koizumi's unusual decision to make his cabinet appointments irrespective of factional politics and to reach policy decisions more independent of LDP councils reflected the predilection of younger party members. Likewise, his appointment of five women—an unprecedented number—to his first cabinet, including the sharp-tongued Tanaka Makiko as foreign minister, further demonstrated his disposition to break with traditional politics.

Young Japanese coming to maturity in the Heisei years are experiencing the kind of decisive change that often gives rise to a new political generation. Born in the 1960s and 1970s, they have no living memory of the war and Occupation. History is much less of a burden for them than it was for their parents. Unlike the progressives of the postwar generation, members of the Heisei generation do not feel guilt or remorse for Japan's imperial past; nor are they defensive about Japan's traditional political values. The issues that divided postwar politics have now receded. Ito Joichi, a young Internet entrepreneur and venture capitalist born in 1966, wrote in 2005, on the sixtieth anniversary of the atomic bombings:

> The bombings don't really matter to me, or, for that matter, to most Japanese of my generation. My peers and I have little hatred or blame in our hearts for the Americans. . . . My grandparents' generation remembers the suffering, but tries to forget it. My parents' generation still does not trust the military. The pacifist stance of that generation comes in great part from the mistrust of the Japanese military. . . . For my generation, the Hiroshima and Nagasaki bombings and the war in general now represent the equivalent of a cultural "game over" or "reset" button. Through a combination of conscious policy and unconscious culture, the painful memories and images of the war have lost their context, surfacing only as twisted echoes in our subculture. The result, for better and worse, is that 60 years after Hiroshima, we dwell more on the future than the past.[15]

The old Left-Right axis of the Cold War period is irrelevant to the new generation.

The Heisei generation, which emerged after Japan was widely recognized as having caught up with the West, is more at home in the world than any earlier generation in modern Japan.[16] The century-long pursuit of equality with the West has not shaped their psychological makeup, with all that that pursuit once entailed in terms of anxiety over status and feelings of inferiority toward their own culture. At the same time, owing to the rising power of other Asian countries and their importance to Japanese interests, members of the Heisei generation are less prone to the instinctive paternalism and sense of superiority that their elders felt toward other Asians. Typically, having studied and traveled abroad, they are less constrained by traditional practices and mores. Instead, they are attuned to the lifestyle changes brought on by globalization and technological change.

They constitute the first generation whose entire schooling has been under the democratic principles mandated by the Fundamental Law of Education of 1947, which the Occupation drafted. During their life span, there has been a growing understanding and acceptance of the fundamental notions of democratic government, albeit in a distinctly Japanese form. Postwar high-school textbooks at first explained democratic values in a way that blurred respect for hierarchy and individualism, but more recently they have been clearer in explaining the concepts of democracy and human rights. As one authority wrote, although the explanations of individual dignity and human rights in the textbooks have changed over time, they still maintain a distinctly Japanese approach:

> At the end of the twentieth century, what has emerged in Japanese textbooks is a sense of communitarian democracy emphasizing social rights. They teach that the central idea of democracy is respect for individuals and protection of their fundamental human rights, and they clearly stress equality, not hierarchy. . . . But they do not encourage people to protect their rights against the government. Rather, they indicate that cooperation between the government and people is the key to bringing a just and fair society for all people. . . . The Japanese seem to be creating their own communitarian version of democracy. While rights should be observed because all people are worthy of respect . . . people are not encouraged to assert their rights against strong communitarian sentiments.[17]

This observation is very much in accord with the view of the legal scholar John Haley. Haley has argued that the spirit of Japanese law reflects the customs and norms of the community and that the Japanese Supreme Court interprets its role as protecting "the informal rules and norms evolved through time and accepted by tacit assent and community adherence."[18] Nevertheless, Japanese encouragement of an active defense of individual rights against government interference is still weak.

The degree to which Japan has absorbed the universal values of democracy and human rights as guiding principles for its foreign policy is debatable. During the Cold War, the values of international liberalism were given lip service by the conservative elite, but there is no persuasive evidence that they exercised substantial influence on policymaking. As a result, as Watanabe Akio, president of Japan's Research Institute on Peace and Security, wrote in 2001, "Japan is frequently criticized as having a foreign policy that is devoid of moral principles."[19] But in the post–Cold War period, Watanabe said, Japanese foreign policy is more congruent with the values of international liberalism. While not so openly assertive and high profile in its defense of human rights as the Americans or Europeans, the Japanese nevertheless have quietly made these values an important principle in their recent diplomacy with other Asian nations. Watanabe identified three characteristics of Japanese-style human rights diplomacy. It is nonconfrontational, pragmatic, and multilateral, he said, in its approach to human rights concerns. Still, one recalls Prime Minister Hosokawa's observation, while visiting Beijing in 1994, that it is wrong to try to impose Western concepts of human rights on other countries. Japan's official position seems characterized by ambiguity and a certain straddling of Asian and Western traditions.

Although democratic values may not have been wholly embraced in Japan, they still have made their mark on the Heisei generation. This generation is more tolerant than earlier generations of diversity and more inclined to respect individuality, freedom, autonomy, and civic-mindedness. The new breed of Heisei politicians is impatient with the earlier emphasis on homogeneity and with the institutions that stressed uniformity and disciplined practices of seniority, requiring the younger generation to defer to their elders. In some respects, they want Japanese institutions to be made more open, flexible, tolerant of diversity, and responsive to the international expectations associated with Japan's status as an advanced economy.

The growing restiveness of the Heisei generation of politicians has momentous implications. These politicians are impatient with the slow pace of change in economic restructuring, in developing a more assertive foreign policy, and in rethinking the constitution. Japan's systemic crisis and declining international prestige has fueled the generational consciousness of the younger politicians. This new breed is deeply interested in policy issues and willing to cross factional and party lines to meet a range of challenges and to develop their legislative agendas. Increasingly, they are prepared to confront bureaucratic resistance to their proposals. "In the old days, the bureaucrats drew up policy," said Takemi Keizō, an Upper House Diet member and one of the most self-conscious of the Heisei generation. "Now, we make the decisions and they have to implement them."[20] Younger members of the Diet are more likely to favor constitutional revision.[21] Disaffection from the old political-economic structure is evident in the election of young, independent, reform-minded governors in many prefectures.

Still, despite this widely acknowledged generational rebelliousness, it would be wrong to miss the elitist dimensions and continuities inherent in the political leadership of the Heisei generation. Many of its prominent members in the Diet are second- or third-generation politicians who have "inherited" their positions from relatives. They are not, for the most part, outsiders to the system. Despite their restlessness, they are still in the tradition of Japanese conservative politics. Although they are open to new influences and want to break with some of the old ways, they are not ideologues. Ideology, in fact, is nowhere in sight. Heisei leaders have yet to define clear new national goals or a sense of national purpose that might someday form the basis of a new national consensus. The status acquired by permanent membership on the Security Council, for example, seems more important to them than what might be accomplished once having become a permanent member.[22] They do not yet have common views on how the constitution should be revised.

Moreover, the extent of their attraction to internationalist influences should not be exaggerated. There are no signs that the Heisei generation wants to radically open Japan and challenge its deeply embedded insularity—an insularity that is still evident in Japan's resistance to foreign direct investment, refugees, and foreign residents. In fact, how this new generation of leaders chooses to deal with such issues as the treatment of foreign workers will be telling.[23] Increasing illegal immigration and a growing reliance on foreign labor for work that the Japanese themselves do not want to do have given rise to a national debate about the implications of "strangers in the land." On the one hand, Japan remains inhospitable to foreign residents. They tend to be shunned, and "because their status and position are unstable they tend to be shut out of Japanese society and discriminated against."[24] It is unclear whether the nation will be content with a "little Japan" that limits these outsiders or will seek to become a "big

Japan" that encourages guest workers—a choice that many observers say would work in the interests of economic dynamism.[25]

In any case, the new generation must decide such issues in the face of the new pressures of globalization. Thus far, in spite of their rebelliousness, they seem more in the tradition of modern conservative politics than they might at first seem. They are realists and pragmatists who instinctively believe that the trends of the time require adapting to the fundamentally changed conditions at home and abroad. Despite the increased power of politicians vis-à-vis the bureaucrats, the bureaucracy, with its prestige rooted in centuries of precedent, remains immensely powerful. The number of political appointees that a new prime minister can make is still small compared to the latitude given to a U.S. president. Thus, the Heisei generation will not only have to contend with the older generation of entrenched politicians, whose ties with the bureaucracy and special interests remain formidable obstacles to reform and change, they will also have to come to terms with the continuing power of the bureaucracy.

Ultimately, the reforms necessary to achieve a viable new political-economic structure will require establishment of a new consensus on national goals. As a late-developing nation, Japan could always perceive in the advanced industrial societies an image of the future to which it could adapt. For the first time in its modern history, Japan lacks a sense of national purpose. If past experience is any guide, the Heisei generation is more likely to redefine Japan's national purpose in response to its perception of the international environment than it is to come up with some innovative new formulation. What is significant thus far about the nascent generation is not a new ideology, but its openness to change; its pragmatic recognition that, in an uncertain international environment, past solutions to the nation's problems are no longer viable; and its readiness to adopt a new course.

JAPAN'S TWENTY-FIRST-CENTURY RESURGENCE

A s the 1990s unfolded and Japan seemed barely able to muddle through its time of troubles, Japan became almost a "forgotten player" in the international system.[1] But it would have been a great mistake to project Japan's future on the basis of this interlude. In retrospect, the fifteen-year period after the end of the Cold War appears as a time of transition. Japanese leaders were gauging the trends, assessing the appropriateness of Japan's institutions to the new conditions, debating the consequences, and achieving a consensus on a new course for the nation. Beneath the surface of confusion and aimlessness, support for reform gathered strength.

The prime ministership of Koizumi Junichirō (2001–2006) was the turning point when reform—that is, the adaptation of Japan's foreign policy and domestic institutions to its new environment—gained irreversible momentum. The reforms that Nakasone had failed to achieve in the 1980s, and that Ozawa had urged early in the 1990s, at last began to materialize. By 2006, when Koizumi chose to step down as prime minister, there were unmistakable signs that Japan had turned the corner in its economic recovery, that its politics were taking a new direction, and that its foreign policy strategy was on the verge of a sea change.

In a series of symbolic events during the last year of his tenure, Koizumi signaled the new direction he had set for the nation. In September 2005, following the Upper House defeat of his proposal to privatize the government's massive postal savings system, he called a snap election, framing it as a litmus test on reform, and won a stunning victory that ousted a large number of the LDP Diet members who had resisted his proposals. He and the other proponents of reform had won a convincing mandate for streamlining the government role in the economy. In July 2006, he made a high-profile visit to the White House (and flew on Air Force One with President George W. Bush to visit the Tennessee home of Koizumi's idol Elvis Presley), dramatizing the much tighter alliance relationship with the United States that he had established. On August 15, the anniversary of Japan's surrender, in the face of intense Chinese and Korean protests, he worshipped at the Yasukuni Shrine, demonstrating his determination that Japan take a self-assertive stance in international politics. Finally, in September 2006 he passed leadership to a new, young prime minister, Abe Shinzo, marking the ascendance of the Heisei generation.

REFORMING JAPANESE CAPITALISM

During the fifteen-year period from 1991, when the Cold War ended and the bubble burst, to 2006, when Koizumi left office, Japanese business and government leaders struggled to determine how to bring the nation's institutions and practices into sync with the globalization of capitalism and its attendant new technological paradigm. Deeply entrenched interests contended with a gathering will for change. Even in the face of prolonged economic decline, the forces of resistance were powerful and determined. But the severity of the crisis and the pressure of the market were unrelenting. The appeal to privatize and deregulate fit the demands of the information technology for greater flexibility. The U.S. model was seductive because of its responsiveness to the increased mobility of capital and corporate activity. Japanese policymakers intensely debated the extent and nature of reform, endlessly arguing the calculation of costs and benefits. It was a time marked by experimentation and by trial and error in adjusting and innovating. The old Japanese economic model had to change. Japan had to become more open and integrated into the global economy. At the same time, the weight of Japanese social values in which Japanese economic institutions were embedded dictated a measured and continuous pattern of adjustment and reform. The long-term employment system, stable supplier networks, and close government-industry ties reflected the value placed on personal and cooperative relationships—relationships the Japanese were instinctively loath to sacrifice.

Thus, what was required for the world's second-greatest economy was not a break with the past, but rather, the adjustment and reshaping of its existing institutions, along with policy innovations to fit the new circumstances. In automobiles, electronics, and other manufacturing, Japanese industries continued to be world-class leaders. Japan was overall abreast of other countries in its technology and science. It had a highly educated workforce, the world's healthiest population, remarkable degrees of social integration, and cooperative patterns within its corporate world. Its economic model still had many proven strengths.

During this period of economic uncertainty and stagnation, institutional reform proceeded incrementally and differentially. The rhetoric of economic reform often seemed to imply emulation of the American liberal model, but the reality was rather a pattern of innovation that followed a distinctive Japanese logic in which "the trajectory of change [was] strongly shaped by existing institutions."[2] While some corporations made significant innovations, others concluded that their past practices were still valid. Toyota, for example, although making some concession to the principle of merit-based wages, chose to adhere to what it regarded as the proven strengths of its past practices in lifetime employment and close collaboration with its workforce and suppliers. In contrast, financially troubled Nissan turned to the French automaker Renault and its Brazilian-born strategist Carlos Ghosn to lead the troubled company and make a sharp break from aspects of the Japanese model. Ghosn's restructuring initially alienated the workforce, and his cost-based approach to suppliers seemed to violate respect for long-standing ties, but in the end his success in engineering a corporate turnaround disarmed his critics. He was even able to preserve some aspects of the Japanese model. Although the number of foreign actors in the economy remained relatively small, their presence had a leavening effect on past practice.

The fifteen-year period proved to be the beginning of a steady adaptation to a radically changed international environment. As the economic recovery emerged, it became apparent that, while not converging with the American liberal model, the Japanese model was receptive to reform and redefinition. There was an ongoing evolution of corporate and government reforms that were implemented incrementally in labor relations, finance, and corporate organization. As reforms took hold, banks succeeded in reducing their debts. Many problems persisted, but, aided in part by China's growing economy, the long-range economic picture brightened. One knowledgeable authority observed in 2006, "Japan won't look dramatically

different in five years, but it will in 15 years."[3] Confidence was returning.
Japan was back.

ADAPTING TO A NEW SECURITY ENVIRONMENT

This fifteen-year period proved even more dramatic in bringing on a
change in Japan's stance in international politics. The change in the approach to military and strategic affairs was bound to be more radical than
the change in the corporate world. The economy had to be remodeled, but
Japan's strategic power had to be organized from the ground up. Step by
step, Japan began undoing its Cold War strategy and constructing a new
one to fit the still emerging order in its region and in the world. First, it
ended the Yoshida Doctrine's prohibition against overseas dispatch of
Japanese forces. After sending Self-Defense Forces on a UN peacekeeping
mission in a noncombat and logistical role to Cambodia in 1992, Japan
participated in other UN Peacekeeping Operations (PKO) missions. Such
activities quickly became accepted practice, causing little stir at home. In
2002, restrictions on the scope of these missions were quietly eased to permit more dangerous functions, including patrol of cease-fire zones and dis-
posal of weapons. As one authority observed, "Japan has the capacity to
undertake considerably more UN PKO in the future, given that its wholly
professional military is comparable in size to that of the UK or France."[4]

Second, the narrow interpretation of the constitution banning participation in collective self-defense was steadily eased to accommodate a greater
cooperative role within the U.S.-Japan alliance. As Japan moved to closer
bilateral military cooperation with the United States, deployment of Japanese forces to Afghanistan and Iraq was handled legislatively on a case-by-
case basis, but there was growing support in the Diet for a reinterpretation
of Article 9 to give participation in collective self-defense explicit legal justification.

Third, a readiness to acquire power-projection capability marked a further change from Cold War–era limitations. Japan purchased Boeing 767
in-flight refueling tankers and had plans to acquire proto–aircraft carriers,
in this case to carry helicopters. The Japanese had not possessed aircraft
carriers since 1945. In the interim, defense capability had been limited to
the minimum necessary to defend the home islands. Now, a new interest
in precision-guided munitions and long-range air transports to carry rapid-
reaction forces for overseas operations provided further evidence of an

impending end to the long-standing limit on military power. The steadfast avoidance of any commitment to regional security was replaced by a broadened geographical range of cooperation with the United States. This was dramatized by Japan's 2005 statement of strategic concern for the peace and security of Taiwan.

Fourth, although the prohibition on possession of nuclear weapons that Prime Minister Satō enunciated in 1967 remained in place, it was no longer taboo to discuss the issue. In addition to keeping a close eye on North Korea's nuclear capability, Japan viewed Chinese nuclear weapons as threatening. In a contentious visit to China's leaders in 2002, Ozawa Ichirō is said to have told them that "if Japan desires, it can possess thousands of nuclear warheads. Japan has enough plutonium in use at its nuclear power plants for three to four thousand. . . . If that should happen, we wouldn't lose [to China] in terms of military strength."[5] Japan's conservative leaders have made no secret of the fact that they continue to study the nuclear option. It gives them leverage in their relationships with potential adversaries as well as with their alliance partner. So long as the U.S. alliance and the nuclear umbrella remain credible, Japan is unlikely to exercise the option.

Fifth, the self-binding prohibition on the sharing of military technology and the export of arms that had been in place since 1976 was set to be breached. In a 2003 decision, Japan announced it would procure a ballistic missile defense (BMD) system from the United States and explore joint development of more advanced BMD technology. This decision was momentous because it would require tighter alliance cooperation, including the two-way sharing of information and technology, to develop the system. North Korean nuclear and missile development, concern for China's military advances, and Japanese business interests all played a role in prodding the allies to take this unusual step. In 2004, Keidanren (the Japan Federation of Business) urged Japan's leaders to lay aside the self-imposed restraint on the export of arms and the sharing of military technology so that Japan could keep abreast of technological progress and open up new markets. Nakasone had allowed sharing of technology with the United States in 1983, but the agreement had never worked well and had never been expanded. By 2006, the director of the U.S. Missile Defense Agency said that Japan had become America's most significant international partner in developing BMD systems.[6] Japan's defense industries were also poised to join with their U.S. counterparts in the development of airborne lasers and other ambitious technologies.

Sixth, Japan's defense budget remained officially at less than 1 percent of GDP, but it has long been recognized that the way in which the government organizes its budget and reports its defense spending masks the actual level of expenditures. The budget leaves out items that in Europe, for example, would have been included, increasing the percentage. Furthermore, Japan's practice of deferring payment for major arms procurement over a five-year period, and the long lead-in times for new weapons systems, helped Japan manage the costs of its military spending.[7] In any case, Japan's military spending is actually estimated to be the third or fourth largest in the world.[8] The extent of public debt in Japan will for the time being militate against sharp increases, but spending is being directed more and more toward new technologies and away from the hardware of the Cold War period.

Finally, the 1969 Diet resolution proscribing the military use of space was about to be openly set aside. A move in this direction had already been taken when Japan chose to put up spy satellites in 2003, but in 2006 an LDP committee prepared a package of measures that would fully engage Japan in the use of outer space for defense purposes.[9]

IMPLICATIONS FOR THE ALLIANCE

The implications of Japan's change of course for the alliance and the regional balance of power are huge. For most of the Cold War, there was no integration, no joint command, no interoperability, and limited consultation between the U.S. military stationed in Japan and the Self-Defense Forces. Beginning in the late 1990s, Japan steadily increased its military cooperation with U.S. forces in piecemeal ways made possible through revision of its military doctrines and defense guidelines as well as through new legislation. Each of these steps strengthened the reciprocity in the alliance. The decision to cooperate fully in missile defense will lead to enhanced coordination, exchange of information, and sharing of technology. Japan will now become an engaged ally. Having the technology and resources of the world's second-largest economy weighing in on the side of American power will give shape to a new regional order.

But U.S. relations with Japan will not be like those with Britain, as the authors of the Armitage Report had hoped. Japan is Japan. It is motivated by different imperatives, values, traditions, and practices. Japan's readiness to tighten cooperation is not so much the result of shared values as it is of the realist appraisal of the value of the alliance. Japan and the United States have different visions of the future character and purpose of the alliance. From an American perspective, the alliance should be expanded to maintain regional stability and to advance the global war on terrorism. Japan will see the alliance differently and in ways that will not always make for its smooth functioning.

Japan will seek maximum autonomy for its own purposes, for example, even as the alliance becomes more reciprocal. It will not wish to be hostage to the global strategy of the United States or to its relations with China and Korea. In addition, Japan will need to tend to its imperatives as an Asian nation. As one of the nation's most influential business leaders, Kobayashi Yotaro, put it in 2005: "Whenever we ask ourselves, 'Where is Japan's home?' we know it is Asia. . . . While Japan's relationship with the United States is vitally important, at this time when geopolitical realities are shifting around us, Japan has to rebuild its ties with Asia and invest those relationships with a depth and reach comparable to our relationship with the United States."[10] Japan has a great interest in promoting multilateral institutions in Asia where it can establish its leadership, compete with China for influence, and press for solutions to a wide range of purely regional problems. Thus far, the Americans have remained on the sidelines and have not committed to a vision of multilateral institution-building that would enhance regional integration and serve Japan's purposes.

Finally, the growing influence of public opinion on Japan's foreign policy will cause times of difficulty. Japan now has an increasingly active and vocal politics at the local level, where the NIMBY (not in my back yard) syndrome will likely become as apparent in relation to U.S. bases as it is in relation to nuclear power plants. The inevitable irritants that come with garrisoning tens of thousands of U.S. troops and with having foreign air and naval bases in close proximity to urban areas will be less tolerable to a more vocal Japanese public. It is remarkable that the large number of U.S. bases, with all they have entailed in terms of control of air space, requisitioning of land, and legal entanglements, have persisted for so long. But in the altered domestic situation, the base structure in Japan is bound to become the source of considerable friction. Prolonged disagreements over the bases in Okinawa have already taken a toll on relations. The decision in 2006 to move 8,000 U.S. Marines from Okinawa to Guam by 2014 reflects the unavoidable need to revise the fundamentals of the alliance.

INSTITUTIONAL CHANGE

As has happened repeatedly at times of momentous change in the international system, the fundamental shift in Japanese foreign policy is leading to an extensive reshaping of domestic institutions. Adopting a more orthodox role in the international politics of a conflict-prone world has required an institutional revolution. Exclusive concentration on economic growth left many political-strategic institutions undeveloped. The internal changes that were made during the fifteen years after the Cold War to support the new foreign policy showed a gathering momentum.

First of all, Japan became seriously engaged in revising the MacArthur constitution in order to define the role of the military, make collective defense legal, and clarify the national purpose. Revision, which requires a two-thirds approval of the Diet followed by a national referendum, lacked the necessary support during the Cold War. When the Socialist Party collapsed after disowning its foreign policy in 1994, the momentum for revision rapidly gained ground. Revisionist sentiment stressed not only the constitution's foreign origins, but also the outdated nature of Article 9 and the absence of respect for Japanese values and traditions in the preamble as well as in various specific provisions. Political parties, Diet committees, the media, and public organizations began to draft revisions. Since the turn of the century, polls have shown that strong majorities of the public favor revision.[11]

Reaching a consensus on how to replace Article 9 and how to define Japanese values and traditions will take time, but it is clear that a newly determined Japan will not be deterred from revision by its neighbors' negative reactions. China's Xinhua News Agency found proposals to revise Article 9 evidence of Japan's "wild ambitions of becoming a political and military power."[12] South Korean President Roh Moo Hyun remarked that Japan should become an "ordinary country" by "acting in conformity with universal standards for conscience and decency rather than seeking to amend laws and reinforcing its military power."[13] Events will dictate the speed at which revision progresses, but there is little question that the pacifist article will be revised and that the values written into the constitution by the Americans will be modified in ways that correspond to Japan's own norms and mores.

In a second type of institutional change, the role of the prime minister is being revised. The prime minister's capacity to provide leadership in foreign policy has been strengthened so that the prime minister can take a more assertive and proactive role in international politics, formulate a strategic vision, manage crises, and respond rapidly to the demands of international security. Important changes in the political process allowed a more top-down leadership style. Revisions in the electoral law in 1994 and subsequent administrative reforms in 1999 and 2001 had the effect of weakening the factional and bureaucratic restraints on the prime minister's role while at the same time increasing the influence of public opinion and younger party politicians on the policy process.[14] Koizumi's extraordinary popular support allowed him to clip the wings of bureaucrats and LDP faction leaders and establish a much stronger cabinet secretariat and core executive leadership during his term. Although these developments did not guarantee success against entrenched interests, they allowed him to respond rapidly and decisively to the post–9/11 crises in deploying forces to support the U.S.-led campaigns in Afghanistan and Iraq. The prime minister's new power was symbolized by the replacement of the old, rundown quarters of the prime minister with gleaming new five-story quarters across the street from the Diet completed in 2005.

Third, the government passed a plethora of new laws relating to national emergency and crisis conditions to prepare for new security threats. These threats included the possibility of missile attacks, incursions into Japanese territorial waters, chemical and biological attacks, and other terrorist acts. In the Cold War period, the government ignored the need for crisis management because it was assumed that U.S. forces would protect Japan in the unlikely event of an invasion. Japan's leaders avoided giving the SDF powers that would limit civilian government even in an emergency. Not until the rise of the new security threats of the 1990s, at a time when America's impatience with Japan's reluctance to provide any backup assistance in a regional crisis grew, did serious work in this area begin.

In 2003 and 2004, the Diet passed a series of laws that gave the government emergency powers to expropriate private property and allow the SDF to use civilian ports, airports, roads, and communication facilities; to inspect foreign ships in Japanese waters; and to provide logistical support to U.S. forces in a regional crisis. The rules of engagement for the Self-Defense Forces were modified to deal more forcefully with incursions into Japanese sea and air space. In 2006, the government carried out a sweeping reorganization of the SDF, placing the army, navy, and air force under a single command for the first time since 1945. Japan quietly proceeded with an impressive modernization of its military, bringing its air force and navy to a capability and sophistication second in the region only to the United States. The heightened attention to emergency legislation left little doubt that Japan, as one authority concluded, "is now contemplating more seriously than at any time in the previous half century the possibility that it needs to ready itself for war fighting."[15]

The fourth impending institutional change at home to support the new trajectory of Japanese foreign policy is the elevation of the Self-Defense Agency to ministry status. The Finance Ministry's domination of the budget-making process will be modified in ways that give strategic military criteria greater influence. The laws establishing the Defense Agency and Self-Defense Forces in 1954 not only ensured their subordination to civilian control but in countless ways subjected them to bureaucratic dominance. This subordination of the military was reinforced by a public revulsion from the militarist past so strong that personnel were discouraged from wearing uniforms off base. In a myriad ways, the pacifist norms of postwar society were reflected in the low regard for the activities of the SDF.[16] The threat perceptions and vulnerabilities exposed in the post–Cold War era gradually improved the popular appreciation of a professional military. Participation in UN peacekeeping missions, which fulfilled a popular wish to see Japan making an "international contribution," enhanced the SDF image. The *Asahi* in May 2006 found that 85 percent of the public held a positive image of the SDF.[17] As alliance cooperation increased, the military began to have a voice in policymaking.

The rising status of the defense forces was reflected in its ability to attract bright, young, strategically sophisticated career bureaucrats. It was also reflected in the Defense Agency's stunning new headquarters. In May 2000, the agency moved into a mammoth new state-of-the-art complex of buildings in the Ichigaya district of Tokyo. Imposing enough to house a corporate giant, the soaring buildings are on the site where the Imperial War Ministry headquarters once stood. At the new complex, the Defense Agency chose to keep and restore two significant pieces of Japanese history: the high-ceilinged room where the War Crimes Tribunal was held in 1945, and a small adjacent building where the novelist Mishima Yukio committed harakiri in 1970 to protest the postwar loss of martial spirit. Despite the disturbing nature of these memorial sites, the new SDF complex is more about the future than about the past—a striking indication of the change that Japan is undergoing.

REGAINING JAPAN'S VOICE

Finally, and perhaps most indicative of its change of course, Japan is regaining its voice. The political will and spirit that had been quieted first by the trauma of defeat and then by the strategic priorities of a mercantilist foreign policy are resurfacing. Japan is becoming more muscular in its rhetoric and posture. A deferential stance was never easy for a proud and spirited people. Economic realism came at considerable cost to self-respect. During the fifteen-year period after the Cold War, Japan began to show a new assertiveness on political issues. Nowhere was this clearer than in the readiness to confront pressure from China on many issues after decades of deference. On a series of border disputes with China over islands and underwater resource explorations, Japan adopted a tough stance. The Air Self-Defense Force began to scramble to meet Chinese military planes approaching Japanese air space.

Perhaps the most high-profile evidence of the new assertiveness was Prime Minister Koizumi's insistence on worshipping at the Yasukuni war memorial shrine in the face of Chinese outcry. Japanese business leaders predictably reacted in alarm, fearing damage to Sino-Japanese trade, and publicly urged him to end the visits. In an earlier time, concern with economic consequences would have carried the day, but Koizumi was determined not to bend to foreign opinion. Instinctively, he was intent on restoring respect for the nation's history. Every nation, he believed, must honor its war dead. The Japanese people were about evenly divided as to whether Koizumi should be making such visits, given the reaction of Japan's neighbors. But there was wide appeal in Koizumi's stubborn determination that Japan no longer needed to wilt before China's pressure.

After such a prolonged period of political passivity, the Japanese may find this new disposition an exhilarating and liberating experience. The new Heisei generation of politicians, in particular, believes that Japan must assert its own identity in international society. The younger politicians are intent on diversifying the tools of Japanese foreign policy. They favor a higher political profile for Japan. In dealing with Sino-Japanese tensions over conflicting territorial claims and energy competition, they are more self-assertive than their elders, who were constrained by the burdens of history. The Heisei generation sees China not as a war victim but as a rival.

Although Japan has become a status-quo power with a substantial stake in existing international rules and institutional governance, its ambition to rise in the international hierarchy of prestige and to establish its national dignity, in its own eyes as well as in the eyes of the world, remains unsatisfied. Japan still seeks its place in the sun. In recent years, it has placed immense importance on gaining permanent membership in the UN Security Council. In May 2005, all of Japan's overseas ambassadors were called home to an unusual meeting to emphasize that this issue was a top priority. The reason was that it was seen as a way to advance national dignity.[18]

Ultimately, Japan must establish a new consensus on national goals if it is to achieve a viable new political-economic structure. The way in which the constitution is revised, the reshaping of the party system and the political structure, and the reform of Japan's economic institutions will be worked out, to a very considerable degree, by external developments that impact Japan's national interest. Japan's characteristic style is to engage in watchful opportunism, adapting to the drift of international events and riding the trends of the time. In the absence of a settled international order, it is these national tendencies that will steer the nation's course. But a purely reactive policy will not be so successful as it was during the more predictable days of the Cold War. As Japan becomes entangled in the tensions and turmoil of international politics, the trends will be more difficult to discern, their meanings harder to decipher, and the foreign policy choices more contentious.

And it will be the Heisei generation that will finally provide the momentum to revise the constitution and adapt it to Japan's new course. This generation will also have to do what the earlier generation failed to do: It will have to come to terms with history in a way that satisfies the nation's need for pride in its past without feeding the nationalism of Japan's neighbors. The Yoshida Doctrine, once proclaimed as Japan's "permanent" (*eien*) strategy, is a dead letter.[19] Japan will not be the "Venice of the East." Nor will it be an "international civilian power." The changes that Japan is making are not peripheral adjustments; rather, they point toward a comprehensive revision of the Japanese system. The transformation of Japan's policies and institutions may be swift, or it may take time as Japan makes incremental adjustments. Presently, it is taking place through a slow evolution, but there can be no question that Japan is on the threshold of a new era.

NOTES

Introduction: The Japan Puzzle

1. See Paul Kennedy, "A. J. P. Taylor and 'Profound Forces' in History," in *Warfare, Diplomacy, and Politics: Essays in Honor of A. J. P. Taylor,* edited by Chris Wrigley (London: Hamish Hamilton, 1986), pp. 14–28.

2. Ezra F. Vogel, *Japan as Number One: Lessons for America* (Cambridge: Harvard University Press, 1979); Jean-Jacques Servan Schreiber, *The World Challenge* (New York: Simon and Schuster, 1980).

3. Henry Kissinger, *Does America Need a Foreign Policy? Toward a Diplomacy for the 21st Century* (New York: Simon and Schuster, 2001), p. 118.

4. Kenneth Waltz, "The Emerging Structure of International Politics," *International Security* 18, no. 2 (Fall 1993), p. 55.

5. *Newsweek,* February 27, 1989, p. 15.

6. Paul Kennedy, *The Rise and Fall of the Great Powers: Economic Change and Military Conflict from 1500 to 2000* (New York: Random House, 1987), p. 467. Italics in original. Although there were some observers who expressed doubts that Japan could achieve true international leadership, they stood outside of the mainstream. See, for example, Bill Emmott, *The Sun Also Sets: The Limits to Japan's Economic Power* (New York: Times Books, 1989).

7. *Newsweek,* October 9, 1989, p. 64.

8. This was the headline for the *New York Times* Sunday Book Review section on February 9, 1992. The issue reviewed a "great tide" of current books that raised fears of "a new evil empire." Among the more prominent were *Agents of Influence* (New York: Knopf, 1990) by Pat Choate, which examined Tokyo's payoffs to influential Americans to achieve "effective political domination over the United States"; *Trading Places* (New York: Basic Books, 1988) by Clyde Prestowitz, which argued that the United States was failing to respond to the Japanese challenge and that as a result, "the power of the United States

and the quality of American life is diminishing rapidly in every respect"; and *The Enigma of Japanese Power* (New York: Knopf, 1989) by Karel van Wolferen, which analyzed the rudderless, amoral governing structure of Japan and the danger it posed for the world.

9. Edward J. Lincoln, "Japanese Trade and Investment Issues," in *Japan's Emerging Global Role*, edited by Danny Unger and Paul Blackburn (Boulder: Lynn Rienner, 1993), p. 135.

10. Prodded by the Japanese, the World Bank in 1993 published a widely read study extolling the Japanese system as the model for Asian development. See *East Asian Miracle* (New York: Oxford University Press, 1993).

11. *Kokuminsei no kenkyū* (Tokyo: Tōkei sūri kenkyūjō, 2004), p. 120, shows the changes in the response to the question "Compared to westerners, are the Japanese in a word superior or inferior?" at five-year intervals beginning in 1953.

12. Shimomura Mitsuko, "'Eikoo aru Amerika' wa doko ni," *Voice*, September 1980; see translation in *Japan Echo* 8, no. 1 (1991), pp. 119–122.

13. Nakasone Yasuhiro, "Takumashii bunka to fukushi no kuni o," *Seiron*, January 1983, pp. 26–37; see translation in *Japan Echo* 10, no. 1 (1983), pp. 12–18.

14. *The Economist* of March 21–27, 1998, devoted a special survey to "The Japan Puzzle."

15. *Financial Times*, February 2/February 3, 2002.

16. *New York Times*, July 6, 2002.

17. Edward J. Lincoln, *Arthritic Japan: The Slow Pace of Economic Reform* (Washington, D.C.: Brookings Institution, 2001), p. 68.

18. Alessandro Valignano, quoted in Michael Cooper, *They Came to Japan* (Berkeley: University of California Press, 1965), p. 229.

19. *Britain and Japan: Biographical Portraits*, vol. 2, edited by Ian Nish (London: Curzon Press, 1997), p. 18.

20. See Edwin Reischauer's "Foreword" to *The Foreign Policy of Modern Japan*, edited by Robert A. Scalapino (Berkeley: University of California Press, 1977), p. xi.

21. R. R. Palmer and Joel Colton, *A History of the Modern World*, 8th ed. (New York: Knopf, 1995), p. 582.

22. John Keegan, *The Second World War* (New York: Penguin, 1989), p. 241.

23. Michael Mandelbaum, *The Ideas That Conquered the World: Peace, Democracy, and Free Markets in the Twenty-First Century* (New York: PublicAffairs, 2002), p. 80.

24. See James C. Thomson, Jr., "The Role of the Department of State," in *Pearl Harbor as History: Japanese-American Relations, 1931–1941*, edited by Dorothy Borg and Shumpei Okamoto (New York: Columbia University Press, 1973), pp. 101–102.

25. Quoted in Roberta Wohlstetter, *Pearl Harbor: Warning and Decision* (Stanford: Stanford University Press, 1962), pp. 264–265.

26. Robert J. C. Butow, *The John Doe Associates: Backdoor Diplomacy for Peace* (Stanford: Stanford University Press, 1981), p. 303.

27. See the essay by Michael Barnhart in *Pearl Harbor Reexamined: Prologue to the Pacific War,* edited by Hillary Conroy and Harry Wray (Honolulu: University of Hawaii Press, 1990), pp. 65–72.

28. Harold L. Ickes, *The Secret Diary of Harold L. Ickes,* vol. 3, *The Lowering Clouds 1939–1941* (New York: Simon and Schuster, 1954), p. 588, quoted in Scott D. Sagan, "The Origins of the Pacific War," in *The Origins and Prevention of Major Wars,* edited by Robert I. Rotberg and Theodore K. Rabb (Cambridge: Cambridge University Press, 1989), p. 335.

29. Dean Acheson, quoted in Sagan, "Origins," p. 336.

30. Hamilton Fish and Winston Churchill are both quoted in Sagan, "Origins," p. 323.

31. Nathan Glazer, "From Ruth Benedict to Herman Kahn: The Postwar Japanese Image in the American Mind," in *Mutual Images: Essays in Japanese and American Relations,* edited by Akira Iriye (Cambridge: Harvard University Press, 1975), p. 161.

32. Ruth Benedict, *The Chrysanthemum and the Sword* (Boston: Houghton Mifflin, 1946), pp. 1–2.

33. Zbigniew Brzezinski, *The Fragile Blossom* (New York: Harper and Row), p. 16.

34. George Ball, "We Are Playing a Dangerous Game with Japan," *New York Times Magazine,* June 25, 1972; Robert C. Christopher, *The Japanese Mind* (New York: Ballantine Books, 1983), p. 55.

35. Samuel P. Huntington, *The Clash of Civilizations and the Remaking of World Order* (New York: Simon and Schuster, 1996), p. 44.

36. The cultural critic John Nathan was surely correct in observing that "Japanese are almost certainly not the people they appear to be when dealing with foreigners outside Japan in languages other than their own. . . . Abroad, the Japanese tend . . . to recede into a formal, tight-lipped impassivity that is actually a kind of resignation about ever making themselves understood. This unfortunate withdrawal is often interpreted as lifelessness." John Nathan, *Sony: The Private Life* (Boston: Houghton Mifflin, 1999), p. 81n.

37. Henry Kissinger, *Years of Upheaval* (Boston: Little, Brown, 1982), p. 735.

38. Henry Kissinger, *White House Years* (Boston: Little, Brown, 1979), p. 324.

39. Walter Isaacson's 600-page study of Kissinger's diplomacy offers only one page reference to Japan in its index. Walter Isaacson, *Kissinger: A Biography* (New York: Simon and Schuster, 1992).

40. The journalist Don Oberdorfer, who covered Kissinger during his term as secretary of state, described Kissinger's slighting attitude. "Kissinger," Oberdorfer wrote, "was going back and forth to Beijing and he would spend about ten days at a time [in China], and maybe ten hours in Japan on the way back. He was enchanted with Zhou Enlai, and he couldn't find anybody in

Japan who was an equal in talking about the affairs of the world." Oberdorfer recounted how Kissinger, who had come to Japan only once before entering government, confided his disdain. "I don't zink they understand me."
He said, "They took me down to a Japanese inn in Kyoto. Vatever I asked
them, they sent a man to press my pants." Don Oberdorfer, "Japan and the
United States: Reflections of a Diplomatic Correspondent," *International
House of Japan Bulletin* 17, no. 2 (Summer 1997).

41. U. Alexis Johnson, *The Right Hand of Power* (Englewood Cliffs, N.J.: Prentice-
Hall, 1984), p. 521; Marvin Kalb and Bernard Kalb, *Kissinger* (Boston: Little,
Brown, 1974), p. 255.

42. Ohira Masayoshi, foreign minister during Kissinger's tenure, later prime minister and one of the most universally respected of Japanese political leaders,
did not escape Kissinger's contempt. "Do you know this guy Ohira?" he
asked Oberdorfer. "Well, yeah," responded the journalist, "I've met him a
few times." Kissinger said, "Tell me something. If he's so smart why doesn't
he ever say anything?" See Oberdorfer, "Japan and the United States." With
a little reflection, Kissinger might have understood why the Japanese would
be wary of him. After all, he was Nixon's national security adviser who had
engineered the secret opening to China without bothering to inform the
Japanese in advance. Years later, in his memoirs, Kissinger would reflect, "It
is a dangerous mistake to think of Japanese leaders as unimpressive and to
confuse their inarticulateness with lack of perception." And he belatedly
came to understand why Ōhira "was not about to reveal his thinking to an
American he did not know and whose record on matters Japanese had revealed the absence of a certain delicacy." Kissinger, *Years of Upheaval*, pp.
738–743.

43. *The Kissinger Transcripts,* edited by William Burr (New York: The New Press,
1998), p. 91.

44. Kissinger, *Years of Upheaval,* p. 693.

45. Michael Schaller, *Altered States: The United States and Japan Since the Occupation*
(New York: Oxford University Press, 1997), pp. 211–212.

46. *Kissinger Transcripts,* p. 276.

47. Kissinger, *Years of Upheaval,* pp. 737–738.

48. Kissinger, *White House Years,* p. 324.

49. Institute for National Strategic Studies, "The United States and Japan: Ad-
vancing Toward a Mature Partnership," *Institute for National Strategic Studies Special Report* (Washington, D.C.: National Defense University, October 11,
2000).

Chapter 1: *New International Orders*

1. G. B. Sansom, *Japan: A Short Cultural History*, rev. ed. (New York: Appleton-Century Crofts, 1943), p. 15.

2. See, for example, Kent Calder, "Japanese Foreign Economic Policy Formation: Explaining the 'Reactive State,'" *World Politics* 40 (1988), pp. 517–541; see also Akitoshi Miyashita, "Gaiatsu and Japan's Foreign Aid: Rethinking the Reactive-Proactive Debate," *International Studies Quarterly* 43 (1999), pp. 695–732.

3. Kenneth Waltz, *Theory of International Politics* (Reading, Mass.: Addison-Wesley, 1979), p. 118.

4. Robert Gilpin, *War and Change in World Politics* (Cambridge: Cambridge University Press, 1981), p. 85.

5. Kenneth B. Pyle, "Advantages of Followership: German Economics and Japanese Bureaucrats, 1890–1925," *Journal of Japanese Studies* 1, no. 1 (Autumn 1974), pp. 127–164.

6. Alexander Gerschenkron, *Economic Backwardness in Historical Perspective* (Cambridge, Mass.: Belknap Press, 1962).

7. As the sociologist Reinhard Bendix observed, owing to the spread of ideas and the political initiative of leaders in the modern world, the understanding of change within societies had to be revised: "The traditional posture of sociological theory conceives of change as slow, gradual, continuous and intrinsic to the societies changing. . . . However, once the eighteenth century [industrial and democratic] revolutions had occurred, subsequent social changes were characterized by a precipitous increase in the speed and intensity of communication. Ideas and techniques have passed from 'advanced' to 'follower' societies. . . . Within a relatively short historical period there are few societies which have remained immune from these external impacts upon their social structures." Reinhard Bendix, *Embattled Reason: Essays on Social Knowledge* (New York: Oxford University Press, 1970), p. 331.

8. For a comparative study of individual Japanese and Italian leaders, see Richard J. Samuels, *Machiavelli's Children: Leaders and Their Legacies in Italy and Japan* (Ithaca, N.Y.: Cornell University Press, 2003).

9. Fareed Zakaria, *From Wealth to Power: The Unusual Origins of America's World Role* (Princeton, N.J.: Princeton University Press, 1998), p. 42.

10. Edwin Corwin, *The President's Control of Foreign Relations* (Princeton, N.J.: Princeton University Press, 1917), is quoted in Peter Trubowitz, Emily O. Goldman, and Edward Rhodes, eds., *The Politics of Strategic Adjustment: Ideas, Institutions, and Interests* (New York: Columbia University Press, 1999), p. 106.

11. Quoted in Michael Mastanduno, "The United States Political System and International Leadership: A 'Decidedly Inferior' Form of Government?" in *American Foreign Policy: Theoretical Essays*, 2d ed., edited by G. John Ikenberry (New York: HarperCollins, 1996), p. 329.

12. Henry Kissinger, *White House Years* (Boston: Little, Brown, 1979), p. 323.
13. Quoted in Theodore H. Von Laue, *Leopold Ranke: The Formative Years* (Princeton, N.J.: Princeton University Press, 1950), p. 167. Ranke counseled the Prussian rulers on the primacy of foreign policy, but he also adopted it in his scholarship, emphasizing international relations as a centerpiece of history. For a time in the twentieth century his concept of the primacy of foreign policy had a bad name, partly owing to disapproval of his role as an "official historian" to the Prussian state. He was the object of criticism by historians because in the hands of many of his disciples his emphasis on foreign affairs crudely cast the writing of history into a narrow political mold chiefly occupied with the external relations of states. One of the strongest reactions from the next generation to this approach came from the eminent German historian Eckert Kehr, who lived through the dark years of German defeat in World War I and the social upheaval of the Weimar Republic. He rejected the notion that Germany's fate had been the result of outside forces and instead traced the debacle wholly to domestic sources. Proclaiming provocatively *"der Primat der Innenpolitik,"* he studied internal sociopolitical alignments as constituting the roots of German foreign policy. See James J. Sheehan, "The Primacy of Domestic Politics: Eckert Kehr's Essays on Modern German History," *Central European History* 1, no. 2 (1967), pp. 166–174. The English historian Herbert Butterfield recalled his own early resistance to the Rankean historiographical tradition because it overlooked the broader range of influences on European history, such as the scientific revolution. He recorded that he came to recognize that a "neglect of military history and war" and the redistribution of power among states resulted in "an anaemic and unreal idea of the deeper processes of mundane history." See Herbert Butterfield, *Man on His Past: The Study of Historical Scholarship* (Cambridge: Cambridge University Press, 1955), p. 119.
14. Quoted in Reinhard Bendix, ed., *State and Society: A Reader in Comparative Political Sociology* (Berkeley: University of California Press, 1968), p. 156.
15. Felix Gilbert, ed., *The Historical Essays of Otto Hintze* (New York: Oxford University Press, 1975), p. 183.
16. Ibid., p. 11.
17. P. C. Emmer and H. L. Wesseling, eds., *Reappraisals in Overseas History* (Leiden: Leiden University Press, 1979), pp. 200–204.

Chapter 2: Japan's National Style

1. Arthur Schlesinger, Jr., "Foreign Policy and the American Character," *Foreign Affairs* 62, no. 1 (Autumn 1983), p. 1.
2. Raymond Aron, *Peace and War: A Theory of International Relations,* translated by

Richard Howard and Annette Baker Fox (Garden City, N.Y.: Doubleday, 1966), p. 279.

3. Ibid., p. 287.

4. Ibid., pp. 289–290. In the years since Joseph Nye and Sean Lynn-Jones observed a persistent neglect of "national styles of strategy," there has developed considerable interest in strategic culture as an explanation for a state's international behavior. Alastair Iain Johnston, *Cultural Realism: Strategic Culture and Grand Strategy in Chinese History* (Princeton, N.J.: Princeton University Press, 1995), chap. 1. See also Joseph Nye and Sean Lynn-Jones, "International Security Studies: A Report on a Conference on the State of the Field," *International Security* 12, no. 4 (1988), pp. 5–27.

5. Ronald P. Toby, *State and Diplomacy in Early Modern Japan: Asia in the Development of the Tokugawa Bakufu* (Princeton, N.J.: Princeton University Press, 1984), p. 111.

6. Toby wrote: "Some modern scholars, for example, credit a perceived threat from the unifying Sui and T'ang dynasties in China, and the Silla unification of Korea, in the sixth and seventh centuries, with catalyzing the emergence of the first unified Japanese state." Ibid., p. 111. Inoue Mitsusada argued that "Japan's direct motive in adopting the *ritsuryo* system [a Chinese-style centralized bureaucratic state] was the foreign rather than the domestic situation." Ibid., p. 111n. See also Inoue's chapter 4 of *The Cambridge History of Japan*, vol. 1, *Ancient Japan*, edited by John Whitney Hall (Cambridge: Cambridge University Press, 1993), p. 201.

7. Edwin O. Reischauer, *Japan: The Story of a Nation* (New York: Knopf, 1970), p. 21.

8. John Whitney Hall, *Japan: From Prehistory to Modern Times* (New York: Delacorte Press, 1970), p. 35.

9. *Cambridge History of Japan*, vol. 1, p. 223. Also, in "The *Ritsuryo* System in Japan," *Acta Asiatica* 31 (1977), p. 111, Inoue Mitsusada wrote that "the imperial court built up the Japanese *ritsuryo* state in the latter half of the seventh century in order to cope with the tense international situation. . . . When the threat from the continent abated, the imperial court lost its zeal for maintaining the *ritsuryo* system, which, in its initial stages, had had a military significance."

10. Delmer Brown in *Cambridge History of Japan*, vol. 1, pp. 39–40.

11. John Whitney Hall, *Government and Local Power in Japan: 500 to 1700* (Princeton, N.J.: Princeton University Press, 1966), p. 61.

12. Kawazoe Shoji, in *The Cambridge History of Japan*, vol. 3, *Medieval Japan,* edited by Kozo Yamamura (Cambridge: Cambridge University Press, 1990), p. 416.

13. See the discussion in Toby, *State and Diplomacy*, p. 172.

14. *Cambridge History of Japan*, vol. 3, p. 437.

15. Toby, *State and Diplomacy*, pp. 225–226.

16. Rushton Coulborn, quoted in *Studies in the Institutional History of Early Modern Japan,* edited by John W. Hall and Marius B. Jansen (Princeton, N.J.: Princeton University Press, 1968), p. 16.

17. See the pertinent discussion in John Gerard Ruggie, "Continuity and Transformation in the World Polity: Toward a Neorealist Synthesis," in *Neorealism and Its Critics,* edited by Robert O. Keohane (New York: Columbia University Press, 1986), pp. 141–148.

18. Albert M. Craig, *Chōshū in the Meiji Restoration* (Cambridge: Harvard University Press, 1961), p. 361.

19. Quoted in John J. Mearsheimer, *The Tragedy of Great Power Politics* (New York: W. W. Norton, 2001), pp. 35–36. Also see Robert Gilpin, *War and Change in World Politics* (Cambridge: Cambridge University Press, 1981), p. 94.

20. Quoted in John Hampton Sagers, "The Intellectual Roots of Japanese Capitalism: Economic Thought and Policy, 1835–1885," Ph.D. dissertation, University of Washington, 2001, p. 52.

21. Luke Roberts, *Mercantilism in a Japanese Domain: The Merchant Origins of Economic Nationalism in 18th-century Tosa* (Cambridge: Cambridge University Press, 1998), pp. 1–3.

22. Joseph Strayer, "The Tokugawa Period and Japanese Feudalism," in *Studies in the Institutional History of Early Modern Japan,* edited by John W. Hall and Marius B. Jansen (Princeton, N.J.: Princeton University Press, 1968), p. 14.

23. Kenneth Waltz, *Theory of International Politics* (Reading, Mass.: Addison-Wesley, 1979), p. 117.

24. Thomas Hobbes, *Leviathan,* edited by C. B. MacPherson (Harmondsworth, England: Penguin Books, 1968), p. 161.

25. Japan's leaders acted according to the fundamental premise of political realism, which holds that "a state is compelled within the anarchic and competitive conditions of international relations to expand its power and attempt to extend its control over the international system. If the state fails to make this attempt, it risks the possibility that other states will increase their relative power positions and will thereby place its existence or vital interests in jeopardy. The severe penalties that can be visited on states for failure to play the game of power politics have exemplified the undeniable value of the realist position to an understanding of international relations." Gilpin, *War and Change,* pp. 86–87.

26. See Craig's discussion in *Chōshū in the Meiji Restoration,* p. 361.

27. My colleague James Palais has pointed out that there is no institution in Japan like the censorate and remonstrance.

28. Fukuzawa Yukichi, *An Outline of Civilization,* translated by David A. Dilworth and G. Cameron Hurst (Tokyo: Sophia University Press, 1973), pp. 135–136.

29. Craig, *Chōshū in the Meiji Restoration,* pp. 373–374.

30. Iriye Akira, *Shin Nihon no gaikō: Chikyūka jidai no Nihon no sentaku* (Tokyo:

Chūkō shinsho, 1991), pp. 13–14. See also Iriye Akira, *Nihon no gaikō: Meiji ishin kara gendai made* (Tokyo: Iwanami, 1966), p. 27.

31. S. N. Eisenstadt in his study of Japanese civilization wrote: "Its religions— above all Shinto, but also the mixture of Shinto, Buddhism, and Confucianism that characterized Japan—seemed to lack a strong transcendental dimension or orientation. . . . This lack of any transcendental dimension in Japanese religion has been asserted both by some Japanese scholars, such as Maruyama Masao, and by Western ones—Kurt Singer, who visited Japan in the thirties, George Sansom, who emphasized in his Columbia lectures on the encounter between Japan and the West that, despite many structural similarities, Japanese civilization lacked those universalistic orientations which shaped many aspects of Western historical dynamics; and later on Robert N. Bellah, John Pelzel, and scholars of Japanese religion such as Joseph Kitagawa and William LaFleur." *Japanese Civilization: A Comparative View* (Chicago: University of Chicago Press, 1995), p. 7.

32. Hajime Nakamura, *Ways of Thinking of Eastern Peoples: India-China-Tibet-Japan,* edited by Philip P. Wiener (Honolulu: East West Center Press, 1964), p. 350.

33. Robert N. Bellah, *Imagining Japan: The Japanese Tradition and Its Modern Interpretation* (Berkeley: University of California Press, 2003), p. 116.

34. Eiko Ikegami wrote that "unlike the medieval Church, which asserted the existence of universal standards of truth and justice that were greater than the secular sovereignty of one European country, the medieval Japanese Buddhist temples did not establish normative and transcendental values to which the secular authority should, in theory, be subject." Eiko Ikegami, *The Taming of the Samurai: Honorific Individualism and the Making of Modern Japan* (Cambridge: Harvard University Press, 1995), pp. 186–187.

35. John W. Hall, quoted in Bellah, *Imagining Japan,* p. 187.

36. Eisenstadt, *Japanese Civilization,* p. 13.

37. Ibid., p. 48.

38. Bellah, *Imagining Japan,* p. 35.

39. This maxim is attributed to H. Stuart Hughes. See David B. Hart, "A Most Partial Historian," *First Things,* no. 138 (December 2003), p. 35.

40. Yasusuke Murakami, *An Anticlassical Political-Economic Analysis: A Vision for the Next Century* (Stanford: Stanford University Press, 1996), p. 426.

41. Ibid., p. 415.

42. Bellah, *Imagining Japan,* p. 185.

43. Quoted in Kei Wakaizumi, "Japan's Dilemma: To Act or Not to Act," *Foreign Policy* 16 (Fall 1974), p. 31.

44. Tahara Soichirō, "Sōren wa kowai desu ka," *Bungei shunjū* (March 1980); Miyazawa Kiichi and Kōsaka Masataka, *Utsukushii Nihon e no chōsen* (Tokyo: Bungei shunjū, 1984); Tahara Soichirō, "Nippon no fumie," *Bungei shunju* (October 1990).

45. Okazaki Hisahiko, "Ajia chōtaiken e no shinsenryaku," *This Is Yomiuri* (August 1992), pp. 4–90; translated as "Southeast Asia in Japan's National Strategy," *Japan Echo* 20 (1993), p. 61.

46. Euan Graham, *Japan's Sea Lane Security, 1940–2004: A Matter of Life or Death?* (London: Routledge, 2006).

47. Cited in Jack L. Snyder, *Myths of Empire: Domestic Politics and International Ambition* (Ithaca, N.Y.: Cornell University Press, 1991), p. 20.

48. Ibid., p. 318.

49. Masataka Kōsaka, "The International Economic Policy of Japan," in *The Foreign Policy of Modern Japan*, edited by Robert A. Scalapino (Berkeley: University of California Press, 1977), p. 224.

50. Quoted in ibid., p. 224.

51. Rōyama Masamichi, *TōA to sekai: shinjitsujo e no ronsaku* (Tokyo: Kaizō-sha, 1941), pp. 52–53.

52. Niccolo Machiavelli, *The Prince and the Discourses* (New York: Random House, 1940), chap. 25.

53. Yanagita Kunio, *Nihonjin* (Tokyo: Mainichi shimbunsha, 1976), pp. 1–2.

54. Maruyama Masao, *Senchū to sengo no aida* (Tokyo: Misuzu shobō, 1976), pp. 347–348.

55. *Itō Hirobumi den*, vol. 2 (Tokyo: Shunbō Kōtsuki Shōkai, 1940), pp. 193–194. See also George M. Beckmann, *The Making of the Meiji Constitution* (Lawrence: University of Kansas Press, 1957), p. 132.

56. Nobutaka Ike, *Japan's Decision for War: Records of the 1941 Policy Conferences* (Stanford: Stanford University Press, 1967), p. xxvi.

57. Nakao Yūji, ed., *Shōwa tennō hatsugen kiroku shusei*, vol. 2 (Tokyo: Fuyo shobō, 2003), pp. 400–401.

58. Iwakura Tomomi, quoted in Marius B. Jansen, "Modernization and Foreign Policy in Meiji Japan," in *Political Development in Modern Japan*, edited by Robert E. Ward (Princeton, N.J.: Princeton University Press, 1968), pp. 158–159.

59. Quoted in Arthur Tiedemann, "Japan's Economic Foreign Policies, 1868–1893," in *Japan's Foreign Policy, 1868–1941: A Research Guide*, edited by James W. Morley (New York: Columbia University Press, 1974), p. 130.

60. Kimitada Miwa, "Fukuzawa Yukichi's 'Departure from Asia': A Prelude to the Sino-Japanese War," in *Japan's Modern Century*, edited by Edmund Skrzypczak (Tokyo: Tuttle, 1968), p. 25.

61. Roger F. Hackett, *Yamagata Aritomo in the Rise of Modern Japan, 1838–1922* (Cambridge: Harvard University Press, 1971), p. 138.

62. Graham, *Japan's Sea Lane Security*, p. 1.

63. Michael E. Barnhart, *Japan Prepares for Total War: The Search for Economic Security, 1919–1941* (Ithaca, N.Y.: Cornell University Press, 1987), p. 50.

64. See the discussion in Erica R. Gould and Stephen Krasner, "Binding Versus Autonomy," in *The End of Diversity? Prospects for German and Japanese Capitalism*,

edited by Kozo Yamamura and Wolfgang Streeck (Ithaca, N.Y.: Cornell University Press, 2003), p. 77.

65. Isaiah Frank, quoted in Michael Mandelbaum, *The Fate of Nations: The Search for National Security in the Nineteenth and Twentieth Centuries* (Cambridge: Cambridge University Press, 1989), p. 336n.

66. Nishida and Maruyama are quoted in Bellah, *Imagining Japan*, p. 189.

67. Ibid.

68. James B. Crowley, "Japan's Military Foreign Policies," in *Japan's Foreign Policy, 1868–1941: A Research Guide*, edited by James W. Morley (New York: Columbia University Press, 1974), p. 3.

69. Peter Duus, *The Abacus and the Sword: The Japanese Penetration of Korea, 1895–1910* (Berkeley: University of California Press, 1995), p. 424.

70. Thomas P. Rohlen, "Learning: The Mobilization of Knowledge in the Japanese Political Economy," in *The Political Economy of Japan*, vol. 3, *Cultural and Social Dynamics*, edited by Shumpei Kumon and Henry Rosovsky (Stanford: Stanford University Press, 1992), pp. 326–327. Italics added.

71. Ibid.

72. See Kenneth B. Pyle, "Advantages of Followership: German Economics and Japanese Bureaucrats, 1890–1925," *Journal of Japanese Studies* 1, no. 1 (Autumn 1974), pp. 127–164.

73. Leon Trotsky, *The History of the Russian Revolution*, translated by Max Eastman (Ann Arbor: University of Michigan Press, 1957), pp. 4–9.

74. Thorstein Veblen, *Essays in Our Changing Order* (New York: Viking Press, 1934), pp. 248–266.

75. Quoted in R. P. Dore, "The Modernizer as a Special Case: Japanese Factory Legislation, 1882–1911," *Comparative Studies in Society and History* 11 (1969), p. 439.

76. "Nihon sonnō ron," in *Kawakami Hajime chōsaku shū*, vol. 1 (Tokyo: Chikuma Shobō, 1964), p. 154.

77. Thomas C. Smith, *The Agrarian Origins of Modern Japan* (Stanford: Stanford University Press, 1959), p. 206.

78. Mearsheimer, on "the well-known realist argument that imitation of the successful practices of rival great powers is an important consequence of security competition," wrote, "While I acknowledge the basic point as correct, I argue that *imitation* tends to be defined too narrowly, focusing on copycatting defensive but not offensive behavior. Moreover, great powers also care about *innovation*, which often means finding clever ways to gain power at the expense of rival states." Mearsheimer, *Tragedy of Great Power Politics*, p. 140.

79. Thomas Hobbes, *Leviathan* (Oxford: Clarendon Press, 1952), quoted in Ikegami, *Taming of the Samurai*, p. 24.

80. Quoted in Gilpin, *War and Change*, p. 31.

81. Ikegami, *Taming of the Samurai*, p. 22.

82. Ibid., p. 363.
83. Eiko Ikegami, "Shame and the Samurai: Institutions, Trustworthiness, and Autonomy in the Elite Honor Culture," *Social Research* 70, no. 4 (Winter 2003).
84. Ikegami, *Taming of the Samurai,* p. 268.
85. Ibid., p. 361.
86. Roberta Wohlstetter, *Pearl Harbor: Warning and Decision* (Stanford: Stanford University Press, 1962), p. 353.
87. Tōgō Shigenori, *The Cause of Japan* (New York: Simon and Schuster, 1956), p. 186.

Chapter 3: The World Japan Entered

1. John Whitney Hall, *Government and Local Power in Japan: 500 to 1700* (Princeton, N.J.: Princeton University Press, 1966), p. 6.
2. See Yamazaki Masakazu and Haga Toru, "Reexamining the Era of National Seclusion," *Japan Echo* 19 (Winter 1992), pp. 73–75. In addition to the well-known trade with the Dutch, considerable commerce with China and Korea was maintained. See Ronald P. Toby, *State and Diplomacy in Early Modern Japan: Asia in the Development of the Tokugawa Bakufu* (Princeton, N.J.: Princeton University Press, 1984), and also Marius B. Jansen, *China in the Tokugawa World* (Cambridge: Harvard University Press, 1992).
3. As Robert Gilpin wrote, "Until the modern era there was no single international system, but rather several international systems, with little or no contact with one another. Thus, except for the modern world, one cannot really speak of the international system." Gilpin, *War and Change in World Politics* (Cambridge: Cambridge University Press, 1981), p. 26.
4. Ibid., pp. 124, 132.
5. In such cases, Peter Gourevitch wrote in his seminal essay, "instead of being a cause of international politics, domestic structure may be a consequence of it. International systems become causes instead of consequences." Gourevitch, "The Second Image Reversed: The International Sources of Domestic Politics," *International Organization* 32, no. 4 (Autumn 1978), p. 882.
6. Paul Kennedy, *The Rise and Fall of the Great Powers: Economic Change and Military Conflict from 1500 to 2000* (New York: Random House, 1987), p. 150.
7. John Gallagher and Ronald Robinson, "The Imperialism of Free Trade," *Economic History Review* 6, no. 1 (1953), p. 13.
8. Gilpin, *War and Change,* p. 138.
9. Quoted in Peter Paret, ed., *Makers of Modern Strategy: From Machiavelli to the Nuclear Age* (Princeton, N.J.: Princeton University Press, 1986), pp. 225–226.
10. Gilpin, *War and Change,* p. 34.
11. Hedley Bull, *The Anarchical Society: A Study of Order in World Politics* (New York: Columbia University Press, 1977), p. 32.

12. Gallagher and Robinson, "The Imperialism of Free Trade," p. 11.

13. Marius B. Jansen, ed., *The Cambridge History of Japan*, vol. 5, *The Nineteenth Century* (Cambridge: Cambridge University Press, 1989), p. 297.

14. W. G. Beasley, *Japanese Imperialism, 1894–1945* (New York: Oxford University Press, 1987), p. 16.

15. *Cambridge History of Japan*, vol. 5, pp. 269–270.

16. Ibid., p. 278.

17. Beasley, *Japanese Imperialism*, p. 24.

18. Kevin H. O'Rourke and Jeffrey G. Williamson, *Globalization and History: The Evolution of a Nineteenth Century Atlantic Economy* (Cambridge: MIT Press, 1999), p. 54.

19. Albert Craig placed great emphasis on the premium the new leaders put on the acquisition of power: "The Meiji leaders, who had won out in the Bakumatsu [1853–1868] struggle for power, represented in an extreme form this concern of the traditional society with power. In their eyes the existence on Japan's doorstep of the superior Western powers was intolerable. Thus, during the early Meiji period, the leaders of Japan were not concerned solely with consolidating their power against internal opposition—a process which would have demanded only a relatively small increase in political rationalization. On the contrary, their main task was to create a state sufficiently powerful to cope with the powers of which they were so conscious. It was this latter challenge that led them to carry out the Meiji revolution." Craig, *Chōshū in the Meiji Restoration* (Cambridge: Harvard University Press, 1961), p. 273.

20. Albert M. Craig, "Kido Kōin and Ōkubo Toshimichi: A Psychohistorical Analysis," in *Personality in Japanese History*, edited by Albert M. Craig and Donald Shively (Berkeley: University of California Press, 1970), pp. 274–275.

21. Albert M. Craig, "The Central Government," in *Japan in Transition from Tokugawa to Meiji*, edited by Marius B. Jansen and Gilbert Rozman (Princeton, N.J.: Princeton University Press, 1986), p. 64.

22. *Cambridge History of Japan*, vol. 5, p. 303.

23. Gerrit Gong, *The Standard of "Civilization" in International Society* (New York: Oxford University Press, 1984), p. 27.

24. Alexis Dudden, *Japan's Colonization of Korea: Discourse and Power* (Honolulu: University of Hawaii Press, 2005), p. 27.

25. Quoted in Masao Miyoshi, *As We Saw Them: The First Japanese Embassy to the United States (1860)* (Berkeley: University of California Press, 1979), p. 143.

26. Dudden, *Japan's Colonization of Korea*, chap. 3.

27. Peter Duus, Ramon H. Meyers, and Mark R. Peattie, eds., *The Japanese Informal Empire in China, 1895–1937* (Princeton, N.J.: Princeton University Press, 1989), p. xx.

28. Kim Key-hiuk argued that the Sinocentric system finally ended in 1882 when the Chinese sent troops to Korea to suppress an uprising and transformed its traditional "moral and ceremonial authority into a political authority." See Kim

Key-hiuk, *The Last Phase of the East Asian World Order: Korea, Japan and the Chinese Empire, 1860–1882* (Berkeley: University of California Press, 1980), p. 348.

29. Dudden, *Japan's Colonization of Korea,* pp. 55–59.

30. Ibid., p. 33.

31. The military historian Correlli Barnett is quoted in Kennedy, *Rise and Fall of the Great Powers,* p. 202.

32. Quoted in Marius B. Jansen, "Modernization and Foreign Policy in Meiji," in *Political Development in Modern Japan,* edited by Robert E. Ward (Princeton, N.J.: Princeton University Press, 1968), p. 175.

33. Prince Iwakura Tomomi, quoted in Marlene J. Mayo, "Rationality in the Meiji Restoration," in *Modern Japanese Leadership: Transition and Change,* edited by Bernard S. Silberman and Harry D. Harootunnian (Tucson: University of Arizona Press, 1966), p. 356.

34. Jansen and Rozman, *Japan in Transition from Tokugawa to Meiji,* p. 67.

35. Quoted in Jansen, "Modernization and Foreign Policy," p. 158.

36. Quoted in ibid., pp. 158–159.

37. Quoted in Irokawa Daikichi, *The Culture of the Meiji Period,* edited by Marius B. Jansen (Princeton, N.J.: Princeton University Press, 1985), p. 55.

38. Quoted in Mayo, "Rationality in the Meiji Restoration," pp. 357–358.

39. Quoted in Joseph Pittau, *Political Thought in Early Meiji Japan* (Cambridge: Harvard University Press, 1967), p. 39.

40. Quoted in Jansen, "Modernization and Foreign Policy in Meiji Japan," p. 175.

41. Fareed Zakaria, *From Wealth to Power: The Unusual Origins of America's World Role* (Princeton, N.J.: Princeton University Press, 1998), p. 38.

42. Gilpin, *War and Change,* p. 42.

43. As Kennedy wrote, Britain's relative position was slipping decisively: "Whereas in 1880 the United Kingdom still contained 22.9 percent of total world manufacturing output, that figure had shrunk to 13.6 by 1913; and while its share of world trade was 23.2 percent in 1880, it was only 14.1 percent in 1911–1913. In terms of industrial muscle, both the United States and imperial Germany had moved ahead. The 'workshop of the world' was now in third place, not because it wasn't growing, but because others were growing faster." Kennedy, *Rise and Fall of the Great Powers,* p. 228.

44. Veblen argued that imperial Germany had become more efficient industrially than its predecessor, England, because of the "merits of borrowing." England was "paying the penalty for having been thrown into the lead and so having shown the way." Thorstein Veblen, *Imperial Germany and the Industrial Revolution* (New York: Viking Press, 1939), pp. 19, 132.

45. Kennedy, *Rise and Fall of the Great Powers,* p. 229.

46. Duus et al., *The Japanese Informal Empire in China,* p. xix.

47. Gilpin, *War and Change,* pp. 140–141.

48. Rejecting the applicability of Leninist explanations, the Marxist economist Takahashi Kamekichi found the sources of imperialism not primarily in domestic economic circumstances but rather in the international environment. Japan was a "petty imperialist" whose external circumstances impelled its expansion. As a late-developing nation-state, Japan was disadvantaged by the previous partition of East Asia and the resulting limited access to essential raw materials and markets. For Takahashi, Japan's was a defensive imperialism required for survival. He was on the right track. See Germaine A. Hoston, *Marxism and the Crisis of Development in Prewar Japan* (Princeton, N.J.: Princeton University Press, 1986), chap. 4.

49. Mark R. Peattie, "The Japanese Colonial Empire, 1895–1945," in *The Cambridge History of Japan*, vol. 6, *The Twentieth Century*, edited by Peter Duus (Cambridge: Cambridge University Press, 1989), p. 218.

50. Ramon H. Myers and Mark R. Peattie, eds., *The Japanese Colonial Empire, 1895–1945* (Princeton, N.J.: Princeton University Press, 1984), p. 15.

51. Quoted in Roger F. Hackett, *Yamagata Aritomo in the Rise of Modern Japan, 1838–1922* (Cambridge: Harvard University Press, 1971), p. 138.

52. Peter Duus, *The Abacus and the Sword: The Japanese Penetration of Korea, 1895–1910* (Berkeley: University of California Press, 1995), p. 424.

53. See Mutsu Munemitsu, *Kenkenroku: A Diplomatic Record of the Sino-Japanese War, 1894–95,* edited and translated by Gordon Mark Berger (Tokyo: University of Tokyo Press, 1982), passim.

54. Dudden, *Japan's Colonization of Korea*, p. 74.

55. Beasley, *Japanese Imperialism*, p. 49.

56. Quoted in John Albert White, *The Diplomacy of the Russo-Japanese War* (Princeton, N.J.: Princeton University Press, 1964), p. 135.

57. Quoted in Kenneth B. Pyle, "The Technology of Japanese Nationalism: The Local Improvement Movement, 1900–1918," *Journal of Asian Studies* 33 (November 1973), p. 51.

58. Marius B. Jansen, *The Japanese and Sun Yat-sen* (Cambridge: Harvard University Press, 1954), p. 211.

59. Roosevelt, quoted in Henry Kissinger, *Diplomacy* (New York: Simon and Schuster, 1994), pp. 41–42.

60. Quoted in Walter LaFeber, *The Clash: U.S.-Japanese Relations Throughout History* (New York: W. W. Norton, 1997), p. 90.

61. For an excellent survey of such views, see Tanaka Akira, *Shōkoku shugi: Nihon no kindai o yominaosu* (Tokyo: Iwanami shoten, 1999).

62. "Shōri no hiai," *Meiji bungaku zenshū*, vol. 42, *Tokutomi Roka shū* (Tokyo, 1966), pp. 366–368.

63. David C. Evans and Mark R. Peattie, *Kaigun: Strategy, Tactics, and Technology in the Imperial Japanese Navy, 1887–1941* (Annapolis, Md.: Naval Institute Press, 1997), p. 148.

64. Cited in Jonathan Haslam, *No Virtue Like Necessity: Realist Thought in International Relations Since Machiavelli* (New Haven, Conn.: Yale University Press, 2002), pp. 203–204.
65. Ikuhiko Hata, "Continental Expansion, 1905–1941," in *Cambridge History of Japan*, vol. 6, pp. 271, 274.
66. Quoted in Zakaria, *From Wealth to Power*, p. 185.
67. For a discussion of the sense of vulnerability and insecurity in the post-Russo-Japanese War period, see Pyle, "The Technology of Japanese Nationalism."

Chapter 4: Stature Among Nations

1. Ernest R. May, *Imperial Democracy: The Emergence of America as a Great Power* (New York: Harcourt, Brace, 1961), p. 270.
2. See Christopher Layne, "The Unipolar Illusion," in *The Perils of Anarchy: Contemporary Realism and International Security*, edited by Michael E. Brown, Sean M. Lynn-Jones, and Steven E. Miller (Cambridge: MIT Press, 1995), p. 153. The calculation is based on Paul Kennedy, *The Rise and Fall of the Great Powers: Economic Change and Military Conflict from 1500 to 2000* (New York: Random House, 1987), pp. 198–209.
3. E. Sydney Crawcour, "Economic Change in the Nineteenth Century," in *The Cambridge History of Japan*, vol. 5, *The Nineteenth Century*, edited by Marius B. Jansen (Cambridge: Cambridge University Press, 1989), p. 616.
4. David Landes, *The Wealth and Poverty of Nations: Why Some Are So Rich and Some So Poor* (New York: W. W. Norton, 1999), pp. 381–382.
5. Quoted in ibid.
6. Kenneth Waltz, *Theory of International Politics* (Reading, Mass.: Addison-Wesley, 1979), p. 77.
7. Alexander Wendt, "Anarchy Is What States Make of It: The Social Construction of Power Politics," *International Organization* 46, no. 2 (Spring 1992), pp. 391–425.
8. Quoted in *Cambridge History of Japan*, vol. 5, pp. 469–470.
9. Marius B. Jansen, *Japan and Its World: Two Centuries of Change* (Princeton, N.J.: Princeton University Press, 1980), pp. 64–65.
10. *Nihon kaika shōshi* is found in *Teiken Taguchi Ukichi zenshū*, vol. 2 (Tokyo, 1928).
11. Quoted in Albert M. Craig, "Fukuzawa Yukichi: The Philosophical Foundations of Meiji Nationalism," in *Political Development in Modern Japan*, edited by Robert E. Ward (Princeton, N.J.: Princeton University Press, 1968), pp. 120–121.
12. Natsume Sōseki, *Sanshirō*, translated by Jay Rubin (Seattle: University of Washington Press, 1977), p. 15.

13. Individuals who are embarrassed about their own civilization can be found in every country at one time or another. Often they are writers, artists, and intellectuals. Henry James, for example, in the 1870s compared the young and relatively undeveloped civilization of his own country, America, with the historic nations of Europe, rich in history and traditions, celebrated achievements, and venerable monuments. He undertook to "enumerate the items of high civilization, as it exists in other countries, which are absent from the texture of American life." The cultural alienation he felt from his own country was apparent in the list of what America lacked: "No state, in the European sense of the word, and indeed barely a specific national name. No sovereign, no court, no personal loyalty, no aristocracy, no church, no clergy, no army, no diplomatic service, no country gentlemen, no palaces, no castles, nor manors, nor old country houses, nor parsonages, nor thatched cottages, nor ivied ruins; no cathedrals, nor abbeys, nor little Norman churches; no great universities, nor public schools— no Oxford, nor Eton, nor Harrow . . . no Epsom nor Ascot!" Quoted in C. Vann Woodward, ed., *The Comparative Approach to American History* (New York: Basic Books, 1968), p. 6. James, with his sense of cultural inferiority that drove him to England and the Continent to write his novels, is an example of the isolated individual embarrassed and alienated from his cultural heritage. What has been striking about Japan through the modern period has been how deep the feelings of alienation and inferiority have run. A sense of ambivalence about Japanese civilization has been widespread among the Japanese.

14. Edwin Arnold, *Seas and Lands* (London, 1891), pp. 240–243.

15. Basil Hall Chamberlain, *Things Japanese* (London, 1891), pp. 3–5.

16. "Datsu-A ron," in *Fukuzawa Yukichi zenshū*, compiled by Keio Gijuku, vol. 10 (Tokyo, 1958–1964), pp. 238–240.

17. "Tōyō no seiryaku hatashite ikan," *Jiji shimpō*, December 1, 1882.

18. Raymond Aron, *Peace and War: A Theory of International Relations,* translated by Richard Howard and Annette Baker Fox (Garden City, N.Y.: Doubleday, 1966), p. 90.

19. Fukuzawa Yukichi, *An Outline of a Theory of Civilization,* translated by David Dilworth and G. Cameron Hurst (Tokyo: Sophia University, 1973), p. 2.

20. The Bakufu's senior minister put it this way: "I am therefore convinced that our policy should be to stake everything on the present opportunity, to conclude friendly alliances, to send ships to foreign countries everywhere and conduct trade, to copy the foreigners where they are at their best and so repair our own shortcomings, to foster our national strength and complete our armaments, and so gradually subject the foreigners to our influence until in the end . . . our hegemony is acknowledged throughout the globe." *Cambridge History of Japan,* vol. 5, p. 279.

21. Peter Duus, ed., *The Cambridge History of Japan,* vol. 6, *The Twentieth Century* (Cambridge: Cambridge University Press, 1989), p. 389.

22. Cited in Inukai Michiko, "Agreeing to Differ—A Report to America," *Japan Quarterly* 8, no. 2 (April–June 1966), p. 182.

23. *Meiroku Zasshi: Journal of the Japanese Enlightenment*, translated by William R. Braisted (Cambridge: Harvard University Press, 1976), pp. 406–407. In the novel *Saka no ue no kumo* (The Cloud Above the Hill), modern Japan's favorite storyteller, Shiba Ryōtarō, compared the shared ambition of the Japanese people at the time of the Russo-Japanese War and their desire for international recognition to chasing a cloud over a hill.

24. Masao Miyoshi, *As We Saw Them: The First Japanese Embassy to the United States (1860)* (Berkeley: University of California Press, 1979), p. 87.

25. See Masao Maruyama, *Studies in the Intellectual History of Tokugawa Japan*, translated by Mikiso Han (Princeton, N.J.: Princeton University Press, 1974), p. 8.

26. Eiko Ikegami, *The Taming of the Samurai: Honorific Individualism and the Making of Modern Japan* (Cambridge: Harvard University Press, 1995), p. 271.

27. John W. Hall, "Rule by Status in Tokugawa Japan," *Journal of Japanese Studies* 1, no. 1 (Autumn 1974), pp. 39–50.

28. Dan Fenno Henderson, *Conciliation and Japanese Law: Tokugawa and Modern*, vol. 1 (Seattle: University of Washington Press, 1965), p. 25.

29. W. G. Beasley, *Select Documents on Japanese Foreign Policy, 1853–1868* (Oxford: Oxford University Press, 1955), pp. 102ff.

30. Quoted in *Sources of Japanese Tradition*, edited by Ryusaku Tsunoda et al. (New York: Columbia University Press, 1958), pp. 608ff.

31. R. P. Dore has suggested that rather than explaining Japan's pursuit of dignity in its foreign policy by reference to Bushido, it is better to see at work a "sociological law" that "as societies become more fluid and mobile . . . the various dimensions by which men are ranked—their power, their family origins, their achievements, their charm or personal effectiveness—cease to correlate as highly as they did. Many people become more aware of relative rankings, more sensitive to them. . . . The ones who have this sensitivity most markedly are likely to be both those who are upwardly and those who are downwardly mobile." Dore, *Japan, Internationalism and the UN* (London: Routledge, 1997), p. 97.

32. These are characteristics rewarded in post–World War II education that Rohlen suggested are "highly indicative of Japanese national character." Thomas P. Rohlen, *Japan's High Schools* (Berkeley: University of California Press, 1983), p. 109.

33. Robert Gilpin, *War and Change in World Politics* (Cambridge: Cambridge University Press, 1981), pp. 30–34.

34. "Idai naru kokumin," *Kokumin no tomo*, May 23, 1891.

35. Alexander Wendt, *Social Theory of International Politics* (Cambridge: Cambridge University Press, 1999), p. 327.

36. "Nihon kokumin no dōkaryoku," *Kokumin no tomo*, October 23, 1893.

37. "Nihon kokumin no hinkaku," *Kokumin no tomo*, June 2, 1893.

38. Gilpin, *War and Change*, pp. 33–34.

39. Carr is quoted in ibid., pp. 32–33.

40. *Fukuzawa Yukichi zenshū*, vol. 15, pp. 333–337.

41. Tokutomi Iichirō, *Sohō Bunsen* (Tokyo, 1915), pp. 312–342.

42. Gilpin, *War and Change*, p. 32.

43. Quoted in David C. Evans and Mark R. Peattie, *Kaigun: Strategy, Tactics, and Technology in the Imperial Japanese Navy, 1887–1941* (Annapolis, Md.: Naval Institute Press, 1997), p. 124.

44. Quoted in Fareed Zakaria, *From Wealth to Power: The Unusual Origins of America's World Role* (Princeton, N.J.: Princeton University Press, 1998), p. 172.

45. Quoted in Shumpei Okamoto, *The Japanese Oligarchy and the Russo-Japanese War* (New York: Columbia University Press, 1970), p. 119.

46. Quoted in Gerrit W. Gong, *The Standard of "Civilization" in International Society* (New York: Oxford University Press, 1984), pp. 27–28.

47. Carol Ann Christ, "'The Sole Guardians of the Art Inheritance of Asia': Japan and China at the 1904 St. Louis World's Fair," *Positions* 8, no. 3 (Winter 2000), p. 677.

48. Quoted in Neil Harris, "All the World a Melting Pot?" in *Mutual Images: Essays in Japanese and American Relations*, edited by Akira Iriye (Cambridge: Harvard University Press, 1975), p. 46.

49. Alexis Dudden, *Japan's Colonization of Korea: Discourse and Power* (Honolulu: University of Hawaii Press, 2005), pp. 135–136.

50. Peter Duus, *The Abacus and the Sword: The Japanese Penetration of Korea, 1895–1910* (Berkeley: University of California Press, 1995), p. 37.

51. Craig, "Fukuzawa Yukichi," pp. 115–116.

52. Quoted in Maruyama Masao, "Fukuzawa, Uchimura, and Okakura: Meiji Intellectuals and Westernization," *The Developing Economies* 4 (December 1966), p. 601.

53. *Kinoshita Naoe shū*, vol. 45, *Meiji bungaku zenshū*, compiled by Yamagiwa Keiji (Tokyo, 1965), p. 337.

54. Miyake Setsurei, "Waga Nihonjin no shokubun," *Nihon oyobi Nihonjin*, January 1907.

55. F. G. Notehelfer, "On Idealism and Realism in the Thought of Okakura Tenshin," *Journal of Japanese Studies* 16, no. 2 (Summer 1990), pp. 353–354.

56. *Tōkyō dempō*, June 12, 1888.

57. Quoted in Joseph Pittau, *Political Thought in Early Meiji Japan* (Cambridge: Harvard University Press, 1967), pp. 177–178.

58. See Kenneth B. Pyle, "The Technology of Japanese Nationalism: The Local Improvement Movement, 1900–1918," *Journal of Asian Studies* 33 (November 1973).

59. Carol Gluck, *Japan's Modern Myths: Ideology in the Late Meiji Period* (Princeton, N.J.: Princeton University Press, 1985), p. 18.

60. Roger F. Hackett, "The Meiji Leaders and Modernization: The Case of Yamagata Aritomo," in *Changing Japanese Attitudes Toward Modernization,* edited by Marius B. Jansen (Princeton, N.J.: Princeton University Press, 1965), p. 249.

61. Quoted in Sheldon Garon, *The State and Labor in Modern Japan* (Berkeley: University of California Press, 1987), p. 30.

62. See Ralf Dahrendorf, *Society and Democracy in Germany* (New York: Doubleday Anchor, 1967), p. 41.

63. Kanai Noburu, "Shakai seisaku to kojinshugi," *Hōgaku kyōkai zasshi* 30 (1912), pp. 1450–1451. Italics added.

64. Sheldon Garon pointed out that "the modern Japanese state has managed its society in peacetime much as Western democracies have done only while at war. The blurring of wartime and peacetime mobilization can be explained in part by the fact that Japan was engaged in hostilities during nearly half of the years between 1894 and 1945: in the Sino-Japanese War (1894–1895), the Russo-Japanese War (1904–1905), World War I (1914–1918), and the 'Fifteen Years' War' (1931–1945). And when not at war, the government was often occupied with 'postwar management' or preparations for the next war." Sheldon Garon, *Molding Japanese Minds: The State in Everyday Life* (Princeton, N.J.: Princeton University Press, 1997), p. 13.

65. Quoted in Gluck, *Japan's Modern Myths,* p. 130.

66. Charles Tilly, ed., *The Formation of National States in Western Europe* (Princeton, N.J.: Princeton University Press, 1975), p. 42. Tilly refined and expanded Hintze's belief that "all state organization was originally military organization." Tilly observed how the major attributes of state formation were made in the crucible of preparation for war: "The building of an effective military machine imposed a heavy burden on the population involved: taxes, conscription, requisitions, and more. The very act of building it—when it worked—produced arrangements which could deliver resources to the government for other purposes. . . . It produced the means of enforcing the government's will over stiff resistance: the army. It tended, indeed, to promote territorial consolidation, centralization, differentiation of the instruments of government and monopolization of the means of coercion, all the fundamental state-making processes. War made the state, and the state made war."

67. Quoted in Miyaji Masato, "Chihō kairyō undo no ronri to tenkai (1)," *Shigakkai zasshi* 79, no. 8 (1970), pp. 4–6, translated in Pyle, "The Technology of Japanese Nationalism," p. 57.

68. Thomas C. Smith, *The Agrarian Origins of Modern Japan* (Stanford: Stanford University Press, 1959), p. 205.

69. See Gluck, *Japan's Modern Myths,* pp. 9–10.

70. Doi Takeo, cited in the book review section of *The Japan Times,* March 20, 2005.

71. I have used the translation by Jay Rubin contained in Natsume Sōseki, *Kokoro:*

A Novel and Selected Essays (Lanham, Md.: Madison Books, 1992), pp. 257–283. See also Kenneth B. Pyle, *The New Generation in Meiji Japan: Problems of Cultural Identity, 1885–1895* (Stanford: Stanford University Press, 1969), pp. 190–191; and *Natsume Sōseki zenshū,* vol. 13 (Tokyo, 1936), pp. 352–380.

72. Quoted from Kenzaburo Ōe, *Japan, the Ambiguous, and Myself: The Nobel Prize Speech and Other Lectures* (Tokyo: Kodansha, 1995), pp. 21–23.

73. See Masaru Tamamoto, "Ambiguous Japan: Japanese National Identity at Century's End," in *International Relations Theory and the Asia-Pacific,* edited by G. John Ikenberry and Michael Mastanduno (New York: Columbia University Press, 2003), p. 198.

74. See Thomas C. Smith, *The Agrarian Origins of Modern Japan* (Stanford: Stanford University Press, 1959), pp. 206–207.

75. Quoted in Donald Keene, *Appreciations of Japanese Culture* (Tokyo: Kodansha, 1971), p. 179.

76. Jun'ichirō Tanizaki, *In Praise of Shadows,* translated by Thomas J. Harper and Edward G. Seidensticker (New Haven, Conn.: Leete's Island Books, 1977), pp. 8, 42.

77. Takeuchi Yoshimi, "Kindai to wa nani ka," quoted in Nobukuni Koyasu, "Nihon no kindai to kindaika-ron," in *Gendai shisō,* vol. 15, *Datsu-Seiyō no shisō* (Tokyo: Iwanami Koza, 1994), p. 133.

78. Hedley Bull, *The Anarchical Society: A Study of Order in World Politics* (New York: Columbia University Press, 1977), pp. 36–37.

79. David Duncan, *Life and Letters of Herbert Spencer,* vol. 2 (New York, 1908), pp. 14–18. Italics in original.

80. *Meiji bunka zenshū,* vol. 6 (Tokyo, 1927–1930), p. 475.

81. Ikegami, *Taming of the Samurai,* p. 23.

82. Quoted in Naoko Shimazu, *Japan, Race and Equality: The Racial Equality Proposal of 1919* (London: Routledge, 1998), pp. 79–80.

83. Ibid.

84. Kōsaka Masataka, cited in Kawachi Takashi, "A New Backlash Against American Influence," *Japan Echo* 25, no. 2 (April 1998), pp. 44–47.

85. Quoted in Mark R. Peattie, *Ishiwara Kanji and Japan's Confrontation with the West* (Princeton, N.J.: Princeton University Press, 1975), pp. 352–353.

86. Ian Buruma, "Back to the Future," *New York Review of Books,* March 4, 1999.

87. Quoted in ibid.

88. Translated in Donald Keene, "Japanese Writers and the Greater East Asian War," *Journal of Asian Studies* 23, no. 2 (April 1964), pp. 209–225.

89. Wendt, *Social Theory of International Politics,* pp. 236–237.

90. Quoted in James B. Crowley, ed., *Modern East Asia: Essays in Interpretation* (New York: Harcourt, Brace and World, 1970), p. 263.

91. Quoted in Ronarudo Dōa, *"Kō shiō" to ieru Nihon* (Tokyo: Asahi shimbunsha, 1993), p. 169.

Chapter 5: The Challenge of International Liberalism

1. This is the thesis of Robert Gilpin in *War and Change in World Politics* (Cambridge: Cambridge University Press, 1981).
2. G. John Ikenberry, *After Victory: Institutions, Strategic Restraint, and the Rebuilding of Order After War* (Princeton, N.J.: Princeton University Press, 2001), p. 257.
3. Charles Tilly, *The Formation of National States in Western Europe* (Princeton, N.J.: Princeton University Press, 1975), pp. 74–75.
4. Paul Kennedy, *The Rise and Fall of the Great Powers: Economic Change and Military Conflict from 1500 to 2000* (New York: Random House, 1987), p. 278.
5. See Gilpin, *War and Change*, pp. 197–198.
6. Ibid.
7. Frederick Dickinson, *War and National Reinvention: Japan in the Great War, 1914–1919* (Cambridge: Harvard University Asia Center, 1999), p. 61.
8. Quoted in Akira Iriye, *Japan and the Wider World* (London: Longman, 1997), p. 25.
9. Akira Iriye, *After Imperialism: The Search for a New Order in the Far East, 1921–1931* (New York: Atheneum, 1969), pp. 6–9.
10. Quoted in Dickinson, *War and National Reinvention*, p. 56.
11. Quoted in ibid., pp. 43–44, 140.
12. Ikuhiko Hata, "Continental Expansion, 1905–1941," in *The Cambridge History of Japan*, vol. 6, *The Twentieth Century*, edited by Peter Duus (Cambridge: Cambridge University Press, 1989), p. 281.
13. Quoted in Charles E. Neu, *The Troubled Encounter: The United States and Japan* (New York: Wiley, 1975), p. 99.
14. Quoted in Richard Hofstadter, *The Age of Reform* (New York: Knopf, 1955), pp. 274–277.
15. Quoted in Henry Kissinger, *Diplomacy* (New York: Simon and Schuster, 1994), p. 51.
16. Walter A. McDougall, *Promised Land, Crusader State: The American Encounter with the World Since 1776* (Boston: Houghton Mifflin, 1997), p. 147.
17. Hofstadter, *Age of Reform*, pp. 274–277.
18. Ikenberry, *After Victory*, p. 124.
19. Ibid., p. 145.
20. N. Gordon Levin, Jr., *Woodrow Wilson and World Politics: America's Response to War and Revolution* (New York: Oxford University Press, 1968), p. 1.
21. See John Gerard Ruggie, *Winning the Peace: America and World Order in the New Era* (New York: Columbia University Press, 1996), p. 12.
22. Kissinger, *Diplomacy*, p. 44.
23. Michael Doyle, quoted in Robert O. Keohane, "International Liberalism Reconsidered," in *The Economic Limits to Modern Politics*, edited by John Dunn (Cambridge: Cambridge University Press, 1990), p. 177.

24. Kissinger, *Diplomacy*, pp. 44, 54.

25. Robert N. Bellah, *Imagining Japan: The Japanese Tradition and Its Modern Interpretation* (Berkeley: University of California Press, 2003), p. 136.

26. Akira Iriye, "The Failure of Economic Expansionism: 1918–1931," in *Japan in Crisis: Essays on Taisho Democracy*, edited by Bernard S. Silberman and H. D. Harootunian (Princeton, N.J.: Princeton University Press, 1974), p. 244.

27. Tetsuo Najita, "Some Reflections on Idealism in the Political Thought of Yoshino Sakuzo," in *Japan in Crisis: Essays on Taisho Democracy*, edited by Bernard S. Silberman and H. D. Harootunian (Princeton, N.J.: Princeton University Press, 1974), p. 40.

28. See Jung-Sun N. Han, "An Imperial Path to Modernity: Yoshino Sakuzo and the Making of a New Liberal Project in Japan, 1905–1937," Ph.D. dissertation, University of Washington, 2003, p. 138.

29. Quoted in Bob Tadashi Wakabayashi, ed., *Modern Japanese Thought* (Cambridge: Cambridge University Press, 1998), p. 168.

30. Quoted in Mitani Taichirō, *Nihon seitō seiji no keisei* (Tokyo, 1967), pp. 19–21. Hara returned from a tour of Europe and America in 1908–1909 convinced that a "fundamental democratization" of politics was the world trend [*sekai no taisei*]: "In every country, the growth of popular influence (*minryoku*) is impressive. Even in Russia where bureaucratic politics has prospered, leaders are now in awe of the popular will. In Germany, also, power is being usurped by the Reichstag. This is material for a great deal of thought with regard to our country's future" (p. 21).

31. Akira Iriye, *Across the Pacific: An Inner History of American–East Asian Relations* (New York: Harcourt, Brace and World, 1967), p. 111.

32. Barbara J. Brooks, *Japan's Imperial Diplomacy: Consuls, Treaty Ports, and War in China, 1895–1938* (Honolulu: University of Hawaii Press, 2000), p. 29.

33. Quoted in Iriye, "Failure of Economic Expansionism," p. 241.

34. Ibid., p. 242.

35. Ibid., pp. 242–243.

36. John W. Dower, *Empire and Aftermath: Yoshida Shigeru and the Japanese Experience, 1878–1954* (Cambridge: Harvard University Press, 1979), p. 79.

37. Thomas W. Burkman, "Nitobe Inazo: From World Order to Regional Order," in *Culture and Identity: Japanese Intellectuals During the Interwar Years*, edited by J. Thomas Rimer (Princeton, N.J.: Princeton University Press, 1990), p. 195.

38. Margaret MacMillan, *Paris 1919: Six Months That Changed the World* (New York: Random House, 2003), pp. 306–307.

39. Naoko Shimazu, *Japan, Race and Equality: The Racial Equality Proposal of 1919* (London: Routledge, 1998), pp. 16–17.

40. Ibid., p. 4.

41. Ibid., p. 115.

42. Shimazu Naoko, "The Japanese Attempt to Secure Racial Equality in 1919," *Japan Forum* 1 (April 1989), pp. 93–94.
43. Levin, *Woodrow Wilson and World Politics,* p. 114.
44. Quoted in Shimazu, *Japan, Race and Equality,* p. 155.
45. Ibid., p. 181.
46. Ibid., p. 184.
47. Brooks, *Japan's Imperial Diplomacy.*
48. Dower, *Empire and Aftermath,* p. 47.
49. Walter LaFeber, *The Clash: U.S.-Japanese Relations Throughout History* (New York: W. W. Norton, 1997), p. 126.
50. Robert Gordon Kaufman, *Arms Control During the Pre-Nuclear: The United States and Naval Limitation Between the Two World Wars* (New York: Columbia University Press, 1990), pp. 15–16.
51. Ibid., p. 1.
52. Ibid., pp. 30–32.
53. Ibid., p. 44.
54. W. G. Beasley, *Japanese Imperialism, 1894–1945* (New York: Oxford University Press, 1987), p. 166.
55. Ian Nish, *Alliance in Decline* (London: Athlone Press, 1972), p. 193.
56. Ibid., p. 221.
57. Beasley, *Japanese Imperialism,* p. 167.
58. Iriye, *After Imperialism,* p. 18.
59. Ibid.
60. Quoted in Neu, *Troubled Encounter,* p. 117.
61. LaFeber, *The Clash,* pp. 144–145.
62. Quoted in Greg Robinson, *By Order of the President: FDR and the Internment of Japanese Americans* (Cambridge: Harvard University Press, 2001), p. 38.
63. Quoted in Ogata Sadako, "The Role of Liberal Nongovernmental Organizations in Japan," in *Pearl Harbor as History: Japanese-American Relations, 1931–1941,* edited by Dorothy Borg and Shumpei Okamoto (New York: Columbia University Press, 1973), p. 468.
64. Randall L. Schweller, "Managing the Rise of Great Powers: History and Theory," in *Engaging China,* edited by Alastair Iain Johnston and Robert Ross (New York: Routledge, 1999), p. 15.
65. *The Cambridge History of Japan,* vol. 6, p. 284.
66. Iriye, *Japan and the Wider World,* p. 53.
67. James William Morley, ed., *Japan Erupts: The London Naval Conference and the Manchurian Incident, 1928–1932* (New York: Columbia University Press, 1984), p. 124.
68. Iriye, "The Failure of Economic Expansionism, p. 245.
69. *The Cambridge History of Japan,* vol. 6, pp. 284–285.
70. Iriye, *Japan and the Wider World,* pp. 55–57.

71. Brooks, *Japan's Imperial Diplomacy*, p. 99.
72. Kaufman, *Arms Control*, pp. 68–69.
73. Ibid.
74. Dean Acheson, *Present at the Creation* (New York: W. W. Norton, 1969), p. 5.
75. Ernest R. May summed up the Sprouts conclusions in his foreword to Erik Goldstein and John Maurer, eds., *The Washington Conference, 1921–22: Naval Rivalry, East Asian Stability and the Road to Pearl Harbor* (London: Frank Cass, 1994).
76. Akira Iriye, *The Origins of the Second World War in Asia and the Pacific* (London: Longman, 1987), p. 2.
77. Quoted in Kissinger, *Diplomacy*, pp. 373–374.
78. Robert H. Ferrell, *American Diplomacy: A History* (New York: W. W. Norton, 1969), p. 567. The verbiage is worth citing because some of it was to turn up again in Japan's postwar constitution, which the Americans drafted during the Occupation. It contained two substantive articles: first: "The High Contracting Parties solemnly declare in the names of their respective peoples that they condemn recourse to war for the solution of international controversies, and renounce it as an instrument of national policy in their relations with one another"; second: "The High Contracting Parties agree that the settlement or solution of all disputes or conflicts of whatever nature or of whatever origin they may be, which may arise among them, shall never be sought except by pacific means."
79. Kissinger, *Diplomacy*, p. 281.
80. Ferrell, *American Diplomacy*, p. 567.

Chapter 6: Japan's Abortive New Order

1. Robert Gilpin, *The Political Economy of International Relations* (Princeton, N.J.: Princeton University Press, 1987), p. 130.
2. Henry A. Kissinger, *A World Restored: Metternich, Castlereagh, and the Problems of Peace, 1812–1822* (Boston: Houghton Mifflin, 1957), p. 1.
3. James B. Crowley, *Japan's Quest for Autonomy: National Security and Foreign Policy, 1930–1938* (Princeton, N.J.: Princeton University Press, 1966), p. 196.
4. Gordon M. Berger, "Japan's Young Prince: Konoe Fumimaro's Early Political Career, 1916–1931, *Monumenta Nipponica* 29, no. 4 (1974), p. 453.
5. Konoe Fumimaro, "EiBei hon'i no heiwashugi o haisu," *Nihon oyobi Nihonjin*, December 15, 1918.
6. Excerpts from Konoe's essay are translated in *Japan Echo* 22 (1955), pp. 12–14.
7. Quoted in John J. Mearsheimer, *The Tragedy of Great Power Politics* (New York: W. W. Norton, 2001), p. 26.

8. Quoted in Akira Iriye, *The Origins of the Second World War in Asia and the Pacific* (London: Longman, 1987), pp. 38–39; also see Yoshitake Oka, *Konoe Fumimaro: A Political Biography*, translated by Shumpei Okamoto and Patricia Murray (Tokyo: University of Tokyo Press, 1983), pp. 10–13.

9. Oka, *Konoe*, p. 17.

10. Peter Duus, ed., *Cambridge History of Japan*, vol. 6, *The Twentieth Century* (Cambridge: Cambridge University Press, 1989), p. 283.

11. See the review of Matsumoto Shigeharu, *Shōwashi e no ichishōgen*, by Marius Jansen, in *Journal of Japanese Studies* 14, no. 2 (Summer 1988), p. 468.

12. Kissinger, *A World Restored*, p. 2.

13. Sadao Asada, "The Japanese Navy and the United States," in *Pearl Harbor as History: Japanese-American Relations, 1931–1941*, edited by Dorothy Borg and Shumpei Okamoto (New York: Columbia University Press, 1973), p. 227.

14. Erik Goldstein and John Maurer, eds., *The Washington Conference, 1921–1922: Naval Rivalry, East Asian Stability and the Road to Pearl Harbor* (London: Frank Cass, 1994), p. 151.

15. Borg and Okamoto, *Pearl Harbor as History*, p. 237.

16. Sadao Asada, "Japanese Admirals and the Politics of Naval Limitation: 'Kato Tomosaburo vs Kato Kanji,'" in *Naval Warfare in the Twentieth Century, 1900–1945: Essays in Honor of Arthur Marder*, edited by Gerald Jordan (London: Croom Helm, 1977), p. 158.

17. Sadao Asada, "From Washington to London: The Imperial Japanese Navy and the Politics of Naval Limitation, 1921–30," in *The Washington Conference, 1921–1922: Naval Rivalry, East Asian Stability and the Road to Pearl Harbor*, edited by Erik Goldstein and John Maurer (London: Frank Cass, 1994), p. 157.

18. Kissinger, *A World Restored*, p. 3.

19. Borg and Okamoto, *Pearl Harbor as History*, pp. 234–240.

20. Michael E. Barnhart, *Japan Prepares for Total War: The Search for Economic Security, 1919–1941* (Ithaca, N.Y.: Cornell University Press, 1987), p. 23.

21. Jack L. Snyder, *Myths of Empire: Domestic Politics and International Ambition* (Ithaca, N.Y.: Cornell University Press, 1991), p. 131. See also Wolfgang J. Mommsen, "Ranke and the Neo-Rankean School in Imperial Germany," in *Leopold von Ranke and the Shaping of the Historical Discipline*, edited by George G. Iggers and James M. Powell (Syracuse, N.Y.: Syracuse University Press, 1990).

22. *Cambridge History of Japan*, vol. 6, p. 287.

23. Barnhart, *Japan Prepares for Total War*, pp. 31–32.

24. Goldstein and Maurer, eds., *The Washington Conference*, pp. 169–170.

25. Quoted in ibid., pp. 172, 175, 183. Italics in original.

26. Michael Mandelbaum, *The Fate of Nations: The Search for National Security in the Nineteenth and Twentieth Centuries* (Cambridge: Cambridge University Press, 1988), p. 341.

27. Crowley, *Japan's Quest for Autonomy*, pp. xiv–xvii.

28. Akira Iriye, *After Imperialism: The Search for a New Order in the Far East, 1921–1931* (New York: Atheneum, 1969), pp. 302–303.

29. Bernard S. Silberman and H. D. Harootunian, eds., *Japan in Crisis: Essays on Taisho Democracy* (Princeton, N.J.: Princeton University Press, 1974), p. 261.

30. Peter Duus and Daniel Okimoto, "Fascism and the History of Prewar Japan," *Journal of Asian Studies* 39, no. 1 (November 1979), pp. 65–76.

31. Peter Duus, Ramon H. Myers, and Mark R. Peattie, eds., *The Japanese Wartime Empire, 1931–1945* (Princeton, N.J.: Princeton University Press, 1996), p. xvi.

32. Ernest R. May, "Foreword," in *The Washington Conference, 1921–22: Naval Rivalry, East Asian Stability and the Road to Pearl Harbor,* edited by Erik Goldstein and John Maurer (London: Frank Cass, 1994).

33. W. G. Beasley, *Japanese Imperialism, 1894–1945* (New York: Oxford University Press, 1987), p. 188.

34. Sadako Ogata, *Defiance in Manchuria: The Making of Japanese Foreign Policy, 1931–1932* (Berkeley: University of California Press, 1964), pp. 165–166.

35. Walter LaFeber, *The Clash: U.S.-Japanese Relations Throughout History* (New York: W. W. Norton, 1997), pp. 169–172.

36. Robert Kaufman, *Arms Control During the Pre-Nuclear: The United States and Naval Limitation Between the Two World Wars* (New York: Columbia University Press, 1990), p. 148.

37. Ibid., p. 172.

38. Barnhart, *Japan Prepares for Total War,* pp. 52–53; Michael Barnhart, "Hornbeck Was Right: The Realist Approach to American Policy Toward Japan," in *Pearl Harbor Reexamined: Prologue to the Pacific War,* edited by Hilary Conroy and Harry Wray (Honolulu: University of Hawaii Press, 1990), p. 66.

39. Quoted in Armin Rappaport, *Henry L. Stimson and Japan, 1931–1933* (Chicago: University of Chicago Press, 1963), p. 106.

40. Sadako Ogata, *Defiance in Manchuria,* p. 179.

41. Akira Iriye, "Introduction," in *Japan Erupts: The London Naval Conference and the Manchurian Incident, 1928–1932,* edited by James William Morley (New York: Columbia University Press, 1984), pp. 238–239. Mark Peattie disagreed. Stressing the role of Nichiren Buddhism on Ishiwara Kanji, he took issue with Iriye's belief that it was military realism that inspired his program. Peattie, *Ishiwara Kanji and Japan's Confrontation with the West* (Princeton, N.J.: Princeton University Press, 1975), p. 47n.

42. Masatoshi Matsushita, *Japan in the League of Nations* (New York: Columbia University Press, 1929), p. 119.

43. Quoted in Ian Nish, *Japan's Struggle with Internationalism: Japan, China and the League of Nations, 1931–1933* (London: Kegan Paul International, 1993), p. 240.

44. Ibid., p. 176.

45. John W. Dower, *Empire and Aftermath: Yoshida Shigeru and the Japanese Experience, 1878–1954* (Cambridge: Harvard University Press, 1979), p. 172.

46. David C. Evans and Mark R. Peattie, *Kaigun: Strategy, Tactics, and Technology in the Imperial Japanese Navy, 1887–1941* (Annapolis, Md.: Naval Institute Press, 1997), pp. 298, 370–374.

47. Akira Iriye, *Japan and the Wider World* (London: Longman, 1997), p. 65.

48. Quoted in Crowley, *Japan's Quest for Autonomy*, p. 188.

49. Quoted in Minamoto Ryoen, "The Symposium on Overcoming Modernity," in *Rude Awakenings: Zen, the Kyoto School, and the Question of Nationalism*, edited by James W. Heisig and John C. Maraldo (Honolulu: University of Hawaii Press, 1995), pp. 212–213.

50. Iriye, *Origins of the Second World War*, p. 103.

51. Royama Masamichi, *Foreign Policy of Japan, 1914–1939* (1941; reprint, Westport, Conn.: Greenwood Press, 1973), p. 169.

52. Crowley, *Japan's Quest for Autonomy*, p. 190.

53. Evans and Peattie, *Kaigun*, pp. 492–493.

54. Quoted in Oka, *Konoe*, pp. 27–28.

55. Daqing Yang, "Convergence or Divergence? Recent Historical Writings on the Rape of Nanjing," *American Historical Review* 104, no. 3 (June 1999), pp. 842–865.

56. Quoted in Iriye, *Origins of the Second World War*, p. 68.

57. During the 1930s, in various complex and often confused ways, Japanese writers sought to recover a sense of Japanese cultural independence from Western civilization. As Yasuda Yojirō, one of the founders of the Japanese Romantic School, wrote, Japan's plight was that although it had become a great power it was still regarded around the world as a "follower country" (*koshinkoku*) because it abandoned its heritage during the Meiji Enlightenment and took the West as its model. To restore cultural integrity, the Romantics advocated a "return" to Japanese traditions. They rejected the universality of Cartesian philosophy; they named their journal *Cogito* to signal their determination to establish a Japanese epistemology grounded in native sensibilities. Kevin Doak, *Dreams of Difference: The Japan Romantic School and the Crisis of Modernity* (Berkeley: University of California Press, 1994), p. xxxi.

58. Miles Fletcher, *The Search for a New Order: Intellectuals and Fascism in Prewar Japan* (Chapel Hill: University of North Carolina Press, 1982), p. 110.

59. Chalmers Johnson, *An Instance of Treason: Ozaki Hotsumi and the Sorge Spy Ring* (Tokyo: Tuttle, 1977), pp. 114–117.

60. James B. Crowley, "Intellectuals as the Visionaries of the New Asian Order," in James W. Morley, *Dilemmas of Growth in Prewar Japan* (Princeton, N.J.: Princeton University Press, 1971), pp. 325–333.

61. *Miki Kiyoshi chōsakushū*, vol. 12 (Tokyo: Iwanami, 1950), pp. 214–215.

62. Silberman and Harootunian, *Japan in Crisis*, pp. 278–279.

63. Fletcher, *The Search for a New Order*, pp. 111–112.

64. Sheldon Garon, *The State and Labor in Prewar Japan* (Berkeley: University of California Press, 1987), p. 212.

65. Fletcher, *The Search for a New Order,* pp. 137–145.

66. Quoted in Waldo H. Heinrichs, Jr., *American Ambassador: Joseph C. Grew and the Development of the American Diplomatic Tradition* (New York: Oxford University Press, 1966), pp. 317–318.

67. Christopher Thorne, *Allies of a Kind: The United States, Britain, and the War Against Japan, 1941–1945* (New York: Oxford University Press, 1978), p. 83.

68. Iriye, *Origins of the Second World War,* p. 156.

69. "The American principle of non-recognition, proclaimed by then secretary of state Henry Stimson in 1932 when Japan conquered Manchuria, prohibited Hull from recognizing any gains acquired through force or the threat of force. A Sino-Japanese settlement that left Japan in control of Chinese territory was a violation of that principle. Yet throughout the negotiations, Hull made it clear . . . that Japan could stay in Manchuria but would have to give up everything else in China proper." Jonathan G. Utley, *Going to War with Japan, 1937–1941* (Knoxville: University of Tennessee Press, 1985), pp. 145–146.

70. Robert Gilpin, *War and Change in World Politics* (Cambridge: Cambridge University Press, 1981), pp. 51–52.

71. Kissinger, *A World Restored,* p. 146.

72. Foreign Minister Tōgō, at the decisive imperial conference of December 1, 1941, concluded (in Robert Butow's words) that "if the government accepted the latest American proposal, the international status of the Empire would drop even below what it had been prior to the Manchurian Incident. Acceptance would endanger the existence of the state. As Tōgō spoke in this vein, his remarks tended to suggest, though never quite openly, that a negotiated settlement would mean forsaking the opportunity to conquer China, to dominate Eastern Asia, to secure the fruits of an Axis victory in Europe, to invade the Soviet Union, and to obtain raw materials at will and in unlimited quantities." Robert J. C. Butow, *Tojo and the Coming of the War* (Stanford: Stanford University Press, 1961), p. 361.

73. Iriye, *Origins of the Second World War,* pp. 164–165.

74. Scott D. Sagan wrote aptly that "if one examines the decisions made in Tokyo in 1941 more closely, one finds not a thoughtless rush to nation suicide, but rather a prolonged, agonizing debate between two repugnant alternatives." See his "The Origins of the Pacific War," in *The Origin and Prevention of Major Wars,* edited by Robert I. Rotberg and Theodore K. Rabb (Cambridge: Cambridge University Press, 1989), p. 324.

75. Marius B. Jansen, *Japan and China: From War to Peace, 1894–1972* (New York: Rand McNally, 1975), p. 202.

76. Quoted in ibid., p. 405.

77. Masao Maruyama, *Thought and Behavior in Modern Japanese Politics* (London: Oxford University Press, 1969), p. 85.

78. Nobutaka Ike, *Japan's Decision for War: Records of the 1941 Policy Conferences* (Stanford: Stanford University Press, 1961), p. xxvi.

79. Thucydides is quoted in Gilpin, *War and Change,* p. 202.
80. Quoted in John Hunter Boyle, *Modern Japan: The American Nexus* (New York: Harcourt Brace Jovanovich, 1993), p. 211.
81. "Never before had such a comparatively large area been conquered in such a short time." Paul Kennedy, *Strategy and Diplomacy: 1870–1945* (London: George Allen and Unwin, 1983), pp. 185–186.
82. Akira Iriye, *Power and Culture: The Japanese-American War, 1941–1945* (Cambridge: Harvard University Press, 1981), p. 64.
83. Ibid., p. 66.
84. Silberman and Harootunian, *Japan in Crisis,* pp. 293–294.
85. Iriye, *Power and Culture,* pp. 68–69.
86. *Cambridge History of Japan,* vol. 6, p. 302.
87. U.S. Department of State, *Papers Relating to the Foreign Relations of the United States: Japan, 1931–1941,* vol. 2 (Washington, D.C.: U.S. Government Printing Office, 1943), p. 786.
88. John W. Dower, *War Without Mercy: Race and Power in the Pacific War* (New York: Pantheon, 1986), p. 263.
89. Ibid., pp. 289–290.
90. Iriye, *Power and Culture,* p. 119.

Chapter 7: The Cold War Opportunity

1. David M. Kennedy, *Freedom from Fear: The American People in Depression and War, 1929–1945* (New York: Oxford University Press, 1999), p. 856.
2. Ibid., p. 853.
3. G. John Ikenberry, *After Victory: Institutions, Strategic Restraint, and the Rebuilding of Order After War* (Princeton, N.J.: Princeton University Press, 2001), p. 163.
4. Cited in Kenneth Waltz, "The Emerging Structure of International Politics," *International Security* 18, no. 2 (Fall 1993), p. 55.
5. Stanley Hoffmann, "An American Social Science: International Relations," *Daedalus* 106, no. 3 (Summer 1977), pp. 41–60.
6. David Calleo, *The Imperious Economy* (Cambridge: Harvard University Press, 1982), p. 1.
7. Kōsaka Masataka, "Tsūshō kokka Nihon no unmei," *Chūō kōron,* November 1975.
8. John Gerard Ruggie, *Winning the Peace: America and World Order in the New Era* (New York: Columbia University Press, 1996), pp. 29–39.
9. John Lewis Gaddis, quoted in Robert A. Pollard, *Economic Security and the Origins of the Cold War, 1945–1950* (New York: Columbia University Press, 1985), p. 10.
10. Quoted in Kennedy, *Freedom from Fear,* p. 805.

11. Quoted in Henry Kissinger, *Diplomacy* (New York: Simon and Schuster, 1994), p. 416.

12. Akira Iriye, *The Cold War in Asia: A Historical Introduction* (Englewood Cliffs, N.J.: Prentice-Hall, 1974), p. 101.

13. Quoted in Kissinger, *Diplomacy,* p. 417.

14. "X" (George F. Kennan), "The Sources of Soviet Conduct," *Foreign Affairs* 25, no. 4 (July 1947).

15. John Lewis Gaddis, *We Now Know: Rethinking Cold War History* (Oxford: Clarendon Press, 1997), p. 72.

16. Ibid., p. 73.

17. Peter Gourevitch, "The Second Image Reversed: The International Sources of Domestic Politics," *International Organization* 32, no. 4 (Autumn 1978), p. 883.

18. Nakao Yūji, ed., *Shōwa Tennō hatsugen kiroku shūsei* (Tokyo: Fuyō shobō, 2003), pp. 400–401.

19. *Life,* July 4, 1947.

20. Kennan and the policy planning staff minutes are quoted in Melvyn P. Leffler, *A Preponderance of Power: National Security, the Truman Administration, and the Cold War* (Stanford: Stanford University Press, 1992), pp. 253–255.

21. George F. Kennan, *Memoirs: 1929–1950* (Boston: Little, Brown, 1967), p. 391.

22. Ibid.

23. Leffler, *Preponderance of Power,* p. 355.

24. Quoted in ibid., p. 393.

25. Ibid., pp. 346–347.

26. Dulles, quoted in Michael M. Yoshitsu, *Japan and the San Francisco Peace Settlement* (New York: Columbia University Press, 1983), pp. 53–54.

27. Quoted in Ronald W. Pruessen, *John Foster Dulles: The Road to Power* (New York: The Free Press, 1982), p. 480.

28. Fred Greene, *U.S. Policy and the Security of Asia* (New York: McGraw-Hill, 1968), p. 74.

29. Kōsaka Masataka, *Saishō Yoshida Shigeru* (Tokyo: Chūō kōronsha, 1968), p. 5.

30. See the observation of Iriye Takanori, cited in the *Journal of Japanese Studies* 19 (Winter 1993), p. 227.

31. See U.S. Department of State, *Foreign Relations of the United States, 1950,* vol. 6 (Washington, D.C.: U.S. Government Printing Office, 1966), pp. 1166–1167.

32. Yoshida's biographer credited me with the earliest use of this term. John Dower wrote that "the term 'Yoshida Doctrine' is of recent coinage, although emphasis on Yoshida's potent legacy has been common since the 1960s. For perhaps the earliest use of 'Yoshida Doctrine,' see Kenneth Pyle, 'Nakasone's Grand Design,' *Journal of Japanese Studies* 13, no. 2." See John W. Dower, *Japan in War and Peace: Selected Essays* (New York: New Press, 1994), p. 238n. Actually, it was an unpublished paper by Nagai Yōnosuke that gave me the idea to use this term to sum up Yoshida's strategy.

33. Leffler, *Preponderance of Power*, p. 393.

34. See Ōtake Hideo, "Defense Controversies and One-Party Dominance: The Opposition in Japan and West Germany," in *Uncommon Democracies: The One-Party Dominant Regimes*, edited by T. J. Pempel (Ithaca, N.Y.: Cornell University Press, 1990), p. 139.

35. Yōnosuke Nagai, "U.S.-Japan Relations in the Global Context" (unpublished paper, 1983).

36. William J. Sebald, *With MacArthur in Japan: A Personal History of the Occupation* (New York: W. W. Norton, 1965), pp. 257–258; John W. Dower, *Empire and Aftermath: Yoshida Shigeru and the Japanese Experience, 1878–1954* (Cambridge: Harvard University Press, 1979), p. 383.

37. Igarashi Takeshi, "Sengo Nihon 'gaikō jōsei' no keisei," *Kokka gakkai zasshi*, nos. 5–8 (1984), p. 486.

38. Chihiro Hosoya, "Japan's Response to U.S. Policy on the Japanese Peace Treaty," *Hitotsubashi Journal of Law and Politics* 10 (1981), p. 18.

39. Dower, *Empire and Aftermath*, p. 315.

40. Miyazawa Kiichi, *Tokyo-Washington no mitsudan* (Tokyo: Jitsugyō no Nihonsha, 1956), p. 160.

41. Okazaki Hisahiko, ed., *Rekishi no kyōkun* (Tokyo: PHP kenkyūjō, 2005), pp. 162–163.

42. Quoted in Ōtake Hideo, *Saigunbi to nashonarizumu* (Tokyo: Chuo koronsha, 1988), p. 133.

43. Ibid., p. 134.

44. Ibid., pp. 136–137.

45. The diary is quoted in Saburo Okita, *Japan's Challenging Years: Reflections on My Lifetime* (New York: George Allen and Unwin, 1985), p. 26.

46. As explained in John Welfield, *An Empire in Eclipse* (London: Athlone Press, 1988), pp. 97–98.

47. Samuels recorded that by resisting the temptation to nurture a large arms industry, Yoshida "played a brilliant game." Richard J. Samuels, *"Rich Nation, Strong Army": National Security and the Technological Transformation of Japan* (Ithaca, N.Y.: Cornell University Press, 1994), p. 152–153.

48. Nagai Yōnosuke, *Gendai to senryaku* (Tokyo: Bungei shunjū, 1985), p. 60.

49. Welfield, *Empire in Eclipse*, p. 107.

50. See Richard J. Samuels, "Politics, Security Policy, and Japan's Cabinet Legislation Bureau: Who Elected These Guys Anyway?" *JPRI Working Paper*, no. 99 (March 2004).

51. Quoted in Tetsuya Kataoka, *Price of a Constitution: The Origins of Japan's Postwar Politics* (New York: Crane Russak, 1991), pp. 122–123.

52. Tahara Soichirō, "Sōren wa kowai desu ka," *Bungei shunjū*, March 1980. Quoted in Kenneth B. Pyle, *The Japanese Question: Power and Purpose in a New Era*, 2d ed. (Washington, D.C.: AEI Press, 1996), p. 130.

53. Yoshitsu, *Japan and the San Francisco Peace Settlement*, p. 40.
54. Yoshida Shigeru, *Sekai to Nippon* (Tokyo: Banchō shobō, 1963), pp. 202–203.
55. Masataka Kōsaka, "The Quest for Credibility," *Look Japan*, September 10, 1981.
56. Dower, *Japan in War and Peace*, p. 213.

Chapter 8: The Yoshida Doctrine as Grand Strategy

1. Igarashi Takeshi, "Peace-Making and Party Politics: The Formation of the Domestic Foreign-Policy System in Postwar Japan," *Journal of Japanese Studies* 11, no. 2 (Summer 1985), pp. 323–356.
2. Takafusa Nakamura, *The Postwar Japanese Economy: Its Development and Structure* (Tokyo: University of Tokyo Press, 1981), pp. 80–81.
3. *Look Japan*, September 10, 1986, p. 4.
4. Ōkubo Toshimichi, the dominant leader of the 1870s, dismissed economic liberalism. A government role, he said, was "absolutely necessary" even if it went "against the laws of political economy." Japan, he added, was "something different" (*ibutsu*) and would advance by "different laws" (*bensoku*). Albert M. Craig, "Kido Koin and Okubo Toshimichi: A Psychohistorical Analysis," in *Personality in Japanese History*, edited by Albert M. Craig and Donald H. Shively (Berkeley: University of California Press, 1970), p. 296.
5. Shigeru Yoshida, *Japan's Decisive Century, 1867–1967* (New York: Praeger, 1967), pp. 15–16.
6. Chalmers Johnson, *MITI and the Japanese Miracle: The Growth of Industrial Policy, 1925–1975* (Stanford: Stanford University Press, 1982), p. 210.
7. Sakakibara Eisuke and Noguchi Yukio, "Ōkurashō—Nichigin ōchō no bunseki," *Chūō kōron*, August 1977, p. 113.
8. Ibid.
9. Ibid. See also Kozo Yamamura, "The Role of Government in Japan's 'Catchup' Industrialization: A Neoinstitutionalist Perspective," in *The Japanese Civil Service and Economic Development*, edited by Hyung-ki Kim et al. (Oxford: Clarendon Press, 1995), p. 112.
10. Michael E. Barnhart, *Japan Prepares for Total War: The Search for Economic Security, 1919–1941* (Ithaca, N.Y.: Cornell University Press, 1987), p. 273.
11. Kozo Yamamura, "The Success of Bridled Capitalism: Economic Development of Japan, 1880–1980," in *The Wealth of Nations in the Twentieth Century*, edited by R. Meyer (Stanford: Hoover Institution Press, 1995).
12. Thomas P. Rohlen, "Learning: The Mobilization of Knowledge in the Japanese Political Economy," in *The Political Economy of Japan*, vol. 3, *Cultural and Social Dynamics*, edited by Shumpei Kumon and Henry Rosovsky (Stanford: Stanford University Press, 1992), p. 327.

13. Richard J. Samuels, "Reinventing Security: Japan Since Meiji," *Daedalus* 120, no. 4 (Fall 1991), p. 54.

14. Quoted in Eric Heginbotham and Richard J. Samuels, "Mercantile Realism and Japanese Foreign Policy, *International Security* 22, no. 4 (Spring 1998), p. 177.

15. Quoted in Donald C. Hellmann, "Japanese Politics and Foreign Policy: Elitist Democracy Within an American Greenhouse," in *The Political Economy of Japan,* vol. 2, *The Changing International Context,* edited by Takashi Inoguchi and Daniel I. Okimoto (Stanford: Stanford University Press, 1988), p. 361.

16. Quoted in Akira Iriye and Warren I. Cohen, eds., *The United States and Japan in the Postwar World* (Lexington: University of Kentucky Press, 1989), p. 97.

17. Stephen D. Krasner, "Vision, Interest, and Uncertainty," in *A Vision of a New Liberalism: Critical Essays on Murakami's Anticlassical Analysis,* edited by Kozo Yamamura (Stanford: Stanford University Press, 1997), p. 53.

18. Selig Harrison, ed., *Japan's Nuclear Future: The Plutonium Debate and East Asian Security* (Washington, D.C.: Carnegie Endowment, 1996), p. 7.

19. *Japan Times,* May 25, 1998, p. 1.

20. *Japan Times,* June 11, 2000, p. 1.

21. Harrison, *Japan's Nuclear Future,* p. 9.

22. Heginbotham and Samuels, "Mercantile Realism," p. 198.

23. See discussion in Robert Gilpin, *War and Change in World Politics* (Cambridge: Cambridge University Press, 1981), p. 215.

24. Quoted in Harrison, *Japan's Nuclear Future,* pp. 17–18.

25. Ibid., pp. 11–13.

26. John Welfield, *An Empire in Eclipse* (London: Athlone Press, 1988), p. 242.

27. Richard J. Samuels, "Politics, Security Policy, and Japan's Cabinet Legislation Bureau: Who Elected These Guys Anyway?" *JPRI Working Paper,* no. 99 (March 2004), p. 3.

28. Quoted in ibid., pp. 6–7.

29. Herman Kahn, *The Emerging Japanese Superstate: Challenge and Response* (Englewood Cliffs, N.J.: Prentice-Hall, 1970), p. 165.

30. See Chapter 10 of this book.

31. Ishihara and Morita are quoted in Samuel P. Huntington, "Why International Primacy Matters," *International Security* 17, no. 4 (Spring 1993), p. 75. Reflecting on Japan's postwar strategy, Huntington observed that "for decades Japan has acted in a way totally consistent with the 'realist' theory of international relations, which holds that international politics is basically anarchic and that to insure their security states act to maximize their power. Realist theorists have focused overwhelmingly on military power. Japan has accepted all the assumptions of realism but applied them purely in the economic realm." Huntington's conclusion was that "Japanese strategy is a strategy of economic warfare."

32. Yamamura, "The Success of Bridled Capitalism."

33. Edward J. Lincoln, *Japan's New Global Role* (Washington, D.C.: Brookings Institution, 1993), p. 62.

34. Huntington, "Why International Primacy Matters," p. 74. Italics in original.

35. Quoted in ibid., p. 74.

36. T. J. Pempel, "Regime Shift: Japanese Politics in a Changing World Economy," *Journal of Japanese Studies* 23, no. 2 (Summer 1997), p. 341n.

37. Heginbotham and Samuels, "Mercantile Realism," pp. 199–200.

38. Ibid., p. 194.

39. Nagai Yōnosuke, "Moratorium kokka no boei-ron," *Chuo koron*, January 1981.

40. Nagai Yōnosuke, *Gendai to senryaku* (Tokyo: Bungei shunju, 1985), p. 67.

41. Amaya Naohiro, "Chōnin koku Nihon tedai no kurigoto," *Bungei shunjū*, March 1980; for a partial translation of this essay, see *Japan Echo* 7, no. 2 (1980), pp. 53–62. See also "Nichi-Bei jidōsha mondai to chōnin kokka," *Bungei shunjū*, June 1980, and "Sopu nashonarizumu o haisu," *Bungei shunjū*, July 1981. Amaya's essays were collected in *Nihon chōnin kokka ron* (Tokyo: PHP bunko, 1989).

42. Amaya Naohiro, "Chōnin koku Nihon tedai no kurigoto," *Bungei shunjū*, March 1980; for a partial translation of the essay, see *Japan Echo* 7, no. 2 (1980), pp. 53–62. See also "Nichi-Beijidosha mondai to chōnin kokka," *Bungei shunjū*, June 1980, and "Sōpu nashonarizumu o haisu, *Bungei shunjū*, July 1981.

43. Naohiro, "Chōnin koku Nihon tedai no kurigoto."

44. Quoted in Tetsuo Anzai, "We Can Still Learn from Europe," *Japan Echo* 2, no. 1 (1975), pp. 128–129.

45. Huntington, "Why International Primacy Matters," p. 76.

46. Quoted in ibid., p. 76.

47. Ezra F. Vogel, *Japan as Number One: Lessons for America* (Cambridge: Harvard University Press, 1979).

48. Iida Tsuneo, *Nippon-teki chikara-tsuyosa no sai-hakken* (Tokyo: Nihon keizai shinmbunsha, 1979), p. 206.

49. *Kokuminsei no kenkyū dai 7-kai zenkoku chōsa: 1983-nen zenkoku chōsa* (Tokyo: Tōkei sūri kenkyūjo, 1984).

50. The political theorist Michael Waltzer observed in his *Just and Unjust Wars*, "The outer limit of what can be legitimately sought in war . . . is the conquest and total reconstruction of the enemy state, and only against an enemy like Nazism can it possibly be right to reach that far. . . . The right does not arise in every war; it did not arise, I think, in the war against Japan." Michael Waltzer, *Just and Unjust Wars: A Moral Argument with Historical Illustrations* (New York: Basic Books, 1992), p. 113.

51. Yasusuke Murakami, *An Anticlassical Political-Economic Analysis: A Vision for the Next Century* (Stanford: Stanford University Press, 1996), p. 415.

52. Amaya Naohiro, *Nippon wa doko e iku no ka* (Tokyo: PHP, 1989), p. 189.

53. Sakakibara Eisuke, "Change and Continuity in Modern Japan," *Japan Echo* 24 (1997), p. 98.

54. Ibid.

55. *New York Times,* September 14, 1994.

56. *The Economist,* June 24, 2000.

57. John J. Mearsheimer, *The Tragedy of Great Power Politics* (New York: W. W. Norton, 2001), p. 140.

58. Quoted in Welfield, *Empire in Eclipse,* p. 251.

59. See Murakami's editorial introduction to *Japan Echo* 17, no. 4 (1990), p. 4.

60. "To be dependent on the continued good will of another sovereign state is demoralizing, because it is a confession of impotence, an invitation to the irresponsibility induced by the conviction that events cannot be affected by one's will." Henry A. Kissinger, *A World Restored: Metternich, Castlereagh, and the Problems of Peace, 1812–1822* (Boston: Houghton Mifflin, 1957), p. 316.

61. John Nathan, *Japan Unbound: A Volatile Nation's Quest for Pride and Purpose* (New York: Houghton Mifflin, 2004), p. 14.

62. Chalmers Johnson, "Reflections on the Dilemma of Japanese Defense," *Asian Survey* 26, no. 5 (May 1986), p. 559. As one of Mishima's biographers, Henry Scott Stokes observed that his suicide struck a responsive chord among Japanese who were "deeply traumatized" by the constitution that was forced upon them and that required the abandonment of ancient traditions of martial valor, replacing them with materialist and merchant values. Mishima, who had organized a small army of rightist students, was privately helped by Satō Eisaku, the prime minister, and Nakasone Yasuhiro, who was at that time director-general of the JDA. Satō's connections to right-wing businessmen facilitated financial support for Mishima's small militia, and Nakasone made it possible for this militia to train at a self-defense base. Satō, Nakasone, and many other prominent Japanese sympathized with Mishima's effort. Henry Scott Stokes, "Lost Samurai: The Withered Soul of Postwar Japan," *Harper's Magazine,* October 1985. Shortly before his suicide, he had written that Japan must recover the essence of its culture, which he defined as *miyabi,* "courtly elegance," as epitomized in *The Tale of Genji.* John Nathan, *Mishima: A Biography* (New York: Da Capo Press, 2000), pp. 232–233.

63. Kōsaaka Masataka, "Tsūshō kokka Nihon no unmei," *Chūō kōron,* November 1975.

64. Tahara Soichirō, "Sōren wa kowai desu ka," *Bungei shunjū,* March 1980.

65. Matsuoka Hideo, "'Nori-okure gaikō' no susume," *Chūō kōron,* March 1980.

66. Kōsaka Masataka, "Yaruta taisei: yonju-nen: Nihon gaikō nokijiku wa dō kawaru ka," *Chūō kōron,* January 1985.

67. Kenzaburo Ōe, "Speaking on Japanese Culture Before a Scandinavian Audi-

ence," in *Japan, the Ambiguous, and Myself: The Nobel Prize Speech and Other Lectures* (Tokyo: Kodansha, 1995), pp. 23–27.

68. Karel van Wolferen, *The Enigma of Japanese Power* (New York: Knopf, 1989), p. 9.

69. Murakami, *An Anticlassical Political-Economic Analysis*, p. 415.

70. Nakasone Yasuhiro, *My Life in Politics* (1982) (typescript).

71. Nakasone Yasuhiro, "Takumashii bunka to fukushi no kuni o," *Seiron*, January 1983, pp. 26–37. See translation in *Japan Echo* 10, no. 1 (1983), pp. 12–18.

72. For a discussion of the mobilization of the Ōhira Research Groups, see Kenneth B. Pyle, *The Japanese Question: Power and Purpose in a New Era*, 2d ed. (Washington, D.C.: AEI Press, 1996), pp. 68–72.

73. Ōhira sōri no seisaku kenkyūkai, ed., *Bunka no jidai* (Tokyo: Ōkurasho, 1988), p. 71.

74. Sekai heiwa kenkyūjō, ed., *Nakasone naikaku shi: shiryō-hen* (Tokyo: Chūōkōron, 1995), pp. 631–632. See also Kamiya Matake, "Japanese Politics and Asia-Pacific Policy," in *The Golden Age of the U.S.-China-Japan Triangle, 1972–1989*, edited by Ezra F. Vogel, Yuan Ming, and Tanaka Akihiko (Cambridge: Harvard University Press, 2002), pp. 69–70.

75. Sekai heiwa kenkyūjō, *Nakasone naikaku shi*, p. 620. See also Matake, "Japanese Politics and Asia-Pacific Policy," pp. 70–71.

76. Sekai heiwa kenkyūjō, *Nakasone naikaku shi*, pp. 383–385.

77. Nakasone Yasuhiro, "Sōri kantei o saru ni saishite," *Bungei shunjū*, December 1987.

78. I owe this observation on Nakasone and the limits of the system to Donald Hellmann, "Japanese Politics and Foreign Policy," p. 376.

79. In an article on Nakasone's "grand design" for reorienting Japan's international role, I described the prime minister as caught between the past and the future in trying to lead his country toward a more activist foreign policy. In a speech to the Asia Foundation in San Francisco on March 10, 1988, shortly after leaving office, Nakasone agreed with this assessment and expressed impatience with the pace of change: "Professor Pyle argues [I] expounded a grand design for transforming Japan's foreign policy—namely, from a policy of traditional passivity to one in which Japan carries growing international responsibilities, involves itself in strategic issues, plays an active role in its national defense, and is supported by a new and liberal nationalism. Although I agree with the way Professor Pyle has formulated the basic design of my foreign policy, the outcome of that design is yet to be seen." Pyle, *The Japanese Question*, p. 188.

Chapter 9: *The Post–Cold War Interval in East Asia*

1. Samuel P. Huntington, "America's Changing Strategic Interests," *Survival* 33, no. 1 (January/February 1991), p. 8.

2. Robert Gilpin, *The Political Economy of International Relations* (Princeton, N.J.: Princeton University Press, 1987), pp. 391–392.

3. Paul Kennedy, "The Eagle Has Landed," *Financial Times*, February 2/3, 2002.

4. Ibid.

5. Quoted in Joseph S. Nye, Jr., *The Paradox of American Power: Why the World's Only Superpower Can't Go It Alone* (New York: Oxford University Press, 2002), p. 1.

6. G. John Ikenberry, *After Victory: Institutions, Strategic Restraint, and the Rebuilding of Order After War* (Princeton, N.J.: Princeton University Press, 2001), pp. 215–216.

7. Francis Fukuyama, "The End of History," *National Interest*, Summer 1989.

8. John Gerard Ruggie, *Winning the Peace: America and World Order in the New Era* (New York: Columbia University Press, 1996), p. 6.

9. Gilpin pointed out that the outcome of great wars do not always give rise immediately to a renovated international order: "As has frequently occurred, the combatants may exhaust themselves, and the 'victorious' power may be unable to reorder the international system. . . . The Pax Britannica was not replaced by the Pax Americana; there was a twenty year interregnum, what E. H. Carr called the 'twenty years' crisis. Eventually, however, a new power or set of powers emerges to give governance to the international system." Robert Gilpin, *War and Change in World Politics* (Cambridge: Cambridge University Press, 1981), p. 198.

10. Masataka Kōsaka, "The International Economic Policy of Japan," in *The Foreign Policy of Modern Japan*, edited by Robert A. Scalapino (Berkeley: University of California Press, 1977), p. 224.

11. Kozo Yamamura, "Germany and Japan in a New Phase of Capitalism: Confronting the Past and Future," in *The End of Diversity? Prospects for German and Japanese Capitalism*, edited by Kozo Yamamura and Wolfgang Streeck (Ithaca, N.Y.: Cornell University Press, 2003), pp. 115–116.

12. See Kozo Yamamura, "The Japanese Political Economy After the 'Bubble': Plus Ca Change?" *Journal of Japanese Studies* 23, no. 2 (Summer 1997), pp. 291–331.

13. Quoted in ibid., p. 304.

14. Nakatani Iwao, *Nihon keizai no rekishiteki henkan* (Tokyo: Toyo keizai shimposha, 1996), pp. 345–346.

15. Quoted in Yamamura, "The Japanese Political Economy After the 'Bubble,'" p. 304. Sakakibara subsequently elaborated his views in *Structural Reform in Japan: Breaking the Iron Triangle* (Washington, D.C.: Brookings Institution, 2003), which places him more in our category of favoring "a third way."

16. Quoted in ibid., p. 304.
17. See the article by Donald C. Hellmann, "Japanese Politics and Foreign Policy,": Elitist Democracy Within an American Greenhouse," in *The Political Economy of Japan*, vol. 2, *The Changing International Context*, edited by Takashi Inoguchi and Daniel I. Okimoto (Stanford: Stanford University Press, 1988), p. 346.
18. Igarashi Takeshi, "Peace-Making and Party Politics: The Formation of the Domestic Foreign-Policy System in Postwar Japan," *Journal of Japanese Studies* 2, no. 2 (Summer 1985), pp. 323–356.
19. Richard J. Samuels, "Politics, Security Policy, and Japan's Cabinet Legislation Bureau: Who Elected These Guys Anyway?" *JPRI Working Paper*, no. 99 (March 2004), p. 7.
20. Nakanishi Hiroshi, "The Japan-US Alliance and Japanese Domestic Politics: Sources of Change, Prospects for the Future," in *The Future of America's Alliances in Northeast Asia*, edited by Michael H. Armacost and Daniel I. Okimoto (Stanford: Asia-Pacific Research Center, 2004), p. 106.
21. Tahara Soichirō, "Nippon no fumie," *Bungei shunjū*, October 1990. As prime minister, Miyazawa later modified his position.
22. Ibid.
23. Nakasone Yasuhiro and Kōsaka Masataka, "Atarashii Nippon no kokka senryaku," *Voice*, May 1991.
24. Ozawa Ichirō, "Hoshuseiji no shissei o tadasu," *Voice*, March 1992.
25. *Asahi shimbun*, November 29, 1991; Ozawa Ichirō, "Waterware wa naze kaikaku o mezasu ka," *Bungei shunjū*, December 1992.
26. *Asahi shimbun*, February 21, 1992.
27. Ichiro Ozawa, *Blueprint for a New Japan* (Tokyo: Kodansha, 1994).
28. See Don Oberdorfer, *The Two Koreas: A Contemporary History* (Reading, Mass.: Addison-Wesley, 1997), pp. 221–222.
29. Don Oberdorfer, *The Changing Context of U.S.-Japan Relations* (New York: Japan Society, 1998; Tokyo: America-Japan Society, 1998), p. 39.
30. See the discussion in Aaron Friedberg, "Introduction," *Strategic Asia: 2001–2002* (Seattle: National Bureau of Asian Research, 2001).
31. See Ōtake Hideo, "Defense Controversies and One-Party Dominance: The Opposition in Japan and West Germany," in T. J. Pempel, ed., *Uncommon Democracies: The One-Party Dominant Regimes* (Ithaca, N.Y.: Cornell University Press, 1990), p. 139.
32. See David Arase, "U.S. and ASEAN Perceptions of Japan's Role in the Asian-Pacific Region," and Steven C. M. Wong, "Japan in Search of a Global Economic Role," in *Japan, ASEAN, and the United States*, edited by Harry H. Kendall and Clara Joewono (Berkeley: Institute of East Asian Studies, 1991), pp. 275, 296–297.
33. Discussed in Kenneth B. Pyle, *The Japanese Question: Power and Purpose in a New Era*, 2d ed. (Washington, D.C.: AEI Press, 1996), pp. 134–135.

34. Edward J. Lincoln, *East Asian Economic Regionalism* (Washington, D.C.: Brookings Institution, 2004), p. 30.
35. Okazaki Hisahiko, "'Ajia chōtaiken," *This Is Yomiuri*, August 1992, pp. 42–90; translated as "Southeast Asia in Japan's National Strategy," *Japan Echo* 20 (1993).
36. Aaron L. Friedberg, "Will Europe's Past Be Asia's Future?" *Survival* 42, no. 3 (Autumn 2000), pp. 147–160.
37. Huntington, "America's Changing Strategic Interests," p. 12.
38. Michael H. Armacost and Kenneth B. Pyle, "Japan and the Unification of Korea: Challenges for American Policy Coordination," in *Korea's Future and the Great Powers*, edited by Nicholas Eberstadt and Richard J. Ellings (Seattle: University of Washington Press, 2001).
39. Ibid.

Chapter 10: Japan and the Rise of China

1. "The widespread perception that intraregional trade is increasing relative to the share of trade between the region and the rest of the world is largely an artifact of the emergence of China." Edward J. Lincoln, *East Asian Economic Regionalism* (Washington, D.C.: Brookings Institution, 2004), p. 8.
2. *Japan Times*, June 3, 1999.
3. Akira Iriye, ed., *The Chinese and the Japanese: Essays in Political and Cultural Interactions* (Princeton, N.J.: Princeton University Press, 1980), p. 3.
4. Michael Schaller, *Altered States: The United States and Japan Since the Occupation* (New York: Oxford University Press, 1997), p. 53.
5. Yoshihide Soeya, *Japan's Economic Diplomacy with China, 1945–1978* (Oxford: Clarendon Press, 1998), p. 21.
6. Quoted in John W. Dower, *Empire and Aftermath: Yoshida Shigeru and the Japanese Experience, 1878–1954* (Cambridge: Harvard University Press, 1979), p. 403.
7. Soeya, *Japan's Economic Diplomacy*, p. 55.
8. Ibid., pp. 97–98.
9. As a percentage of Japan's world trade, its Asian trade was still a small 3 percent. Ibid., p. 2.
10. Aruga Tadashi, cited in Walter LaFeber, *The Clash: U.S.-Japanese Relations Throughout History* (New York: W. W. Norton, 1997), p. 358.
11. Sadako Ogata, *Normalization with China: A Comparative Study of U.S. and Japanese Processes* (Berkeley: Institute of East Asian Studies, 1988), pp. 104–105.
12. Selig Harrison, ed., *Japan's Nuclear Future: The Plutonium Debate and East Asian Security* (Washington, D.C.: Carnegie Endowment, 1996), pp. 14–16.
13. Ibid., p. 11.

14. William Burr, ed., "The National Security Archive: Negotiating U.S.-Chinese Rapprochement," www.gwu.edu/nsarchiv/NSAEBB/NSAEBB70/.
15. Henry Kissinger, *White House Years* (Boston: Little, Brown, 1979), p. 334. See also the discussion in William Bundy, *A Tangled Web: The Making of Foreign Policy in the Nixon Presidency* (New York: Hill and Wang, 1998), p. 236.
16. LaFeber, *The Clash*, pp. 355–358.
17. Henry Kissinger, *Years of Upheaval* (Boston: Little, Brown, 1982), p. 693.
18. Ijiri Hidenori, *Amerikajin no Chūgokukan* (Tokyo: Bunshun shinsho, 2000), pp. 8–17, 230–231.
19. Schaller, *Altered States*, p. 236.
20. Ibid., p. 241.
21. Harrison, *Japan's Nuclear Future*, p. 17.
22. See Wakamiya Yoshibumi, *The Postwar Conservative View of Asia* (Tokyo: LTCB International Library Foundation, 1999), pp. 130–131.
23. Chae-Jin Lee, *Japan Faces China: Political and Economic Relations in the Postwar Era* (Baltimore: Johns Hopkins University Press, 1976), p. 124.
24. Zhu Jianrong provided a persuasive account of the factors influencing Chinese thinking in the decision to waive reparations. See *Gaikō foramu*, October 1992.
25. Chae-Jin Lee, *China and Japan: New Economic Diplomacy* (Washington, D.C.: Hoover Institution Press, 1984), p. 113.
26. Hasegawa Keitaro, "Should We Leave China in the Lurch?" *Japan Echo* 8, no. 3 (1981), pp. 97–109.
27. Allen S. Whiting, *China Eyes Japan* (Berkeley: University of California Press, 1989), p. 158.
28. David Arase, *Buying Power: The Political Economy of Japan's Foreign Aid* (Boulder: Lynn Rienner, 1995), pp. 18ff.
29. The words of Sun Pinghua, president of the China-Japan Friendship Association, in 1988, quoted in Kojima Tomoyuki, "Japan's China Policy: The Diplomacy of Appeasement," *Japan Echo* 15, no. 4 (1988), p. 27.
30. See Caroline Rose, *Interpreting History in Sino-Japanese Relations* (London: Routledge, 1998).
31. Quoted in Michael H. Armacost, *Friends or Rivals? The Insider's Account of U.S.-Japan Relations* (New York: Columbia University Press, 1996), p. 139.
32. Although there is speculation that Jiang had personal reasons for harping on Japanese militarism, his biographer wrote that "so far as we know, Jiang lost no close family members in the war with Japan. . . . [He did] not harbor any of the instinctive, visceral anti-Japanese hatred." Bruce Gilley, *Tiger on the Brink: Jiang Zemin and China's New Elite* (Berkeley: University of California Press, 1998), pp. 14–15.
33. Michael H. Armacost and Kenneth B. Pyle, "Japan and the Unification of Korea: Challenges for American Policy Coordination," in *Korea's Future and the*

Great Powers, edited by Nicholas Eberstadt and Richard J. Ellings (Seattle: University of Washington Press, 2001), p. 134.

34. *Japan Digest,* October 31, 1997.
35. Armacost and Pyle, "Japan and the Unification of Korea," p. 143.
36. *New York Times,* March 9, 1990.
37. *New York Times,* July 10, 1999.
38. Christopher B. Johnstone, "Japan's China Policy: Implications for U.S.-Japan Relations," *Asian Survey* 38, no. 11 (November 1998), p. 1081.
39. Ibid., p. 1081.
40. *Far Eastern Economic Review,* July 22, 1999, p. 22.
41. The one exception was a statement in the U.S.-Japan Joint Communiqué in 1969, when Prime Minister Satō said that "the maintenance of peace and security in the Taiwan area was also a most important factor for the security of Japan."
42. Euan Graham, *Japan's Sea Lane Security, 1940–2004: A Matter of Life or Death?* (London: Routledge, 2006), p. 6.
43. See the discussion in Kenneth B. Pyle and Eric Heginbotham, "Japan," in *Strategic Asia: Power and Purpose, 2001–2002* (Seattle: National Bureau of Asian Research, 2001), pp. 71–128.
44. These impressions are partly based on interviews that Michael Armacost and I conducted with a cross-section of Japanese leaders in September 2000.
45. Sakakibara Eisuke, writing in the "Seiron" (opinion) column, *Sankei shinbun,* May 2, 2004.

Chapter 11: *The Prospect of a New East Asian Order*

1. John Lewis Gaddis, "Grand Strategy in the Second Term," *Foreign Affairs* 84, no. 1 (January/February 2005), p. 2.
2. Masashi Nishihara, "Japan's Receptivity to Conditional Engagement," in *Weaving the Net: Conditional Engagement with China,* edited by James Shinn (Washington, D.C.: Council on Foreign Relations, 1996), p. 187.
3. See the extended discussion in Yutaka Kawashima, *Japanese Foreign Policy at the Crossroads: Challenges and Options for the Twenty-First Century* (Washington, D.C.: Brookings Institution, 2003), pp. 86–91. There is the additional concern over what would happen if the Americans were to reach an accommodation of sorts with North Korea. How secure would Japan be? The thoughtful and otherwise cautious president of the National Defense Academy raised this issue in terms of Japan's nuclear option. Writing in November 2003, Nishihara Masashi observed that if the U.S. nuclear umbrella were compromised, "the question would be whether to rely on conventional weapons, including a missile defense system, or to decide that since a missile defense system cannot

provide complete security, Japan must acquire its own nuclear capability." Nishihara worried that anti-American sentiment in South Korea might lead the Americans to pull back their forward-deployed troops: "Americans are now moving toward projecting their power globally while shifting toward increased reliance on high-tech weaponry and scaling back their ground forces. . . . In Northeast Asia . . . the United States could do everything it needs to do by itself. Japan should consider its own position in this light." Nishihara Masashi, "The Peril of a US-North Korea Nonaggression Pact," *Japan Echo* 31, no. 1 (February 2004), pp. 13–16.

4. This is the proposal of Michael H. Armacost, former ambassador to Japan. See Armacost, *Friends or Rivals? The Insider's Account of U.S.-Japan Relations* (New York: Columbia University Press, 1996), p. 246.

5. Erica R. Gould and Stephen Krasner, "Germany and Japan: Binding Versus Autonomy," in *The End of Diversity? Prospects for German and Japanese Capitalism,* edited by Kozo Yamamura and Wolfgang Streeck (Ithaca, N.Y.: Cornell University Press, 2003), p. 53.

6. *Washington Post,* March 27, 1990.

7. *Japan Digest,* February 25, 2000. Kanemaru told his colleague Takeshita Noboru that he coined the term after reading that the Duke of Wellington had once said that "a great general should be considerate about the conditions of his soldiers' boots."

8. Quoted in Roger Buckley, *U.S.-Japan Alliance Diplomacy, 1945–1990* (Cambridge: Cambridge University Press, 1995), p. 4.

9. *Gaikō Forum* 2, no. 1 (Winter 2002), pp. 29–30.

10. Henry Kissinger, *Does America Need a Foreign Policy? Toward a Diplomacy for the 21st Century* (New York: Simon and Schuster, 2001), p. 119.

11. Okazaki Hisahiko, "'Ajia chōtaiken' e no shinsenryaku," in *This Is Yomiuri,* August 1992, pp. 42–90; translated as "Southeast Asia in Japan's National Strategy," *Japan Echo* 20 (1993), p. 61.

12. Umemoto Kazuyoshi, "The Last Holdout: Impediments to Reform of Japan's Security System," *Gaiko Forum* 2, no. 1 (Winter 2002), p. 32. Italics added. This was a roundtable discussion, and Umemoto Kazuyoshi is director of the Policy Coordination Division in the Ministry of Foreign Affairs.

13. Ozawa Ichirō, "Hoshu-seiji no shissei o tadasu," *Voice,* March 1992. In 2006 when he was chosen leader of the Democratic Party of Japan, Ozawa said, "Recently, I have recalled a famous line in the climax of *The Leopard,* a film I watched during my youth: "We must change to remain the same." *Yomiuri shimbun,* April 8, 2006.

14. See the discussion in Kenneth B. Pyle and Eric Heginbotham, "Japan," in *Strategic Asia: Power and Purpose, 2001–2002,* edited by Richard J. Ellings and Aaron Friedberg (Seattle: National Bureau of Asian Research, 2001), pp. 113–117.

15. Joichi Ito, "An Anniversary to Forget," *New York Times,* August 7, 2005, p. 12.

16. A prescient observer of generational differences, Takemi Keizō, an LDP member of the Upper House and formerly parliamentary vice minister for Foreign Affairs, confirmed many of the observations made here. He pointed out that among young people under thirty years of age there is a notable strain of individualism. From the time they were born, he wrote, Japan was already an advanced country rich in material terms. They are much less affected by the older psychological complex toward the West. At the same time, they do not feel the same sense of superiority toward Asia that was common in earlier generations of Japanese. In fact, during their lives Asia has come to command more respect for its economic growth and assertiveness. Takemi further observed that many younger Japanese do not have quite the same guilt-consciousness toward Asia that their elders feel. Thus, while older Japanese are often inclined to give aid to China out of a sense of remorse for suffering caused during the war years, many younger Diet members are more inclined to put relations with China on a new basis. (In a recent interview that I had with former Prime Minister Miyazawa Kiichi, he also noted the new attitude that younger Diet members have toward China, which he characterized as less based on idealism or guilt.) Among younger Japanese, Takemi noted a new trend that supports international as well as domestic NGO volunteer activities. Independent-minded politicians, such as the governor of Kochi Prefecture, Hashimoto Daijirō, and the governor of Nagano Prefecture, Tanaka Yasuo, are skillfully appealing to these people. These younger people thus are manifesting new attitudes toward both the West and Asia. Takemi Keizō, "Shinrai kankei o do kochiku suru ka," *Sekai* (March 2001), pp. 88–93.

17. Kyoko Inoue, *Individual Dignity in Modern Japanese Thought: The Evolution of the Concept of Jinkaku in Moral and Educational Discourse* (Ann Arbor: Center for Japanese Studies, University of Michigan, 2001), pp. 226, 230.

18. John Owen Haley, *The Spirit of Japanese Law* (Athens: University of Georgia Press, 1998), p. 199.

19. Watanabe Akio, "Japan's Position on Human Rights in Asia," in *Japan and East Asian Regionalism,* edited by S. J. Maswood (London: Routledge, 2001); see also the same author's "Toward a Middle Path in Human Rights Policy," *Japan Review of International Affairs* 11, no. 2 (Summer 1997), and Watanabe Akio, ed., *Ajia no jinken; kokusai seiji no shiten kara* (Tokyo: Nihon kokusai-mondai kenkyūjō, 1997), pp. 1–27.

20. See the interview of Takemi and other young politicians in the *Wall Street Journal,* June 28, 2005.

21. It is noteworthy, for example, that already in a 1998 *Yomiuri* poll among Diet members, 90 percent of the politicians under fifty years of age favored constitutional revision, whereas only 60 percent of all Diet members supported revision.

22. Reinhard Drifte, *Japan's Quest for a Permanent Security Council Seat: A Matter of Pride or Justice?* (New York: MacMillan, 2000), pp. 95–99. Drifte's exhaustive study of Japanese attitudes concludes that Japan's quest "has been presented almost exclusively in terms of Japan's financial contributions . . . rather than political merits and readiness, and strongly backed by perceptions about the country's status and prestige as a result of these contributions" (p. 111).

23. Haruo Shimada, *Japan's "Guest Workers": Issues and Public Policies* (Tokyo: University of Tokyo Press, 1994), chap. 8.

24. Ibid.

25. Sakanaka Hidenori, "Gaikokujin no ukeire seisaku wa hyakunen no kei de aru," *Chuo koron*, February 2004.

Epilogue: Japan's Twenty-First-Century Resurgence

1. See Michael J. Green, "The Forgotten Player," *The National Interest*, June 22, 2000.

2. Ibid., pp. 217ff.

3. Stevan Vogel, "Japan Reforming Incrementally," *The Oriental Economist*, May 2006.

4. Christopher W. Hughes, *Japan's Re-emergence as a "Normal" Military Power*, Adelphi Paper 368 (New York: Oxford University Press; London: International Institute for Strategic Studies, 2004), p. 125.

5. Ibid., p. 93.

6. Testimony of Air Force Lt. Gen. Henry Oberding III, House Armed Services subcommittee hearing, March 9, 2006.

7. Hughes, *Japan's Re-emergence*, pp. 78–79.

8. CIA World Fact Book, www.cia.gov/cia/publications/factbook.

9. *Asahi shimbun*, March 15, 2006.

10. Kobayashi Yotaro, "A Time to Rebuild: A New Era for Japan-China Relations," *Gaiko Forum* (Winter 2006), p. 14.

11. For five years beginning in 2000, *Yomiuri*'s annual poll showed just over 60 percent of respondents favoring revision. Nakanishi Hiroshi, "What the Constituents Say," *The Japan Journal* (June 2005), p. 17.

12. November 19, 2004. Quoted in J. Patrick Boyd and Richard J. Samuels, "Nine Lives? The Politics of Constitutional Reform in Japan," *East-West Center Policy Studies*, no. 19 (2005), p. 63.

13. *Japan Times*, March 2, 2006, p. 2.

14. See Tomohito Shinoda, "Koizumi's Top-Down Leadership in the Anti-Terrorism Legislation: The Impact of Political Institutional Changes," *SAIS Review* 23, no. 1 (Winter–Spring 2003).

15. Hughes, *Japan's Re-emergence*, p. 76.

16. Personnel were known as "special public servants" and not "soldiers," and the unit of deployment was "the workplace" rather than the "battalion" or "brigade." In giving orders, an officer might well add "please" (*onegai shimasu*). To distinguish themselves from the violence of the prewar military and blur their separation from civilian society, the defense forces publicly stressed only their efforts to enhance the collective public good, such as performing disaster relief and humanitarian aid. Sabine Fruhstuck and Eyal Ben-Ari, "'Now We Show It All!' Normalization and the Management of Violence in Japan's Armed Forces," *Journal of Japanese Studies* 28, no. 1 (Winter 2002), pp. 1–39.

17. Cited in David Pilling, "Tokyo Faces Tough Questions over US Troop Deal," *Financial Times,* May 3, 2006.

18. Security Council membership is a priority because, as Ronald Dore observed, "there is a strong desire among the Japanese public for an advancement in national dignity . . . probably stronger than among the publics of any other major country." Ronald Dore, *Japan, Internationalism and the UN* (London: Routledge, 1997), p. 98.

19. Nagai Yōnosuke, *Gendai to senryaku* (Tokyo: Bungei shunjū, 1985), p, 67.

INDEX

PublicAffairs is a publishing house founded in 1997. It is a tribute to the standards, values, and flair of three persons who have served as mentors to countless reporters, writers, editors, and book people of all kinds, including me.

I. F. STONE, proprietor of *I. F. Stone's Weekly*, combined a commitment to the First Amendment with entrepreneurial zeal and reporting skill and became one of the great independent journalists in American history. At the age of eighty, Izzy published *The Trial of Socrates*, which was a national bestseller. He wrote the book after he taught himself ancient Greek.

BENJAMIN C. BRADLEE was for nearly thirty years the charismatic editorial leader of *The Washington Post*. It was Ben who gave the *Post* the range and courage to pursue such historic issues as Watergate. He supported his reporters with a tenacity that made them fearless and it is no accident that so many became authors of influential, best-selling books.

ROBERT L. BERNSTEIN, the chief executive of Random House for more than a quarter century, guided one of the nation's premier publishing houses. Bob was personally responsible for many books of political dissent and argument that challenged tyranny around the globe. He is also the founder and longtime chair of Human Rights Watch, one of the most respected human rights organizations in the world.

·   ·   ·

For fifty years, the banner of Public Affairs Press was carried by its owner Morris B. Schnapper, who published Gandhi, Nasser, Toynbee, Truman, and about 1,500 other authors. In 1983, Schnapper was described by *The Washington Post* as "a redoubtable gadfly." His legacy will endure in the books to come.

[signature]

Peter Osnos, *Founder and Editor-at-Large*